DATE DUE

95

CRIME, LAW AND THE SCHOLARS

GERHARD O. W. MUELLER

Professor of Law, New York University

Crime, Law and the Scholars

A HISTORY OF SCHOLARSHIP IN AMERICAN CRIMINAL LAW

UNIVERSITY OF WASHINGTON PRESS

SEATTLE

Published in England by Heinemann Educational Books Ltd
as Volume XXVI of Cambridge Studies in Criminology,
edited by Leon Radzinowicz

To
MORRIS PLOSCOWE
and
the memory of
PAUL TAPPAN
and all their predecessors at New York University
who labored to turn Criminal Law
into a reputable science
and a successful instrument of social control

Contents

Part 1

'Antiquity': Seventeenth to Nineteenth Centuries

Part 2

'The Middle Ages': Nineteenth to Twentieth Centuries

Part 3

The Present

Synopsis

'If Criminal Law is an empirical art let us throw the pen away, and cease meditating upon the mysterious beginnings that, as such, it does not have. If it is a science, and if we want to maintain it on that level, it must have some principles, and these cannot be recognized when they are not accepted on the basis of logical deductions because truth is unitary and must appear as such in all its various forms.' CARRARA, *Programma 1* (1860).[1]

Foreword

by Leon Radzinowicz

Tremendous changes have taken place over the last twenty years in academic attitudes to the criminal law in the United States: in teaching, in research and in the whole standing of the subject. They are changes which those of us who are fortunate enough to have close links with America, yet who view it from outside, have been specially well-placed to observe.

Before the Second World War, criminal law, both substantive and adjective, was grossly neglected even amongst the leading law schools of the country. Few teachers of ability were prepared to take it up, and penal problems were debated without reference to empirical research. The apathy of teachers was matched by the apathy of students. The very few enlightened Deans and Professors who wanted to bring the subject to life fought what seemed to be a losing battle. Now the situation has changed out of all recognition.

Like most radical changes, the new outlook and the new practice cannot be attributed to any one cause. It is the product of several. The movement for civil liberties has brought criminal procedure into a central position and has indirectly affected concepts of criminal law as a whole. Thus, for example, the powers of the police, the protection of the accused, the conflict between the legal rights of the individual and the powers of state intervention have all come to the fore. The growing social conscience of the country recognizes criminal as well as civil law as a potential instrument of social justice. The pervasiveness of crime creates an unrelenting pressure for more to be done to improve the effectiveness of the law and its administration. Existing systems of criminal justice appear rigid, old-fashioned, resistant to experiment and adaptation. The searching enquiries of criminologists, and indeed of lawyers themselves, bring a critical and empirical approach, challenging deficiencies in procedure, questioning the effectiveness of punishment and treatment.

Formerly criminology found its only foothold in Departments of

Sociology. If the wider aspects of the criminal law were not studied there they were not studied at all. Only eight years ago I was deploring the neglect of criminology by virtually all the Schools of Law: now it is finding its way into several of their most forward-looking faculties.

The effect of this ferment upon the teaching of criminal law is nowhere better reflected than in the contrast between the old legal casebooks and the new. Compare, for example, the earlier books by Perkins and Harno with those by Wechsler and Michael, George Dession or Kadish and Paulsen.

The same trend appears in the activities of professional bodies. The American Bar Association has of late devoted much of its energy, and added much prestige, to empirical studies of criminal justice. As a result two volumes have already appeared and several others are in the making. Attempts are also being made to reformulate minimum standards. 'Sentencing Alternatives' reflects from another angle the new approach to the criminal law. Here lawyers have concerned themselves not with the processes of adjudication but with the processes of sentencing, with the principles that should govern procedure and decision in a part of the court's duties that had, until recently, received only the scantiest attention from them.

At the other end of the professional scale is the genuine interest evinced by students. In contrast to the old expectation that all they would want would be the training in specific branches of the law necessary to make them competent members of well-established and lucrative law firms, they are now eager to know about the wider implications of the law and its enforcement: about criminal behaviour and the phenomenon of crime; about their connection with other aspects of deviance and social pathology; and about the way legal institutions, procedures and penalties really work. (Whether this critical interest will be swallowed up in rejection of everything associated with social control remains to be seen.)

The issues have been focused and dramatized by the three great presidential commissions which have followed each other in close order. First there was the President's Commission on Crime, then the Commission on Civil Disorders and now the Commission on Violence. The National Commission on the Reform of Federal Criminal Laws is also forging ahead.

We are witnessing a movement of renovation in the teaching of criminal law and procedure; in bringing criminology closer to them; in planning and supporting, at the federal level, an organised attack upon crime; and in social and political pressures to find solutions. All these things react upon each other. Whatever the future of this movement, it has a very substantial and relevant past. It is this that Professor Gerhard Mueller's book is all about.

He presents the parts in their relation to each other, as a whole great movement developing from its very beginnings to the present day. He shows the impact of Blackstone on American criminal law and penal thought. He looks at the long delay in developing a genuine scholarship of criminal law in the United States and the rejection of premature efforts in codification, even of the far-sighted work of Edward Livingston. He points out that rising crime, and the multiplication of *ad hoc* legislation, challenged the assumption that the common law could adapt itself better than any code to the needs of a changing society. He traces the way the initiative in legal reform, neglected by legal scholars, was taken up in experiments by practical penologists and later by the younger science of criminology. He illustrates the dawning awareness of a few great lawyers of the need to draw these disciplines together in the task of bringing the law and its administration into line with current social facts and social needs. He recalls the severe, though only partially justified, criticisms of those lawyers who, in the 1930s, questioned the value of what he calls the 'criminological hubbub' of the time.

From this widening of the gap between criminologists and lawyers he proceeds to the great enterprise in codification after the war, led by Herbert Wechsler and drawing in the majority of professors of criminal law on one hand, but also psychiatrists, sociologists, criminologists, on the other. Although empirical research was not undertaken as part of this project, it brought the teachers of criminal law, the judges, and the explorers of criminal behaviour and the penal system back into the same stream of endeavour. Finally, balancing this functional approach, he refers to the work of Jerome Hall, and to international comparative studies, both seeking to identify and clarify the principles of the criminal law, the principles which should underlie any attempt to construct a coherent and acceptable system.

So we see all these movements, some of them stemming from far back in the past, some of them much more recent but nonetheless vigorous, now advancing together in the attempt to understand the phenomenon of crime, to identify faults in the law and its administration, and to devise better solutions.

We already have separate descriptions of parts of this movement but no one until now has attempted to depict it as an organic whole. To trace the whole story adequately would be a life's work. Because the enterprise is so vast, it is no surprise that what we have here is a sketch rather than a finished painting. Inevitably the strokes are broad, sometimes too broad, the generalizations perhaps too rapid, the judgments often open to dispute. Professor Mueller is obviously more at home in law than in psychiatry or sociology and he himself states that his emphasis has been upon legal rather than behavioural scholarship. He has not, therefore, explored the trends in these other fields very thoroughly. What he has done, however, is to bring out the crucial points at which they have made contact with the criminal law and the lawyers, whether in terms of co-operation or of conflict. Shortcomings in some directions may be the price to be paid for the boldness and sweep of his approach.

This book will be extensively used wherever criminal law and criminology are being taught, and wherever the impact of developments in the criminal law and criminology of the United States is being felt. And it is being felt in many parts of the world.

Our publishers are to be congratulated on having produced a book which will satisfy needs on both sides of the Atlantic.

L. R.

INSTITUTE OF CRIMINOLOGY,
UNIVERSITY OF CAMBRIDGE.
February 1969.

Preface

This is a report sponsored by and directed to the Walter E. Meyer Research Institute of Law. The report, written during the academic years 1960–1966, deals with the history and status of American criminal law *scholarship*, as evidenced by mature publications directed to the professional public. This includes books, articles, reports and other means of publication about criminal law and about activities concerning the criminal law. It excludes internal legislative committee reports, case briefs and other published materials intended to reach only restricted audiences. The report deals with the body of criminal law only as far as it is necessary to demonstrate the impact of scholarship upon the positive law of a given period in American history. Matters pertaining to criminology have been drawn upon throughout, but the emphasis is on legal rather than on behavioral scholarship.

The year 1966 marks a convenient and important cut-off point in the history of American thought on crime and criminal justice. The civil rights crisis, following the death of a president, the riots in the ghettos, the proliferation of violence, and the awakening of a desire for peace and social justice, all sparked a flurry of activities, soon reaching landslide proportion, which in one way or another sought to change the aim and structure of criminal justice in the United States. Prior to 1966, largely as a result of Supreme Court *fiat*, scholars and lay observers of criminal justice alike felt that the American scene was in motion. But after 1966, all felt involved in the rapidly changing scene. Presidential and Congressional committees and commissions, study groups and seminars, state agencies and private groups and foundations, all focused on criminal justice. Around a dozen major foundation grants were made to universities and private groups, to support research, education, and action and demonstration projects in this field. Never before had American scholars been so deeply involved and so clearly in demand. This development is wholesome. The emerging trend is desirable. But this new focus should not detract from the needs uncovered and discussed in this book: needs which are not dependent on the exigencies of the moment, purposes unrelated to 'ad hocism'. The do's and don'ts themselves are what lies behind all the talk about the problems of administration. Not only must those do's and don'ts be reconsidered in light of modern social and moral conceptions, but they must be cast in the form which is most capable of application in a society of mass administration. And in this respect I firmly believe that the history of American criminal law scholarship points the way to the next step of evolution, which is likely to be a new law phenomenology, cast in a logic capable of being computerized. The pragmatism of the nineteenth century was good enough to make us fact-conscious. But the twentieth century points the way toward a logical organization of human behavior stimuli and responses which, then, in the twenty-first century, will direct man's destiny with the aid of man-manipulated electronic computers.

The approach of this report is as much objectively historical as it is subjectively evaluative. This does not make it a book of history with a message. Rather, it should be understood as a book on contemporary criminal law scholarship, endeavoring to fathom the meaning of today's events in terms of its antecedents.

Except for passages in quotation and with citation of authority, no part of this book has been previously published in English. It is only fair to mention, however, that the theme of the book was the subject matter of lectures delivered at the University of Tübingen, Germany, and at the Free University of Berlin,[2] and that, in preliminary form, the various sections dealing with penal codification in America formed an article in French published in Belgium.[3]

Acknowledgements

I wish to extend my special gratitude to Messrs John E. V. Pieski, Jerry Shames and John Spain for their untiring research assistance, to Miss Judith Chazen for efficiently performing the herculean task of handling the manuscript, and to Miss Virginia Gray and her colleagues then at the Law Library of New York University for indefatigable service in providing me with needed books. Professor Ralph Brown, acting as a colleague, rather than in his official capacity as the director of the Institute which commissioned this book, as well as Professor Fred Cohen, University of Texas School of Law, have made many useful suggestions as to form and substance, for which I am deeply grateful.

With the kind permission of the Walter E. Meyer Research Institute, a mimeographed preliminary version of this book was used as text for an experimental seminar on the history of American criminal law, given to the Root-Tilden class of 1965 at New York University, in the spring semester 1963. The Root-Tilden scholars—never in need of urgings in such matters—offered constructive criticism and thus bared many weak spots which, thus, could be improved in this final edition. Their enthusiasm is gratefully acknowledged. Lastly, I want to record my deep indebtedness to that great fellow worker in the vineyard, Professor Louis B. Schwartz, of the University of Pennsylvania, who mercilessly forced me to clarify matters which the mimeographed edition had left uncertain.

Obviously, the author takes sole responsibility for everything stated in this report, and the Walter E. Meyer Research Institute should in no way be deemed to have approved any part of this book.

On the Tradition of Scholarship

As is customary, this introduction was written after completion of the book itself. Custom also seems to dictate that the introduction be filled with apologies, and that it anticipate conceivable criticism. Knowing that criticism will follow regardless of introductory anticipations, I had decided at this early point to part with custom and embrace law. This, however, entails the risk of turning the introduction into the mere digest of the book, a task I should leave to digesters. To set the appropriate mood for the reception of the unfamiliar, writers have frequently introduced their subjects by a description of the familiar. Such would here require me to reproduce a condensed history of civilization—a rather forbidding task. There remained, then, only one way in which to turn for a useful introduction, namely to the plausible, albeit established, analogy. Hence, I turned to the history of medicine, the sister 'Science'— *quod erat demonstrandum*—of law, the sister faculty of the university, the rival in the market-place for bright and eager students and, traditionally, the rival in all human efforts to cure frail man's woes.[1]

A diseased limb or organ is to the body what deviant man is to the body politic. More closely analogous yet, a diseased man may be regarded as dangerous to society—rightly or wrongly—as much as a violator of the laws may be regarded as dangerous to society— rightly or wrongly.

Is it not odd that we should learn of an initially identical societal reaction to the sick man and to the deviant man? For the primitives medicine and law were matters of mystery, not of science. Both were practiced by pontifical *honoratiores*. Magic and wonder dominated the explanations of physical and of social deviancy, and witchcraft and sacrifice were the remedies for both—except in cases of complete failure, when expulsion was resorted to for both the incurably ill and the unforgivably criminal, as the *ultima ratio*. But just as practical observation taught the early priests of medicine that rest, pressure, heat or cold can give relief from physical suffering, it must have taught the early priests of law that pain-fearing man may forgo forbidden short-term pleasure for fear of promised long-term pain. And, thus, medicine and law became teleological instruments in an effort to insure for man all that which he regards worth living for. From then on man's progress in medicine corresponded as nearly to his progress in law as it did to his progress in civilization and culture in general.

Let us turn to Greece as an ontogenetic example of the philogenesis of medical history. When medical art was still in the hands of the physician-priests of Aesculapius' family, it consisted of little more than magic and incantations. The human anatomy and its functions remained closed to the priest's intellect. Next, man became curious and experimental. But progress could not come until Pythagoras studied the human frame and its reactions to outside stimuli. And with Hippocrates' patient and accurate observations, detailed record-keeping and theorizations, Greek medicine became a rational, albeit as yet incomplete, science. The rest, as far as ancient Greece goes, is commonly known. Plato's lofty intellect added philosophy, systematism and humanity to Greek medicine, while Aristotle added that and more, namely correct anatomical knowledge, such as the discovery of the difference between arteries and veins, the recognition of the optical nerve and so on. Not long thereafter, the human mind had contributed to medical knowledge all it was then capable of contributing, as we may now judge objectively in terms of the over-all body of knowledge available in classical times. At just that time the first theoretical schools of medicine can be recognized. Dr Allen put it this way:[2]

> [T]he medical profession became divided on the method of the treatment and study of disease—the Dogmatists and later the Empirics. The Dogmatic school professed to set out with theoretical principles which were derived from the generalization of facts and observations and to make these principles the basis of practice. Although this is now considered the correct method to pursue the study and practice of medicine, it is a method which if not carefully watched is exposed to the greatest danger of being corrupted by ignorance and presumption. This occasioned the slow formation of the opposing sect—the Empirics —who defended the principle of 'experience' as being of chief importance in the development of the methods of medical investigation and treatment. The Empirics rejected as useless all search after the theoretical causes of disease and all knowledge of anatomy—certainly a grave mistake—but, on the other hand, in their emphasis on experience caused the formation of the conception of the physician, not only as a scholar and a student, but also as a man of ripe judgment and understanding.

The history of classical Greek medicine is but a microcosmic example of the world history of medicine—and of law.

The Europe which emerged from the dark ages was as much determined by demonism in medicine and law as pre-Hippocratic medicine had been in Greece. Luther, the enlightened reformer, and Paré, the great physician, were as convinced of the necessity of dealing with devils and witches in medicine, as was Charles V in the case of law. His penal code of 1533, the great *Constitutio Criminalis Carolinae*, eminently demonstrates this proposition. Yet by then man had been sufficiently freed from the bonds of determinism to permit him to turn to experimentation for answers. The results of the following experimentations and observations led to theorizing— to compilation of the findings, in the manner of realism, in medicine and law. In the eighteenth century, finally, mankind liberated itself completely from its demonological past and pursued the path of science. As Harvey, in the outgoing seventeenth century, dealt the death blow to the doctrine of the 'spirits' in the heart, the naturalists of the law banned witchcraft from the list of crimes.

But from this point the two nascent sciences went their somewhat different ways. It is true that for both there followed a classificatory phase, with Hale and Blackstone in English law, more particularly penal law, and with the systematizers in medicine, such as Boerhaave the eclectic, George Stahl, Frederick Hoffman, Franz Messmer, John Brown, Philippe Pinel the realist, and others. But while for Anglo-American penal law the systems of Hale and Blackstone constituted terminal points for two centuries to come, the contemporaneous systems of medicine served as mere beginnings. They were but hypotheses, based on the best possible knowledge of the times. They were indices of a constantly growing body of knowledge, with the parts of the whole gradually being rejected, replaced and enlarged. The foundation of systems marked an era of growing and vigorous scholarship in anatomy and histology before equally vigorous subsequent endeavors in exploratory and directed pathological investigation. Today, medicine may no longer resemble the systems of the eighteenth century, but it is a seamless web of largely validated dogma which covers the breadth and the depth of man's ills. The 'where-it-is' and the 'what-it-is' and the 'what-to-do-about-it' have been harmoniously assembled in such a fashion that the practitioner called upon to cure an ill has easy access to—in most cases—an effective remedy. Can the prosecutor turn with equal ease to an equally effective remedy for the ills he is called upon to cure? But it is not systematism alone which is at stake, for if it were, the lawyers of today could easily reorganize the body of human knowledge called penal law. That type of organization would not lift penal 'science' to the level of medical science—unless all the hypotheses were then to receive the best validation man is capable of today, followed by a rephrasing, reorganizing and reassembling of all that knowledge.

In criminal law most of us have not yet left the era of the common-sense assemblage of common-sense propositions, a stage which both sciences had reached in the eighteenth century. That is what, as it now appears, this study tends to document. But it also documents the change in legal science which is currently taking place, which all of us can feel and sense, which has been prophesied and conjured up many times, but which, in my opinion, has never been properly identified and described.

We live in the exciting era in which American criminal law scholars are trying to make up for two centuries of failure and neglect. In contemporary American criminal law we are reliving the classic Greek era of the struggle between the medical dogmatists and empirics. We are similarly experiencing the combat between eclectics and dynamists, and that between realists and analysts. Indeed, it is an exciting time. But we should not merely witness the event—we should take part and promote that which a seemingly capricious history appears to have selected as the proper course.

Advisedly I have referred only to Anglo-American penal law so far, for not all bodies of criminal law have stopped their development in the eighteen-hundreds, as ours nearly did. On the European continent there existed in all sciences the tradition of the medieval scholastics, i.e., a scholarly tradition with inclinations toward thoroughness and theory. To a somewhat lesser extent this tradition prevailed in England, though not in law, for in the struggle for supremacy between the anti-scholarly common law and the scholarly romanized civil law, the former had carried the victory. This means that in England the scholar, rounded in the traditions of thorough analytical and theoretical pursuit, was virtually barred from further participation in legal development. On the continent, however, all sciences, including law, remained in the hands of those whose work was deeply affected by these scholarly traditions, consisting of their own rules of conduct, methods, and even ethics, but governed, most of all, by a drive to know and to discover, to penetrate deeper and deeper, which drive had been passed on from generation to generation of scholars working at the universities.

The victory of the common law over the scholarly civil law was complete with Coke, though it is remarkable that the man most responsible for the ultimate victory was at the same time perhaps more learned—not to say steeped—in scholastic scholarship than any of his contemporaries. It was possibly because he knew the adversary so well that he could carry the victory. (It is remarkable, furthermore, that subsequent works of relative perfection were, like those of Coke's, the products of writers with at least some grounding in the tradition of the civil law, for example Blackstone, Bentham, Austin.)

On the continent, at the same time (now in the age of enlightenment), the scholarly tradition came to full fruition in all of the then extant spheres of human knowledge, in political theory (with repercussions as far away as America), in medicine, and in law. In Germany, during the romantic decades of the early nineteenth century, there was even an overflow of these traditions: the medical scholars went beyond philosophical medicine and reached a medical philosophy, and the legal scholars, quickly fired by their own imagination and enthusiasm, were all too ready to generalize and to philosophize, although as yet they lacked a full knowledge of the basic ingredients of their imaginative schemes. But such excesses soon gave way to more sober reflection in the second half of the nineteenth century, when piece by piece all the organs of the grand organism of law, and especially of criminal law, were identified, classified and assembled by such giants of the law as von Feuerbach, von Grolmann, Carl Stooss, the great Swiss reformer, and the analytical scholars and codifiers of the second half of the nineteenth century: Binding, von Liszt, Merkel, and others.[3]

It was at this time that most, if not all, sciences became analytical and descriptive, or, at least, received the impress of analytical and descriptive effort—the material outgrowth and product of the scholarly tradition. As a result, criminal law had become a manageable body of well understood principles by the time the classical codifications of the late nineteenth century occurred. This was true not only in Germany but in other nations as well—Italy, Belgium, Denmark, Norway and others. But nothing of that sort could take place in the common law world. Stephens' ambitious but humble effort was the work of but one man, himself not fully versed in scholarly traditions, and lacking the scholarly milieu essential for such an endeavor to come to fruition. In sum, at the beginning of the twentieth century, continental criminal law had in effect been reduced to its principles, so that it was theoretically ready for examination and manipulation by the nascent empirical sciences. Put differently, the study of the anatomy and physiology of the criminal law had been substantially completed. A study of its pathology could now begin. However, the auxiliary sciences, as the tools with which such a study might be made, were not yet up to the task.

It is clear, then, that American criminal law—and English criminal law for that matter—branched off from the main stream of scientific development in the nineteenth century, for lack of the scholarly tradition in law. No effort can be made here to describe and trace all the anti-scholarly movements in the America of the eighteenth and, especially, the nineteenth centuries, which affected all sciences. Jacksonian democracy and its continuing effects are still with us. Memory still lingers on of the American image of the 'professor' who sells patent medicine out of a saddle bag. Nowadays, more likely, his image is that of a long-haired, weird-looking, foreign-accented, utterly impractical 'mad scientist', creating Frankensteinian monsters.

Of course, it is not the purpose of this investigation to trace, explain or improve the *image* of the American scholar of criminal law. The object is to find the men throughout America's history who devoted their lives and labors to the pursuit of scholarship in criminal law. This calls for an at least tentative definition of the concept of *scholarship*.

For the purposes of this book I define scholarship as *the rational and mature pursuit and exposition of knowledge or truth in a given sphere of human endeavor, meant to serve the advancement of humanity by seeking perfection—however difficult to attain—in that given sphere.* Scholarship may be evaluated only in terms of relative success, *i.e.,* in relation to previous or alternative modes of proceeding, for the purpose of human improvement in that given sphere. If a given scholarship were ever to reach ultimate success, by solving all its problems, it would cease to be scholarship and become simply knowledge.

In this report I shall constantly evaluate the scholarship pertaining to the sphere of crime, of given periods and given men. It is my own endeavor to be scholarly in this regard, yet if knowledge is truth I am bound to hurt the feelings of friends and esteemed colleagues. May they forgive me or even take subsequent opportunity to prove that I am wrong by my own standards. My scruples have been sufficiently strong to impede rapid and irreverent progress in producing this report. More than once the fear that my evaluation may be slanted in accordance with personal predilection, that, therefore, criticism of the work of colleagues, past and present, may be unjustified, has produced strong frustrations, serious soul-searching and three years of delay in publication.

Part 1

'ANTIQUITY'
SEVENTEENTH TO NINETEENTH CENTURIES

Part 1

ANTHOLOGY

CHAPTER I

The Molds and the Mass

1. *In the Colonies*[1]

Recently a foreign colleague said to me, 'You Americans have an easy job in relating your legal history, because you do not have to go back as far as Hammurabi, or The Twelve Tables, or even to Moses.' Unfortunately, this is not accurate, at least in so far as American criminal law is concerned. Here, indeed, we must begin with Moses. For, as much as historians may debate the question whether the early settlers brought the common law as their treasured birthright from England to the coast of their new country *in partibus transmarinis*, the fact that all early American penal law was determined by the Pentateuch stands out clearly. But it would be false to view the Biblicism in early American penal law as a purely indigenous American phenomenon. As Goebel said, 'Calvinism . . . had burned its way generally into English intellectual life during the reign of Elizabeth. Its brand is on Anglican as well as on Puritan thinking. It fired the legal pietism of Coke as much as it did the outbursts of Cartwright'[2]—after which Goebel demonstrated how Calvinism manifested itself in the growth of Biblicism and the exaltation of Mosaic law, resulting in 'definite ideas for law reform among the radical dissenting groups in England. They are the inspiration for the demands that the law of Moses be part of the law of the land. . . .'[3]

That these ideas for law reform along Biblical lines could find no free expression through the dissenters is, of course, the single most significant factor for the settlement of New England. This Bible-law attitude may have been weakest in Virginia[4] and strongest in Plymouth,[5] but it was prevalent in every settlement and influenced almost every action of the settlers of Massachusetts Bay.[6]

Just as the replacement of the common law by the law of Moses had been advocated in England, the first draft code of Massachusetts Bay, by the Rev. John Cotton, was based upon the law of Moses, with literal references to the punishments of the Pentateuch. It was a harsh and severe penal code.[7] While it never gained the force of positive law, many of its provisions found their way into the Body of

Liberties of 1641, and the Code of 1648, as permanent law of the colony.[8]

In view of this incisive influence of fundamentalist-Biblical scripture on the attitude of America's earliest settlers toward law and order, it is rather difficult to accept the frequently held notion that the English common law of crimes was transplanted to, and continued an uninterrupted existence in, America.[9] Indeed, the very purpose of the immigrations seems to speak against such a theory. Many of the settler groups had left England because of overt or covert oppressions, particularly because of their dissentient religious ideals and goals. Others, like the Massachusetts Bay settlers, simply wanted to assert their independence, in order to follow their separatist principles and carry out their divinely-inspired mission. In any case, their departures were marked by dissatisfaction with the common law as applied in England. 'Seventeenth-century English law provided few of the safeguards that are presently regarded as essential to the fair conduct of a criminal trial.'[10] The English rule of law in criminal law and procedure, as we know it today, gradually emerged during the seventeenth and eighteenth centuries,[11] but that was too late to be brought along by the policy-making settlers. In a sense, however, the settlers improved over the English state of affairs. Rights which in England had merely been the demands of the reformers, became positive laws in the colonies. It is only in this sense, and only if we keep in mind the Puritan premise as to the force of the law of God, that we can speak of an importation of the traditional common-law rights and liberties of Englishmen by the settlers.[12]

> Most of the colony's improvements on English law in the area of civil liberties were not radical innovations but embodied ideals which were widely held, both in England and in Massachusetts, to be the rights of Englishmen. Many of these rights were not legally recognized in England, but most of them were claimed at one time or another there, and their denial was widely regarded as a grievous irony. The legal recognition of such rights in Massachusetts Bay owed much to the influence of the deputies, whose distrust of arbitrary powers in the hands of the magistrates had its roots in unhappy memories of disregard of due process, particularly by the prerogative agencies of the crown.[13]

Thus, among the procedural safeguards more liberal in Massachusetts than in England, we find protections as to bail, double jeopardy, the right of confrontation, the guarantee of orality of proceedings, the equal protection of the laws, appeal rights, vigorous disapproval of torture and self-incrimination, and other 'due process' guarantees.[14] In this respect, then, the settlers brought with them *more* than the common law.

The progressive notion of the Massachusetts Bay settlers also extended to matters of penal policy. While, on the one hand, the penological notions of the settlers were biblically talionic, they were, on the other hand, progressive, in relying as well on the teleological function of punishment as a deterrent, with power over soul and mind, true to protestant ideology.[15] The deterrent purpose of the law was made to rest on an insistence of the knowledge of the law, on the supposition that a rational mind will respond to the command of the law if it be known, and that to punish in the face of ignorance is unjust.[16]

If we add to such common-law ideals—which were so much ahead of the common law of England—the fact that in the establishment of their primordial legislative and judicial bodies, the pioneers likewise showed an astounding ingenuity and seeming familiarity with the common law, de lege lata and de lege ferenda,[17] we may well be driven to conclude with Haskins that 'for a supposedly simple frontier community, the colony's judicial system was both elaborate and comprehensive'.[18]

Haskins goes so far as to exclaim with a certain amount of exuberance that in Massachusetts Bay 'the law was neither rude nor untechnical'.[19] At least for the law of the colony of Plymouth, Goebel came to the seemingly contradictory conclusion that 'we are dealing . . . with the crude imitation of inaccurately remembered things',[20] citing as evidence 'the absence of clear-cut lines between the legislative and judicial functions, and the failure to distinguish entirely between civil and criminal jurisdiction'.[21] Some of these examples of crudeness or lack of sophistication are almost as much inherent in the law of Plymouth as they are in that of the English county or manorial courts. This led Professor Goebel to the conclusion that because the early settlers had been more familiar with the law and procedure of English manorial courts than with those of the courts of Westminster, at least as much manorial law went into the early positive law of Massachusetts as common law and Bible law.[22] In view of Goebel's vast and meticulous documentation, this conclusion seems hardly subject to dispute. Haskins, who warns against generalizations about the uniformity of law in New England,[23] nevertheless seems to be in basic agreement with Goebel on that point.[24] Hence we can conclude with Haskins that

> both the magistrates and the deputies were well aware, despite their assertions to the contrary in the famous declaration of 1646, that the Massachusetts legal system was not that of the common law. Dissatisfaction with various aspects of the common law, particularly with its delays and its technical pitfalls, and distrust of lawyers as a class, was constantly voiced by Puritan writers under the early Stuarts . . .

and it is therefore hardly surprising—or even inconsistent—that the colonists viewed some aspects of the common law with hostility and others with veneration.[25]

In addition, we must keep in mind the changes which took place in the attitudes toward the common law of England and towards the class of men representing it. If, on the whole, the settlers' attitude toward the positive common law of England was originally only tolerably unfavorable, the state of affairs probably worsened as new tides of settlers arrived in New England, many of whom held outspokenly heretical views.[26] The lip-service which had been paid to the common law turned into outright hostility with the onset of civil war in England in 1642.[27] The common law then reached its nadir in New England, and things were not to change until peace in England, and the growing commercial and political significance of the colonies, made it possible and desirable for the crown to send Royal Commissions to Plymouth, in 1664. This put the common law on the ascendency in the colonies.

But before turning to these late developments we should take a brief look at the salient characteristics of men who put the early imprint on American criminal law. All had in common a devotion to religious principles derived literally from the Bible, and all subscribed to a Godly mission. All were versed in the Bible and took its strictures and commands more literally than their fellow-Englishmen. This explains one facet of the new American law, and of the attitude toward it.

As for the importation of common-law precepts, we find a plausible explanation in Professor Haskins' book:

> Examples of wholesale importation into the colony of common-law doctrine . . . are remarkably few. Nevertheless, as Professor Plucknett has observed, by 1648 there had been a voluntary reception of a considerable amount of common law, but its doctrines had been tempered or adapted to what was deemed suitable or expedient for the colony.[28]

And who was capable of importing and expediently adapting common-law rules? We learn that at least three of the men on the committee which drafted the Massachusetts Code of 1648 were 'men of substantial legal experience'.[29] Indeed, Winthrop and Ward had been trained at the Inns of Court,[30] and unquestionably were quite familiar with contemporary English law books, whose alphabetical arrangements they copied in their own code.[31]

Hills, not a lawyer, but also a committee member of substance, who had done much of the preliminary drafting for the Code, revealed that he had perused 'all the Stat. Laws of Engl. in Pulton at large out of which I took all such as I conceived suitable to the condition of this commonwealth which with such others as in my observation Experiences & serious Studies I thought needful'.[32] Estate inventories revealed that several colonists in Massachusetts possessed statute compilations. Governor Dudley owned an abstract of the English penal statutes.[33] But it would be folly to conclude from this evidence of relative competency in matters of law, and of the availability of some law books, that the attitude of the colonists in general, and of the legal sophisticates in particular, was favorable to a common-law-type system of penal law. Quite to the contrary: while the few law-trained men of Massachusetts Bay could not help being aided in their tasks by their professional background, their own, and even more, their fellow immigrants' attitudes were anti-common law for the most part. Lawyers *qua* lawyers were not welcomed in the colonies.[34] *Officially* law books do not seem to have been regarded as essential for a long time. Merely by way of example, the Catholic immigrants who founded Maryland in 1634 do not seem to have been in official need of law books for a generation and a half. In 1678 an order was finally sent to England for the acquisition of two legal textbooks: 'The Statute Books of England to these times, named Keeble's Abridgments of the statutes, and Dalton's Justice of the Peace.'[35] The Massachusetts General Court had purchased its first law books forty years after settlement, namely two copies of *Coke on Littleton*, two copies of the *Book of Entries*, and two copies of *Coke's Reports*.[36] It was not until 1687 that a law book was printed in America, a reproduction of Magna Carta of 1215, together with the basic law of the colony of Pennsylvania.[37] But, as Aumann reports, by 1700 there were some quite respectable law libraries in the country, especially in Maryland and Virginia,[38] and in the post-revolutionary period there were approximately two hundred fairly complete law libraries in America. This may well be indicative of the fact that by then the common law had become firmly entrenched as a political and social institution.

But religion and the common law were only two of four ingredients of America's earliest penal law, and devotion to God and a modicum of common-law sophistication were only two characteristics of the men who were to determine the policy of law-makers and law-thinkers for a long time to come.

The third element, then, is the settlers' experience with English manorial law, *i.e.*, the penal law of the manor, as well as the penal law of the realm—but as applied in manorial courts.[39] Most settlers had had no contact with the law of Westminster, particularly those among the Plymouth group. But most had had to deal with county justice. Indeed, some 'had had experience as justices of the peace in the English Quarter session'.[40] Whenever we find radical departures from the common law of crimes which are not dictated by spiritual postulates, the source of the departure frequently turns out to be one of county law.[41]

Last, and most importantly, the settlers were pioneers, willing and accustomed to work with primitive tools, ready and able to adjust to new conditions, to fashion their own tools and to adapt old ones. Such tools—whatever the model—are bound to be crude. So were the settlers' own laws. And whatever legal rule came to America was remolded in laymen's hands, and reduced to the same vulgate level as those few legal institutions which originated in America. This process of remolding lawyer's law into laymen's law certainly continued until the middle of the eighteenth century.[42]

The pronounced hostility toward the legal profession continued for a century and a half, thus prolonging the era of crude law. Perhaps America never really did overcome her attitude of rejection of the professional lawyer.[43]

Lawyers *qua* lawyers obviously could not be kept out of the colonies for ever. Growing commercial complexities, increasing internal transactions—particularly as to realty—and perhaps the growing significance of royal government in the colonies, all contributed to the need for a legal profession. But the first professionals in law were themselves pioneers of their profession, and their tools were as primitive as the settlers' plows and wagons.[44] To substantiate the point, my students of a course on the History of American Criminal Law, at New York University, made a thorough search of the earliest reported colonial criminal decision, in quest of evidence of scholarly—or even only professional—sophistication. They found that for the entire seventeenth century only one reported criminal case had relied on cited authority.[45] In addition, the seventeenth century reveals a curious lack of concern for the reasoned reaching of conclusions. Explanations are usually totally wanting.

This is almost equally true for at least the first half of the eighteenth century. To the extent that judicial opinions were published at all, they consist simply of statements of facts and the decision. Other forms of learned expression in law were virtually unknown. During the early part of the century the penal law was still quite local, and heavily biblical. Only in the middle of the eighteenth century do we find a significant impact of the common law of England. It may be true, as Goebel and Naughton suggest, that—at least in New York— the early lawyers 'took the law still warm from the hands of Coke and Hale, but they were fully and not too happily aware that what they made of it was an imitation. . . .'[46] We find little ingenuity and little skill in the perusal of source material until the last third of the eighteenth century, when English and some American precedents and the writings of English jurists began to be relied upon and professionally perused with greater frequency.

From what has been said, it seems quite clear that there was neither the climate nor the personnel for the development of any legal scholarship in this country. Indeed, there is not the slightest trace of legal scholarship in America for one hundred and fifty years after the first settlements. Characteristic of American law for the entire era is the famous description by the Lords of Trade of the Laws of Rhode Island: 'the blots in some places, the blanks in others, the want of sense in some expressions, the want of titles to the Acts, and the disorderly placing of them.'[47] Thomas Lechford, America's first lawyer, disbarred, disillusioned, and returned to England, caustically remarked in 1642: 'Take heede my brethren, despise not learning, nor the worthy Lawyers of either gown, lest you repent too late.'[48] But a century and a half is a long time for the formation of habits and patterns.

2. *In the Mother Country*

Mr Lechford's parting remarks would give one the impression that the law of the colonists was a poor reproduction of a magnificent original. The fact is that the original English law was superior only if compared with the state of affairs in colonial America.

The repositories of English law were the law reports, of every variety, 'good, bad and indifferent'.[49] Nothing but confusion and doubt lay in the yearbooks.[50] The phase of English legal history from Henry VII to the Restoration has been termed 'hard to characterize, for it is full of shifting scenes, the result of great economic and some social progress. It is marked by opportunism on the part of the Government. The winds of chance or circumstance blew hither and thither, and the threads of legal development were swayed by the varying fortunes of the age.'[51] 'In the foreground this period is one of conflict of institutions.'[52] The criminal law, as mentioned, was in a deplorable condition in the sixteenth century, and was only gradually being subjected to humanizing efforts in the seventeenth.[53] The Council, the Chamber, and analogous courts such as the Court of Requests, exercised 'arbitrary, and sometimes unprincipled, jurisdiction'.[54] Proceedings in Equity and at Common Law were marked by unconscionable delays of justice.[55] The Common Law and the Law Merchant suffered from archaism.[56] Both Equity and Common Law suffered from the clash of rules created in eras of differing philosophical speculation, which rendered reconciliation a frustrating task. In Equity, first principles were hard to grasp.[57] The 'complex mass of settled rules . . . had not prior to the Commonwealth been rationalized'.[58] The law of contract was in a rather fluid state,[59] and 'the present flexibility and uncertainty of the law of torts' has been attributed 'to the fact that the sixteenth- and seventeenth-century lawyers adopted a nebulous form of Action [Case] capable of indefinite expansion'.[60] In exasperation, Cromwell had called the law 'an ungodly jumble'.[61] The trouble was that English law had not experienced the ordering hand of a scholar for three hundred years. From Henry de Bracton (thirteenth century)[62] to Sir Edward Coke (1552–1633)[63] there exists a vacuum in English criminal-law scholarship.[64]

Under such circumstances it was quite natural that a movement should be born under Henry VIII to receive the Roman law of the *Corpus Juris Civile*. 'Roman Law had something much more than the charm of its latinity, because it had attained in the hands of Justinian's jurists a completeness to which the incomplete Common Law system could offer no parallel in that day . . . It was the law of scholars, and the Common Lawyers had too long remained outside the schools of the universities to have any claims to scholarship recognized beyond their Inns of Court.'[65] But the threat of Roman law only caused the practitioners of the Common Law to draw more tightly together in defense of the belovedly obscure object of their devotion, and to find the man who could defeat the Latin monster. They found their man in Coke, in whose hands 'the Common Law forged the axe which beheaded Charles I'.[66]

Professor Potter ventures the thought that by the end of the sixteenth century there was 'a real mass of material capable of being stated in the form of coherent principles'.[67] According to him:

> This era naturally showed development in its textbooks, which in turn pushed forward the growth of scientific law. The fierce heats and controversies of the seventeenth century made men turn to their authorities and attempt to state the law in a logical sequence. Such attempts were mainly one-sided and unscientific, but when the cries died down the technique was increasingly used to state the results of an ever-increasing mass of legal material. Coke's Institutes, as a monument of industry and learning, and Bacon's Maxims, as a philosophical and scientific model in advance of its age, led the way. . . .

It will remain a puzzlement that the great Sir James Fitzjames Stephen would subsequently so totally misjudge the accomplishment of the man who rescued English law, particularly English criminal law, from the shops of pettifogging tradesmen of the law, and elevated it to an object of scientific—albeit infantile scientific—study and perusal. But Stephen thought that 'a more disorderly mind than Coke's and one less gifted with power of analyzing common words it would be impossible to find'.[68] Quite to the contrary, it is evident that 'Coke seems to have set himself no less a task than that of stating in systematic and historical form the principles of English law as they arose in litigation before him'.[69] Surely, the time was ripe for such an effort. The method which Coke employed in his Reports was far from ideal, but it amounted to the clever perusal of an established institution for an entirely new purpose, that of systematization. 'Sheer weight of learning' made all of Coke's writings the virtual law of the land.[70] The Reports, in Plucknett's words, were an 'uncertain mingling of genuine report, commentary, criticism, elementary instruction, and recondite legal history'.[71] From the Reports, Coke turned to the casting of his Institutes. Having mastered the Year Books so well, having recast English law through his editorial reporting in the Reports, and being equipped with a none too moral bent of mind which was easily capable of means-ends accommodations, Coke could through his Institutes turn a jumble of law into an astonishingly complete, reconciled, organized body of propositions which concealed all the 'inconsistencies and difficulties which were inherent' in his position'.[72] Coke was fond of Latin maxims, some of which he invented in order to give his own propositions the air of antiquity. But through it all, there speaks an ardent desire to attain the triumph of a law of which he was fond, and which he wanted to see developed into a body of jurisprudence as good or better than that of Justinian.

Stephen's characterization of Coke's mind as 'disorganized' is justified only in twentieth-century terms, or by comparison with that of Justinian's draftsman Tribonian, or the nineteenth-century classicists. In seventeenth-century terms, Coke was an extraordinary theoretician and scholar, without whose influence Anglo-American penal law today might be a shambles. I need remind the reader only of the fact that it was Coke who rediscovered and gave prominence to the ancient maxim *actus non facit reum nisi mens sit rea*.[73] Coke thereby evidenced his power to think in terms of generalizations about a seemingly unrelated mass of knowledge. The maxim quite clearly amounts to a pronouncement that all crime consists of two primary aspects, namely the *actus reus* and the *mens rea*, coupled with the recognition that both must concur (*nisi . . . sit*) in order to be punishable. This is a recognition which places Coke far above the average barrister of his day, who was capable of little more than solving the problem at hand without regard to the totality or structure of the system.[74]

Coke did not find the leisure to complete his system. The Institutes are perhaps only half as good as they should have been as a work of synthesis, in order to compete with the Roman law. But Coke had

pointed the way for the future. His ambition led to a whole movement of textbook writing, under the titles of 'Abridgements', nearly
all of them inferior to his own work. These were alphabetical in
arrangement, 'unscientific and incapable of being used to express
the principles of any branch of the law in a consecutive and logical
form'.[75] But two of these test writers are of more than passing significance for the criminalist, namely those of Sir Matthew Hale (1609–
1676), whose *History of the Pleas of the Crown* appeared posthumously in 1678, and of William Hawkins (1673–1746), who published
his famous *Pleas of the Crown* in 1716.[76] Both were superb treatises
for their time, but neither author had Coke's analytical ability. Both
books remained authorities on English criminal law into the nineteenth century,[77] and became obsolete only with the beginning of
criminal law reform in England, particularly the codification efforts
of Bentham[78] and Stephen.[79] As a form of legal scholarship, Hale
and Hawkins became obsolete only with the arrival of the genuinely
analytical textbook, in the form of Kenny's tentative effort, in 1901,[80]
and Glanville Williams' definitive effort in 1953.[81]

And what is the significance of these English events as far as the
developments in North America are concerned?

In view of the characteristics of the men who settled our shores,
American criminal law, and the attitude towards criminal law and
scholarship, could not possibly have been more favourable here
than in the mother country. If English law was 'an ungodly jumble',
and if its devotees were 'practicers' of obscurantism, the colony
was bound to suffer very much from such conditions. These were
the determinants of the developments in America. And all subsequent American imports bear the mark of conditions in the mother
country. And so, when conditions improved in England, with Coke,
Hale and Hawkins, the colony was bound to profit proportionately.
When in England the first academician began to record the criminal
law, the colonists reacted instantly. And thus we have reached the
age of Blackstone, a convenient point of re-entry into American
developments.[82]

3. And Back in America

There is much evidence that the work of Coke was in considerable
use in America.[83] In fact, it may have provided the backbone of
American criminal jurisprudence prior to the enormous impact
which the work of Blackstone was to have.

In 1753 William Blackstone was appointed Vinerian Professor of
Law at the University of Oxford. This appointment underlines not
only the fact that Blackstone must have brought some scholarly

traditions to the task, but that, in addition, in the scholarly atmosphere of Oxford University he would develop a system for the teaching of law and, therefore, a system for the law. Blackstone's first London edition of the natural-law-minded *Commentaries on the Laws of England* sold more than one thousand copies in America. From 1765 to 1773 the first American edition of Blackstone was printed. The second edition appeared in 1779. Prior to the peace treaty with England in 1783, there were approximately two thousand five hundred copies of Blackstone's *Commentaries* in America. It is no exaggeration to say that to this day Blackstone's *Commentaries on the Laws of England* has been the most influential law book in America. While earlier books had extolled the virtues of the rule of law concept of English criminal procedure, none did it as well as Blackstone's *Commentaries*. As such, the *Commentaries* had an indirect influence on the American Revolution which, after all, demonstrated the effort of the colonists to gain for themselves those rights which their cousins in England had achieved during the seventeenth century, as Blackstone so splendidly described. Blackstone, as a royalist, was not universally hailed in America. Thomas Jefferson had strong objections to his anti-republican approach.[84] But any resistance was doomed to failure, and Blackstone eventually did win out in America.[85]

We are here particularly interested in the Blackstonian approach (in the fourth book of the *Commentaries*) to criminal law. Stephen rightly says:

> Blackstone first rescued the law of England from chaos. He did, and did exceedingly well, for the end of the eighteenth century, what Coke tried to do, and did exceedingly ill, about one hundred and fifty years before; that is to say, he gave an account of the law as a whole, capable of being studied, not only without disgust, but with interest and profit.[86]

Blackstone begins his volume IV, *Of Public Wrongs*, with the following Introduction:

> Of the Nature of Crimes; and their Punishment. We are now arrived at the fourth, and last branch of these Commentaries; which treats of *public wrongs*, or *crimes* and misdemeanors. For we may remember that, in the beginning of the preceding volume, wrongs were divided into two sorts of species; the one *private*, and the other *public*. Private wrongs, which are frequently termed civil injuries, were the subject of that entire book; we are now, therefore, lastly, to proceed to the consideration of public wrongs, or crimes and misdemeanors; with the means of their prevention and punishment. In the pursuit of which subject I shall consider, in the *first* place, the general nature of crimes

and punishment; *secondly*, the persons capable of committing crimes; *thirdly*, their several degrees of guilt, as principals or accessories, *fourthly*, the several species of crimes, with the punishment annexed to each by the laws of England; *fifthly*, the means of preventing their perpetration; and, *sixthly*, the method of inflicting those punishments, which the law has annexed to each several crime and misdemeanor.[87]

However crude this analysis may now appear, it represented a rather sophisticated departure from the current practice of listing crimes alphabetically. May the difference between the criminal sciences which were to emerge independently in England and America be attributed to the fact that America was more receptive to Blackstone than England.[88]

If we attribute to Blackstone the power of synthesis and analysis in the treatment of law, especially criminal law, we must not forget, however, that this was but a rather primitive beginning. We should add, furthermore, that, at least during this early phase, American lawyers did not accept Blackstone's theories, though they constantly applied the rules of law he expounded. In this connection, it is noteworthy that Blackstone may be regarded as not only having laid the cornerstone for a building or a structure of a systematized American criminal law (as it is being completed today), but that he also laid the cornerstone of American criminology. He was outspoken in the rejection of retribution and vindication as goals of punishment. He strongly favored penitentiaries and penitence and spoke firmly of punishment as 'a precaution against future offenses of the same kind'.[89] It was, after all, in America that the first penitentiaries were to be built, not in England.

Much has been written and said about Blackstone which need not be repeated in this context. His strong influence helped provide our law with its unique mixture of natural law and primordial analytical order, humanism, popularity and sophistication. Blackstone wrote his book for laymen, *i.e.* students who were not members of the Inns of Court—precisely the type of people who longed to peruse his book in America.[90]

Looking beyond the structure of the criminal law which Blackstone adopted we necessarily detect that he was not very original in his molding of the law. As Hall rightly pointed out, the principles discussed by Blackstone are those which Hale had already discussed.[91] The point to be made, however, is that it was Blackstone rather than Hale who put criminal law into the frame of scholarship.

The subsequent development of the English literature of the criminal law is of some interest in the tracing of American developments. Blackstone was followed by writers of specialized criminal law treatises in England, many of which soon were copied and published in America, frequently without prior authorization of their English publishers.[92]

Among the English books which thus appeared in America was *Russell's Treatise on Crimes and Misdemeanors*.[93] This book was exactly what the title announced, a treatise on crimes and misdemeanors. It evidenced no principled organization and contained no general part, or discussion of general principles. Another representative English textbook in use in this century was *Chitty's Criminal Law*.[94] The reviewer of the third American edition noted with questionable exuberance that 'the notes and references by Mr Perkins, to the present edition, deserve a special mention. They place their author, among American annotators, by the side of Story and Metcalf.' He also noted that the American editions were outnumbering the English editions.[95]

Neither Chitty's nor Russell's work could claim to be more than form-book-type exposition of practical criminal law, including an enormous bulk of procedure. This is particularly true of *Russell*, whose only coverage of substantive law is contained in forms of indictments. It is, therefore, stating the obvious simply to record that such books certainly did not contribute to the emergence of an American criminal law scholarship.

4. *The Forerunners of American Criminal Law Scholarship*

Blackstone's elevation to a professorship of law at Oxford led to imitations in America. On the urgings of Thomas Jefferson, his teacher, George Wythe, was appointed Professor of Law at the College of William and Mary, which had been founded in 1696 as the second institution of higher learning in America.[96] (While Harvard University antedates the College of William and Mary by sixty years, it did not inaugurate its first chair of law until 1815.) Was it not to be expected that once law became of concern to the universities, there might develop some interest in an orderly arrangement and organization of the law, especially of the criminal law?

Unfortunately, law teaching at the College of William and Mary was subsequently interrupted. Even the second attempt to create academic legal education, the Litchfield Law School in 1784, was not of permanence. Nevertheless, teaching at the Litchfield School continued until 1833, and if we judge from the notes of Litchfield students, that teaching, including the teaching of criminal law, proceeded in a fairly systematic manner. This, in itself, may have contributed to a better understanding of the interrelationship of principles on the one hand, and crimes on the other.

Academic law teaching was initiated in rapid succession at many other universities, for instance, in 1790 at the College of Philadelphia (abandoned in 1792); in 1794 at Columbia University by Chancellor Kent, subsequently interrupted and resumed; in 1799 at Transylvania University in Lexington, Kentucky.[97] In 1800 a 'New Haven Faculty of Law' was founded, but subsequently abandoned. Yale University began an uninterrupted teaching of law in 1801. Harvard followed in 1815. The University of Maryland assumed the teaching of law in 1816, the University of Virginia in 1826, and New York University in 1838, following Benjamin Butler's plan of 1835.

Few of the early teachers of law were to have any permanent influence on the development of American criminal law and its academic structure.[98] But among those who were to exercise such an influence, Chancellor Kent deserved first mention. As early as 1795 he published some of his lectures delivered at King's College, later Columbia University.[99] Harno rightly said of Kent's work, 'These were the beginnings of legal research and scholarship in America'.[100]

James Kent, Chancellor of New York, held his first professorship at Columbia University, New York, from 1793 to 1797. His second professorship began in 1823. At the age of fifteen, Kent had studied Blackstone's *Commentaries* and acquired a life-long respect for his work. Kent's classnotes, published in 1826 under the title *Kent's Commentaries on American Law*, are in some respects a direct American parallel to Blackstone's English work. Like Blackstone, Kent expounded (but not in his *Commentaries*) a natural law of crimes: 'It is impossible to define, expressly and literally *every offence that ought to be published*; and if you ask me, what is the evidence of its being an offence if not defined in the code, I answer the laws of nature, of religion, of morality, which are written on the heart of every son and daughter of Adam, declare the offence.'[101]

With respect to the aims of penal law, Kent deviated materially from Blackstone's teleological position, and advocated 'real, genuine, vindictive punishment for all cases of malicious crime, springing from a thoroughly corrupt and devilish heart'.[102] Kent further differed with Blackstone in that nowhere in his commentaries does he give criminal law any special treatment. That is, there is no Blackstonian Book Four on 'Public Wrongs' in his *Commentaries*. While Kent may be said to have contributed materially to the systematic presentation and organization of American law, his influence on criminal law was but slight, since he confined himself to a few chance and passing remarks in his *Commentaries* and, perhaps even more significantly, in a few letters which he sent to Edward Livingston, concerning the latter's proposed penal code.[103]

These letters indicate that Kent's feelings on criminal law were strong and that he had more than a passing acquaintance with the criminal law. The coverage of his *Commentaries*, however, seems to indicate that he did not deem criminal law to be significant enough as a subject of university instruction.

Blackstone's and Kent's Commentaries were by no means the first scholarly law books used in America. David Hoffman, a scholar who played a major role in establishing the University of Maryland, was the first to publish a systematic and instructional treatise on law in this country. He occupied the first chair of law at the University of Maryland, beginning in 1817, although, according to some sources, his teaching activities probably did not start until 1823. The book of lectures which he published in 1817 (probably before they had ever been delivered) was hailed by Justice Joseph Story.[104] His approach was imbued with the spirit of the continental scholarly tradition. It was not ascertainable whether David Hoffman was educated in America or in Europe. He did spend frequent vacations in Europe, and Oxford and Göttingen Universities granted him honorary doctorates. Hoffman's approach is neatly summarized by an excerpt from his book: 'Method places in our hands a torch and clue which guide us through the surest and easiest ways: it agreeably impresses the mind with the most distinct and lively pictures of everything worthy of notice, and at least brings us to the end of our journey, improved, invigorated, and delighted.'[105]

Hoffman disparaged dependence upon memory, unlike the practice-minded teachers who required their students to memorize Blackstone's *Commentaries*. He tried to establish 'general and pervading principles of science', meaning a science of law. His original strong endeavour to found the University of Maryland and its chair of law was meant to lay the groundwork for a national renaissance of learning.

The proliferation of American law and the difficulty of studying the obscure and displeasing style of the writers convinced Hoffman of the urgent need for a structure which could accommodate the development and study of legal principles and doctrines.[106] Hoffman functioned in the apparent belief that if American law, including criminal law, was to achieve any status, it had to create its structure before the ever-increasing number of reported decisions created utter chaos.

In Hoffman's view, legal decisions should rest on principles and doctrines of which the cases are mere evidence and example. Hoffman's plans were ultimately frustrated, and the attempt to reduce American criminal law to its principles was not to be successful for another hundred years or more thereafter. Nevertheless,

Hoffman anticipated the pattern for the style of systematization which a modern and successful law must possess.

While criminal law seems to have been regarded as a field of minor significance by all those of influence and academic authority at that time, as early as 1804 a truly 'all-American' criminal law book was published. This earliest textbook on criminal law was written by Harry Toulmin and James Blair, and printed by W. Hunter at Frankfort, Kentucky, and published by the State of Kentucky in 1804 under the title *Review of the Criminal Law of the Commonwealth of Kentucky*. This is a unique publication in that it was ordered to be written and published by a state legislature for the purpose of assessing the existing common and statute law of the state as a foundation for anticipated revision of the Commonwealth's law. In their research the two writers frequently ventured outside the Kentucky borders and the result may be regarded as a concise treatise of contemporary American criminal law. This work is almost entirely textual and relies largely on Blackstone, Hawkins, Hale, Foster and other English writers of the common law. It has relatively few references to cases, but is virtually complete in its citation of Kentucky statutory authority. The text is long and involved but, viewed as an historical document, makes for interesting reading. One of the authors' aims was to present their treatment of the law with a minimum of foreign terminology. Wherever possible the authors avoided Latin and legal French terms, substituting instead American or English equivalents. As might have been expected, this first effort was not successful enough to encourage others to do likewise. In their introduction the authors wrote:

> In treating upon the criminal law of this Commonwealth, we shall in the first place consider the offenses . . . themselves, which are punishable by [the] laws; and in the second place, delineate the course of proceedings in bringing an offender to justice.
>
> In considering the offenses punishable by our laws, we shall begin with taking a view of those which immediately affect individuals in their persons, characters, and property; and shall then proceed to those which relate more especially to the Commonwealth or public at large.[107]

This Introduction is quite revealing in that it documents implicitly the ignorance of lawyers concerning the body of general principles of criminal law. We may conclude that what we now consider to be the crucial 'General Part' of criminal law was viewed merely as 'matters of defense'.

Of further interest is the order in which the crimes were listed, namely, beginning with those affecting individuals, and ending with those relating more specifically to the Commonwealth or public at large. This is certainly indicative of an individualist, libertarian attitude, and differs markedly from the arrangement of the European penal codes of that time which, almost universally, began with the offenses against the state and the sovereign.

These early American efforts did not result in any meaningful conceptualization of the criminal law. No development of principles, theories or empirical validation of criminal law had taken place in America. Were it not for the peripheral work of a few scholars, one would have to characterize this era as an academic vacuum.

Among these few, Joseph Story deserves a very special place. He was appointed Dane Professor at the Harvard Law School in 1829. The list of subjects on which he published treatises, including the criminal law, is indeed a very impressive one. In an anonymous article for volume 4 of the Encyclopaedia Americana,[108] Story addressed himself to a brief and systematic presentation of American criminal law, showing a strong Blackstonian influence, but no originality.[109] In having established several precedents for scholarship, however, Story's influence cannot be overestimated.[110]

5. Incipient Scholarship in Codification

England had not been a country of codified law, and, thus, America was not destined to become one. In Louisiana, however, the French tradition of codification prevailed. Its greatest exponent and master was the displaced New Yorker Edward Livingston. Livingston had studied the classics such as Bentham, Montesquieu, Franklin, Bacon, Cicero, Blackstone, Beccaria, Erasmus, Pothier, Howard and Kent. His encyclopedic knowledge was not a burdensome bulk of helter-skelter curios. It had been assembled in orderly fashion, and stored for use. Intellectually, Livingston was superbly fitted to draft a penal code when appointed by the Louisiana legislature to do so. It became his object 'to remove doubts relative to authority . . . to put into one body, to abrogate reference to foreign law, and to organize a connected system for the prevention as well as the prosecution and punishment of offences'. Livingston began the Louisiana Draft Code in 1820 and completed it in 1824. It was revoked and republished in 1833. As for penal theory, Livingston believed in modern and moderate punishments, imposed under consideration of the criminal as well as the crime, but with a strong insistence on legality and preventive ideal. Philosophically, Livingston was utilitarian in his approach, and justly has been ranked as the American Bentham.[111]

Much has been written about the Livingston Code, and we need not be unduly repetitive here.[112] It is no exaggeration to say that

Livingston foresaw everything of concern to the criminal law of today. 'Livingston had drunk deeply from the springs of continental thinking which may partially account for the attention it aroused and the discussion it provoked there.'[113] Intrigues and machinations at the Louisiana Bar prevented the adoption of the Louisiana draft penal code. Nevertheless, Livingston was highly honoured in Louisiana and elsewhere, and his direct influence can be traced to codifications in Guatemala, Brazil, and Russia. While not supportable by standards of modern criminology, the Livingston code certainly takes an eminent place in the history of penal codification, side by side with Napoleon's *Code Pénal*, the codes of Bentham and Stephen in England, the Model Penal Code in America, the Ferri draft of Italy, and the Radbruch draft of Germany. Kent had taken a great theoretical interest in Livingston's work of codification.[114] Ultimately positive law itself felt the impact of the theoretical trend toward codification: 'Webster, as chairman of the Judiciary Committee, guided successfully through the House the Criminal Code of the United States, revised by him and Mr Justice Story, which was passed also by the Senate and signed by the President on March 3, 1825.'[115] Perhaps, though, it is not advisable to designate this primitive federal statutory compilation as a codification. It simply did not come anywhere near a work deserving that designation.

6. The First Inventory-taking

The code movement failed. For many decades thereafter Americans were to suffer the consequences of their neglect. In this connection it is noteworthy that during the era of abortive attempts at codification Americans took their first interest in comparative criminal law. Peter S. DuPonceau, for example, published a translation of the French *Code Pénal* in the American Review.[116] Indeed, the influence of those lawyers who were watching the continental development was strong, in no small part owing to the grave dissatisfaction with English politics and English law. But, as in the days of Coke, the common law lawyer was to carry the victory.

What, then, was the state of learning with regard to the law in America during these formative years of the nineteenth century? Law reporting at that time was in a deplorable condition. 'While formal opinions . . . did become common in the first decade of the nineteenth century,'[117] they were not regarded as law but merely as *prima facie* evidence thereof.

In the absence of orderly case collections, and owing to the general lack of extensive law libraries, it remained a matter of chance whether a precedent could be found. Moreover, the practitioner of that era all too frequently lacked the requisite skill, for want of analytical training.

Writing in 1833, one analyst of contemporary legal problems remarked:

> . . . this nursery of practical skill [the law office] is not and cannot be a complete seminary of jurisprudence. It is vain to expect, that the most able and faithful student should gain in the office that fundamental and comprehensive knowledge of the law, without which the most consummate practical discernment still retains the character of instinct, which is useful chiefly in case of common occurrence, but never conducts to a thorough understanding of the science. . . . [A] knowledge of the law, which distinguished the scientific lawyer from the empiric, cannot be derived from the office of a successful practitioner, but it requires an ample and judicious collection of men and books, such as a well organized law school, or law academy, is intended to comprise.[118]

If the law, especially criminal law, was in such a state of confusion, and the universities would not assume the task of organizing and ordering it, and if codification was not undertaken to reduce law to its principles, what then was the solution?

It was during the first half of the nineteenth century—a dark era of American criminal law history—that one scholar finally did undertake to state in a relatively systematic manner not only the criminal law, but the entire law of America. He was Nathan Dane, for whom Story's professorship at the Harvard Law School had been named. In 1823 to 1824 Nathan Dane published an eight-volume work entitled *A General Abridgement and Digest of American law, with occasional notes and comments*.[119]

Dane was the first American who applied a systematic mind to the task of discerning the basic propositions, the few fundamental and distinct common characteristics, of American criminal law. His twenty-first division, 'Crimes and Punishments', therefore, deserves our close attention. Dane's outline of American criminal law in the early nineteenth century, here reproduced from the table of contents of his work, deserves to be regarded as the first precedent of analytical criminal law scholarship in America.

Chapter CXCVII, Crimes and Punishments,
Article I, General Principles;
Article II, Criminal Law;
Article III, Maxims, etc.;
Article IV, The Law of Nations;
Article V, Municipal Criminal Law;
Article VI, Punishment By our Law Generally, Kinds of, Ends of, Variations in; Persons not Punishable, Minors, Chance, Necessity, Subjections, etc., in Eleven Heads;
Article VII, Malice;

Article VIII, Who are Principles, Who Accessories;
Article IX, Act of Congress as to Crimes;
Article X, Proceedings as to Principles and Accessories, and notes;
Article XI, Extracts from the New Penal Code of France, and Remarks
on Them.

This constitutes what today we would call the General Part of the criminal law. Dane's order was outstanding for its day, which is partially attributable to his knowledge of the French Penal Code. In the first of the chapters devoted to specific crimes, Chapter CXCVIII, Dane dealt of crimes, etc., against religion and morality, thereby revealing his position that religion and morality were the values of highest regard at the time. In Chapter XCCIX he treated of crimes against the state, in the nature of treason, and in Chapter CC of crimes against the state in the nature of felony, followed in Chapter CCI by crimes, etc., against public policy. The remaining chapters follow the English custom and treat the various crimes in alphabetical order.

Throughout Volume VI, in which we find the treatment of these topics, we note an expected heavy but not exclusive reliance on Blackstone's arrangement. Among the other sources quoted we find Beccaria, Burlamaqui, Holt, Hale, Foster, East and many others. Numerous English precedents were cited, and beginning at Chapter CXCVIII also a considerable number of American cases. In these chapters we note Dane's particular attention to American tradition, custom and precedent. The treatment is mostly narrative and is heavily natural-law flavored. With much research, Dane's work (especially a comparison of Volume VI and Volume IX) might tell us in what respects during these critical years American courts veered away from English criminal law. Unfortunately, no one as yet has undertaken this scholarly task.

Dane paid special attention to the laws of France. In the preface to Volume IX he paid homage to French codifications.[120] Parenthetically, it may be worth noting that in Volume IX, Dane, the first American work to do so, refers to the rule of law which prohibits the torture of a person accused of crime to extort a confession. Dane writes that this 'would be contrary to the constitution and to the laws of Vermont, and is an indictable offense'.[121]

7. *Pound's View*

In summing up this period, which covers the American scene from the first settlement to the middle of the nineteenth century, it is only fair to say that the state of legal scholarship was comparable to that which prompted Justinian to undertake his vast codification. Few people in the country knew the rules of law. Not a lack of precedents —perhaps there were too many—but the elusiveness of precedents made justice a matter of chance. Nobody had reduced the legal system to concise and precise principles. The criminal law was as much affected by this diffuseness as any other field. As yet, nobody, with the exception of the visionary Edward Livingston, had developed a meaningful criminal law scholarship in America. But he was so far ahead of his time that few could understand him. Hence, his influence was fleeting. The raw material of an expanding body of criminal law was there, along with the basic premises of scholarship as stated by Hoffman, Livingston, and Dane.

Yet there simply were not enough men of similar opinion and of influence in this country who could have channeled the course of events in the right direction. Consequently, American criminal law continued to be scattered over an ever-increasing number of cases and statutes, and the substantive law of crimes remained buried in the interstices of criminal procedure.[122]

On several occasions Dean Pound has stated that there were, in essence, seven factors which have shaped our law:

1. The original substances of Germanic legal institutions and jural ideas.

2. The feudal law.

3. Puritanism.

4. The contests between the courts and the Crown in the seventeenth century.

5. Eighteenth-century political ideas.

6. The conditions of pioneer or agricultural communities in the first half of the nineteenth century.

7. The philosophical ideas of America at the time the English common law was made over for us.[123]

Pound aptly stated:

[T]he Anglo-American common law is a law of the courts. Its oracles are judges. It was taught in the Inns of Court, societies of lawyers, by practising lawyers and it was developed in the courts. The Continental law is a law of the universities. Its oracles are professors. It has been taught and developed in the universities from the Middle Ages. In consequence, the common law is little systematized. Principles are cautiously and tentatively derived from details. On the other hand, Continental law is highlt systematized. Details are subordinated to broad principles. The law books of Anglo-American common law are typically alphabetical abridgments, digests and cyclopedias. The law books of the Continental law are systematic treatises.[124]

For the 1850's this is an apt description of American criminal law. Coke, Blackstone, Kent, Story, and Dane were the principal sources of all law, including the criminal law, in America. Legislation was as yet insignificant.

As to Pound's formative factors, it may suffice to say that by the middle of the nineteenth century little if any trace of the original substratum of Germanic legal institutions remained in American criminal law. And, but for the sheriff (the shire-reeve), the jury and a few other such institutions, this is also true for criminal procedure, which was materially altered by factor number two, the feudal law. Puritanism, however, was still paramount in American criminal law, especially in legislative enactments. The contests between the courts and the Crown in the seventeenth century had materially influenced the system of American criminal procedure, i.e., in the due process notion, but had no significant influence on substantive criminal law outside the punishments. Eighteenth-century political ideas, on the other hand, had a profound influence on the shaping of American criminal law. The Jacksonian ideal of democracy, resting on seventeenth-century pioneer conditions, worked against the creation of a class of criminal law scholars on this continent. As to the conditions of pioneer agricultural communities in the first half of the nineteenth century, it may suffice to refer to the studies of Blume who found no frontier influence on the shaping of criminal law scholarship.[125] If there was any influence, it was strictly negative in that, owing to the absence of scholars or a scholarly tradition in agricultural frontier communities, no systematization of the criminal law could occur. With reference to the philosophical ideas in America at the time the English common law was made over for us, the only significant aspects pertain to constitutional doctrine, with little significance for substantive criminal law, and indeed little significance for the rest of the law. The criminal law in use in early nineteenth-century America does not differ materially from that in the mother country. In fact, differences which had arisen in colonial America were increasingly eliminated as men trained in law assumed the actual administration of justice, and increasingly relied on English precedent. Material differences did not exist between the substantive criminal law of England and that of America. While one cannot say that this law was firmly in the hands of American practitioners, one can surely say that it was not firmly in the hands of scholars, for there were none in criminal law.

CHAPTER II

The First Casting of American Criminal Law Scholarship

1. *Once More Codification*

With the proliferation of precedents and statutes, and owing to the lack of scholars ready to assume leadership in the organization of the criminal law, American lawyers once again became eager to promote codification as a possible remedy. The history of federal legislation may serve us as an example. By the middle of the nineteenth century federal criminal statutes had multiplied over the number created in the outgoing eighteenth century.[1] Throughout the nineteenth century federal penal law typified the general *ad hoc* or stop-gap approach to American penal law. Ordinarily it took the initiative of ingenious entrepreneurs or a crisis to stimulate legislators into action. It is precisely that which an academically conceived, methodologically sound penal code seeks to avoid. Such a penal code rests its provisions not merely on consideration of the experiences of the past or the troubles of the moment, but projects itself into the future by anticipating what is likely to occur. Clearly, such a code cannot be drafted except by academic experts in criminal law. No systematic penal law ever has been created either in the process of adjudication or solely on the floor of a legislature. Livingston in America, Macaulay in India, and Bentham in England had demonstrated, and Stephen was to demonstrate, how a common law could be transformed into a code, yet, as successful as their scholarship was, as singularly unsuccessful was their political ambition or ability to make their scholarship a political reality in the mother countries.

By the middle of the nineteenth century it had become clear to the federal government that in order to effectuate the policies expressed by federal criminal law, at least a consolidation of statutes was in order. Americans had very little experience with consolidation. And if consolidation, why not codification, about which so much had been heard from Europe? With these thoughts in mind the President of the United States ordered the chargé d'affaires of the United States in Paris, Hon. H. S. Sanford, to write an extensive report on 'The Different Systems of Penal Codes in Europe'. Mr Sanford traveled throughout Europe and gathered valuable information on the penal law in the various European countries, including the systems of penal law administration. His report was published in 1854 as Executive Document number 68, 33rd Congress, First Session, 1854. It included extensive descriptions of the penal codes in France, Prussia, Bavaria, Saxony-Weimar, Baden, Austria, Switzerland, the Italian Republics, Russia, Sardinia, Turkey, Belgium, Holland, Denmark, and Sweden. Greece, Portugal, Spain, France, and Prussia were specially emphasized. Sanford's approach to his task may be gathered by his concluding remarks in the introduction to the report:

> Let me be permitted, however, to say, in answer to the objection that we do not require and cannot adopt European systems of penal law, that while undoubtedly the criminal law of a country should be intimately connected with the moral and religious opinions, as well as in a manner the development of the traditions of the people, rather than being, as in France, a direct emanation from the authority, the experience of other nations, even if they differ greatly in their religious and political institutions, and in the usages and intellectual development of the people, may be useful in perfecting the legislation of any state.

> Those principles or provisions, which the experience of other States had proved to be practicable or advantageous, certainly merit consideration. Majores nostri quod unique apud socios aut hortes idoneum videbatur, cum summo studio exequebantur, imitari quam invidere bonis malebant.[2]

Unfortunately, Sanford did not find it advisable to make specific recommendations. Rather, he said,

> it would be unbecoming in me to give an opinion as to the advantages to our country of adopting or improving upon some of the principles or details which have been given. If it shall have served to attract the liberal and enlightened attention of those who guide the councils or deliberate on the laws of our country to the subject of the codification of our own criminal laws, I shall feel that the labor bestowed thereon has met with an ample return.[3]

Regrettably, the report did not attract the 'liberal and enlightened attention of those who guide the councils or deliberate on the laws of our country'. While it is impossible to assess the influence which the five thousand printed copies of Sanford's report had on the further development of federal criminal law, it is noteworthy that not until 1866, twelve years after its publication, did Congress appoint a commission for the re-examination of the entire federal penal law, and for the creation of an orderly system of revised statutes of the United States. This Commission, including not a

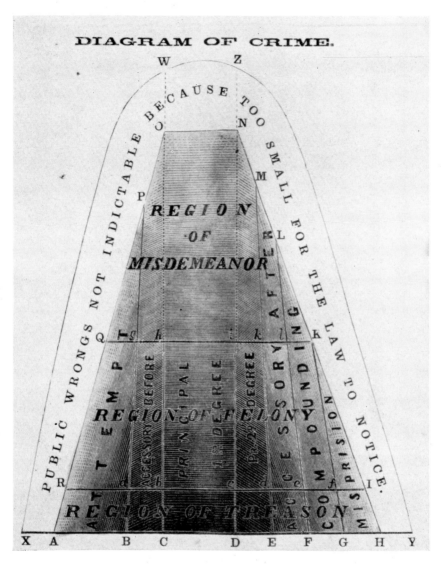

Joel P. Bishop's 'Diagram of Crime' (See page 38)

Taft's Skyscraper (See page 199)

THE FIRST CASTING 33

single academician, did fulfill the limited task assigned to it and did create the Revised Statutes of the United States, Title LXX of which included crimes. Even that work, however, was insufficient to create an orderly system of federal criminal laws, so that Congress, in 1897, again found itself forced to revise and codify the federal criminal law in order to meet the demands of the time.[4]

In 1901 a further law extended the jurisdiction of the commission to other spheres of federal public law as well.[5] This commission concluded the penal law reform in 1909. By law of March 4, 1909, chapter 321,[6] Congress gave the Federal Penal Code the force of law. It is only from this day on that we can speak of a Federal Penal Code, provided, however, that we are not very demanding and exacting in the definition of the word 'code'. While, on the whole, this penal code followed the pattern of the original Revised Statutes of the United States, of 1878, the organization of the new penal code was much more sensible and covered in five chapters and three hundred and forty-five sections the entire federal criminal law.

After 1909 Congress passed innumerable laws, most of which could be found only with the greatest diligence, so that in 1940, finally, a revision and codification commission, the third one, was appointed.[7] This commission completed its assigned task in 1948 and submitted its draft code to Congress, which enacted it without further difficulties.[8] This is now Title 18, United States Code, and covers most of the federal criminal law. But in the over one hundred years from Sanford to date, federal criminal law did not once feel the impact of sound theory and criminal law scholarship. Title 18, as it looks today, might just as well have been drafted in this form immediately following Sanford's report, or, for that matter, before Sanford ever wrote his report. There is in our federal code not a trace of the enlightened code-drafting technique which had been developed through the various European codifications. Yet, the practicing attorney's task in finding a given piece of penal legislation has been eased by the compilation of Title 18. But today, many years after this codification, much of the new criminal legislation must be found outside of Title 18, and much, especially in the General Part of criminal law, is treated neither by Title 18 nor by any other statute. To this day there is not a single public index which can lead the researcher to all penal provisions of federal law. Thus, the so-called code cannot even be said to fulfill the most rudimentary objectives of a code.

The development was not materially different in the various states of the union. As an example, the Massachusetts legislature, as early as 1836, had created a criminal code commission which counted among its members Joseph Story, Thorin Metcalfe, Simon Greenleaf,

Charles E. Forbes and Luther S. Cushing. The report of this commission was received in 1837, but met with no success. A second commission was then appointed. Its work resulted in the draft of a code in 1844. Luther S. Cushing was the only member of the first commission who also served on the second one. The labors of the second commission likewise were fruitless.

New York did not fare much better when thirteen years later its first code commission was created. It included such experts at the bar as David Dudley Field, its dominating chairman, William Curtis Noyes, and Alexander W. Bradford. Their task was the drafting of a political code, a civil code, and a penal code. There followed years of investigation, and years of research and of consultation, with frequent reference to other experts. The draft of the penal code was introduced for enactment in 1865, but it was not until 1881 that the New York legislature adopted a modified version of it. The penal code which expired in 1967 did not come into existence until 1909, although in most respects it conformed to that of 1881. A reviewer of the Field-Noyes-Bradford draft, writing in 1870, characterized it as a competent job, covering and describing all the crimes. But he added, 'inasmuch as the code aspires to the dignity of a scientific production, it is of primary importance that its plan and arrangement should be philosophical. In this respect we believe the commissioners have been only moderately successful.' The reviewer compared it with the French code pénal and came to the conclusion that the New York penal code did not compare well with it. Even in the special part the reviewer found many shortcomings, and he launched a blistering attack on the commissioner's proposed definitions in the law of homicide.[9]

The failure of codification should not be thought to have been due solely toward enmity to codification. To some extent, of course, the generally negative attitude of the bar was due to distrust of codification, and sheer conservative pride in common law. But there is much indication of a strong desire for the benefits of clarity and certainty which only a code can provide, vide these codification-friendly quotations from a contemporary writer:

It was tyranny in Caligula, which has been held up to the scorn of all good men from that day to this, to publish his decrees in such a manner as not to be understood by his subjects, and then punish them for violating one of these as crime.[10]

There is little show of justice in punishing as a crime in a citizen what he did under an error of judgment, if in so doing some of the very judges who by him could not themselves then have known that he was thereby violating any rule of law.[11]

Yet, the desire for a code was not articulate, the conception of a code was warped or imperfect, and even where, as in the next following quotation, there was a relatively clear idea of the functions of a code, either there was no qualified draftsman to be entrusted with the formidable task, or no politicians willing to do the entrusting.

All that can be desired in a code is to leave the common law to its free play, as to what is future; while so far as it has been fixed by judicial decision, it should become a solemn declaration of what the law is, in an authoritative form, and save us from being obliged to hunt for it in a thousand and one volumes through which these decisions are scattered. This we believe, may be done as well as the many volumes of our statute laws can be reduced to a single one.[12]

2. American Autodidactic Scholarship: Joel P. Bishop

While a publication by Francis W. Wharton preceded Bishop's first major publication, theoretical American criminal law scholarship cannot be said to have started until the appearance, in two volumes, of Bishop's work *Commentaries on the Criminal Law* in 1856 and 1858. Who was Bishop, the first American criminal law scholar? Let us have his personal report, published on the occasion of the conferring of an J.U.D. (*honoris causa*) degree upon him by the University of Berne, Switzerland.

I was born March 10, 1814, in Volney, Oswego county, New York, in a small log cabin in the woods, remote from all other habitations but one. While yet a babe, my mother being sick and soon to die, I was taken to my father's former place of residence, Paris, Oneida county, in the same State and I have no remembrance of Volney. My father was a farmer of small means, yet owning his fertile sixty acres, and I worked with him, attending a remote district school three or four months in the year, and finally graduating into 'the academy'. The schoolmaster of the district school was changed every term; and, regularly at its close, the retiring one visited my father and urged him to send me to 'college'. My own aspirations grew, and at about the age of sixteen an arrangement was made with my father to permit me to leave the farm and get an education by my own exertions. I found poverty to be no obstruction. While yet sixteen I taught a public school. And by such and other means I readily obtained the money for clothing, tuition and books. I could always earn my board without hindrance to my studies. But health soon failed, and then began the struggle. I did everything to baffle disease; relinquished study, returned to it under circumstances thought to be more favorable, broke down again, varied the experiment, and so on, for how many times I do not remember. When twenty-one I became fully satisfied that the struggle was useless, and gave it up. I did not, like Blackstone, write a 'Farewell to the Muse', but a 'Farewell to Science'. It was dated July 19, 1835, and published in 'The Literary Emporium', of New Haven, Conn., near which place I then was, in the number for October 3, 1835. I made, in the 'Farewell', one reservation, expressed in the following words:

> Though thus I bid adieu to Learning, where
> She sits in public places, or bows and waves
> Her plumes from off her star-clad height to meet
> The gaze of millions, still I may invite
> Sometimes her presence in a humble garb,
> To cheer me in my lone, obscure retreat.

Acting on this reservation, and otherwise letting 'Learning' alone, and having drifted to Boston, I entered a law office in the fall of 1842, hoping to obtain a little useful information, but with no idea of having health to practice the law. Here came another, yet agreeable, disappointment. At the end of a year and four months, I had fully supported myself by literary work outside the law, undergone an examination by the judge as to my competency in law, taken the proper oath for admission to the bar, opened an office, and entered upon legal practice. Indeed, legal practice with me began six weeks after I was enrolled as a student, when required by circumstances to draw, without other help than a little preliminary explanation, a special declaration in an important case which went through the courts and 'stood'. And afterward I had managed all the small-court business of the office, consulting with clients, and trying their causes. During this period also, I tried and won my first jury case in the higher court. So practice had become familiar to me, and, considering how slowly my short preparation compelled me to work, there was no lack of clients.

My business was divided between large and small, but most of it was the latter. This, preferring the former, I determined to get rid of; and, as a side exercise during the change, to write a law book. Hence my 'Marriage and Divorce', which was published in one volume just ten years after I entered a law office as a student. It brought me a constant succession of requests and advice to write other books. I saw that I could not both write books and practice; so, with the approbation of the only person entitled to object, I made the great sacrifice of my life by relinquishing practice, and entering upon legal authorship—whether for the benefit or injury of mankind time only can disclose.

Ever since the 'Farewell' spoken of, I have adhered to its promise by keeping clear of Learning's 'plumes'. I never flourished the appendate of 'A.B.', or 'A.M.'; nor did I ever expect or desire the opportunity of waving the more magnificent 'LL.D.' But the manner and source of its comings were such that I could not refuse. I did not go after it, nor was it bestowed on personal grounds. So far as I know, there is not in the country whence it came a human being whom I ever saw. On its face, it was a tribute to my labors in legal authorship from a country where the standard of legal authorship is higher than with us. 'The Faculty of Law,' I was informed in a letter after the degree was conferred, 'feels happy to improve the occasion [of the special celebration of the founding of the University] to confer the title of *Doctor Juris Utriusque* upon some gentlemen who by their learning and their works rendered great service to their land and to the science of the law.' Yet it was not meant for me individually, but rather as an act of international courtesy. This was shown by its being announced in the presence of the representatives of the principal universities of Europe, and the specially invited presence of the American Minister, and the diploma transmitted through the State Department at Washington. Under these circumstances, to decline would have been an act justly deemed offensive both to the people of our own country and to those of foreign friendly powers.

In my books, I have followed a new rendering of the Golden Rule, 'Do unto others as they do not unto you', by abstaining from stealing. And on the question whether our profession will sustain the new rendering, together with what it implies, or go back upon it, hangs the other, namely, whether my life shall prove, to the future of the law, a blessing or a curse.

JOEL P. BISHOP.

Cambridge, March 26, 1885.[13]

Mr Bishop may have been born in a log cabin, yet his treatise, published by Little, Brown and Co. of Boston, puts him among the royalty of legal scholarship. He proceeded with a remarkable scholarly care and an unprecedented meticulousness. In the preface to his fourth edition, for instance, he remarked: 'I find, however, that I have omitted one important case, much to my regret'.[14]

More significant than this attention to detail is the grand sweep of organization and the thoroughness of his analysis and classification. In Volume I of Book 1 he deals with the outlines of the subject and with general divisions. In Book 2 he deals with jurisdiction and locality, in Book 3 of statutory and other like interpretation as respects the criminal law, in Book 4 with *intent*, and in Book 5 with the *act*, under the title 'General Doctrines Concerning the Act'. In Book 6, he covers the 'General Doctrines Concerning the Consequences which Flow from Crime', i.e., sanctions and punishments. Book 7 details some specific human relationships—domestic relations and slavery—and their treatment by the criminal law. In Book 8, Bishop discusses the separation of criminal events into specific crimes, and the consequences thereof. Here he deals with such problems as the elemental morphology of crime and the doctrines of merger and double jeopardy. In Book 9, he discusses the question of what constitutes crime considered with respect to specific offences, with particular attention to protected interest, or its reverse, the harm, and the policies for the creation of penal law, i.e., the prevention of specific harms. In Volume II Bishop addresses

himself more particularly to the specific offenses, admirably organized. His analytic skills and his ability to convey his thoughts were
most powerful. By way of demonstration, I include his diagram of
crime (see plate facing p. 32), and his explanation thereto:[15]

> 'Diagram of Crime'. The idea of the diagram is as follows: Everything
> criminal, in the sense of indictable, is supposed to be included within
> the lines A O N H, resting on the base AH. Without those lines, and
> within the lines X W Z Y, are supposed to be things of a criminal
> nature; but, as there expressed, 'too small for the law to notice'. Those
> crimes which are of the heaviest nature lie upon the base, and occupy
> what is there called 'Region of Treason'; the 'Region of Felony' comes
> next; and the 'Region of Misdemeanor', where are represented the lesser
> crimes, is at the top.
>
> But the reader perceives that not all the things found in the 'Region of
> Treason' are treason; not all within the 'Region of Felony' are felony;
> though, of course, all within the 'Region of Misdemeanor' are mis-
> demeanor. This leads us to a consideration of the upright lines. A P B
> covers the region of 'Attempt'. An attempt to commit a treason is,
> according to the diagram, what it is in the facts of the law, not treason
> but misdemeanor. And the same is true of an attempt to commit a
> felony, represented by R O g a. An accessory before the fact, in treason,
> is guilty of treason, as shown by the coloring in the diagram; and,
> in felony the accessory before the fact is guilty of felony.
>
> It is not deemed necessary to go over the whole diagram with these
> explanations; the reader, having seen the idea upon which it is made,
> can study it for himself. The engraver cast his heaviest shades in the
> center and to the bottom; for there the heaviest guilt is supposed to lie;
> while, where the lines separate the indictable wrong from the wrong
> which is not indictable, the shading vanishes toward the light. The
> coloring, put on with a brush, distinguishes the treason, felony, and
> misdemeanor proper from one another. A careful study of this diagram
> will be very helpful to the learner. Indeed, there is no way in which he
> can so easily, accurately, and surely impress his memory with the main
> distinctions recognized in the criminal law, as by studying this diagram
> till everything upon it is seen and comprehended in its minutest as well
> as amplest extent.[16]

Bishop's diagram and an excerpt from his text are included to
demonstrate the master craftsmanship with which he handled matters
of utmost conceptualism and technicality and how, with equal
mastery, he conveyed his knowledge with ease, grace, and simplicity,
yet with no forfeiture of technical accuracy. It shows, moreover, how
Bishop succeeded in teaching his lessons in *context*, a context which
obviously always had been there, but one which it took a Bishop to
describe.

The most surprising aspect of Bishop's accomplishment is that he
proceeded virtually without scholarly guidance. There was little

precedent in American or in English criminal law on which he could pattern his own work. He completely rejected the primitive alphabetical schemes which he found masquerading as criminal law texts. In analyzing the common law of crimes he succeeded so well that he uncovered every element of the crime concept which we can think of today and defined them all with the utmost accuracy. He created his own categories of harm for the purpose of organizing the discussions on specific offenses. Perhaps most astonishing is the fact that Bishop published with equal vigor in other fields of law. Bishop's, then, is the first great statement of the American common law of crimes, and if, indeed, there is such a thing as the American common law of crimes, it certainly is what Bishop said it is.

His two volumes met with great success. Within ten years his work saw four editions, and the volumes did not cease publication until they saw the thirteenth edition in 1923.[17] It is a pity that just during those crucial decades of the twentieth century there was no analytical scholar able enough to carry on the work which Bishop had started, and the thirteenth edition was a far cry from Bishop's original masterpiece. Bishop's fame was world-wide and he received international recognition when in 1884 the University of Berne, Switzerland, conferred the honorary doctorate to which he refers in his autobiography quoted above.

The award of the J.U.D (*h.c.*) from the University of Berne was hailed in America as well. The *American Law Review* wrote:

> It is no exaggeration to say that in what he has done toward illustrating, expounding and reducing to form and system the law on several of the most intricate subjects, he has conferred lasting benefits upon his country. In all his writings he has studiously avoided appropriating, even in a slightest degree, the labors of other contemporaneous writers. His researches have been so original and exhaustive that his literary life affords a pattern to those who aspire to be called learned men. But he has spent his life under the very shadow of the greatest American university, and has not received the slightest recognition from it, any more than though he had been a Fiji Islander living in a hut within sight of its walls.

The 'greatest university' referred to by the *American Law Review* is none other than Harvard University. The negative attitude taken by this university—policy-determinative as always—toward Bishop and criminal law scholarship, was to have unfortunate results for the fate of American criminal law scholarship for a long time to come.

With increasing age Bishop apparently became a quarrelsome old gentleman, at least so we can judge from several reviews in the 1890s. One reviewer of the eighth edition of Bishop's *New Criminal*

Law (two volumes, 1892) called him the greatest living author on law, 'exceeding the stature of Kent, but a man of enormous vanity and ignorance in matters of practical life, a man out of touch with the bar'. The attribution of vanity refers to Bishop's own statement that between Hawkins in 1716 and Bishop in 1856, over a period of one hundred and forty years, there had not been a single new book on the criminal law, only rehash. With the detachment made possible by the intervening several generations, we can perhaps affirm that Bishop was right in his assessment. If that is vanity, then Bishop was entitled to it. And even the quoted reviewer admitted that 'no law writer, not even Kent, has done as much for the jurisprudence of his country'.[18]

There were times when Bishop was almost unreasoning in his attacks on such contemporary writers as Wharton, and Bennett and Heard. He sued them, and others, for literary piracy, sometimes successfully, sometimes not, and frequently with settlements. Whether or not Bishop in his later life suffered from litigious paranoia does not interest us today.[19] What is of interest is that his uncompromisingly ethical views on matters of literary authorship and on the ethics of research have helped create the standards to which all of us should aspire.[20]

Here we are especially interested in Bishop's pattern-setting views on the active development of criminal law, especially as to the nature of scholarly effort, research and possibly codification. Let us begin with this last topic.

Bishop took the conservative position on codification: 'Let me suggest, therefore', he said, 'that we suspend our quarrel over this question of codification until our law has received such juridical culture as to inform us, and enable us to agree among ourselves, just what and how many are its elementary principles, reduced to their smallest proportions. We have already seen that to ascertain this is the proper work of the jurist; it is absolutely outside the functions of the judge.'[21] In all my reading on criminal law, throughout the period of American history, I have not found a finer statement of the task of the legal scholar than this: 'Every lawyer acknowledges that there is no such number of legal principles as of judicial decisions.'[22] 'Hence', he continued, 'it is the task of the scholar to "find the elementary principles, reduced to their smallest proportions".' In England, Stephen had just published his Draft Code. Said Bishop: 'Let our American advocates of codification do the same, and when they have produced what all our courts accept as the embodied principles of the common law, reduced to their smallest proportions, the further question of their legislative enactment will present itself. . . .'[23] His point was obvious: Once all the principles are agreed upon by the courts, why bother to give them a legislative stamp of approval? It follows, according to Bishop, that if the work of the jurist has met with success it would be nonsense to give it the stamp of official approval. If it has not met with success it is too immature for codification and will probably be rejected anyway.

To illustrate: If one brings suit for building a fence which is the hypotenuse of a right-angled triangle, for which he was to be paid an agreed sum per rod, and the lengths of the perpendicular and base are severally proved, but not that of the hypotenuse, the length of the latter is matter of law, and the proofs are adequate. Now you enact a code providing that the square of the hypotenuse of a right-angled triangle shall equal the sum of the squares of the perpendicular and base. You will remember that, under the old system, if a boy in a class asked his master how this could be, the latter would draw the triangle on the blackboard, extend his lines, and show how the problem is reasoned out. The boy's brain would be stirred, a step would be taken in teaching him to think. Under the new system, the master would say, 'This is provided for by the one thousand three hundred and fiftieth section of our glorious code. It was explained by an old Greek named Euclid. Perhaps it was discovered before; at any rate, it has long been settled. In the year 1886, there was a meeting of great lawyers at Saratoga, and fortunately the best minds were in the majority. Saratoga, please note, is a place of water; hence it is certain that these best minds were not drunk. They resolved that whatever is settled should be enacted into a statute. Our legislature had the wisdom to follow the light; therefore, until the statute is so changed as otherwise to provide, the sum of the squares of the perpendicular and base shall be and remain the square of the hypotenuse. Now, boys, remember that this is the rule for what are termed the braces in all buildings. It is understood that the wicked political party, to which we do not belong, propose to change this statute, and make the square of the perpendicular equal to the sum of the squares of the hypotenuse and base. That change, it has been ascertained, will overturn every building in the State, and it is uncertain whether people can protect themselves by digging holes in the ground and getting into them. The better opinion is that, in this event, all things on the surface of the earth will be precipitated into its internal fires. To avoid this, as soon as you are old enough to vote, go to the polls; and, under the pressure of dire necessity, you may be required to vote, not only early, but often.'

It will be the same with all the rest of your code. You have slipped from reason, and settled on bare legislative command.

Law is the only profession which teaches the sort of reason that governs the State. The lawyers, as already said, are the judges, and they are the great majority also of the executive and legislative branches of the government. Should the cry for codification, under the eternal aspiration for laziness, prevail, and the element of reason which the practice and administration of the common law have carried into governmental affairs, be banished therefrom, the hitherto common-law nations will quickly cease to be the leaders of the civilized world.[24]

There is, of course, a flaw in Bishop's reasoning. If the jurist discovers what is right, it will be well to give it the force of enacted law so that it may not be forgotten and so that some ignorant judges, practitioners, or teachers, of whom our part of the world abounds, will not put their own conception of right above that of the rest of the world. This has happened, for example, when the courts ignored Bishop's statement of truth about the fallacies of absolute liability in regulatory penal law. Bishop made a good point[25] when he called the ignorant lawmaking by non-lawyers in the regulatory field 'sewer justice' (from a wrongfully handled sewer assessment case). It would surely be wrong, he argued, to condemn the entire common law as stop-gap injustice or ignorance. The point remains, nevertheless, that it would be wiser to clip judicial and legislative wings against flights of fancy.

But Bishop firmly believed that only evil could come from codification. As the true remedy against the disintegrating common law of crimes, he demanded scholarly discipline. He feared that 'the other remedy is to jump this ditch, and to codify the law while yet it has not had a single jurist, and make sure that it shall not have a jurist hereafter'.[26]

We shall have occasion to return to Bishop shortly, but will now focus on Bishop's contemporary and worthy competitor, Wharton.

3. *American Autodidactic Scholarship: Francis W. Wharton*

Francis W. Wharton had his first fling at the law in 1847 when he published a book entitled *A Treatise on the Criminal Law of the United States*. A reviewer remarked that the contents were disappointing. The book was neither novel in thought nor complete, nor did it 'suggest anything for the systematizing or statute amelioration of our present diversified defective penal law'.[27] This assessment of Wharton's first work is in accordance with that rendered by his contemporary, Bishop—and we must confirm those opinions about Wharton's first work today.[28]

When Francis Wharton later became cognizant of Bishop's success, he swiftly imitated Bishop's approach and in many respects surpassed him. Wharton was not only a first-rate lawyer, especially in the criminal field, but also a man of universal interests extending over all spheres of political endeavor. He was a competent historian and an excellent comparatist. He had a great interest in political economy, thus foreshadowing the work of the realists of the twentieth century. As we shall see later, he was a criminologist and penologist as well. The following brief biography, published on the occasion of his death in 1888,[29] is worth reproducing.

Francis Wharton, D.D., LL.D., solicitor of the State Department of the United States, . . . died at his residence in Washington on February 21 [1888]. He was long a sufferer from partial paralysis of the larynx, and recently submitted to tracheotomy, which gave him comparative relief. He continued his work for the Department of State and also his literary labors until the day before his death, and only a few hours before read proofs of his latest literary work, 'Diplomatic History of the United States in the Revolutionary Period', of which he had been appointed editor under a resolution of Congress. Dr. Wharton was a descendant of Thomas Wharton, Governor of Pennsylvania in 1735, whose father emigrated from Westmoreland, England, about 1683, and was the founder of the family in Philadelphia. Dr. Wharton was born in that city March 7, 1820, graduated at Yale in 1839, studied law, and was admitted to the bar in 1843. Three years later he was Assistant Attorney-General. He practiced fifteen years in Philadelphia, and from 1856 till 1863 was professor of logic and rhetoric in Kenyon College, Ohio. In the last-mentioned year he was ordained in the Protestant Episcopal Church, and became rector of St. Paul's Church in Brookline, Massachusetts, and professor of ecclesiastical and international law in the Cambridge Divinity School, and in Boston. In March, 1885, he was appointed solicitor by Secretary Bayard and examiner of international claims, succeeding the Hon. William H. Trescott, of South Carolina. The degree of D.D. was conferred on him by Kenyon College in 1883, that of LL.D. by the same institution in 1865, and by the University of Edinburgh in 1883. Dr. Wharton began his literary career early in life, and attained eminence as a writer on account of his perspicuous style and scholarly research. With Charles E. Lex he edited the *Episcopal Recorder* in Philadelphia, and contributed to periodicals. He edited ten volumes of reports of the decisions of the Supreme Court of Pennsylvania from 1835 to 1841, and in 1846 published 'A Treatise on the Criminal Law of the United States'. It comprised three volumes and ran through half a dozen editions. From that time until 1887 he published various works on legal and religious subjects, of which the following list is believed by the *New York Times* to be complete: 'The Law of Contracts', 'Criminal Law', 'Criminal Pleading and Practice', 'Criminal Evidence', 'Precedents of Indictments and Pleas', 'The Law of Evidence in Civil Issues', 'The Law of Negligence', 'The Law of Homicide', 'Conflict of Laws', 'Commentary on the Law of Agencies and Agents', 'Medical Jurisprudence', 'Commentaries on American Law', 'A Treatise on Theism and Modern Sceptical Theories', 'The State Trials of the United States during the Administrations of Washington and Adams', 'The Science of Scripture', 'Treatise on Private International law'.

We find in Wharton those essentials of industry which mark the scholar. We must regard him, together with his contemporary,

Bishop, as having inaugurated the patterns of American criminal law scholarship. He possessed 'love of learning, untiring industry, intense enthusiasm, deep piety, and a natural vivacity of mind'.[30] In many respects Wharton's career differed from that of Bishop. He was well-endowed by his family. He had a splendid education and in early years won a professorship in Divinity. Ultimately he attained the status of professor of law, but, like Bishop, he was to live in the shadows of the Harvard Law School without ever having his existence recognized by that venerable institution which, through this second example of neglect of criminal law scholarship, compounded the American law schools' negative attitude toward the cultivation of criminal law.[31] But what derived to the detriment of Harvard University accrued to the benefit of Boston University, where Wharton taught criminal law and other subjects.

Like Bishop's, Wharton's eminence was recognized abroad. In 1883 the University of Edinburgh bestowed an honorary doctor of laws degree on him for his vast accomplishments in scholarship and the analysis of the criminal law. Like Bishop's, Wharton's contributions, in the form of books and legal periodicals, were vast. On many issues his erudition remains unsurpassed. Adhering to Bishop's pattern-setting scholarship and meeting with increasing success, his criminal law treatise expanded from one to three volumes. It became a source of enlightenment in matters of criminal law. It is Wharton's theoretical insight into intricate problems which still commands our attention, and it should be a great matter of sorrow to all of us that the latest edition of his work no longer follows this original pattern.[32]

Later editions were crammed with references to foreign law. Wherever feasible he would point to the solution which theoretical scholarship had provided in Europe. He visited Europe at least twice, and one of his law review articles was in fact written in Heidelberg, Germany, in November, 1882, on the topic of comparative criminal jurisprudence.[33] In it, he showed how the American law on infancy and intoxication allowed, in effect, a sliding scale for the determination of capacity or responsibility, while it did not permit this flexibility with insanity. Why not? he asked, and noted that with the Germans this was long established practice. While there are other instances in which Wharton could extol the logic and advance of German criminal law scholarship,[34] his work nevertheless remained thoroughly American and deeply grounded in the traditions of the common law of crimes.

Even before Wharton had shown himself to be an expert in criminal law, he had made a reputation in forensic medicine. In assessing American criminological scholarship, Professor Fink wrote in 1938:

American courts followed (the M'Naghten) rulings which were early presented by the celebrated lawyer and writer, Francis Wharton, in 1855. (Francis Wharton, A Monograph on Mental Unsoundness, Philadelphia, 1855). Wharton's treatise was a model for close reasoning, scholarly grasp, and succinct presentation, being the first of many treatises on medical jurisprudence written by American lawyers. Indeed Wharton's book may be regarded as being as able a work for the legal profession as Ray's seventeen years earlier was for the medical.[35]

And to his interest in law and medical jurisprudence—an interes which Boston University has preserved—we must add Wharton's interests in practical matters of penology, criminology and even economics.[36]

CHAPTER III

The Mainstream of Development

1. *Stars of Lesser Order*

No original criminal law textbook of analytical or theoretical dimensions was produced from the times of Wharton and Bishop to the middle of the twentieth century. Criminal law scholarship and research in the theory of criminal law were quiescent during that period. This is not to say that no criminal law books were published during that time. Indeed, many books on criminal law made their appearance. Criminal procedure and pleading were favorite topics for law writers.[1] Most of the criminal law texts copied the pattern established by Bishop and Wharton, although never achieving equal competency. Only a few are worth mentioning. Several of these books were produced by law professors for the primary purpose of serving as class books in schools operating with the lecture method.

Emory Washburn (Cambridge, Mass.) produced a *Manual of Criminal Law*, designed for the use of students, which was published posthumously in 1877 by Marshall D. Ewell, LL.D., M.D.[2] Ewell first taught at the Union College of Law and later was Dean of the Kent School of Law in Chicago. The Washburn-Ewell manual was a throwback to a more primitive era. The entire general part of the criminal law, i.e., the elementary principles, was covered in eighteen pages. The bulk of the book dealt with the specific crimes and with procedure. Most of the materials were adapted from other standard textbooks.

In 1882 Robert Desty wrote *A Compendium of American Criminal Law*. His introduction indicates that he believed 'the elements common to all crimes are so blended with fraud, deceit, and violence, that a logical classification is extremely difficult'.[3] This quotation from Desty's book certainly sums up the general attitude then prevailing, Wharton and Bishop always excepted: criminal law is just too difficult for logical analysis! Nevertheless, Desty had a reasonable part, and a relatively sensible grouping in his special part, and in that sense he had improved over Washburn.

The first criminal law 'hornbook' appeared in 1894. 'This book is intended to contain a concise, but full, statement of the general principles of the criminal law.' Procedure was omitted. For better understanding the author 'endeavoured to classify the crimes according to their nature, and to treat kindred crimes together'.[4] One might anticipate that here was emerging analytical scholarship, but again the work was not very original. What its author, Clark, attempted to do had long been achieved by Wharton and Bishop. Indeed, Blackstone and Dane had already accomplished as much as Clark. The first hornbook, then, amounted to little more than an unauthorized and abridged version of Wharton's and Bishop's treatises, nicely reduced, though, and properly stated.

Another work deserving mention is Eulin McClain's book, *A Treatise on the Criminal Law*.[5] In his preface, Professor McClain writes about the changing functions of the text writer:

> When authorities are few he may be to some extent a prophet and an originator; but as the ground is more fully covered in detail by judicial decisions, he necessarily limits himself more strictly to an orderly arrangement and concise statement of that which has been determined; and finally when the number of adjudications on the subject which he is considering has become so great as to cover practically all the important questions which are likely to arise, his function is to put all in order and preserve a proper perspective which shall make general and well-established principles stand out boldly among the bewildering details of complicated cases, without obliterating distinctions which may be of the greatest importance. . . .[6]
>
> The law in almost any subject may be so stated by generalization that there can be no conflict in the decisions cited, or it may, on the other hand, be so technically and minutely stated that as to almost any proposition conflicts among the decisions shall appear.[7]

This is a rather authoritative assessment of the work of criminal law scholarship as perceived in the last years of the nineteenth century. There is no doubt that McClain was proceeding in the direction which history and experience were indicating, though it is a pity that the younger McClain had been unable to improve over the older Bishop and Wharton. It had taken McClain seven years to prepare his book. After eight years of teaching he had published a 250-page outline of criminal law and procedure which, in turn, formed the basis of his book. McClain made frequent references to the casebook by Bennett and Heard of which we shall have more to say a little later. Although he rarely relied on Bishop, he made use of Wharton, Wilson, Holmes, Russell, Blackstone, Hale, Hawkins, Stephen and Foster. His book contained a few analytical tables, e.g., on homicide, and, on the whole, it was very good in its analytical grasp and arrangement. The general part, without being so labeled, was presented at the outset. An incipient modern scholarship is definitely there, but the author himself seemed not fully conscious of it.

Among the more original of these late nineteenth-century criminal law textbooks was a brief handbook written by Professor Minor of the University of Virginia and published in 1894. This little volume presents the material of criminal law and criminal procedure in a highly organized and abbreviated fashion, although with many references. Everything Professor Minor stated was kept in its most succinct terms so that, perhaps, one could more aptly regard it as a grand outline of the criminal law rather than as a textbook.

His organizational scheme was quite traditional. The general part remains relatively small and the special part extremely lengthy and involved. In the preface to his work Minor wrote:

> The exposition of the law of crimes and punishments contained in this little volume is brief, but the writer has spared no pains to make it as perspicuous and as complete as the space which he had prescribed himself would in any way admit; and he flatters himself that the student who would master these few pages will find himself prepared to *enter upon* the practice of the law in the criminal courts. But he is earnestly advised not to make this book the limit of his studies, but to keep within his reach, and to read, as opportunity serves, some or all of the following, namely: Hale's, Pleas of the Crown, East's, Pleas of the Crown, Hawkins', Pleas of the Crown, Archbold's, Pleading and Evidence in Criminal Cases, Roscoe's, Criminal Evidence, Wharton's, Criminal Law, Bishop's, Criminal Law, together with such cases as he may find from the citations of them to be *leading cases*.[9]

One of the most prolific periodical writers of the period was Irving Brown, 1835–1899, probably best known through his editorial management of the American Reports, the *Albany Law Journal* and the *Greenbag*, but also known through his contributions to several other journals.[10] But perusal of many of his articles leads one to conclude that Brown failed to give in-depth treatment to his subjects. He definitely did not have the requisite analytical grasp. At least one book carries his authorship, *The Elements of Criminal Law, Principles, Pleading and Procedure*, 1892. Here he deals with the subjects mentioned in the title in a reasonably adequate, but terse and hardly challenging manner. His treatment of the insanity issue in this book is among his best academic accomplishments. Sensing that the terminology employed by the House of Lords in M'Naghten was no longer properly descriptive of the scope of the test, he proposed to rephrase the test by changing the word 'know' to 'understand', and the phrase 'nature and quality of the act' to 'nature, character or consequences of the act'. By modern psychiatric standards, as shall

Joel P. Bishop (See page 42)

Francis W. Wharton (See page 43)

be demonstrated in Ch. X, this is a considerable improvement over the outdated original language of 1843. This proposal indicates that Brown was fully aware of the bipartition of each offense into *actus reus* and *mens rea*, a separation which Wharton and Bishop earlier had made. In thus restating the M'Naghten test, Brown foresaw subsequent developments and hardships many jurisdictions would face. Unfortunately, the perception which Brown usefully employed in his discussion of insanity was not utilized anywhere else in the book.

Brown was also keenly aware of penological problems. He advocated that deterrence be employed through certainty of punishment rather than severity,[11] and he commented on such matters as the death penalty and the newly created institution of probation. Brown also seemed quite at home in the special part of criminal law, showing a particular interest in the analysis of sexual offenses and of obscenity.

Seymour D. Thompson was another well-known writer of this era, although his interest was more particularly directed to criminal procedure. This he had in common with many contemporaries, and especially Hochheimer, whose book *Crimes and Criminal Procedure* (1st Edition, State Attorneys' Edition) 1897, is still being cited in Pennsylvania.

Other writers, of lesser renown, made some contribution to criminal law. Among them are Spear and Speranza, as well as W. W. Thornton, all of whom evidenced interest in substantive criminal law. Perhaps we can briefly focus on the latter, as typifying the scholarship of the legal writers of that time. Thornton, in his many articles, displayed a tendency either to comment too generally, or merely to reiterate what had been said before by more eminent colleagues, in either case failing to take a deeply probing approach to the problems. Most of Thornton's criminal law articles utilized cases and the works of others (which he at least credited, in contrast to some of his contemporaries who did not) in order to arrive at what he believed the criminal law to be. Frequently he commented on cases in the Criminal Law Magazine and Reporter, and more than once provided insight into judicial decisions. Unfortunately, he never really rose above the rank of a case commentator. In one of his better articles, 'Intent in Crime',[12] he showed the embryo of an attempt to contest the emerging doctrine of absolute liability, and he quite correctly perceived the underlying theoretical considerations. This, however, is but a dim spark in the 39-page article.

Since it is impossible to comment on the work of all writers of the second half of the nineteenth century, a summary assessment is in order. We must emphasize that there were relatively few writers, and most of them were not connected with the universities. As busy practitioners or editors of (private) law reviews, they evidenced virtually no interest in the general part of criminal law. There were few comments on general problems, and, as the following examples demonstrate, these rarely showed deep insight.

In 1870 a notewriter portrayed a better than average appreciation of legal analysis when he wrote:

> And the intent and the overt act must both concur *in point of time* in order to constitute a legal offense. A person who retires to rest with the deliberate purpose of rising during the night to take the life of another inmate of the same house and who does so in a state of somnambulism, clearly established, is no more guilty of murder than if he had never entertained such an unlawful purpose. There was an original evil intent, and an overt act of homicide, but they did not co-exist.[13]

While today a psychoanalyst might think differently on this issue, the law itself still stands firmly grounded on the requirement that *mens rea* and *actus reus* must both concur, and hardly anybody has stated the issues more clearly than the writer of this note.

Continuing in the analytical vein, an author by the name of Endlich took issue with a statement by Judge Manisty that '*actus non facit reum nisi men sit rea* is more like a title of a treatise than a workable maxim' (from Regina *v*. Tolson).[14] Endlich argued:

> A maxim is neither a definition nor treatise. It is a formula for a principle. No matter how valuable, in order to be useful, it must be understood. For centuries this utterance of Lord Coke's has stood as a recognized formula for a most valuable and most cherished principle. It would seem to be part of wisdom rather to facilitate the understanding of its meaning and application, than to attempt the impossible task of blotting it out of our jurisprudence.[15]

While such sound argument was rare, it does justify us in the observation that on the whole, although grossly deficient and in need of cultivation, American criminal law scholarship was not non-existent.

Mr Endlich was rather sound in his general approach to the doctrine of *mens rea*. He was one of a small group of scholars who struggled to make modern sense of inherited doctrine. How far the writers fell short of their ultimate task is demonstrated by the following passage in Mr Endlich's paper: 'The *mens rea* or guilty mind, of which the law speaks, is that mental state in which the actor, voluntarily doing an act, is conscious of the existence of facts, from which it follows as a matter of law that the thing done by him is an infraction of a duty prohibition.'[16] This definition, of course, failed to consider the emergence of regulatory penal law. The maxim which was sound at a time when all criminal prohibitions were known as moral wrongs, now no longer made sense. In fact, by this well-intentioned statement, Endlich endorsed the doctrine of *versari in re illicita*, or absolute liability, to which nearly all regulatory legislation was tending at that time.

In earlier days immorality coincided with illegality, and everyone might know from the very nature and character of his conduct that what he did was wrong. But when statutory criminal law seeped into the body of penal law, it no longer followed as a matter of fact or law that where the actor is conscious of the existence of the facts he also must have an awareness of wrongdoing. Quite the contrary would seem to follow. Thus, for lack of analytical scholarship, as the Endlich example demonstrates, the doctrine of absolute liability and many other dubious concepts crept into our penal law. Neither heated legislative debate nor the issue and time restrictions of a lawsuit are well adapted to fundamental analysis. This task is best allocated to the legal scholar, and in the second half of the nineteenth century the American scholar failed in this respect.

To take another example from Mr. Endlich's paper, he believed that insane persons and infants could not be responsible for any crime, including regulatory offenses, because such persons do not have any *mens* at all. In other words, such persons are so demented that the issue of *mens rea* does not even arise. This is an improper and illogical argument. The M'Naghten test is quite clearly phrased in terms of *mens* as well as *mens rea*, and it exculpates persons who lack a rational mind (to appreciate the nature and quality of their act) or a *mens rea*, to wit, the awareness of wrong-doing. Surely an infant may lack full appreciation of wrong-doing yet have a rational mind. Indeed, a child may act rationally even though below the age of seven. The same argument applies to insane persons. A person who is psychotic may engage in crime fully aware of the physical nature of his acts and yet lack all appreciation of wrong-doing.

Let us compare Endlich's analysis with that of Elliott.[17] Elliott fully recognized the cultural criminal law on the one hand, i.e., the body of law in which the voluntary doing of an act supplies full evidence of *mens rea*, and the regulatory criminal law on the other hand, where such is not the case. Yet, and here again is evidence of inaccurate analysis, he accepts absolute liability without any apparent qualms! If there is one major complaint about the scholars of the nineteenth century it is that they were much too ready to accept what the courts propounded, whether sense or nonsense, and to go along with legislative trends.

Cowper may have spoken his famous words on *stare decisis* much earlier, but they certainly characterize the attitude of the law theoreticians of the second half of the nineteenth century:

The slaves of custom and establish'd mode,
With packhorse constancy we keep the road,
Crooked or straight, through quags or thorny dells,
True to the jingling of our leader's bells,
To follow foolish precedents, and wink
With both our eyes, is easier than to think.

Consider yet another example of legal writing during the second half of the nineteenth century. An author identified only by initials reviewed the concept of malice and determined what it meant in morals and various contexts of the laws.[18] He went on to note that while matters were changing in his time,

> The old terms and phrases will, doubtless, be retained, yet, like many others in language at large, they will be formal and meaningless. This tendency is in harmony with a healthy progressiveness of the age. The allowance to any man or set of men of the right to judge by what internal purpose, action is in a given case, controlled, places in their hands a dangerous engine of power, which can only be restrained by inflexible rules of evidence. The doctrine [of malice] was originally unnecessary; with a few exceptions, it belongs to the past.

Is this Jacksonianism in substantive criminal law? Be that as it may, it certainly amounts to an endorsement of the trend to emasculate the well-developed terms of the common law and to render them formalistic and meaningless. It was this tendency which resulted in the watering-down of such concepts as malice aforethought, premeditation and deliberation, *mens rea* and intent.

Hardly any of these writers distinguished himself in portraying or promoting scholarship. Only a few, with Wharton the notable exception, combined their writing with teaching—on or off the printed page. All of them were deeply attached to the common law, and it was an attachment which permitted little intellectual freedom.

What were the objects of inquiry of this generation of writers? The era of the sociologist was just being inaugurated, but few of the scholars of the period were yet fully aware of this development. They were content to debate the old issues which had been debated for hundreds of years, foremost among them the question of capital punishment. Reams of paper were written on that subject: Is it right for the state to take the life of a murderer? Will capital punishment deter? Is it necessary for the state to practice capital punishment in order to uphold the sanctity of the criminal law?

There was little development in criminal law theory, with 'insanity' being one of the few hotly debated issues. Most writers on insanity lacked an adequate grasp of the crime concept. The surprising fact is that the judges of the nineteenth century, on the whole, were beginning to conceptualize the problem properly and with *little guidance from scholarship*. 'Power and Capacity' came into vogue, in addition to the term insanity, and for a time it appeared that this correct analysis would win the upper hand.[19] Many jurisdictions, in this case with academic urging, adopted the 'irresistible impulse test'.[20] It is generally not realized that the 'Durham Test' (of 1954) —not the superficially similar New Hampshire Test—was well known as early as 1880. Witness this statement by an unidentified New Jersey author: 'It is suggested that the proper test is this: "Was there any disturbing element in the mind such that the act would not have been done but for its presence; and was that element disease?" or, more shortly, "Was disease the cause of the act?" '[21]

It is worth repeating that the legal writers of the nineteenth century were much more concerned with the problems of the Special Part, the specific offenses, than with those of the General Part of criminal law, the more abstract principles and doctrines. This tradition stood in the way of the emergence of a sound criminal theory. For the most part the articles of that time were superficial and descriptive.[22]

The literature of this era reveals some concern about the multitude of so-called public welfare offenses. Yet, again the writers preferred either to complain about, or to hail the development, depending on their point of view, rather than to examine such new offenses with the critical tools of scholarship.

In sum, the condition of the criminal law was worsening. While the number of statutes was rapidly increasing, the number of published opinions was even greater. The situation was close to chaotic. Bishop had clearly stated that the number of principles is much smaller than the number of decided cases of existing statutes. This was obviously not enough to convince American law-makers that the task of simplifying the law and reducing it to its principles was a job for scholars, or, indeed, was a goal worth pursuing at all! Whatever the reason, politicians did not avail themselves of the services of the few scholars who could have helped. Codification in the modern sense of that word had failed as well. What then was the answer?

If the textbook scholars, the courts, and the politicians did not attempt to provide any solutions to a worsening state of American law—especially criminal law—who then would or could? The solutions began coming from two entirely unrelated institutions, the law schools, which should have been involved much earlier, and the law publishing houses, which were never expected to engage in any theoretical work.

2. *Professors and Casebooks*

In 1835 the Attorney General of the United States, Benjamin F. Butler, gave an apt description of the method of legal instruction in the United States: 'Instruction in Law Schools is usually communicated through the medium of lectures . . . usually in writing . . . and not unfrequently prepared with such accuracy and precision, as to fit them for the press on the completion of the series'.[23] Butler credited Blackstone, Kent, Woodeson and Story with having produced admirable works of this sort. But he deemed the method suitable only 'when the elements of a science are few and simple' and 'when they admit of demonstration to the eye'.[24] In Butler's opinion, by then

> the rules of Law . . . [were] too numerous and sometimes too abstruse, to be treasured in the memory without the aid of notes and memoranda which cannot be made whilst listening to a fluent reader. Many legal principles are also so artificial and refined, and others qualified by distinctions so subtle, as not to be understood without the closest attention, even when presented to the mind in a written page—much less when pronounced with the rapidity of ordinary reading.[25]

In these comments of Butler's we uncover an important turning point in the history of American legal scholarship. In the past it had been thought feasible to reduce the sprawling rules of law to their basic elements for orderly comprehension and accessible placement in the store of legal knowledge. But through a process of proliferation law had become all too unwieldy for this kind of easy management. In retrospect it appears that to the leaders of the profession at that time, two paths seemed open: first, proliferation might have been replaced by reduction of the mass to manageable principles; second, a new method of transmitting the proliferated mass could have been developed. The second seemed the more natural course to take for a pragmatic case law. Butler pioneered a quasi-Socratic method for American legal education. The students were to be guided by syllabi, which not only would organize the subject-matter of the course (hence, not an entire abandonment of the benefits of theoretical analysis!) but which also would lead the student to his preliminary reading on each topic. The reading consisted of 'selections from the most approved elementary books, with references to the statute law . . ., and to one or more leading authorities from the Reports.'[26] The lecture itself was no longer to be a formalistic recital of doctrine. The speaker was not to be 'confined to the precision of written language, nor to a strictly scientific examination of his subject, . . . his great object being to expound and illustrate . . . and . . . [to] amplify and report, in a manner which may be very useful to his hearers, but which would not be allowed in written composition.'[27] Butler recommended that the instructor intersperse

> appropriate questions, at the pleasure of the Professor, in such a manner as to put at least one question, during the lecture, to each member of the class. . . . The answers to such interrogatories, if correct, will furnish instruction to the whole class; and in proportion to their fulness and accuracy, and to the promptitude and clearness with which they are given, will confer honor on the students from whom they come. If wrong in whole or in part, they will indicate the topics on which full and accurate illustration is particularly needed, and thus draw out such remarks from the Professor as will be likely to make a lasting impression upon the understanding and memories of all. . . .[28]

Butler maintained that such oral give-and-take between instructor and student 'will not only give animation and excitement to the lecture; but accomplish other and more important purposes. . . . They will frequently be obliged to reflect, to reason, and to judge; their minds will be brought into contact with each other and with the mind of their teacher.'[29]

Somewhat optimistically, Butler thought that 'lectures, more or less of this nature, are now taking the place of the written dissertations formerly read in Law Schools'.[30] In fact, however, Butler's was a rather startling innovation in legal education. No legal educator of the past had abandoned the formal lecture and placed such emphasis on an informal oral method requiring colloquii between instructor and student, and on the case and statute as the principal focus of preparation and class attention. Thus was born today's method of American legal education.

The increase of students at the law schools soon over-burdened the small school libraries where many of the students endeavored to read and brief the same few cases in preparation for their next class. Thus, the publication of casebooks containing these leading cases became mandatory. But it was almost twenty years after Butler put his socratic case-method into practical operation at New York University (1838) that the first successful casebook in criminal law appeared on the market. A law publishing house whose name has been connected ever since with a solid line of leading casebooks, Callaghan and Co., in 1856–57 published the first criminal law casebook. The book, edited by Bennett and Heard, was entitled *A Selection of Leading Cases in Criminal Law*. A second edition appeared in 1869. This book was specifically designed for use in legal education. The selected cases were arranged in the order in which they were meant to be discussed in law-school instruction, and we can judge from collateral reference that Bennett and Heard's casebook was used by students and instructors at a number of law schools. For example, we find in McClain's *Treatise on the Criminal Law*, previously discussed, a constant reference to the cases included in Bennett and Heard's casebook. In a book by Professor William C. Robinson, of the Yale faculty, entitled *Elementary Law* (1888), there are many cross-references to Bennett and Heard, and there are several other such examples. It could not be clearly established, however, whether either Bennett or Heard were members of law faculties. Probably they were members of the faculty of the long extinct Chicago College of Law.

Bennett and Heard's *A Selection of Leading Cases in Criminal Law* was not followed by another casebook in any field of law for almost half a generation. Then Professor Christopher Columbus Langdell's *Selection of Cases on the Law of Contracts* appeared on the market (1870–71). Ever since, the casebook method of instruction has been linked to Langdell's name, for it was apparently he who propagated its use.

Several other important casebooks in criminal law appeared during the last decades of the nineteenth century. Professor Lawson of the University of Missouri Law School published his casebook, entitled *A Collection of Leading Cases in Criminal Law*, in 1884. In 1885 Albert Phelan, who practiced law in Chicago, published a two-volume book entitled *Criminal Cases*, and in 1886 to 1891 Walter S. Shirley's *Selection of Leading Cases in the Criminal Law*, published in England, was brought out in an American edition with American notes by Horace W. Rumsey. Chaplin's *Cases in Criminal Law* appeared as a temporary edition in 1891, and the permanent edition was published in 1896. In 1893–94 Joseph H. Beale, then assistant professor at the Harvard Law School, published the first edition of his *Casebook in Criminal Law*, which saw four successful editions, the last one in 1928.

The theoretician of the criminal law had found a new outlet for his energy. Frustrated about the unmanageable mass of the criminal law, he abandoned efforts at theoretical refinement and structuralization, and made the decision to confine instruction and theorization to 'selections of leading cases'. In my opinion, this decision now appears as a most unfortunate capitulation in the face of adversity. Instead of feeling challenged to multiply the efforts at ordering the criminal law, law teachers lessened their efforts and reverted to a level of lesser sophistication and to a more crude theory. Of course, even the modest scholarly activity of editing a casebook compels the editor to do some basic thinking on the general classification and organization of the unruly mass of the subject. Thus, however reluctantly, the criminal law professor was forced to theorize a bit about a subject-matter which had predominantly come to be understood as merely a practical exercise in forensics and oratory. And so we find in the casebooks of the late nineteenth century an incipient, although primitive, classification of the body of criminal law, not measuring up to the far superior classification and intrinsic understanding which the two leading texts had achieved shortly before. In essence, the American casebook in criminal law was dry and uninspiring, as were most of the minor texts previously discussed. In fact, it is safe to say that in this respect no change took place until the middle of the twentieth century.

Beale had learned something about the synthesis and morphology of crime, but his book was still a relatively poor teaching tool. That defect did not prevent it from being widely imitated. Roscoe Pound wrote that 'His [Beale's] *Cases on Criminal Law* (1894, 4th ed: 1907) [*sic*] is the foundation of more than one subsequent book still in use.'[31] That Beale's work was considered worthy of imitation was to prove most unfortunate for the further development of criminal law in America.

With a twentieth-century assessment of the effect of casebook writing having previously been interspersed, it will be well, in conclusion, to recall the words of a nineteenth-century contemporary. In 1888, several years before Beale's casebook on criminal law appeared at Harvard, but after five other criminal law casebooks were already widely in use, Mr Bishop addressed himself to this new vehicle for teaching law, and this new expression of academic diligence. He said:

> This method is sometimes inaccurately termed the teaching of the law by cases. But the use of the decided cases in elementary instruction has always been common, and I believe universal; yet not heretofore commonly practiced to the exclusion of such books as Blackstone's Commentaries, Kent's Commentaries, Greenleaf on Evidence, and Story's Equity Jurisprudence. So that the new method consists simply in banishing books like these. And the brief explanations of the reason of the change demonstrate that, while the university does not choose to pronounce in words the common law's utter lack of jurists, it believes it to have none, and adapts its curriculum to this belief.[32]

Moreover, Bishop was convinced that case-oriented academics, spending their time on the pedagogical task of teaching law by the case method, could not possibly succeed in reducing the mass of common law precedents to a workable and coherent system. Bishop then commented on a speech by the President of Harvard University, a chemist, to the effect that scientists must go to the very source of their object of inquiry and 'in law that means go to the case'. Here is Mr Bishop's answer:

These words, also, when taken in connection with the fact that all text-books are banished from the school, are the university's clear and emphatic declaration that the common law has not so much as a solitary jurist; for jurist writings are 'original sources'. They are not the stolen productions, the 'second-hand treatises', I have described, or the joint work of men and boys;[33] but are the 'original memoirs of the discoverers', arrangers and condensers of the principles of law. They are not the apple which suggested to Sir Isaac Newton the law of gravitation, but his Organon. An adjudged case is the apple, and the showers of apples, and the glorious ingatherings of the fruit, not unfitly emblem the vast accumulations of our reports of adjudged cases.[34]

It was Bishop's conviction that the new case method pronounced the death sentence upon juristic works. If we examine the quality of post-Bishop juristic writings, during the first blossoming of the case method, we must concede that Mr Bishop's fears were not without justification.

For an overall assessment of the criminal law scholarship—or mere academic output—of the university teachers of the Victorian age, Bishop should again be consulted. He condemned, as we have seen, the then existing university scholarship in every respect: its case method and casebook, its textbook and its work method. His attacks on those so-called illustrious jurists who, if we believe him, produced innumerable works by student authorship, without giving credit to their helpers, were well founded. In his flowery language he suggested an interesting analogy to this type of juridical scholar-ship, which still has a few followers in the second half of the twentieth century. Suppose, Mr Bishop suggested, you want your portrait painted by a great artist and the artist suggests: ' "My dear Sir, the heavenly hand is still with you; it has led you to me. I have a hundred students, every one of whom is itching to get hold of the brush. From ardent cooperation of them and me, you shall have your picture." To this overture you do not need so much as to scratch your head for an answer; you say: "Great sir, the proposed work would undoubtedly be amazing, but it is not the sort for which I am looking." '[35] This caution is no less appropriate today. True, the demands upon scholars have so increased that frequently the scholar will find himself unable to proceed without the help of competent research assistants. But such assistance should be on the technical or tactical rather than the truly intellectual and strategic level, and should never go unaccredited.

It might be suggested that Mr Bishop should not have been so harsh on his contemporaries, especially since he, as an outsider, had no knowledge of the difficulties with which education itself was confronted. After all, legal education had only recently been made a matter of university study, and perhaps the early law professor were much too busy raising the scholarly requirements of schools and students to find time for scholarly preoccupations.

This suggestion may be borne out by the fact that the first school to solve the problem of academic standards and requirements was also the first school to produce any scholar of note, Joseph Henry Beale, Jr. If we disregard Wharton for the moment, then Beale, of the Harvard Law School, was the first criminal law professor who aspired to scholarly accomplishment. Born in Massachusetts on October 12, 1861, Beale was awarded an A.B. degree by Harvard in 1882 and an LL.B. degree in 1887. After having been a master at St Paul's School at Concord, New Hampshire, and having practiced at the Boston Bar for five years, in 1890 he became an assistant professor of law at Harvard University, where his tenure continued for forty-eight years.

Beale was well grounded in the theory of law, as evidenced by his editorship of the second edition of John Wilder May's *Law of Crimes*, 1893. But in this text, as well as in his casebook and articles, he gave an inordinate amount of attention to the specific offenses and tended to avoid the general principles.

Beale also published a treatise on criminal pleading and practice in 1899, and a mimeographed booklet, *Criminal Law; Its Origin, History and Purpose*. His analytical writings include outstanding articles on Criminal Attempts, 16 Harv. L. Rev. 491 (1903) and Homicide and Self-Defense, 3 Colum. L. Rev. 526 (1903), in which he proved himself to be a case-law master of the substantive law of crimes. He did succeed in accurately stating the law in the subjects he dealt with. His articles were logical but, frankly, lacked imagination.

Nevertheless, with Dean Pound, we must acknowledge that Beale 'first gave his attention to Criminal Law, which had been much neglected, and gave the teaching of that subject a needed development.'[36] Nor should it be forgotten that Beale was humble enough to recognize the outstanding accomplishments of those few who had labored successfully before him, for he once said—without mentioning names—: '[F]or the first time since the modern world began . . . the work of these scholars has at last made possible the intelligent statement of the principles of law.'[37] It is unfortunate that Beale himself participated so little in the statement and further development of these principles.

3. *The Contribution of Private Enterprise*

While Beale was laboring at Harvard there was yet another development under way. In previous eras, whenever private initiative failed in the accomplishment of a societally necessary task, government itself had stepped into the picture. But American government seemed most reluctant to assume any positive role. Laissez-faire was the mood of the time and, as mentioned earlier, even on so simple a task as consolidation of widely dispersed statutes, government failed to achieve any significant results. Such an environment provides the conditions where private enterprise may flourish and even assume a formative role. This is exactly what happened in the field of law, including the field of criminal law, in the second half of the nineteenth century. The same law-publishing companies which had produced the textbooks and the casebooks of which we have just spoken, which continued to publish the various so-called codes and statutory compilations, which, through their own initiative, had so materially contributed to the growth of the enormous mass of judicial precedent, these very same publishing companies now assumed the task of a theoretical ordering of the mass of American law. In the 70's and 80's of the last century these firms began with the publication of 'digest' systems. It was simply a matter of necessity to organize the mass of law in such a fashion that the practitioners of the law could determine *quid sit juris*, what is the law, in a given case. Classification and organization of the law was not urgent when precedents and authorities were few in number. But the expanding legal system of the late nineteenth century could no longer rely exclusively on the memory of man. Since there was neither scholar nor government to perform the task of classification and organization for our system, the law publishers, under the leadership of the West Publishing Company, assumed this function.

If the rule of law itself, *quid sit juris*, is the most basic level of sophistication in law, it is readily apparent that organization and classification constitute the next higher echelon of abstraction.

This is the level of theory, as distinguished from that of positive law. It is obvious to anyone who has used a digest that it rests on a fairly unsophisticated theoretical level. The digest may be a mere alphabetical ordering, and while that may be sufficient for the purpose of making law accessible, it has little to do with legal theory. Actually, the effort to order the mass of the law through commercial endeavor did help somewhat in the better refinement and organization of our law; and this was a welcome incidental effect of the creation of digests. By way of contrast, the law digests were a far cry from the scientific classification systems developed for biology or chemistry. The digest classification was neither continuous nor dynamic. It was predominantly static in structure and purpose. The classification system adopted by the digest writers was perhaps as good as any other, although in evaluating scholarship such a notion in itself is insupportable. Worst of all, these classifications did not attempt to discover the basic distinctive units or data comprising their subject matter—law. Significant uniformities and relationships were not discovered. The digest systems never proceeded beyond a common sense, so-called practical classification, devised to enable the practitioner to locate precedents.

By way of example, the titles of the American Digest classification are broken down into seven grand categories: Persons, Property, Contracts, Torts, Crimes, Remedies and Government.

If we study the sub-analysis of category five, Crimes, we find an intriguing list of subject headings which are so hopelessly mixed that one wonders whether anything at all has been achieved. The subject headings are: Criminal Law, Suicide, Homicide, Mayhem, Abortion, Rape, Sodomy, Kidnapping, Abduction, Arson, Fires, Malicious Mischief, Burglary, Robbery, Threats, Extortion, Larceny, Embezzlement, False Pretenses, False Personation, Receiving Stolen Goods, Forgery, Counterfeiting, Adulteration, Vagrancy, Disorderly Conduct, Disturbance of Public Assemblage, Common Law Blasphemy, Obscenity, Fornication, Incest, Miscegenation, Adultery, Bigamy, Lewdness, Prostitution, Disorderly House, Breach of the Peace, Dueling, Prizefighting, Affray, Unlawful Assembly, Riot, Compounding Felony, Obstructing Justice, Bribery, Embracery, Perjury, Escape, Rescue, Insurrection and Sedition, Treason, Neutrality Laws, and Piracy, in that order. Such a hopelessly garbled list of subject headings was actually believed to be a scientific, theoretical organization!

Some old articles by John A. Mallory, author of the American Digest Classification Scheme and employed by the West Publishing Company, throw a rather interesting light on the technique for preparing business digests. In 1904 Mallory published an article in the *American Law School Review* entitled 'Philosophical Classification of Law'.[38] The article adopted a very high-sounding style and conveyed the idea of being scientifically conceived. Mallory traced the development of philosophical classification of law from the Institutes of Justinian to Hale and to Blackstone, followed by subsequent authors, regarding all these efforts, however, as somewhat arbitrary, and declaring his intention not to feel bound by their precedent. In contrast, he pursued the goal of classifying *all* 'the subjects to which laws relate', and he felt obliged to express his satisfaction with the fact that the West System of classification had by then successfully emerged, and that most lawyers were gradually abiding by it. In a subsequent article, Mr Mallory considered the divisions of law as applied by scholars as arbitrary. Nevertheless, he found that a large amount of uniformity in indexing had been achieved: '[D]ifferences have not been fundamental but have involved mere matters of detail and of form rather than principles and matters of substance.'[39] And he quoted from Wambaugh's *Study of Cases*, section 115: 'In preparing a digest, the first step is an attempt to make classification of logics. What is aimed at is not a classification satisfactory to an analytical jurist, but one useful to a practicing lawyer.'[40] This approach, among other shortcomings, creates a vicious circle. The practicing lawyer was not analytically minded, and he could not be because the books and the professors were not analytically minded, and the books and the professors were not analytically minded because the works they produced were for the practicing lawyers who were not analytically minded.

In essence, Mallory's digest classification scheme rested on a few vast categories, within which he then resorted to alphabetical arrangement at best, common sense arrangement at second best, and no arrangement whatsoever for the most part. When Mallory quoted from Abbott 'let practical convenience always override theory', it seems to me he had his own convenience in mind, rather than that of those who in the future would have to operate within the legal system. Abbott, however, at least had begun with a theory, and this theory Mallory found expressed in one simple sentence of Abbott's:

> Law is the effort of society to protect
> *Persons*,
> including
> *Corporations*,
> in their rights and relations, to guard them in their
> *Property*,
> enforce their
> *Conveyances*,
> and
> *Contracts*,
> and redress or punish their
> *Wrongs*
> and
> *Crimes*,
> by means of judicial redress, judicial
> *Remedies*,
> founded upon,
> *Evidence*,
> and administered by the civil arm of
> *Government*.

This maxim, intended to encompass the entire order of the legal system, was indeed of profound influence upon Mallory. He took it as his credo, worked his entire classification system around it and created a pattern from which we still suffer.[41] The negative impact of this classification scheme on the subsequent development of American criminal law is second only to the failures of the nineteenth-century professors of criminal law.

With all this there were some signs that the time was ripe for effective legal scholarship. Consider this excerpt from the Introduction to Langdell's *Selection of Cases on the Law of Contracts*: 'Law, considered as a science, consists of certain principles or doctrines ... Each of these doctrines has arrived at its present state by slow degrees; ... the number of fundamental legal doctrines is much less than is commonly supposed; the many different guises in which the same doctrine is constantly making its appearance, and the great extent to which legal treatises are a repetition of each other, being the cause of much misapprehension.'[42] This of course is the same thought earlier expressed by Bishop.[43] Yet for criminal law the recognition remained academic, if that is the right term, since Bishop was never an academician.

Part 2

'THE MIDDLE AGES'
NINETEENTH TO TWENTIETH CENTURIES

CHAPTER IV

Forebodings of a Change

1. *What Great Change? A Premature Proclamation*

Unless forces were at work which have totally escaped the archivists' attention, we are driven to the conclusion that the events just described precipitated an increasing and nation wide drive for greater order in the system of criminal law, its administration and its auxiliary sciences. An astute observer of that era, the great legal educator J. B. Ames, assessed the past events in similarly critical terms. But he also spoke hopefully of the presence of forces which he expected to build a different future. On the occasion of the dedication of the University of Pennsylvania Law School building, Professor Ames said: 'Some of our law-books would rank with the best in any country, but as a class our treatises are distinctly poor. The explanation for this is to be found, I think, in the absence of a legal professorial class. We now at least have such a class. . . .'[1]

If Mr Ames had the criminal law in mind, there were only two books which the world had ranked with the best. As for the existence of a professorial class, history attests to the existence of a growing number of law schools, and thus professors. Whether these professors constituted a class is a debatable question. The notion of a class would seem to carry with it the connotation of common interest (distinct from that of other classes or groups), common power and common influence. In those terms, I am confident that there was no class of law professors in criminal law, but only a teachers' appendix to the profession-dominating common law judiciary. In spirit, and often in practice, apprentice training was viewed and practiced with nostalgia. In such an atmosphere tactics win out over strategy, and law cannot become legal science. I view it as one of the tragedies of the nineteenth century that no independent class of law professors did come into existence in the United States, and that the judiciary continued to dominate the scene. Had it been otherwise, our law would have been turned from common law to system law, as it happened with continental criminal law during just that century.

Ames realized all this when he said:

It is the function of the law to work out in terms of legal principle the rules, which will give the utmost possible effect to the legitimate needs and purposes of men in their various activities. Too often the just expectations of men are thwarted by the action of the courts, the result largely due to taking a partial view of the subject, or to a failure to grasp the original development and true significance of the rule which is made the basis of the decision.[2]

From the nature of the case the judge cannot be expected to engage in original historical investigations, nor can he approach the case before him from the point of view of one who has made a minute and comprehensive examination of the branch of the law of which the question to be decided forms a part. The judge is not and ought not to be a specialist. But it is his right, of which he has too long been deprived, to have the benefit of the conclusions of specialists or professors, whose writings represent years of study and reflection, and are illuminated by the light of history, analysis, and the comparison of the laws of different countries. The judge may or may not accept the conclusions of the professor, as he may reject or accept the arguments of counsel. But that the treatises of the professors will be of a quality to render invaluable service to the judge and that they are destined to exercise a great influence in the further development of our law, must be clear to every thoughtful lawyer.[3]

Ames then defined the role which the legal scholar must play in society in these terms:

If the professor renounces the joy of the arena, and the intellectual and moral glow of triumphant vindication of the right in the actual drama of life, he has the zest of the hunter in the pursuit of legal doctrines to their source, he has that delight, the highest of purely intellectual delights, which comes when, after many vigils, some original generalization, illuminating and simplifying the law, first flashes through his brain, and, better than all, he has the constant inspiration of the belief that through the students that go forth from his teaching and by his writings, he may leave his impress for good upon that system of law, which, as Lord Russell has well said, 'is, take it for all and all, the noblest system of law the world has ever seen'.[4]

But if as yet there were no scholars of the criminal law, at least none admitted to influential chairs, how could scholars be produced? If as yet the common law, no matter how noble, was not sufficiently systematized in the criminal law field, who would be qualified to accomplish the systematization? If criminological ideas had been generated, and indeed ideas which gained the respect of the entire world, who would there be to test these ideas through practical experimentation, to solidify them, to reconcile them, and to provide for their proper operation within the framework of a law perhaps yet to be created?

By this time all civil law countries had succeeded, through arduous scholarly work, in gaining insight into the basic premises of their criminal law, and they had made the best use of such insight by putting into statutory form all these basic premises and rules of the criminal law. France produced some of her greatest criminal law scholars during that era in Blanche, Cheaveau, Faustin-Hélie, Garcon and Garraud.[5] Germany's and Austria's criminal law had been fashioned in the shops of the greatest *Dogmatiker* of the nineteenth century, from Feuerbach, Grolmann and the elder Mittermaier to Franz von Liszt and the vast body of brilliant students he was to mold, among them von Hippel, Rosenfeld, Kohlrausch, Liepmann, Graf zu Dohna, Hafter, Exner, Delaquis, Radbruch, Engelhardt and Schmidt.[6] There was not a nation in Europe which at that time did not witness the ascent of the greatest criminal law scholars in national history: to proceed from North to South, Getz and Hagerup in Norway,[7] van Hamel in the Netherlands and Prins in Belgium, Pacheco and Silvella in Spain, Stooss in Switzerland, and Carrara and Pessina in Italy.

America lagged far behind. While there was no dearth of ideas, especially as to criminological matters, America lacked the apparatus, the men and the intellectual-emotional readiness to put these ideas to work. In retrospect, it is easy to say that perhaps it was nothing but myopia which prevented our predecessors from moving ahead in the right direction. It is easy to say that had the American Bar remembered the admonitions of Lechford, Hoffman, Bishop, Langdell and Ames, we would never have become known the world over as a criminogenic and, in matters of criminal law, anti-intellectual nation. Of course, we can derive comfort from the fact that in more than one piece of writing in old books and law reviews we find fully reasonable accounts of the basic properties of the criminal law as then in existence. We could make much of the fact that we had our prophets who proclaimed that no revolutionary revamping of the law was needed, as long as we followed the sound traditions of the law by preserving its dynamic quality of constant adaptability to new conditions. But the dynamics of the common law of crimes had expired. At the crucial time, the common law of crimes did not proceed to that stage which every other legal system in world history had to traverse in the development from the common law of an unsophisticated rural society to the code law of sophisticated modern society. I refer to the stage of practical stock-taking and reduction of the unorganized mass of common law, supplemented by stop-gap legislation, to its basic principles, the phase of theoretical abstraction. Did the bar—apart from its few sages—not realize that the common criminal law had not appropriately grown with the society it was to serve, that it could no longer cope with its task?

The crime problem increased constantly. One did blame the quality of the administrators, the press, and the general public for their attitude toward crime and delinquency, but one did not blame the outmoded *law* of those who should have kept it youthful.[8]

Surely, the basic premises had all been discovered, albeit crudely. But there was nobody to develop them further and to counteract the real evils: the dangerous trend of seeking a solution for every problem in a piece of *ad hoc* legislation, the endless rounds of usually abortive reform proposals, the willingness of every public speaker to advocate reform, and the unwillingness of every other individual to follow up. In the years prior to World War I public opinion was uniform to the effect that the American machinery of criminal law enforcement and the criminal law itself had broken down.[9] We take it from an account in the *Law Times* (England) that the situation in America was then alarming, that there were, for example, more homicides in Georgia in one year than in the entire British empire, and that corruption and lawlessness prevailed everywhere.

> America is cursed with a corrupt oligarchy composed of three classes: 1. The salonkeepers and gamblers, 2. The contractors, capitalists and bankers 'who can make money by getting franchises and other property of the community cheaper by bribery than by paying the community'. 3. The politicians who live by the conspiracy with the other two classes.[10]

In America crime was not confined to the lower economic strata of an immigrant population. Crime had become a common adjunct of life, involving even the leading citizens. If the state of affairs in America regarding crime and the criminal law was only half as bad as the English thought it to be,[11] it would have been bad enough to call for drastic remedial measures. Was there anybody to inaugurate such measures? What of the class of criminal law academicians whom Ames had conjured up?

Necessarily we must now focus on the men of academic stature in whose hands the fate of criminal law lay at the time. In these decades before World War I the following men held sway in the field: Professor Mikell at the University of Pennsylvania, Professor, later Dean, Kirchwey at Columbia University (who was soon to become Warden of Sing Sing Prison), Dean Wigmore at Northwestern University, Dean Pound, who would shortly resign as the Dean of the University of Nebraska and go to Harvard University, and Edwin R. Keedy, then of Indiana University. But most of these were young men and as yet not influential. Those who actually made the policies can hardly be said to have had the circumspection necessary for finding the proper path through the jungle in which American criminal law found itself.

In the early volumes of the American Law School Review, a preponderance of the statements and articles expressed a preference for the so-called 'practical approach', deprecating the 'academic approach' which looked for principles. While all of the men just mentioned were soon to become significant scholars intent upon devoting their efforts to a solution of problems of principle, those who were presently in the leading positions showed no signs of great scholarship. They were the *artisans* who knew all the stones of the mosaic, but not the *artists* capable of designing the whole mosaic picture.

Let us mention but a few names, merely by way of example. Among the more prolific writers (the word scholar is intentionally avoided) of the period there was J. M. Sullivan, a legal author who at times took a sociological look at some aspects of the criminal law, but who usually failed to probe critically the problems which he discussed. One of the topics which he took to his heart was that of juvenile delinquency.[12] He saw the answers to juvenile delinquency in upholding the old standards of morality and in a return to an apprentice system, which he considered to have been abolished solely because of the selfish motives of the unions. He expressed such romantic notions as education by good example, and life by the golden rule, but never managed to rise above the trite. Yet he was one of the most influential writers of his time.

Then there was R. Ferrari, a member of the New York City Bar, who frequently wrote about aspects of crime in a sociological manner. He was fond of the comparative approach, particularly with reference to France, and usually wrote in an energetic and zealous style. Among those mentioned, Ferrari was probably the most prolific and most thoughtful criminal law writer. He advocated several innovations which have become commonplace with us today. For example, he proposed the creation of a public defender system in the belief that 'the difference in cost could well be sustained by the state because of the advantages to the individual, to society and the law'.[13] He also stressed the need for better appeal rights and not only for 'those who can afford several hundred dollars'. In criticism of the privilege against self-incrimination, he wrote that in America 'We . . . are tender of the rights of the defendant, and are neglectful of the rights of society'. He clearly perceived the need for criminological re-evaluation of our penal system when he wrote: of the 'three elements to be considered in the punishment of a person guilty of an act called by society a crime . . . the act, the individual and society', our present law only considers the first and third.[14] This view puts Ferrari in the camp of the emerging criminological positivists who at that time had set out to conquer the criminological world. He advocated, among other innovations, that a course in criminology, covering all phases of law enforcement, be taught at the law schools. But Ferrari was not willing to give up the bailiwick of criminal law to the emerging profession of the sociologist.

> This work cannot be left to the criminal anthropologists. Scientists are adapted to discover truths, not to disseminate them or embody them in legislation. The lawyers will in great part have to depend on the scientists for their material, but they will be the great popularizers, and the appliers of the truths of science. To use a phrase now common in the philosophy of pragmatism, they will make ideas work.[15]

With the vision of a statesman, Ferrari warned against the then current trend, when he said: 'The height of a nation's civilization is in one way measured by the quality of its law. . . . [T]here is no element of the social structure which, more than the law, colors people's opinions concerning the whole structure in which they live.'[16] Ferrari, then, belongs both to the few who intelligently perceived the current needs and to the many who would do nothing about them.

G. C. Speranza, like Ferrari, concerned himself chiefly with sociology and its relation to the penal law, but his efforts were far less strenuous than Ferrari's. Nevertheless, Speranza, a positivist like Ferrari, left us some publications which are valuable today for the purpose of evaluating the eventual progress of positivistic criminology.[17] Speranza's approach demonstrates the beginning of an attitude which has prevailed with criminal law and criminology scholars in America ever since—as soon as the sounds of a new 'scientific' approach have been heard, there is a certain group of lawyers which will immediately clamor for the application of the new 'scientific' approach.

There is at least one more writer who should be specially mentioned as among the professional leaders in the field of that era. He was V. V. Anderson, Director of the Psychopathic Laboratory in the Municipal Court of Boston, Mass.. Anderson, by all standards, was a rather careful researcher, and particularly interested in the mental and emotional make-up of offenders. While it may go too far to proclaim him as the first scholar to use a scientific method for the study of criminals, it is not difficult to say that Anderson was among the first to do so in America. As one might anticipate, he developed a tendency to find mental and emotional defects in offenders. But his claims, based on statistics, were not as exaggerated as the claims of many others to follow later. His specific findings do not interest us today, but his careful empirical method is certainly worth noting.[18]

2. The Evolution of American Criminology

Nobody expressed the Anglo-American philosophy of *laissez-faire* better than Ferguson Bowe:

> The rain it raineth on the just
> And also on the unjust fella;
> But chiefly on the just, because
> The unjust steals the just's umbrella.[19]

Only a blind *laissez-faire* advocate would conclude that a society of 'just fellas' should surrender all its umbrellas to the unjust, as only a blind utilitarian could condone and defend the planned, gradual erosion of the legality and *mens rea* notions of common law by the ('public welfare') penal legislation of that era.[20] The *laissez-faire* attitude was probably even more deeply entrenched among the theoreticians than among the administrators of the criminal law. For, while the scholar may have been justified in the early part of the nineteenth century in letting the criminal law take its own course, he certainly should have changed his attitude during the second half of the nineteenth century when American society had to grapple with problems of prime political importance in the criminal law, when new statutes were passed *en masse*, when new methods for the administration of criminal justice were invented, and when a correlation between criminality in fact and criminological sophistication became more than suspect. To continue an attitude of non-intervention under the guise of *laissez-faire* at such a time was a most dangerous non-feasance. Perhaps the development of the American criminal law proceeded much more vigorously than that of English criminal law, but that is little consolation. The English law, for instance, had not even endeavored to create modern gradations of crime in terms of severity, and, for a much longer period than the American law, it had permitted the continuation of relatively cruel or harsh punishments. All these things had changed during the first hundred years of American criminal law development.[21] Moreover, the introduction of procedural protections for the defendant proceeded much more liberally in America than it did in England. But, on the whole, Americans continued to follow Anglo-Saxon law, practice, and tradition. For a society growing ever more complex this meant, of course, that more criminals than before were bound to escape, often on technical grounds. America responded to this with the emergence of lynch justice, of vigilante committees and of an attitude of general disrespect for the law, comparable with similar English phenomena seventy-five to one hundred years earlier.[22] This need not have been the result of the earlier and greater humanity of our legal system. In a legal system resting on long-range planning, such is not likely to happen. But long-range planning can be expected only from the scholars of law and its auxiliary sciences.

In this chapter we shall turn from law to what today we would call the social sciences. The social science of criminology had its beginning in America during the nineteenth century, more particularly during the latter half. In this era, the master scholars among our criminologists were much more active than were the legal scholars in creating and utilizing new ideas.[23] American criminology was soon to find world-wide acclaim—and it was to maintain its reputation. But there were others, good and plain people without legal training, who engaged in criminological speculation, if not study. They were practical men, acting positively at a time when in America the word 'academic' assumed a negative connotation. No one school of thought grew up to be strong in nineteenth-century American criminology, perhaps for lack of a central clearing-house of criminological ideas.[24] Among the early American pioneers in criminology we find such illustrious names as Charles Caldwell,[25] Benjamin Rush,[26] Isaac Ray,[27] Charles Doe,[28] T. D. Crothers,[29] and G. Frank Lydston.[30] For penology, as a separate sphere of inquiry, a similar listing would include the names of Louis Dwight, Richard Vaux, Francis Lieber, E. C. Wines, T. W. Dwight, F. B. Sanborn, S. J. Barrows, C. R. Henderson, G. W. Kirchwey and T. M. Osborne.[31] This is not the occasion to assess the merits of their contribution to criminology and penology. However, it is in order to note that their impact on the substantive criminal law was but slight, and most of their ideas have not stood the test of time. For us today, all these early American criminologists and penologists are important only as pioneers in the sense of having created an *attitude* which is still with us.

After a period of pat convictions on matters of crime and criminals, centering around biological (hereditary) speculation, there had followed a period of doubt and suspicion in the second half of the nineteenth century. But such doubts and suspicions were to exercise a positive influence. Experimentation and renewed wild speculation followed, but ultimately there emerged such valuable institutions as the indeterminate sentence, probation and parole, and a relatively sophisticated approach to the problem of the juvenile offender. Indeed, some of the articles published during that period sound so thoroughly modern that, if they were placed before a criminological reader in the twentieth century, he occasionally might be unable to tell whether the publication appeared in 1860 or 1960. This is particularly true of writings on juvenile delinquency.

In brief, the highlights of the development in the criminological field are as follows.[32]

Coincident with American independence, the American system of imprisonment underwent a major reform through the introduction of the penitence (penitentiary) scheme, as conceived and developed by the Quaker Society of Pennsylvania. Solitary confinement and a regime of absolute silence were introduced in the belief that this would aid the offender in soul-searching and in making his peace with his Creator. The penitentiary system, of course, had its forerunners in the Royal Palace of Bridewell, England, established in London in 1555, in the proposals of John Howard (1726–1790), and those of his contemporaries, toward the establishment of a penitentiary system,[33] and even in Blackstone's praise of penitentiaries under rejection of the ideas of retribution and vindication. It was in Blackstone's treatise that the penitentiary movement, or system, found its first philosophical explanation and rationalization.[34]

The Pennsylvania development has been reported on many occasions, and it will suffice to mention the establishment of the Philadelphia Society for Assisting Distressed Prisoners, in 1776, the name of which was changed in 1787 to 'Philadelphia Society for Alleviating the Miseries of Public Prisons'. This movement was crowned by the establishment of the Western Penitentiary in Pittsburgh in 1827 and the Eastern Penitentiary in Philadelphia in 1829. Here we mark a significant turn in American penal philosophy, from an attitude of reaction (vengeance) to one of action (rehabilitation and, thus, stimulation against repeated crime). Here is one example of a successful wedding of the humanitarian dogma of natural law (as propagated by Blackstone) and the ethically more neutral dogma of utilitarianism (for example, that of Bentham).

Pennsylvania did not stand alone in the reform movement. New York also experienced a major change. In New York, Calvinist and Lutheran religious principles, coupled with remnants of the archaic Germanic outlaw theory, led to the establishment in 1823 of the so-called Auburn system of prisons. The New York prisoner spent his long day at work and his nights in utter silence. The total environment was one of very pressing discipline, enforced by Captain Elaine Lynd who, fully equipped with whip, for a long time remained the prototype of the prison warden. But the Auburn system was no less 'criminological' or pseudo-scientific than the Pennsylvania system.[35] The New York penological ideas were solidified in an 1828 New York Commission Report which proposed that the initial incarceration of the prisoner be in solitary confinement, to test his character ('probation'), followed by an assignment to common work,[36] to promote his betterment. In 1868 New York introduced the 'good time' system and it was only at this point that the New York penitentiary movement may have turned into a true reformatory movement.

While criminological textbooks have regarded many names as worthy of mention in connection with nineteenth-century American penological experimentations, there is not a single outstanding 'father of the thought'. Few American academics, and even fewer lawyers, of that era would have desired to have their names associated with the improvement of the penal system. But the unsophisticated, unbridled and bold American criminological experiments had considerable success and generated an enormous amount of interest abroad.[37]

The Swedish criminologist Klas Lithner recently listed the following distinguished foreign visitors to the early Pennsylvania penitentiaries;[38] from France: Gustave de Beaumont and Alexis de Tocqueville (1831);[39] from England: William Crawford (1832), who introduced the Pennsylvania system into England;[40] from Germany: Nicholas Heinrich Julius[11] and G. M. Obermaier,[42] who, likewise, became instrumental in publicizing American penological ideas in Europe, though Obermaier, apparently, had not been favorably impressed. A third German, Francis Lieber, came to America as a political refugee, and concerned himself widely with penology. He held professorships at South Carolina College and Columbia College. While on a visit to Germany, Lieber lectured widely on American penal practice and even intervened with Friedrich Wilhelm IV, King of Prussia, on behalf of the Pennsylvania-type penal system.[43] Many others came to America to study the new criminological movements, among them von Mittermeyer[44] and Tellkampf.[45]

Yet another German scholar, Karl Roeder, devoted a greater part of his life's effort to the study and propagation of American penitentiary ideas in Germany. In Germany too, preoccupation with penitentiary methods was regarded as somewhat unscholarly, and so it resulted that Karl Roeder had to wait until he was seventy-three years old to receive an appointment as an adjunct professor! He obtained his title only a few months before he died, in 1879. But during his lifetime he did manage to publish widely on the American penitentiary system,[46] and became influential in the introduction of the cellular and the Pennsylvania system in Germany.[47]

It was at this time, too, that the suspended sentence and the suspended judgment were institutionalized in America. The origin of the suspended sentence and, incidentally, of probation, is not traceable to scholarly invention, but rather to judicial ingenuity: since a judge acted as a general conservator of the peace, he could place a defendant under a peace bond, and he could command sureties to keep the peace and sureties for good behavior. Hence, so it was reasoned, he could also suspend the imposition or the execution of the sentence. Since the American states had long made use of the power to suspend sentence, with or without peace bonds, but usually with sureties, the innovation actually consisted only of dropping the requirement of sureties.[48] It was Adolph Lenz who, early in the twentieth century, gave us a magnificent interpretation of this American development. In his opinion, the origins of our modern criminological ideas of the suspended sentence, indeterminate sentence, and of probation and parole, are completely non-academic. Nor, he said, are they traceable solely to the wide discretion which the common law had traditionally accorded its judges. Rather, they, like the penitentiary system, are attributable to America's great sense of philanthropy and private concern about the common weal, which flourished in a society where the state and the local prosecutors did not enjoy a monopoly of crime control. Thus, according to Lenz, criminality in America was viewed as a community responsibility, rather than as an individual one.[49] As early as in the 1840's, Boston judges, at the urging of John Augustus, a cobbler, took it upon themselves to place delinquent children with responsible foster parents and in private foster homes. This practice would have been inconceivable in continental Europe.[50] After 1870 this practice was regulated by law.[51] Subsequently, Massachusetts adopted the system of visiting agents and, in 1878 for Boston, and 1884 for all of Massachusetts, probation officers for juvenile offenders were introduced. This fabulous idea spread quickly through America and by now has found acceptance in the rest of the world. Soon the juvenile probation system was expanded to an adult probation system, corresponding to the increasing practice of suspending the sentence for probation.

Similarly, parole was developed entirely without scholarly participation; and, though it subsequently crystallized in statutes, it was a judicial and administrative innovation.

Perhaps in nineteenth-century America it was still possible for judges to generate such revolutionary ideas, ideas which on the European continent could have come only from the universities— but did not! The entire criminological superstructure developed by a method of trial and error and, at least initially, solely on the local level. Thus, in Suffolk County, Massachusetts, in 1870, and in New York in 1892, the courts began to hold separate sessions to deal with charges against juveniles. In 1899 Cook County, Illinois, made conventional history when it established the first juvenile court in the world.[52]

As a result of all these fascinating activities, by the turn of the century Americans had created such an abundance of penological innovations that their development and study could no longer be left to the unguided discretion of 'practical' men. The time had arrived for an inventory-taking and for an academic assessment of all these advances. If the academics had not been particularly instrumental in all that which now constituted 'criminology', might they at least bring some belated order to the field?

3. *Wigmore at Northwestern: Scholarship on the Frontier*

It was at this time that a highly regarded American legal scholar, not yet distinguished in criminal law and criminology, saw the need for intelligent action. This scholar was John Henry Wigmore. Born in San Francisco on March 4, 1863, Wigmore had received his Harvard A.B. in 1883, the A.M. degree in 1884, and an LL.B. in 1887. He practiced law in Boston for two years from 1887 to 1889 and then, strangely enough, taught law at Tokyo University from 1889 to 1893, after which he assumed a professorship in law at Northwestern University, where he became dean in 1901. The stream of his accomplishments was nothing short of spectacular and magnificent. The academic profession rewarded him richly. Among his early honorary doctorates we find a University of Wisconsin LL.D. in 1906 and a Harvard LL.D. in 1909. This is not the place to review John Henry Wigmore's enormous contribution to American legal science, his *opus magnum Wigmore on Evidence*, his *Panorama of the World's Legal Systems* and his *Kaleidoscope of Justice*. It is John Henry Wigmore the organizer of American criminology who interests us here.

Wigmore readily perceived that American criminal law had a sound heritage. He was also fully aware of the fact that, for whatever reason, this sound law had not kept pace with social developments and psychological insights, and that it could no longer cope with the growing crime situation in America. It was apparent to him that 'auxiliary sciences' had come into existence and that these sciences might well be usefully employed not only to rejuvenate and to reorganize our criminal law, but to contribute methods hitherto unknown or barely envisaged. Wigmore was willing to do something about it, and that set him apart from all the others of similar perception. In addition, Wigmore probably feared that if these new 'sciences' were to continue to develop outside the framework of the law, the result might well be detrimental to the leadership of law.

Wigmore may have had no firm idea of what had to be done, but it is clear that he knew that *something* had to be done, something to awaken the sleeping scholars.

The energetic, frontier-like City of Chicago was to serve as the host city for a historic conference, arranged by Wigmore, on the occasion of the fiftieth anniversary of the Law School of Northwestern University in 1909. Those who attended could testify that never before on the North American continent had there been a gathering of more eminent criminologists and criminal lawyers. It was Wigmore's plan to turn this criminological gathering into the inauguration ceremony of modern American criminology. This was not a conference after which the participants would leave simply satisfied with the wonderful speeches they had heard and made. This was an entirely different conference. Whether the participants liked it or not, John Henry Wigmore had roped them, and they were now intimately and intricately involved in a national effort of scientific and intelligent coping with the American crime problem. An unheard-of flurry of activities resulted from this Conference on Criminal Law and Criminology. An American Institute of Criminal Law and Criminology was founded which, during the many years of its activity, was to produce more enlightenment in matters of criminal law and criminology than had any previous effort. The Institute held many successful conferences, operated through the participation of the most eminent experts in the nation, and issued many distinguished publications which reflect the enthusiastic collaboration Wigmore inspired. The Conference also established the *Journal of the American Institute of Criminal Law* and *Criminology*, which later became known as the *Journal of Criminal Law and Criminology*, and still later became the present *Journal of Criminal Law, Criminology and Police Science*.

The conference had several direct and indirect effects, of which the continued success of the Journal and Northwestern University's continued emphasis on criminal law administration are the most obvious. It is no exaggeration to claim that the *Journal of Criminal Law, Criminology and Police Science* has not only provided the sounding board for the development of criminal law and criminology in America, but has played a leading role throughout these years. Through its staff and its contributors, it has guided the development of criminal law and criminology in America for the last fifty-three years. The first editor of the Journal was Professor J. W. Garner of the University of Illinois. One year later he was succeeded by Dr Robert H. Gault, who retired only after nearly half a century of service, in 1960. For his long and distinguished editorship he received many honors, including a tribute from the entire editorial

board, and an international *Festschrift*.[53] For the next five years the
Journal was edited by Professor Claude R. Sowle, who was succeeded
by its long-time managing editor, Professor Fred E. Inbau.

Indeed, the *Journal of Criminal Law, Criminology and Police
Science* assumed the functions which had been assigned to the
Institute, but which the latter, in the mid-20s, owing to a lack of
continued vigorous leadership, could not perform, namely, the
furtherance of the scientific study of crime, criminal law and procedure, the formulation and promotion of measures for solving the
problems connected with crime, and the co-ordination of efforts of
individuals and organizations interested in the administration of a
certain and speedy justice. During the few years of its functioning
the Institute itself established branches in Wisconsin and Pennsylvania, and worked on problems of its own organization and the
organization of the courts and of criminal procedure. Here is a slate
of committees in existence in 1916–1917:

  Committee A—Insanity and Criminal Responsibility
  Committee B—Probation and Suspended Sentence
  Committee C—Classification and Definition of Crime
  Committee D—Modernization of Criminal Procedure
  Committee E—Crime and Immigration
  Committee F—Sterilization of Criminals
  Committee G—Drugs and Crime
  Committee I—State Societies and New Membership
  Committee II—Promotion of Institute Measures
  Committee III—Publications

There were, furthermore, the committees on translation of treatises
on criminal law (which published nine volumes of the Modern
European Criminology Series),[54] the committee on employment and
compensation of prisoners, the committee on indeterminate sentence,
release on parole and pardon, the committee on criminal statistics,
the committee on teaching of criminalistics in universities and
colleges, and the committee on the public defender. While the work
of the Institute succeeded in largely co-ordinating the many nation-
wide efforts, and in turning the variegated phases of criminology into
a functioning discipline of criminology, and while the work carried
on under the auspices of the committees occasionally led to the
direct solution or resolution of problems and questions (for instance,
the myth of immigrant criminality was destroyed),[55] the real merit of
the Institute lay more in the mobilization of efforts and in the
establishment of the criminological tradition which is still with us.[56]

We can also regard it a result of Dean Wigmore's successful 1909
conference that an American section of the International Union of
Criminal Law was established at Northwestern University. Professor

Charles R. Henderson of Chicago was the Chairman of this American group, and Professor Edwin R. Keedy, then of Northwestern University, its Secretary. This was the second major effort on the part of American criminological scholars to join the world movement toward criminological progress.[57] Unfortunately, American participation in the International Union of Criminal Law was short-lived. World War I intervened and damped the spirit of world-wide co-operation as far as Americans were concerned, and no similar effort was made until 1960. In retrospect, this American failure to join the world-wide exchange of ideas in criminal law proved to have long-range negative consequences. An appreciation of continental ideas in criminal law, and of European aims in scholarship, remained foreclosed for another half century. The Monroe Doctrine, dead in politics, continued in criminal law. This failure to maintain the nexus to world criminal law development and scholarship was a major cause for the continuing low state of sophistication of American criminal law.

In fact, we might regard this failure of the criminal law scholars, as contrasted with the criminology scholars, as symptomatic. The success of both the Institute and the Journal was much more pronounced in the criminological field, especially in drawing together the various criminological sciences, than it was in the criminal law field. This is easily explainable: the criminal law was static, its scholarship practically non-existent. Criminology, on the other hand—although yet unco-ordinated and somewhat aimless—was dynamic. It was much easier for the Institute to direct criminology into a channel than to dig a well from which to draw criminal law scholarship.

CHAPTER V

Criminology Takes the Lead

1. *In the Beginning—There was Imbecility*

Within the first few years after its coming-out party had been so exuberantly celebrated in Chicago, the young 'science' of criminology could book but few lasting accomplishments. The best known—and most typical—of these was the creation and subsequent refutation of the theory of feeble-mindedness as a major cause of crime.[1]

Through the labor of such eminent medical doctors as Henry M. Hurd,[2] Isaac N. Kerlin,[3] Martha Louise Clark,[4] but particularly Walter E. Fernald[5] and Charles W. Burr,[6] a respectable body of knowledge had been built up, suggesting the close—if not causal—relationship between low intelligence and criminality. These theoretical and classificatory accomplishments then found eminent support through psychometric research on prison inmates. While early researchers proclaimed three, four, or five per cent of prison inmates to be mentally defective, the figures began to increase startlingly over the years to twelve, twenty-one, and twenty-three per cent,[7] until they reached their maximum of sixty-eight per cent in the published reports of Hugo Münsterberg of Harvard.[8] Crude methods of psychological testing were soon replaced by the newly developed Binet scale, widely used by Henry H. Goddard and his research assistant, Helen F. Hill,[9] and the figures steadied at fifty per cent, although Goddard listed other, and presumably reliable, prison estimates of the frequency of feeblemindedness among convicts as high as eighty-nine per cent.[10]

> Many thought the sources of criminality had been uncovered [wrote Dr Gault in retrospect]. There was fear that we should have an institution in every city block to take care of potential jail birds! There was no encouragement there for correctional workers. You can't doctor up low basic intelligence.
>
> Strange that it did not immediately occur to the pioneers that they had examined only a small sample of caught and convicted offenders; that a host of equally wicked ones had been smart enough to go un-

caught, and that a large proportion of low-level people were living honestly, each in his own simple way. But the testers were quite sure of themselves. It took World War I to set them right. For drafted psychologists assigned to personnel service in the United States Army made new tests and techniques. Some of them found later in civilian life that several reformatory populations were closely like draftees and the people generally in respect to intelligence—age for age—though, again, the prisoners were only those who had not got away.

We probably could have got along without a World War to correct the testers, for Dr William Healy,[11] director of what was then called the Juvenile Psychopathic Institute, was accumulating psychological data from juvenile court cases in Chicago during a five year period ending in 1917. He had reported that low intelligence was a major factor in about ten per cent of the examinees—not seventy or eighty per cent. Maybe that figure was misleading because Healy, too, like examiners of reformatory populations, was dealing with a selected group. The correctionalists lacked a good conception of the criminal nature. But basic intelligence was fading from the picture—which was something.[12]

And thus, the young 'science' of criminology had learned its first lesson—by trial and error.[13] The result was negative: the finding was not 'what', but 'what not'. Nevertheless, much had been learned about low intelligence and criminality. But now comes the question which is of paramount significance for this treatise. What had the *law* learned from this criminological experience and experiment? Unquestionably the law *should* have learned something, for if even only ten per cent of the criminal population is feeble-minded, the law must deal with this ten per cent as much as with the remaining ninety per cent who might not be feeble-minded. As early as 1867, an unsigned article in the *American Journal of Insanity*—attributed to Isaac Ray[14]—had pointed out how the law might deal with feeble-mindedness. This article protested at a jury finding of guilty of murder, of one Gregor MacGregor, with the words: 'But he had not that degree of mental activity and energy which an enlightened common sense should deem necessary to a criminal intent.'[15] Indeed, does it not stand to reason that if a fully normal perpetrator incurs full responsibility for his crime, one who falls short of the mark in intelligence or psychic power should incur less responsibility? If the natural age of human beings is taken into account in the assessment of liability, should not the mental age be taken into account as well? The American criminal law took no notice of the events on the other side of the campus. Perhaps it was due to Mr Justice Holmes' dogmatic proclamation of the common law's ancient objective standards of conduct: 'They require him of his own peril to come up to a certain height. They take no account of incapacities, unless the weakness is so marked as to fall into well-known exceptions, such as infancy or madness.'[16] Perhaps it was sheer conservatism. Perhaps, and that is not at all unlikely, it was the legal profession's vast ignorance on matters of science. In any event, nothing, absolutely nothing, happened in law as a response to the major scientific convulsion in criminology. It was not until 1962 that somebody picked up the trend to come forward with a reasonable application of psychological experience resulting from the intelligence studies, to the substantive criminal law. This recent proposal would analogize intensity of psychological power with intensity of *mens rea*, coupled with a series of presumptions, and could result in the recognition of the concept of diminished responsibility.[17] The law's labor-pains followed fifty years after criminology's conception! This was to remain typical.

Perhaps the law's conservative reluctance to even consider the studies of feeble-mindedness was a wholesome thing, for if once the studies had been credited, the criminologists' proposed cure might have been credited as well. This proposed cure was 'asexualization' on a grand scale.[18] How unfortunate if the law had gone on an all-out rampage to sterilize 'mentally defective' criminals, only to see the theoretical bases of such an irreversible remedy reversed within a few years![19]

2. *Biological Theories*

It is impossible in this work to follow the criminological causation theories, one by one, along the entire winding road of criminological research. But two further way-stations along this road should be mentioned.

(a) *Body Types and Delinquency*. Lombroso's theory of the born criminal, identifiable by atavistic body features,[20] celebrated some late triumphs in the United States.[21] However, 'the existence of the criminal brain was not proved',[22] and no strong group of Lombroso followers ever existed in America. This was perhaps due to the early successful refutation of Lombroso by the Englishman Charles Goring.[23]

The relationship between somatotypes and criminal propensity continues to hold some fascination for American researchers.[24] None probably has equaled Hooton's extreme claims[25] that criminals as a group are sociologically and biologically inferior and require the creation of tightly segregated areas where they could establish their own social organizations. This demand is as close as the anthropological theory of criminology ever came to the law.

Still more recently, Sheldon and Eleanor T. Glueck have revived the anthropological theory in *Physique and Delinquency*.[26] Their studies revealed that among over several hundred delinquents, sixty per cent were mesomorphs, thirteen per cent endomorphs, fourteen per cent ectomorphs and thirteen per cent balanced. The authors, with scientific caution, regarded their detailed studies as 'at least suggestive concerning the implications of body structure in the prevention and control of juvenile delinquency'.[27]

Parenthetically, a recent count, conducted by this author and a visiting Dutch criminologist, of a class of twenty-five nationally selected honor students (Root-Tilden and Snow Scholars) of the New York University School of Law, revealed a strikingly similar distribution of body types as those found among the Gluecks' delinquents, namely fifty-five per cent mesomorphs, sixteen per cent endomorphs, twenty per cent ectomorphs, nine per cent balanced. Obviously, the small number examined and the limited examination itself deprives this finding of any scientific value.

Even with the aid of the generally respected scholarship of the Gluecks, the anthropological school has had no impact on the law, and none can be imagined. Data of much greater scientific value, encompassing socio-cultural as well as biological factors, as suggested by the Gluecks, is needed before the law can legitimately consider the theory at all.

(b) *Endocrinology.* To the biochemist, human behavior is the resultant of body chemistry. Since the commission of crime is a matter of human behavior, it must be the resultant of body chemistry. The question is whether the fact that some conduct happens to be legislatively prohibited while other conduct is not, has something to do with the 'chemical composition' of behavior. An entire school of criminology continues to maintain that it does.[28] The earlier endocrinologists were mocked by their brethren in medicine and law, as evidenced by this poem:

MODERN CRIMINOLOGY

The wizard feeds and carves and saws
His rats and gophers till he gleans
The knowledge that crime's only cause
Is maladjusted endocrines.

How happy you should be to know
That when some yeggman smacks you double
It is not crime that prompts the blow
But merely pancreatic trouble.

Or if some low-browed, slinking lad
A knife between your ribs should bury,
Don't mind him, he's not really bad;
It's just a sick pituitary.

Perhaps you've been pumped full of lead
Until the light can through you filter
No crime was done, although you're dead;
'Twas but a thyroid out of kilter.

And so, whatever be your lot:
By some plug-ugly to be socked or
Maybe throttled, stabbed or shot,
Don't call a cop, just a doctor![29]

But we have not heard the last of endocrinology, as yet still an
infant science. Paul Tappan recently said: 'From the evidence
already at hand, however, it is very clear that the endocrines may
profoundly affect . . . feelings, emotions, and behavior through their
influence upon . . . the brain and nervous system in particular. . . .
[Podolsky's] findings suggest interesting possibilities for future
improvements in our understanding of the offender and in our
treatment measures.'[30]

Indeed, if a definite relationship between glandular functioning
and natural or artificial stimulants is demonstrated, the very concept
of personal responsibility, the pillar of our criminal law, would
tumble. As yet, the findings are only disturbingly suggestive, and
much more scientific, i.e. biochemical, work is needed before the law
can take cognizance of endocrinology.

3. *The Psychiatric School*

After the psychology of feeblemindedness, and contemporaneously
with anthropological and endocrinological theories, it was psychiatry
which made the headlines in the criminological journals of the 1920s.
The stage for American developments had been set as early as 1901
when Maurice de Fleury's work *The Criminal Mind* appeared in
English translation. This was the first book of psychoanalytic
dimensions which interpreted criminality on the basis of neurology.
'It will be the glory of this present time', wrote de Fleury, 'to have
recognized that Free Will does not exist, that there is no moral
responsibility, that the criminal belongs to nervous pathology, that
he is the result of an unhealthy heredity and a bad education. And it
will also be a great error of our epoch to have devised to suppress
every vengeful reflex of our minds at this period, to substitute reasoning for natural impulses, as though we were now really civilized!'[31]
The theories of Freud, Adler, Jung and Klein were soon reflected in
the sphere of criminology. In this country, after a series of perhaps
less solid publications, the immediate post-World War I era saw the
emergence of a strong 'psychiatric' school of criminology. Dr

William A. White, the brilliant superintendent of St Elizabeth's Hospital in Washington, D.C., published two significant books in those years.[32] Among 'contemporary' positivists, Dr Robert H. Gault wrote in 1932,[33] 'Dr William Healy should be given a large share of credit for pioneering in respect to reviving and redirecting this interest'. Having done considerable work on the intelligence of criminals and delinquents,[34] he and his renowned associate, Dr Augusta Bronner, became later interested in the whole gamut of psychologic phenomena, including particularly the emotional life.[35]

The third man of the triumvirate of pioneer forensic psychiatrists was Dr Bernard Glueck,[36] who inspired his nephew Sheldon Glueck and thus gave direction to his career.[37]

I mentioned the word 'triumvirate' in connection with White, Healy and Glueck, because none other than Clarence Darrow picked these three psychiatrists for his defense of Leopold and Loeb, the case which would bring the psychoanalytic theory of criminology to public attention. They provided Darrow with the data which allowed him to raise propositions such as these with Judge Caverly in Chicago, and the lay public all over America:

> Was their act one of deliberation, of intellect, or were they driven by some force such as Dr. White and Dr. Glueck and Dr. Healy have told this court![38]

> Do you mean to tell me that Dickie Loeb had any more to do with his making than any other product of heredity that is born upon the earth?[39]

> To believe that any boy is responsible for himself or his early training is an absurdity that no lawyer or judge should be guilty of today.[40]

> If there is responsibility anywhere, it is back of him; somewhere in the infinite number of his ancestors, or in his surroundings, or in both. And I submit, your Honor, that under every principle of natural justice, under every principle of conscience, of right, and of law, he should not be made responsible for the acts of someone else.[41]

Perhaps Darrow's exploitation and sensational use of as yet untested psychoanalytical premises was against the better judgment of White and his colleagues. White was consistent in advocating moderation and co-operation between law and psychiatry.[42] Even the official stand of the American Psychiatric Association at that time was relatively moderate and conciliatory.[43] But that did not keep extremists on both sides from sharpening the issues and accelerating a seemingly inevitable clash.

It is not easy to give a brief statement of the basic tenets of the psychiatric, especially the psychoanalytical, school of criminology, for the views of individual psychiatrists, of schools, and of groups of disciples, vary widely.[44] However there would probably be psychiatric concensus on these propositions put forward by Gregory Zilboorg, one of the most orthodox analysts and a prolific author:

> ... Criminal behavior is not a rational process. It has little to do with intellect, and less with deliberate ill will which the law usually ascribes to criminals without any sense of psychological discrimination. Crime is deeply rooted in the instincts of man, and it is usually an act of the instinctual, impulsive life of the criminal individual.[45]

> With the exception of a very few cases indeed, criminal behavior might be considered a special, antisocial if you will, elaborated extension of the neurotic behavior which is rooted in the aberrations, developmental and accidental, of the instinctual growth and integration of man.[46]

Obviously, these excerpts cannot do justice to the elaborate structure of psychoanalytical criminology. Nor is it necessary to fully depict this structure on these pages. We are interested in the reaction of lawyers and scholars to the vociferously announced psychoanalytic tenets. The general public was as much startled as enamored by psychoanalysis. Indeed, the roaring twenties were the era in which everybody psychoanalyzed everybody else and himself, inside and outside prisons. Lawyers, for the most part, were frightened by the prospect of a complete destruction of the values of orthodox criminal law, as psychoanalytic theory seemed to posit, and as its advocates demanded. Zilboorg himself proclaimed many times that one cannot 'prevent' crime 'by mere intimidation or punishment, as centuries of criminal history prove, any more than one can cure a neurosis by these means. ... Therefore one cannot establish a scale of punishments—a dosage of punitive measures to fit the given scale of crimes—without violating the fundamental principle of human psychology'.[47]

Zilboorg's claims are demonstrative of the zeal with which many analysts advanced their ideas. Proceeding from a sound scientific basis, many of them soon lost themselves in exaggerated claims. (For example, history had obviously not proved anything resembling the thesis that one cannot prevent crime by intimidation and punishment.)

Dr Benjamin Karpman, of St Elizabeth's Hospital, Washington, D.C., a pioneer forensic psychoanalyst and one of the most prolific and successful authors in the field, went as far as to demand that: 'we should replace guard and jailer by nurse; judge by psychiatrist.'[48] If anybody was justified to make claims as extravagant as these, it was Dr Karpman, for he indeed had studied 'criminals', hundreds of them, and in greater detail and greater depth than perhaps anybody else, though with no more success.[49]

While Freud and his contemporaries had directed their attention to the study and treatment of middle-class psychoses and neuroses, and while, in the footsteps of the master, most leading European[50] and American[51] analysts had attempted, more or less, to regard criminality as a form of neurosis, and to treat it as such, to Karpman belongs the credit of first having discovered the distinctness of the psychopathology of various types of criminals. Karpman converted a psychiatric 'wastepaper' category of 'psychopathy' into a syndrome group of relatively well-defined dimensions. Shortly before his death he wrote:

> I came to St. Elizabeth's in the Fall of 1919 and in the Spring of 1920, at my request, I was transferred to Howard Hall, the criminal division. It wasn't long before I realized that the patients there differed in some significant way from those found on the other wards. I was particularly struck by the presence of a large number of patients who couldn't very well fit into the cardinal classifications but instead were called psychopaths. It was a wastebasket and catchall of everything we didn't understand. Thus impressed, I tried to clear up the situation by organizing in 1923 a symposium on psychopathy which was published in *Mental Hygiene* in 1924. Thereafter I have published a good deal on the subject of psychopathy in an attempt to determine its position in the nosological scheme of psychiatry.[52]

Thus, Karpman realized early that 'the psychoanalytic approach has as yet failed to contribute significantly to the solution of the problem because it gratuitously went on the assumption that the same mechanisms operated in criminals as in neurotics. . . . In the present state of our knowledge the great majority of the professional and habitual criminals must be approached by a method different from that used for neurotics'.[53]

In his own words, Karpman's method was

> essentially empirical, which is the method of medicine and of natural sciences in general. We try to understand a social situation through the study of its individual components. We take here the life history of each individual criminal as it presents itself to us, attempting to trace it to its early beginnings, noting the stages of its development, the influences that shaped its progress, points of arrested development, deviations and retrogressions. We further attempt not only to describe the phenomena presented, but to find reasons for their appearance and existence; that is, we search for the underlying mechanisms and processes. It is a study in criminal psychogenetics.[54]

Karpman's careful studies and analyses stand in severe contrast to the socio-political claims which he and other analysts frequently made. Thus, if it is true, according to Dr Karpman, that the human being, in infancy, goes through a 'criminal phase', and that 'the majority of mankind escapes carrying this trend into adulthood . . . because culture and civilization prohibit it',[55] does it follow that the value-upholding sanction-mechanism of the criminal law is useless and should be replaced by a psychoanalytic mechanism? To the contrary, nothing would seem more clear than the necessity to maintain the value-structure of the criminal law, for it is that which shapes, and finds its repository in psychoanalysis' own construct, the super-ego.

It can, then, be readily seen, that when psychiatry, especially psychoanalysis, was not yet firmly established, it made claims and demands greater than were justified by the record of its achievements and accomplishments. While these claims had a resounding echo among the populace in general, the legal profession, either felt threatened or apathetic and, in either event, responded very hesitatingly, where at all.

The scholars of law should have responded with a very careful inquiry into the nature of the psychiatric claims, their foundation, and the extent of the usefulness of psychiatry in explaining, and perhaps modifying, the dogma of our criminal law. No such work was produced. However, in 1931 two important books were published in America, with the highest blessings of American criminological scholars. Both authors were foreigners, one an Englishman, one a Russian refugee. The first author was the eminent British physician, scientist and author Charles Mercier, of whom Professor Osman of Columbia, in the Introduction to the book *Criminal Responsibility*, said:

> He was known as one of the most eminent of scientific interpreters and teachers in the province of mental disease.[56] A trained, scientific mind, he possessed an indomitable determination to search out thoroughly and explain as clearly and fully as his power allowed, the subject chosen for the chief task of his life. Alert and trenchant, he displayed a vastness of knowledge that, at times, passed understanding.[57]

Mercier did produce a significant volume in which he not only displayed a superb knowledge of the intricacies of criminal law, especially the elements of crime, and particularly *mens rea*, and, of course, a unique familiarity with then contemporary psychiatry (of which he was one of the chief practitioners and scholars), but he succeeded where no predecessor had in propagating his thorough understanding of the two fields. In outlining the task he had posed for himself, Mercier said: 'The discovery of the state of mind that accompanies an act, no more than the discovery of the geological constitution of a stone, can be effected by the unaided common-sense of the uninstructed. It demands a knowledge of the constituents of mind, and of the laws of operation of mind.'[58] Mercier clearly had the knowledge, and he displayed it humbly and with great ability. The failure of the legal profession, both English and American, to put this accomplishment to good and large scale use is certainly not Mercier's fault. And why did American scholars and lawyers fail to utilize Mercier's important message, a message to the effect that psychiatry and law are complementary rather than inimical to each other? This is beyond comprehension, especially since Mercier demonstrated that 'the supreme authority of the law would be maintained and the impartiality and publicity essential to the administration of justice would be insured'.[59]

The second work of this sort was produced in America, by Boris Brasol, with the direct advice of John H. Wigmore, Robert H. Gault, William A. White and Franklin F. Russell. A more qualified advisory board could hardly have been suggested for a psychologically oriented book on *The Elements of Crime*.[60] Brasol had been a lawyer in Russia, and from all reports a good one. He proved equally good in understanding the human psyche. A partial description cannot possibly do justice to Brasol's superb accomplishment of assaying the structure, content and purpose of the criminal law in the light of psychological recognitions. No work since his has equalled that accomplishment. Indeed, if ever we are to make headway in creating greater effectiveness of our criminal law, we must follow the pattern of Mercier and Brasol in interpreting psychological knowledge and the rules of law. But only a scholar who understands both spheres of human knowledge equally well could produce a work of that sort today. As long as the scholar understands only one of the spheres, his prejudices, his fears, and his ignorance are likely to turn to intolerance and lessen the prospects of success. In sum, Brasol's work stands out for his highly successful utilitarian explanation of the structure and content of our penal law and the criminal and non-criminal responses thereto;[61] for his superb explanation of the formation of criminal habits or ways of life, particularly in terms of sociologically significant factors;[62] his definition, circumscription and proof for the necessary maintenance of the positive law of crimes,[63] but, most importantly, his unrivalled explanation of the psycho-physical nature of crime.[64] Dean Wigmore wrote in the Introduction to this book:

[W]hat the times need is an exposition which will take into account both points of view [psychological and legal],—will synthesize them pragmatically,—will reconcile for us the principles and experience of psychology with the principles and experience of criminal law.

That situation is met by the present book.

The author brings to its composition a long practical experience in administration of the criminal law, yet with none of the limitations of the mere lawyer in his horizon. He brings to it a thorough mastery of the literature of modern psychiatry, yet free from the bias of the psychiatrist inexperienced in law. Additionally, he takes full account of the contributions of anthropology and sociology to the problem of criminal repressions; and in general brings to bear a comprehensive acquaintance with all sources of relevant data. In every chapter he reveals a broad and balanced judgment.[65]

In addition to the advantages hailed in the Wigmore introduction, the book has special value through its comparative approach, in law as well as the behavioral sciences. Brasol was not so presumptuous as to lay claim to having found final solutions:

> In this treatise it is sought to inquire into the nature of crime itself. There is still much to be learned in this field: The genesis and development of the criminal propensity; the social factors contributing to its structuralization; the inner mechanism of the growth of the criminal intent; the psychic contents of the delinquent act; the problem of criminal responsibility in cases involving the issue of insanity, and a number of other equally important problems, are still awaiting solution. So long, however, as the nature of crime continues to be obscure, the various experiments in the realm of social hygiene and prevention of crime are, in a large degree, derived from 'guesswork' and promoted by philanthropic sentimentalism.[66]

Yet, many of Brasol's hypotheses still remain unchallenged.

For American lawyers the book is as new today as it was in 1927. Few lawyers have seen fit, so it seems, to read it. Despite Dean Wigmore's hope to the contrary, the book has not been of dominating influence on the development of American criminal law. Yet it is there, for everyone to read, and it should be read. Brasol argued that a mastery of the concept of crime, in its many-dimensional and inter-disciplinary aspects, is required before the foundation grants and government subsidies will succeed in solving the problem of criminality.

Within American law schools there was no rush whatever to respond to psychiatry's challenge.[67] Professor Sheldon Glueck's thesis *Mental Disorder and the Criminal Law* (1925) and Professor Henry Weihofen's first of several good books, *Insanity as a Defense in Criminal Law* (1933), were the sole—and sober—responses. The significance of these books lies not so much in their content as in the direction in which they caused their authors to proceed in their subsequent careers. But these are matters to be taken up in the next chapter. Both books, however, were masterly efforts at integrating legal doctrine and psychiatric knowledge, by authors who were subsequently to prove themselves as masters of criminal law theory; Glueck by his book *Crime and Justice* (1935), and Weihofen by his authorship (with Professor Kenneth C. Sears) of the fourth edition of J. W. May's *Law of Crimes* (1938).[68] As indicated, both authors retained their interest in solving the vexing doctrinal and practical questions of the defense of insanity and of the relation of law and psychiatry in general.

Indeed, to the extent that the law school scholars responded at all to the psychiatric challenge, such responses were primarily within the confines of the insanity defense. The foremost example, besides Glueck and Weihofen, is probably the work of the Committee of the American Institute of Criminal Law and Criminology, chaired by Professor Edwin R. Keedy. This Committee succeeded in drafting a reformation of the insanity defense entirely in terms of the objectives and elements of the criminal law, thus avoiding entanglement with psychiatric doctrine. By confining the test to the effect of the disease on the mental elements of crime, the Committee left the question of *what* disease may constitute a defense entirely open to the triers of fact, as guided by the judgment of psychiatry.

> No person shall hereafter be convicted of any criminal charge when at the time of the act or omission alleged against him he was suffering from mental disease and by reason of such mental disease he did not have the particular state of mind that must accompany such act or omission in order to constitute the crime charged.[69]

While not perfect, the bill is a strong assertion of the correctness of the law's traditional approach, while yet largely catering to psychiatry's demands for leadership in determining the definition and existence of the 'disease' itself. This accommodation of psychiatry is a far cry from the frantic surrender-attitude displayed by later generations of lawyers.

How did the law itself, as distinguished from a few legal scholars, react to psychiatry's loudly proclaimed assertions? In view of the nature, frequency and vociferousness of the psychiatric attacks upon the law, one would not expect the law to respond happily. And it did not. No major concessions were made,[70] and virtually the sole accommodations were in the restricted realm of insanity procedures.

As early as 1921, a book[71] and other endeavors by the prominent Boston physician Dr L. Vernon Briggs had moved the Massachusetts legislature to enact the so-called Briggs Law, providing for the mandatory pre-trial psychiatric examination by the Department of

Mental Diseases of anybody charged with a capital crime, or who has been previously indicted on more than one occasion, or who has been previously convicted of a felony.[72] The Briggs Law marked psychiatry's first major victory on the battlefield of law. It was an almost premature victory, and obviously a surprising one. But some regard it as of the utmost significance, witness the fact that Dr Winfred Overholser devoted his chapter on 'Psychiatry and the Law' in Branham and Kutash's *Encyclopedia of Criminology* entirely to the Briggs Law.[73] This law had the wholesome effect of reducing the ferocity of the traditional battle of experts on trial, and, while thus terminating the ritual slaughter of alienists in the court-room, made for a greater objectivity in the determination of criminal incapacity.[74] While certain provisions of the Briggs Law proved to be problematic, and while the law is such that much depends on the good-will and capacity of its administrators,[75] 'the Briggs Law has become a fundamental part of the administration of criminal justice in Massachusetts',[76] and, in modified form, in a few other jurisdictions. It continues to point the way to successful co-operation between law and psychiatry.

On a somewhat more popular front, psychiatry made major inroads into legal doctrine with the passage of the so-called sexual psychopath laws in a number of states.[77] Traditionally, sex crime prosecutions have been statistically quite insignificant in this country. But a few sensational sexual offenses are ordinarily sufficient to excite the popular fancy, and thus to cause a clamor for 'bigger and better' laws. The so-called criminal sexual psychopath laws provide for a simple civil procedure under which two psychiatric experts may commit a person until cured, for example, for life (on evidence less than that requisite for a criminal conviction) if they establish that the suspect is a criminal sexual psychopath. '[A]lthough the number of persons incarcerated under these statutes is relatively small', wrote Jerome Hall, 'very serious abuse of fundamental rights is prevalent'.[78]

Indeed, these statutes are a typical example of the hysterical yielding to the not yet properly established demands of a young science. Is it not noteworthy that the title of these acts alone is devoid of any scientific content? Certainly the use of the term 'criminal' in the title of the act is inappropriate in view of the fact that criminal conviction is not a prerequisite for commitment. Nor is the term 'psychopath' appropriate, since perhaps most sexual perversions, i.e. paraphelias, are in the nature of neuroses rather than psychopathies.[79]

Sutherland probably rendered the right diagnosis of these laws when he wrote:

Certain psychiatrists have stated that they are interested in the sexual psychopath laws principally as a precedent; they believe that all or practically all criminals are psychopathic, that all should be treated as patients, and that psychiatrists should have a monopoly on professional advice to the courts. These laws are dangerous precisely from this point of view; they could be passed over in silence otherwise, as a product of hysteria.[80]

While psychiatry had some other impacts on the solutions and procedure of the criminal law in the two decades between the great wars, these few samples are characteristic of the nature of this first impact of an essentially 'alien' body of knowledge on criminal law.

In fine, it seems appropriate to refer to a survey made by Dr Winfred Overholser in 1928, to measure the impact of psychiatry on American criminal law administration. Dr Overholser addressed a questionnaire to 2,194 American judges in all states of the union save one, asking how many courts in the country made use of 'psychiatry'. The 1,168 replies indicated that 9·4 per cent of the courts were regularly served by psychiatrists, full-time or part-time, and six per cent were occasionally served by psychiatrists. In a majority of the cases, these services had been initiated since 1921.[81] Barnes and Teeters concluded: 'These figures indicate that there is at least a beginning. . . .'[82]

Perhaps it is noteworthy that, while law professors Michael and Adler, in their irreverent study *Crime, Law and Social Science*, disapproved of and rejected nearly every criminological claim to scientific accomplishment—including those of psychology—[83] they evidenced a rather tender regard for the efforts of the psychoanalysts:

Psychoanalytical psychology is both a theory of human biography and historical knowledge of a vast number of human biographies collected in recorded and analyzed case histories. The concepts of psychoanalysis may be useful in the development of an empirical science such as psychometrics. Psychoanalysis provides insight which may direct the formulation of problems for empirical research.[84]

4. *Sociology's Advance Upon the Law*

(a) *Mass Surveys*. While a psychiatric school of criminology came into existence without any positive assistance by legal scholars, a competing sociological school made its appearance in the same era in response to the demands of the most eminent of all law professors, Roscoe Pound, the father of the 'sociological school of jurisprudence'.

In his 'Outline of Lectures on Jurisprudence' (Third Edition, 1920, p. 37), Dean Roscoe Pound outlines the program of the Sociological School in the following language: 'The Sociological jurist insists upon six points: (1) Study of the . . . actual social effects of legal institutions and legal doctrines. . . . (2) Sociological study in preparation for law making. . . . (3) Study of the means of making legal rules effective. . . . (4) A sociological legal history. . . . (5) The importance of reasonable and just solutions of individual cases. . . . (6) That the end of juristic study, toward which the foregoing are but some of the means, is to make effort more effective in achieving the purposes of law.' When [Sheldon Glueck] . . . was privileged to attend Dean Pound's truly inspiring lectures and seminar in Jurisprudence in 1922–1923, Dean Pound added the following important items to the agenda of the Sociological School: (7) The study of judicial method. (8) A Ministry of Justice.[85]

And thus was launched a continuous series of unprecedented mass inquiries into the 'actual social effects of legal institutions'. But legal scholars were not the principal actors in this sociological game. Whether for this reason, or because Dean Pound was not fully understood, or because of ignorance and incompetence, the flood of large-scale studies on the administration of criminal justice was devoid of significant references to the substantive law of crimes, concerning itself primarily with criminal procedure and the general condition of law enforcement—not, however, without occasional words of disparagement about the substantive law of crimes.[86]

Following some earlier and relatively minor surveys, the Cleveland Foundation Survey *Criminal Justice in Cleveland* was the first of the long list of factual field studies on the regional state of criminal justice. Other surveys swiftly emulated the Cleveland study. Here is a list of all the important surveys:

Annual reports of Baltimore Criminal Justice Commission, 1923–1929.

Report of the California Crime Commission, 1929. Published California State Printing Office, Sacramento, 1929.

The Bail System in Chicago, by Arthur Lawton Beeley, under the auspices of the University of Chicago and the Chicago Community Trust.

The Cleveland Crime Survey, conducted by the Cleveland Foundation and published by that Foundation in 1922.

Report on a Minor Survey of the Administration of Criminal Justice in Hartford, New Haven, and Bridgeport, Conn., under the auspices of the American Institute of Criminal Law and Criminology and published in the Journal of that Institute for November, 1926; also other articles or reports on special phases of the administration in Connecticut in the same number of that Journal.

'Crime and the Georgia Courts': prepared by the Department of Public Welfare, Atlanta, Ga., for the *American Journal of Criminal*

Law and Criminology, June, 1924. Published in the said Journal in the number of August, 1925.

The Illinois Crime Survey: made by the Illinois Association for Criminal Justice in co-operation with the Chicago Crime Commission in 1929.

A Study of Crime in the City of Memphis, Tenn., conducted for the American Institute of Criminal Law and Criminology and published in the Journal of that Institute, August 1928 number.

Report of the Commission of Inquiry into Criminal Procedure, State of Michigan, 1927.

Report of the Minnesota Crime Commission in 1926. Published as the January 1927 number of the Minnesota Law Review.

The Missouri Crime Survey: conducted by The Missouri Association for Criminal Justice. Published by the Macmillan Co., New York, in 1926.

Report of Crime Commission of the State of New York: submitted to the Legislature of that State in 1927. Legislative Document [1927] No. 94.

Report of the Crime Commission of the State of New York for the year 1928. Published in Albany in 1928 and known as Legislative Document (1928) No. 23.

Report of the Crime Commission of the State of New York 1929.

Preliminary report of Survey of the Administration of Criminal Justice in Oregon, conducted by the University of Oregon School of Law, prepared for and submitted to the Governor and Legislature of Oregon, January 1931; Survey Director Wayne L. Morse, associate professor of law, with assistance by Ronald H. Beattie.

Report to the General Assembly of the Commonwealth of Pennsylvania, Meeting in 1929, of the Commission appointed to study the Laws, Procedure, etc., Relating to Crime and Criminals. Published in Philadelphia, January 1, 1929.

Report of Crime Survey Committee of the Law Association of Philadelphia. Published by that Association in 1926.

First Annual Report of the Criminal Law Advisory Commission made to the General Assembly of Rhode Island at its January Session 1928. Published Providence, R. I., 1928.

Criminal Justice in Virginia, a survey conducted by the Survey Committee of the Institute for Research in Social Sciences of the University of Virginia, under the direction of Hugh N. Fuller, Associate Professor of Criminal Procedure, University of Virginia: published by the Century Company, 1931.[87]

These surveys are fairly similar in scope and approach so that it will suffice to direct attention to two of them.

The Cleveland Survey was directed by the very father of the thought, Roscoe Pound, aided by his critical Harvard colleague, Professor, later Mr Justice Frankfurter. 'The task is that of diagnosing the causes of a system whose origins must be traced back to social, economic, and political conditions distant in time and different from the present, and whose consequences cannot be understood apart from the civic standards and economic pre-occupations of today', wrote Professor Frankfurter. ' "Head-hunting" was from the first disavowed. The search for causes rather than for victims had repeatedly to be insisted upon as the only aim of the survey. . . . [T]he survey was in the hands of men whose professional interest is the scientific administration of justice adapted to modern industrial conditions. . . . [But] this survey represents a collective effort of the community. . . .'[88]

Professor Frankfurter put it very bluntly in his preface to the published report, when he said that the report did not establish anything startlingly new. 'Doubtless, to a considerable extent, the survey proved what was already suspected by many and known to a few. The point is that the survey *proved* it. Instead of speculation, we have demonstration.'[89] Later reviewers attributed even more benefit to the survey than that. In the Wickersham report we read: 'This was a pioneer piece of work in this field, and out of this grew the technique and methodology of statistics of the administration of criminal justice which were availed of in the later surveys and which are producing a science of statistics of this nature. . . .'[90]

However much the Cleveland Survey may have contributed to uncovering the crime situation in Cleveland, and to the development of criminal statistics, it is impossible to avoid concluding that the only certain conclusion to be drawn from it is that law enforcement will fail if the law is not, or not properly, enforced. Such tautology obviously focuses on the quality and reliability of enforcers, and we are again confronted with the age-old riddle: *Quis custodiet enim custodes*—who watches the watchmen? It is not surprising, therefore, that of nine specific general conclusions, the Cleveland surveyors devoted eight to remedial answers to the 'watchman' question.[91]

Subsequent experience demonstrated the validity of these recommendations. The art of 'judicial administration' had definitely benefited by the Cleveland Survey. As for the substantive criminal law, the only recommendation was this:

(3) A statute on the lines of the New York Indeterminate Sentence and Parole Law should replace the present statute in Ohio, which is a typical product of hasty legislative striking in the dark at evils that are attracting public notice for the moment.[[92]]

As to the appropriateness of this recommendation, it may be well to keep in mind what experience has taught us since: while few will doubt the wisdom of the parole laws, properly administered, 'the wholly indeterminate sentence has appeared an inappropriate correctional device ("[e]xcept for psychotic and feeble-minded offenders"), not merely because of the reluctance of the bench to relinquish its control over disposition of the offender but, more especially, because of the grave danger of injustice'.[93]

On the last page of their report the surveyors felt competent to conclude that 'our law is better organized, more accessible, and much more complete than that on which Marshall and Kent and Story labored'.[94] This conclusion was probably based on Dean Pound's contribution to the Cleveland Survey: 'Part VIII, Criminal Justice in the American City—A Summary',[95] a well-prepared historical sketch, most of which, however, could equally have been produced without the benefit of the Cleveland Survey. Several ideas advanced by Dean Pound were to be reiterated in his subsequent writings, to which we shall allude later. And, of course, there was to be found Dean Pound's recurring theme:

> What we have to do is nothing less than to reshape the substantive criminal law so as to maintain the general security of social institutions, and at the same time maintain the social interest in the human life of every individual, under the circumstances of the modern city; and we must do this upon the basis of traditional rules and principles in which the latter was chiefly regarded, and yet were warped in their application by those who regarded only the former.
> This is too large a subject for the city. As things are it calls for nothing less than a ministry of justice. . . .[96]

While the Cleveland Survey was directed by two eminent legal scholars, and while most of the other surveys had prominent law teachers on their staff,[97] the Missouri Survey, sponsored by the Missouri Association for Criminal Justice—organized specifically for that purpose—proceeded without the benefit of advice by criminal law academics. The social sciences, however, were well represented. 'The laws defining crimes and their punishments were not considered.'[98] Hence, the 'Missouri Crime Survey' really turned out to be only a Missouri crime-detection survey.[99] But in thus focusing on law *enforcement* in Missouri, the surveyors did a splendid public service. They lifted the carpet under which the dirt had been swept in the past.

In order to assess the impact of all these surveys on American criminal law, and their nature as a conceivable expression of and contribution to scholarship, we must consult at least two sources: the Wickersham Commission Report and the Michael and Adler Report. According to the Wickersham Commission Report, their single aim was accomplished by concisely stating the prevailing conditions in the administration of criminal justice in various regions of the United States of America.[100] The findings of all the surveys were almost exclusively procedural as, of course, had been the research direction. While the surveys had the beneficial effect of taking a number of criminal law academicians out of their ivory towers into the pulsing life of crime and criminal law enforcement, it also gave to these young academicians and their subsequent students a bias toward procedural and enforcement problems which would continue for almost a generation.

In addition to their procedural findings, the surveyors came to the conclusion that the crime phenomenon, including crime causation, is a terribly complex affair.[101] In the face of this, Mr Bettman, of the Wickersham Commission, also felt justified in reporting the general findings of the surveys in the aggregate, as follows:

> (13) Effectiveness of criminal justice as a preventive of crime is dependent upon the disposition or treatment of the offender; and there is need of the development and adoption of *principles* and *concepts* concerning the objectives of criminal justice, to which principles and concepts the whole system, its organization and procedure, should be adjusted. [Emphasis added.][102]

But in his 'Summary of Major Subjects or Topics Requiring Further Study or Research' we find only a very weak implementation of his general finding number 13.[103] And thus it was that scholarship in substantive criminal law remained dormant for another long period. A major opportunity had been missed.

Michael and Adler probed the surveys with relentless skill and logic. Point by point, their superb reasoning laid the basis for the following conclusion:

> In short, it seems impossible to measure the efficiency of criminal justice or any of its processes; and if this is true, it is obvious that we cannot measure comparative efficiency, that is, the efficiency of the same process or of the same variety of a process as executed at different times or places, or relative efficiency, that is, the efficiency of alternative processes or of different varieties of the same process.[104]
>
> Most of the quantitative research, completed and projected, is not only insignificant; it is also unnecessary and pretentious . . . it has little practical utility.[105]

But Michael and Adler conceded that 'the non-quantitative descriptive knowledge in which research in criminal justice has resulted, has a greater theoretical significance . . . and is of greater theoretical significance' because 'our common sense tells us that institutions which are badly organized or administered, or which have inadequate facilities, will not function efficiently'.[106]

That is the upshot of all the practical results of millions of man-hours devoted to the surveys of criminal justice. Moley, one of the principal surveyors, in effect conceded that 'their chief value' is 'that they serve the purpose of arousing public interest in the enforcement of the criminal law'.[107]

(b) *The Wickersham Commission.* The 'survey to surpass all surveys' was that of the famous Wickersham Commission, the United States National Commission on Law Observance and Enforcement (1929–1931), directed by the Attorney General of the United States, George W. Wickersham. Its original purpose was to enquire into law enforcement problems arising out of the legislation under the 18th Amendment, but it was soon expanded to extend to virtually every aspect of law enforcement and observance in the United States. Among the ten Commissioners we find four judges and a by now experienced surveyor, Dean Roscoe Pound. But that was not the extent of the law scholars' participation in commission work. Professor Sam B. Warner worked on the Report on Criminal Statistics (no. 3), and a young man who was soon to acquire fame as one of the ablest scholars of criminal law, Morris Ploscowe, wrote the critique of federal criminal statistics. In doing so, Mr Ploscowe felt constrained to append to his report a 'Criticism of the Federal Penal Code', a scathing indictment of the chaotic federal compilation of penal laws, and some of the best sense yet written on that subject.[108] The same author also prepared a Report of 161 pages, *Some Causative Factors in Criminality—A Critical Analysis of the Literature on the Causes of Crime.*[109]

But the largest assembly of law school scholars of criminal law was to be found in the group studying the federal courts. Here we find Robert Maynard Hutchins (who in 1929 moved from the deanship of the Yale Law School to the Chancellorship of the University of Chicago), William O. Douglas and Charles E. Clark (both then of the Yale Law School), Orrin K. McMurray (then of the University of California School of Law), Edmund M. Morgan (then of the Harvard Law School), Thurman Arnold (then of the West Virginia University College of Law), Henry M. Bates (then of the University of Michigan Law School) and Henry K. Medina (then of Columbia University School of Law). Fourteen District Supervisors conducted the actual analysis of the business of the federal courts—Deans Rogers (Colorado), Clark (Yale), Bigelow (Chicago), Harris (Tulane), Bates (Michigan), McCormick (North Carolina) and Arant (Ohio State), and Professors McMurray (California), Douglas (Yale), Puttkammer (Chicago), Atkinson (Kansas), Morgan (Harvard), Medina (Columbia), Harris (Ohio State) and Fordham (West Virginia). This certainly is a rostrum of subsequently distinguished judges and legal educators. Oddly enough, not one of these was to emerge as an outstanding scholar of the substantive criminal law, though several established a reputation in criminal procedure.

If the local crime surveys had revealed dirt under the carpet, the inquiry of the National Commission produced a dust storm! But what remained after the dust had settled?

1. The vast labor of the commission staff showed beyond any doubt the futility of employing the criminal sanction (and sanction machinery) in the enforcement of a law clearly rejected by a vast portion of citizens and law enforcers alike. (The folly of prohibition was terminated with Utah's ratification of the repeal of the 18th Amendment on December 6, 1933.)

2. Less directly, procedural and enforcement reforms were instituted in federal and state jurisdictions.

3. The need for federal codification of the criminal law was demonstrated.[110]

President Hoover, in his message to Congress, expressed the belief that the procedural changes advocated on the basis of the Commission finding 'will contribute to cure many abuses'.[111] But he continued:

> Beyond these immediate questions are others which reach deeply into the whole question of the growth of crime and the enforcement of the laws. The causes of crime, the character of criminal laws, the benefits and liabilities that flow from them, the abuses which arise under them . . . all require further most exhaustive consideration and investigation, which will require time and earnest research as to the facts and forces in action before sound opinions can be arrived at upon them.[112]

This was a bit of an overstatement. Little, if anything, had been undertaken to study the substantive law itself. Not 'further' consideration, but 'consideration', is what the substantive criminal law needed. In so far as the Commission had gone into problems of causation, the commissioners themselves were prudent to point out the following:

> We found it impossible comprehensively to discuss the causes of crime or factors in nonobservance of law. Criminology is remaking, the social sciences are in transition, and the foundations of behavior are in dispute. It would serve no useful purpose to put forth theories as to criminality or nonobservance of law.[113]

A vigorous dissent was filed by Commissioner Henry W. Anderson,[114] who disagreed with the majority's defeatist attitude. The conclusions of this farsighted dissenting report deserve to be quoted in full:

As a means to this end it is recommended that there be established in the appropriate department of the Federal Government, an *Institute of Human Research* under a director who should be a scientist of unquestioned ability, with adequate scientific and other assistance, which institute shall be charged with the following duties, among others:

1. To make thorough and scientific studies and investigations in this and other countries of the factors of human personality and environment in their relations to each other, the influence of these factors upon individual and social attitudes and conduct, with special reference to the crime problem, and to suggest appropriate remedies in the light of these investigations.

2. To coordinate, so far as may be practicable, the work of the various agencies, private and public, now engaged in such studies or undertaking to deal with these problems.

3. To collect, classify, and from time to time to publish and distribute to and through appropriate agencies the information so collected in the form of scientific and authoritative data.

4. When so requested, to advise the State and local agencies dealing with these problems as to any of the various aspects of the subject as to which the institute may have knowledge or experience.

5. The general purpose of the institute should be scientific investigation, the coordination of the studies and efforts of existing agencies, and the dissemination, in simple, but scientific form, of the available knowledge in relation to these questions. It should be confined to study and instruction. Matters of administration or control should be left to other appropriate agencies.

'Nine-tenths of wisdom is in being wise in time; and, if a country lets the time for wise action pass, it may bitterly repent when a generation later it strives under disheartening difficulties to do what could have been done so easily if attempted at the right moment,'* This expression from a statesman of great foresight and of large human sympathies is fully sustained by the records of history which show one nation after another arising to play its short part in the great drama, seeking to expand its influence by power and to maintain domestic order by repressive laws, only to crumble in the end as a result of social disease and internal weakness.

The general and increasing prevalence of crime gives adequate warning that America should be 'wise in time' in devising effective measures to meet this problem by removing the deeper causes to which it is due. The economic results will more than justify the expenditure and effort, but the results in social security and human happiness will be far more important in their bearing upon the future of American civilization.[115]

This recommendation was supported by Morris Ploscowe, in the conclusion to his scholarly summary on causation of crime. Mr

* Theodore Roosevelt, letter to Sir Edward Grey, Nov. 15, 1912.

Ploscowe wrote: 'It would be desirable for the Federal Government to devise a system for a thorough study of the individual criminal through careful routine examinations and further laboratory study. Such a program would be a model which State governments might find it advisable to follow. If it were well planned and intelligently directed, it could not fail to provide a body of knowledge of the individual criminal from which considerable advance in the ascertainment of causes of crime might be made.'[116]

Once more the nation and its scholars as a group had missed their chance to engage in a major effort aimed at the *discovery* of the crime phenomenon and at examination of the theories which have been built up around crime. Collectively the criminal law scholars may have been remiss in their duty. Perhaps they just did not recognize it. But as we shall discuss, several of the active academicians subsequently turned in the proper direction. The nation as a whole, and surely the scholars, should have learned that the raw empiricism of mass inquiries is next to futile, except in arousing (or calming) public clamor. That the nation did not learn is demonstrated by two further mass studies of national dimensions—produced in the post-World War II era—both with little effect in improving that law with which we must attack crime.[117] Obviously, these remarks are not intended to cast any disparagement on the enthusiasm with which all those working for the Commission went to the task. Nor are they meant to deprecate the political usefulness of the revelations. Without public clamor a democracy cannot be stirred into action, even action aimed at improving law enforcement. Nor are these remarks intended to deny the usefulness of the report in revealing existing conditions of law observance and enforcement, for nothing is more clear than that action aimed at improvement requires a knowledge of what is to be improved. Nor, lastly, are these remarks intended to deny that the Wickersham Commission Report did result in temporary as well as permanent improvements in the administration of criminal justice, especially by elevating the humaneness of law enforcement. These remarks are simply intended to point out that the endeavor was *not* an expression of criminal law scholarship, had no positive impact on criminal law scholarship of any consequence, and did not bring us anywhere nearer to a solution of the crime problem.

5. *Empirical Research*

Dean Albert J. Harno wrote in 1951:

The encouraging fact today is, that research on crime and criminal behavior is beginning to produce reliable data. . . . The period of greatest productivity has been during the last thirty-five years. Beginning with Healy's pioneering work, *The Individual Delinquent*, published in 1915, and continuing to Sheldon and Eleanor Glueck's studies, *Unraveling Juvenile Delinquency*, published in 1950, a wealth of facts and information has been placed at the disposal of lawmakers and others charged with the planning of programs of crime repression and control.[118]

At the half-way point of this thirty-five-year period the situation did not look nearly so rosy. Only a few law professors had produced anything in the nature of empirical research. Among these was Professor Sheldon Glueck, of the Harvard Law School, who, in collaboration with his wife, published his first work of empirical dimensions in 1930: *500 Criminal Careers*. Two criminal law professors, Andrew A. Bruce and Albert J. Harno, had joined with an outstanding sociologist, Ernest W. Burgess, in a 'Committee on the Study of the Workings of the Indeterminate Sentence Law and of Parole in the State of Illinois'. This major study, using all known methods of field, library, and statistical research, resulted in a 306-page report, published in the *Journal of Criminal Law and Criminology*. Here the reporters could confidently state:

On the basis of its findings the Committee recommends that the Parole Board seriously consider the placing of its work on a scientific basis by making use of the method of statistical prediction. . . .

The Committee wishes to express the opinion that in the wisdom of its legislation on the indeterminate sentence and parole, Illinois is not surpassed by any other state. . . .[119]

The authors of the reports had been partially released from their teaching obligations in order to accomplish their research mission. The entire file system of the Illinois Parole Board was open to them, and they made an extensive study of the entire criminal and penal record of two thousand men paroled from Illinois penal institutions.[120]

This study contributed much to the development of reliable parole prediction methods and, thus, to a better understanding of the state sanctioning machinery. Dean Harno derived lasting benefit from his work on the Commission, as demonstrated by his sense for the factual in his subsequent scholarly works in criminal law.

Indications of an awaking to the responsibilities of scholarship were becoming visible on a broad front. Professor J. Hall, displaying an inclination toward realism, wrote his first articles: 'Social Science as an Aid to Administration of the Criminal Law',[121] and 'Law as a Social Discipline'.[122] A political scientist, an economist, and a psychologist were appointed to the law faculty at Yale.[123] Rumblings were heard from 'legal realism' and 'sociological jurisprudence', subjects to be taken up in the next chapter.

Until the lawyers reached the phase of 'realism', all non-library research, all 'fact' studies, had been undertaken by social scientists, whose incursion into the field of law may well be due to the legal scholars' failure to take the initiative.[124] It would lead too far afield to discuss this extra-legal research in any detail. It must suffice to point to some representative examples. One of the best, unquestionably, is the report prepared for the Wickersham Commission, 'Social Factors in Juvenile Delinquency—A Study of the Community, the Family, and the Gang in Relation to Delinquent Behavior', by Clifford R. Shaw and Henry D. McKay.[125] Other examples are Elio Monachesi, *Prediction Factors in Probation* in 1932; John Slawson, *The Delinquent Boy* in 1926; P. N. Furfey, *The Gang Age* in 1928; Herbert Asbury, *The Gangs of New York* in 1927. Many other *classic* works were to appear soon thereafter.[126]

In retrospect we have little difficulty in pointing to the common error of most of these studies. As Ploscowe put it at that time:

> The mistake common to [all these studies] . . . has been the tendency to oversimplify the problem and to overemphasize the causative role of some one particular factor. . . . The soundest data on crime causation seem to have been contributed by the literature which has studied the criminal in terms of the demoralizing social influences which have acted upon him.[127]

But Ploscowe found a 'definite value' in all the studies.[128]

As might be expected, any such value was denied by Michael and Adler:

> The absurdity of any attempt to draw etiological conclusions from the findings of criminological research, is so potent as not to warrant further discussion. . . . The assurance with which criminologists have advanced opinions regarding the causes of crime is in striking contrast to the worthlessness of the data upon which those opinions are based.[129]

When Michael and Adler turned to their evaluation of researches in treatment, they had 'only [to] reiterate the conclusions of the previous chapters' on causation,[130] and on the problem of prevention they found that the researches had yielded 'data which are neither valid nor significant'.[131]

That such a book as Michael and Adler's would have some impact on theoreticians and researchers throughout the country is self-evident. Most of the impact probably does not reveal itself even to the historian. Still, how much upset, disappointment and disgust their report must have created among those whose work had been labelled useless and insignificant! How many potential researchers were scared away from further research by this report? How much alienation between theoreticians of law and social scientists did the report create? But some of the reactions to Michael and Adler's indictment were as blunt as the indictment itself. Professor Beardsley Ruml, of the University of Chicago, wrote:

> . . . [W]hat of the private theme of the book? What is the relation of law to the social sciences? . . .
>
> It would have been interesting indeed had the text of *Crime, Law and Social Science* been germane to this conclusion. Most of the discussion is irrelevant; the argument in assuming criminology as a typical empirical social science *in potens* is error. As other than a precise and brilliant statement of how Messrs. Michael and Adler conceive the relation of law to the social sciences, the book makes no substantial contribution to the elucidation of what the authors define as their private theme.[132]

Professor Llewellyn found it 'as stimulating, irritating, vitally wise and hopelessly absurd a book as I have ever read.' He thought 'the authors ill-advised in their conceptions of "crime", of "law", and of "social science"; yet *Crime, Law and Social Science* is a book of penetrating power'.[133] The book was 'written as if with a battle axe'; it was 'brash and insolent'.[134] 'The emotional result is that of a visit to a Chicago slaughterhouse.'[135]

Richard McKeon, of Columbia University, found less fault and more benefit.

> The authors have provided a starting point and criteria which any future investigator of the phenomena of crime would be wise to use. Even more, the critical chapters of this book would serve as a valuable *vade mecum* for investigators in any of the fields of the social sciences. But the importance of the book does not center in its criticisms. It offers the first attempt in recent years, to the knowledge of this reviewer, to analyze carefully and state with some show of system the requirements and characteristics of a social science.[136]

This was a note of hope, a hope which Michael and Adler themselves had expressed when, after denying the existence of any science of psychology and sociology, they wrote:

> The urgency of the practical problems of crime impels us, therefore, to seek their solution not by the kind of research which has so far prevailed in criminology, but by an effort to create empirical sciences of psychology and sociology in hope that when these prerequisites have been satisfied, we shall be able to proceed to an etiology of human behavior.[137]

Michael and Adler used 'Himalayan' standards in defining 'science'. By these standards only 'mathematical economics' was found to be a science.[138] They were obviously correct in stating that 'A science cannot come into existence in a given field until a theory or an analysis has been constructed.'[139]

> Since scientific research cannot be accomplished in the absence of a problem, and a problem cannot be formulated except in terms of problematic propositions, and since a problematic proposition is always a theorem and, as such, a constitutent proposition in a theory or analysis, it follows that scientific research in any field cannot be accomplished in the absence of a theory of analysis of the subject matter of that field.[140]

At the beginning of this chapter I referred to Dean Pound's call for scientific research, and suggested that he may have been largely misunderstood. I think the point is now substantiated, assuming that Michael and Adler were on target. It was as if someone had shouted 'gold', and the multitude had rushed into the surrounding fields to dig for gold with kitchen implements and sand-box toys. To be sure, a nugget or two had been found in the melee, but the sparkling veins were yonder in the mountains, waiting for men with man-sized tools. The researchers had tried to solve the crime problem before it had occurred to them that 'crime' was, as yet, a largely unknown entity, and the researchers as yet lacked the requisite experience in the use of scientific methods.[141]

Tempting as it is to trace the challenges of Michael and Adler into the social 'sciences'—though both would deny that adjunct—the topic of this inquiry is legal scholarship and not social science scholarship. It must suffice here to state that Michael and Adler had probably widened the rift between law and the social sciences. Thus, Thorsten Sellin, in a very sober response to the Michael and Adler challenge, posited:

> If a science of human conduct is to develop, the investigator in this field of research must rid himself of shackles which have been forged by the criminal law.[142]

> The unqualified acceptance of the legal definitions of the basic units or elements of criminological inquiry violates a fundamental criterion of science. The scientist must have freedom to define his own terms.[143]

After this lawyer-precipitated exit of the 'scientist', few sociologists had the courage to insist on the truth that criminology is the science concerned with crime, and that crime is defined and definable by law. Paul Tappan had been such a stalwart;[144] and recently a few others have joined him.[145]

Ultimately, sociologists themselves would lose the initiative in criminology to social workers and public administrators,[146] but that is an entirely different story.

It is now time to return from the criminologist to the lawyer, more particularly the legal scholar.

CHAPTER VI

The Criminal Law Scholars

Conservatism amidst turbulence—the time between the great wars

Dissatisfaction and pessimism pervaded the foregoing chapter. Despite such figures as Pound, Michael, Adler, Glueck and Ploscowe, despite such efforts as those of the Wickersham Commission, little satisfaction could be expressed with criminological scholarship and the role of legal scholarship in the era bounded by World Wars I and II. Why? In the first place, the legal scholars mentioned were but a few of the hundreds of professors who taught criminal law throughout the country. In the second place, with the few exceptions which have been noted, those who engaged in scholarly criminological activity did little to promote and apply the practical benefits derived therefrom, either then or in the future. In the third place, the result of the criminological hubbub was of only questionable value for future development.

1. *The casebooks*

Having introduced the era from one perspective, let us now concentrate on the already mentioned criminalists *qua* legal scholars, survey the activities or inactivities of all the others, and assess the progress of criminal law and its scholarship in the period between the wars.

I had previously noted, with some regret, that the American Institute of Criminal Law and Criminology did not emphasize the field of substantive criminal law, despite the presence, shortly after World War I, of criminal law professors who to this day are held in high esteem. These professors were the authors of the better law review articles of our field—most of which were of but fleeting value—and of the casebooks. We have previously reviewed the first casebooks of the second half of the nineteenth century. No one is likely to disagree with the proposition that the criminal law casebooks of this formative era are nothing but dry recitals of streams of unedited cases. Naturally, the compilation of the cases into chapters called for some organizational ingenuity and, thus, in an indirect way casebook scholarship contributed to the gradual creation of a theoretical system for subdividing the criminal law into its coherent parts. Could it be expected that with the rapid development of criminology, the casebook writers would incorporate some of those newly established hypotheses in their casebooks and thus create an awareness among young or prospective lawyers of the societal implications of the substantive and procedural criminal law? While the answer seems to be yes, the casebooks of the early twentieth century are indistinguishable in their organization and basic content from those of the late nineteenth.

The previously discussed casebook of Professor Joseph H. Beale is representative of the entire output,[1] especially since it scored as the pacemaker. The first edition of Beale's *Casebook in Criminal Law* appeared in 1893–1894. It was widely used and led to a second edition in 1907, a third in 1915 and a fourth and last in 1928. Until quite recently the book was listed among the current casebooks on the advertisement pages of the Harvard Law Review. It does not appear likely that Beale's purpose in publishing the casebook exceeded its sole virtue, namely to save the student the time of looking up ancient landmarks of the criminal law in the original reports.

Professor Jerome C. Knowlton, of the University of Michigan, published a similar book in 1902.[2] This was followed by *Cases on Criminal Law* by Professor William E. Mikell, of the University of Pennsylvania, in 1903—a casebook which had three further editions (1925, 1933, 1935, and one abridged (1908)). The last appeared under the title *Criminal Law and Procedure*, which change in title indicates the only significant difference in approach through the various editions.[3] This book was also in use until relatively few years ago.

In 1909, William L. Clark, 'of the Faculty of the American Institute of Law', added to his 'Hornbook' a casebook on *Criminal Law*, published in a series of pamphlets.

Professor Augustin Derby published his *Cases on Criminal Law* in 1914. Professor Derby, who had served as Secretary to Mr Justice Holmes from 1906 to 1907, and as Assistant to the Attorney General of the United States, was professor of Law at New York University from 1908 until his retirement in 1931. Derby's second edition appeared in 1917, the third in 1930, the fourth edition in 1933, and the book was entirely revamped in 1950 and published jointly by Professors Augustin Derby and Lester Orfield under the title *Cases on Criminal Law and Procedure*. As such the book is still in current use. Judging simply by the number of editions and the length of service at schools, this was the most successful of the books of that era. This was the first American casebook on criminal law which (in its fourth edition) benefited from the *Annual Survey of American Law—Criminal Law and Procedure*, through which forty per cent of the cases included had been uncovered.

The last book falling into this era is that by Professor Thomas W. Hughes of Washburn College, *Cases on Criminal Law and Procedure*, published in 1922 without subsequent editions.

There was little variation of approach in all these casebooks. Nor, by modern standards, were they particularly 'good'. They presented the law as it always had been deemed to be, using the now traditional device of representative or leading cases, and seemingly without concern for the changing world outside the law schools. Substantive criminal law was archaic and its presentation to law students was dry and uninspiring. As such, it was totally unsuited for a society which now rode in automobiles and committed a major share of its crimes therewith, psychoanalyzed itself, and had undertaken to develop a science about itself—sociology.

That such a state of affairs would produce angry reactions from Roscoe Pound was to be expected. Mephistopheles-like,[4] Dean Pound had to shout three times at America's criminal law professors before he succeeded in tearing them away from their preoccupation with producing dry copies of case reports and of teaching their students ancient history. Neither Ames nor Wigmore could spark a modern criminal law scholarship. It was left to Roscoe Pound to do so. Pound was convinced that only the law-school scholar could hold the law in such an order that society would truly benefit thereby. Since the legislature will act only if aroused by public ire, and then usually hastily, and since the judge is too preoccupied with the resolution of narrow issues, no one but the professor can calmly and prudently plan the betterment of criminal law. On all three occasions Pound complained about the lack of interest which criminal law had received in the law schools and in the profession. Specifically, he demanded that the law schools open their eyes and their curricula to better instruction in criminal law and, thus, ultimately work for the benefit to be derived by society through better criminal laws.[5]

It was with the utmost justification that Dean Pound could say in 1926: 'We . . . have all but left the field to charlatans.'[6] The situation was gloomy indeed. Wigmores and Willistons were contributing greatly to law and legal education in the private and procedural fields, but they had no counterparts in criminal law. The last edition of Bishop's *Criminal Law* had appeared in 1923 and did not approximate to the standard which the book had enjoyed under Bishop's personal editorship. Wharton's textbook, too, had been neglected and was no longer even comparable to the current encyclopedic works in other fields of law.

Following the first appeal by Roscoe Pound, a few criminal law scholars had attempted to meet some of his demands. Francis B. Sayre's casebook, *A Selection of Cases on Criminal Law* (1927), became the first to depart from the basic pattern. Though Sayre, in selecting his cases, relied heavily on those already chosen by his Harvard colleague, Beale, it was Sayre who had the greater appreciation of the crime concept, so that his book could become the first with an analytical and detailed organization. Moreover, statutes were reproduced, and even a few French and Italian code sections were included. There were quotations from the then current literature: Roscoe Pound, *Criminal Justice in Cleveland; Report and Preliminary Project for an Italian Penal Code;* Jerome Hall, *Crime in its Relation to Social Progress;* and Walter Lippman and Aristotle, Hale and Blackstone were quoted. But that did not render it a book which would have shocked Christopher Columbus Langdell. Basically, the book was still extremely normative in approach. It merely evidenced the fact that Sayre thought something of the ideas of Dean Pound, who had 'kindly looked over the manuscript'.[7] Dean Pound also wrote the introduction, primarily a historical one, which ended by pointing out the problems of the current American criminal law. There is no allusion to whether the book faced those modern problems. Pound, however, did discuss what 'a complete study of the subject would take up . . .'[8] That did not refer to the contents of the book. His concluding sentence was: 'The student of law ought to do more than merely prepare for a bar examination in criminal law, even if he never enters a criminal court room in his professional career.'[9]

The net result of Dean Pound's first call for a greater consideration of the current social interests at stake, and for the creation of a criminal law scholarship, was rather negligible.

The situation was not much different in England. Mr Justice Du Parq, of the Court of King's Bench, devoted his inaugural address as president of the Society of Public Teachers of Law to 'The Place of Criminal Law in Legal Education'. Criminal Law, he said, is being taught like 'the medicine of the operating table'.[10] But just as medical students must be trained in preventive medicine, so law students must be educated in preventive law. Above all, let criminal law cease to be the cinderella of the academic. Du Parq proposed that, as a matter of teaching practice, much of the law of 'criminal' evidence ought to be transferred to the course of criminal law, which would help make the subject and the method realistic.[11]

This was the time when legal educators began wondering about ways and means to make the law more realistic. What is law really like? What can it really accomplish? What really moves judges to

decide as they do? What is the real impact of society upon the law
and of law upon society? 'Realism' became the order of the day—
of the decade—in America. 'The term "legal realism" emerged
about 1930 as a label for the lively and somewhat heterodox legal
theories of a group of American law teachers and lawyers who
diverged from each other in many respects and yet had much in
common.'[12] These 'common' ideas are 'skepticism of tradition,
reverence for science and faith in man's ability to make his world
better by inquiry and effort. . . . In these respects legal realism was
not very different from pragmatism and sociological jurisprudence'.[13]
In fact, as far as the criminal law is concerned, the influence of
pragmatism, sociological jurisprudence and realism are indistinguishable. They came as one, although they came on cat's paws—in-
audibly. Unless one seeks to classify Karl N. Llewellyn, Thurman
Arnold and Underhill Moore as criminal law scholars—simply
because they all wrote bits and pieces of interest to criminal lawyers—
there was, indeed, no criminalist at all among the founders of legal
realism in America. Columbia was the 'hotbed of academic realism',[14]
yet her criminal law teacher, Jerome Michael, was not 'one of the
boys'. As if with delayed action, Columbia's response to the challenge
of realism was not to come until a decade from its emergence.
This holds even more true for Yale where 'a nucleus of realists . . .
produced more striking changes in the law school curriculum than
occurred at Columbia'.[15] Yet it took Yale eighteen years to give
mature evidence of the impact of legal realism on criminal law.

The rebels at Columbia University accomplished one immediate
change in the method of instruction of law schools. Realizing that
not all the materials of value in the teaching of law are to be found
in the cases,

> 'Cases and Materials' became the standard heading for the coursebook,
> revised to include, besides the traditional collection of reported judicial
> decisions, 'materials' showing economic or social theory or fact,
> relevant business practices, excerpts from works on psychiatry, forms
> of contracts, and frequently just straight legal text from law reviews or
> treatises. The realist drive for 'factual' or 'extra-legal material' to be
> studied in connection with reported cases, as a means of 'integrating' law
> and the social sciences, or as a means of showing the place of law in
> society . . . concurred with a movement toward the use of textual
> material in casebooks, a heterodoxy to Langdell's earlier followers.[16]

While law and legal education thus experienced a major revamping
by 'realism', criminal law, at least at the outset, was at best a fringe
beneficiary of the movement, and that despite Roscoe Pound's
demand for action![17]

C.L.S.—9

The criminal law casebooks which followed Sayre's were as yet very cautious about the new fad. Was it due to the fact that case-books had to cater to the market and that the market was dominated by the conservative elements? I suppose that at that time it was even regarded as daring to publish a casebook devoted entirely to criminal procedure, as did Professor Keedy of the University of Pennsylvania.[18] This book was thought to be liberal and practical, else there would be 'little justification' for a course or a casebook on criminal pro-cedure, one reviewer noted.[19] The books which had been continued from the foregoing period, Beale's, Derby's, and Mikell's, now appeared in a somewhat modernized form. Beale now included some statutes and cases dealing with the growing number of crimes against the United States. The book, as expressed in the preface, was now aimed at training students ready to work toward reform. Beale had also joined criminal law and procedure and Dean Pound thought that Beale's book was the first to have done so successfully.[20] How little all these new editions departed from the customary approach is reflected in the reviews.[21]

In 1933, 1935 and 1937, concurrent with 'realism' and Dean Pound's second appeal 'Toward a Better Criminal Law',[22] three entirely new casebooks made their appearance. Livingston Hall and Sheldon Glueck, in *Cases on Criminal Law and Its Enforcement* (1933), sought to cater to realism, yet, only in 1951 did they succeed in accomplishing what they had sought to do in 1933.[23] Harno's *Cases and Materials on Criminal Law and Procedure* (1935), the first criminal law casebook to emphasize the 'materials' in its title, was a direct competitor of Hall and Glueck's and did not differ materially in content and coverage.

John Barker Waite, of the University of Michigan, in 1937, called his book *Cases on Criminal Law and Its Enforcement*, thus emphas-izing that aspect of criminal law, enforcement, in which he had already labored with considerable success. Yet he, too, confined classroom coverage to the more orthodox problems of criminal law and procedure. The book was norm-minded, in the traditional sense, but skilfully combined cases and textual materials, and extended its attention to juvenile-court proceedings.[24]

A fourth book must be mentioned in this section which, although published in 1942, is closely akin to the three already-mentioned books of the 1930s. This is Professor James J. Robinson's *Cases on Criminal Law and Procedure*. Robinson's book was normative but presented an extremely interesting and versatile approach. Common law, statutes, and the constitution were included with an eye on the training of criminal law practitioners, for which purpose indictments and pleadings were reprinted. The selection of cases was considered rather good. Robinson had a sound grounding in the teachings of Coke and Blackstone.[25]

The 'social jurisprudents', the 'pragmatists' and the 'realists' must have been a bit disappointed about the minimal response to their challenge among the professors of criminal law, at least in so far as their classroom life was concerned. However, before rendering final judgment, we should ascertain in what other conceivable forms the scholarship of the professors might have found expression.[25]

2. Scholarship Between Hard Covers

There are to be considered, first of all, the textbooks. Anyone looking at these dusty tomes today cannot but do so with a certain degree of sadness. Perhaps this is not due to the incompetence of those who must have slaved for years to get those lengthy manuscripts between hard covers. Rather, it is due to the fact that a generation ago the criminal law teachers simply did not recognize the purpose of a treatise, nor the power it may have in directing the destiny of a nation through its criminal law. In the opinion of those who wrote the texts, criminal law scholarship had a very limited purpose. The few better known criminal law texts simply aimed at reciting the basic rules of criminal law, in a common-sense arrangement, without criticism and without witicism. The law professors' textbooks of that era are indistinguishable from those of the late nineteenth century.

The first twentieth-century hornbook on criminal law was that by Dean Hughes of the Washburn College of Law, *A Treatise on Criminal Law and Procedure*. It was the author's design 'to produce a book that would state systematically, concisely and with a reasonable measure of completeness, the rules and principles of both the substantive and the adjective law of crimes, and their application'. It is undeniable that the author achieved a certain measure of success in at least separating a few basic problems in accordance with essential differences between them. The book saw no subsequent edition.

Of similar historical importance was the book by Clark and Marshall, *A Treatise on the Law of Crimes*, which, as previously noted, had first appeared in 1900. The second edition, signed H.B.L., appeared in 1905, and a third by Judson Crane in 1927. The fourth edition, in 1940, was by Professor Kearney, who also prepared the virtually indistinguishable fifth edition in 1952. Clark and Marshall purported to present the general principles of the common law in relation to specific crimes, showing, in a general way, the extent to which the common law was modified by statute.

Clark and Marshall's book, like Hughes', was influenced by Professor Joseph Henry Beale, to whose case selections the book was geared. Far from presenting any material of extra- or meta-legal importance, the book was, and up to and including its fifth edition, remained, a dry but accurate statement of the law. It was hardly ingenious either in organization or in presentation.

There was little deviation in approach when Dean Miller's *Handbook of Criminal Law* appeared in 1934. Justin Miller, then Dean of the School of Law of Duke University, at least confessed his limitations when he observed:

> ... the law is not capable of clear statement in many of its particulars; that it may be highly desirable to indicate its uncertainty in such respects and so far as possible to explain the reasons therefor, in order to encourage growth; that the black letter approach, instead of leading the reader to a more complete investigation of the subject, may actually mislead him into an assumption that the law is really clear and simple and that text-books are definitive in their statements of law as an exact science.[27]

Dean Miller 'found that . . . the law is unsettled or uncertain, or that it is, in particular respects, inadequately developed, particularly with reference to new concepts, arising out of new economic and social conditions.'[28] Miller's book was as modest as it was honest. Miller based his text on Mikell's edition of Clark's *Criminal Law*, retaining the old text in many places, but rewriting much of it. By the then current standards the book was probably quite 'modern' in approach, as it extensively cited the periodical literature, the digest system of the West Publishing Company, and other sources of non-case law. I understand that copies of this book are still being purchased by law students.

A fourth textbook worth mentioning was the completely rewritten fourth edition (1938) of May's *Law of Crimes*, by the late Professor Sears of the University of Chicago, and Professor Henry Weihofen, then of the University of Colorado. This book, which had seen constant rewritings and new editions between 1881 and 1938, was one of the most highly accurate law books of its time. While, according to the custom of the day, the general part was condensed to a single chapter, the authors' sophistication on the general principles and doctrines was greater than that of their competitors. There is no doubt that Professors Sears and Weihofen had improved considerably over the original work of May, or of his successors Joseph Henry Beale and Harry A. Bigelow.

The last book of that era is the book on *Crime and Criminal Law* by Professor Morris Ploscowe, now of New York University. This book, published in 1939, did not pretend to be a student textbook.

Yet, while written as one volume of a general law encyclopedia for general use, it, more than any of the other books mentioned, portrayed a keen understanding of the social environment in which criminal law functions. Perhaps owing to Judge Ploscowe's exposure to the criminal law of the civil-law countries, it was arranged in a theoretically supportable analytical fashion.[29]

3. *Popular Books*

As regards coverage and contents, Ploscowe's book is representative of a number of works by legal scholars, produced principally for the benefit of interested laymen in allied disciplines, the correctional and therapeutic professions and the police.[30] These books represented one of the then predominant types of scholarly expression. It cannot be ascertained how successful they were in alerting the public and conveying a general knowledge of the problems of the criminal law. But, as a class, they represent a valuable and interesting aspect of the evolution of American scholarship.[31]

In this class of books, those by Professor John Barker Waite deserve a principal place. Perhaps the mere fact that J. B. Waite was immortalized as Prof. J. B. White in the best-seller *Anatomy of a Murder* is proof of some impact. Among Waite's leading books are *Criminal Law in Action*, published in 1934, and *The Prevention of Repeated Crime*, published in 1943.[32] 'To understand the spectacular failures of criminal law in action, or its less flamboyant but more commonplace inefficiencies,' Professor Waite wrote, 'one must comprehend the parts played by policemen, lawyers, commissioners, clerks, jurors, judges and all the other persons on whose authorities its effectiveness depends'.[33] This sentence really sums up the objective of all the books in this category. Roscoe Pound himself contributed to this literature when in 1930 he published his *Criminal Justice in America*, a reprint of lectures delivered seven years earlier. And several other legal scholars engaged in the same type of scholarly expression, essentially in the nature of establishing the criminal law's 'public relations'.[34]

4. *Hard Covers without Scholarship in between*

The writing of practice books is frequently called a scholarly activity. Only rarely, however, have criminal law professors produced 'practice books' of the twentieth-century variety. When Bishop and Wharton produced their works, the term 'practice book' had not yet acquired a desultory meaning, for their books were as practical as scholarly. In the twentieth century, however, the term 'practice book', at least in criminal law, became the pejorative for any guide (or misguide) to the law which lacked scholarly insight and ingenuity. Most of these books have been compiled, perhaps after consulting case syllabi, by enterprising practitioners. We have looked at a great number of these books, particularly those with the better reputations among the practicing bar, although by no means at all of them, and can say with confidence that they have nothing at all to do with the topic of criminal law scholarship, although they are, to be sure, printed books, and purport to cover the criminal law of a given state. A list of these books, published elsewhere,[35] may strike some readers as a gallery of horrors. Perhaps all of them can be characterized by a few quotations from a book review by Professor Francis Allen, of the University of Chicago, who reviewed the most recent edition of Wharton's *Criminal Law*, which, in effect, is the national exemplification of all the local efforts:[36]

> First, one would expect to discover something about the nature and character of contemporary American criminal law. What one discovers, I believe, is disquieting. Second, scrutiny of a leading and long established treatise in the field should throw some light on what lawyers and judges expect and demand in their law books. A profession tends to get the kind of treatises it deserves. . . . The problem here is not that material is repeated but that the discussion in the introductory chapters is often woefully inadequate, so inadequate that one may wonder what useful function it performs.

The reviewer then finds that the editor of the work has employed neither the historical nor the analytic nor the comparative method. 'There is to be no nonsense in these volumes, let theory and philosophy fall where they may.' The reviewer complained about the 'absence of any particular theoretical vantage point'. He found the book to be devoid of 'critical judgment, good or bad'. The treatise is 'remarkable for its tolerance and passivity in the face of absurdities in the current law'. 'The determination to eschew "abstract principle" not only diverts the treatise from sober consideration of what the criminal law ought to be, it leads to error and inadequacy in its presentation of the law as it is.' 'Instances of competence do not occur frequently enough.' And so the review goes on citing shortcoming after shortcoming,[37] to which we may add one further comment of our own: the book constantly incorporates passages from American Law Reports, and other annotations, without citing these authorities.

It is clear, then, that progress was not to be found in the practitioner's books, although a major proportion of the law writers' time was spent on them. Practitioners were simply not prepared to engage in scholarly activity, and even the pseudo-philosophical outbursts for which certain practitioners at the bar became famous are a far cry from scholarship. Let us name but one example, Clarence S. Darrow, who became something of a national idol for winning many seemingly hopeless cases. No wonder people would prick up their ears when the great Darrow had something to say on crime and justice. Today we may pick up any one of his many contributions to legal periodicals in order to test the accuracy of his ideas in light of what we now know. And we find that his vast and sweeping statements are either wholly unsupported by scientific evidence, or they are lucky guesses, or they are so commonplace as to require no validation. To be sure, Darrow and his contemporary orators at the bar were astute observers of social phenomena and had keen minds and, frequently, a superior knowledge of the criminal law. But never once in all their bar addresses and arguments did they rise above the level of tacticians.[38] It was, therefore, with good reason that Learned Hand, in 1926, exclaimed to the law professors:

> [W]e [the judges] must look to you, as we have increasingly come to do, as the sources of the only adequate learning in this part of our common work. The reports during the last quarter century are proof enough of the truth of what I say; they show an increasing tendency to accept as authoritative the conclusions of the great writers. It is, I think, entirely clear that we have here a new differentiation, that you will be recognized in another generation anyway, as the only body which can be relied upon to state a doctrine, with a complete knowledge of its origin, its authority and its meaning.[39]

Similarly, Cardozo[40] stated: '[T]he sobering truth is that leadership in the march of legal thought has been passing in our day from the benches of the courts to the chairs of universities.'[41]

Yet, little of this scholarship, as far as the criminal law is concerned, was to be found between hard covers! Where, then, would it be found? One of the theories of evolution is that the philogenesis corresponds to the ontogenesis. How does a young man grow to be a scholar? After having mastered the basic rules of the game, and the basic premises of his field, he will turn to the writing of articles, then perhaps to a little book, and ultimately perhaps a big one. Perhaps American scholars of criminal law, in the aggregate, have followed, or are following, this evolutionary principle! And so, the writing of articles was the principal scholarly endeavor in the substantive law of crimes in the period preceding World War II, the nascent phase of modern American criminal law scholarship. This stage in the philogenesis of American criminal law scholarship was sustained and significant, for Americans seem to turn directly from the writing of articles to the writing of 'big books', there being no intermediate stage of 'little books' or monographs.

Professor Max Rheinstein has described the situation aptly as follows:

> In the development of American law the role of learned writing has been constantly increasing. Such writing has become so significant that American law has reached a stage at which it no longer exhibits exclusively those traits which are characteristic of a purely judge-made law. It has assumed new aspects which reflect the systematic thought of the law teacher or the deeply cutting analysis of the scholar. There is yet missing, however, a kind of writing, which has for generations constituted an essential, if not perhaps the principal, part of the legal literature of the continental countries—the legal monograph. The cause is entirely external. The high cost of printing has limited the production of law books to those types for which a wide market can be expected—the text and case book for law students, and the reference book for the practitioners. In rare cases the author of a learned inquiry into a topic of limited scope has been fortunate enough to obtain the subsidy necessary to pay for the cost of publication. As a rule, however, authorship must be adjusted to the facilities of the law reviews.[42]

We shall therefore turn next to an examination of criminal law scholarship as found on the pages of the ubiquitous law reviews.

5. *Scholarship between Soft Covers*

The *Index to Legal Periodicals* indicates that the number of those who contributed more than a few scattered articles on criminal law to the growing number of American law reviews is quite small. And, as would be expected, the number of those with significant contributions is smaller yet. In search of the strategians, in this section we shall discuss the half dozen or so scholars whose concern lay with the most fundamental aspects of substantive criminal law: classification, organization, and clarification of the basic issues.

James De Witt Andrews was one of those who believed in first things first. In 1920 he published a significant article on 'Classification and Restatement of the Law'.[43] He recognized that no draftsman can work unless he has his tools handily assembled and unless he has the job sized up before starting to chisel away on it. Recalling the heritage of Blackstone, Marshall, Swift, and Dane, he complained about American provincialism which prevented a national uniformity and classification of law. He reminded his readers of the fact that in the 1890s the bar considered classification of the law one of its principal tasks, and that as late as 1916 Mr Elihu Root, in an address to the American Bar Association, considered the classification and simplification of the law as a principal and mandatory task, but one which it had shirked thus far. Andrews saw the origin and progress of classification and restatement of the law in the efforts of

Aristotle, the synthesizer of all human knowledge, in the works of Justinian, and of Blackstone. 'As to Blackstone's classification of English law, the following may be safely affirmed', he said:

> (a) The classification is dominated by reasons more carefully and clearly explained than any prior attempt. . . . (b) It is more comprehensive in scope than any that had appeared in Europe. (c) The method of treatment is more fundamental than any earlier English treatise. (d) It combines the historical and analytical methods in a manner never before attempted elsewhere. As an example and model of juristic exposition (not now having regard to the validity of legal and political theories) it has not yet been excelled on the continent.[44]

He then embarked upon outlining his technique of classification, stating as his purpose: 'We think that our whole *written law* should be comprised under appropriate titles; that those titles should be classified in their natural order; and more especially, that the various provisions of each statute should be arranged in the clearest and most scientific method.'[45] Andrews found ample precedent for a theoretically sound system of classification in the New York State Assembly Journal of 1825, Appendix D, pp. 2, 3, 4, as quoted from the Preface to the Consolidated Laws of New York, 1909, a laudatory reference with which we might quarrel.

Classification, indeed, was one of the principal interests among those who had the ability to think in the abstract. I need remind readers only of Roscoe Pound's system of classification of social interests.[46] Pound classified the social interests protected by the law as follows:

(1) Interests in the general security,
   the general safety, health, peace and order,
   the security of transactions,
   the security of acquisition.
(2) Interests in the security of social institutions, domestic, religious, political, economic.
(3) Interests in the general morals,
(4) Interests in the conservation of social resources,
(5) Interests in the general progress, economical, political, cultural,
(6) Interests in the individual life,
   (a) that the individual will shall not be subject to the will of another;
   (b) the interest in securing to the individual the possibility of a human existence.

Following this outline he then arrived at a classification for purposes of the special part of criminal law as follows: (1) Crimes against property; (2) Crimes against public peace and order; (3) Crimes against religion; (4) Crimes against the family; (5) Crimes against the morals; (6) Crimes against the resources of society. Professor MacDonald commented upon the classification scheme as follows:[47]

> Alphabetical arrangements and organization based on type of crime have been discredited. Statistical groupings have been shown to be of little assistance in redrafting legislation. In most cases the proposals of criminologists are so sweeping that the criminal law as it is known might disappear in the process of such reorganization. It is inconceivable that the legislature would sanction a reclassification based on the motive of the offender, for instance, if it were desirable. It is obvious that if the subject is approached from the objective which rules the present inquiry, none of the foregoing are necessarily models for our purposes.

> The following are tests of the validity and workableness of any new classification, seeking to effect a simplification of the statutory law of crime as it stands in New York today:

> 1. It should assist in attaining the underlying purposes of codification. Thus, it should be flexible enough and comprehensive enough to assure the inclusion and proper arrangement within the statute of all offenses now recognized. It should prevent inconsistencies, uncertainties, and duplications among these offenses. It should minimize the possibility of too much detail; it should encourage the use of general sections covering broader situations, thus preventing loopholes which defeat the purpose of the law.

> 2. It should rest on some basis to be uniformly applied to all sections. Its theory should be a test on the inclusion or exclusion of any particular offense within a given group.

> 3. By its own test, it should be a method of determining the social necessity of continuing the penal sanction for a particular offense.

> 4. It should be of practical assistance now imperative in the task of reconstructing an all-inclusive penal statute, consistent in itself and logically subdivided into accessible subheads. The breaking down of the present law into the form of separate, disunited offenses has created a bewildering mass of chaotic material which cries aloud for its reduction into some form of logical consistency through reclassification.

> 5. It should be so organised as to be of assistance to workers in the field of criminal law other than lawyers: statisticians, sociologists, criminologists, etc.

Such are our objectives. It is submitted that a reclassification on the basis of Pound's classification of interests is the only proposal which would attain these objectives. Such an organization founded on such a theory should be comprehensive, consistent, and a test of the inclusion and presence of each offense with which we must deal. With this point of view the following classification is proposed as a basis for the continuance of this study:[48]

A Proposed Method of Classification for the Purpose of the Simplification of the Penal Law

    1 Crimes against the person of individuals.

    2. Crimes against the general morals.

        a. Sexual morality.

        b. Other moral questions enforced with a penal sanction.

    3. Crimes against the general security.

        a. Crimes against the general safety.

        b. Crimes against the general health.

        c. Crimes against the general peace and order.

        d. Crimes against the security of acquisitions.

            aa. Gainful with violence.

            bb. Gainful without violence.

            cc. Malicious.

        e. Crimes against the security of transactions.

    4. Crimes against the security of social institutions.

        a. Against the family.

        b. Against organized government.

            aa. The government itself.

            bb. The administration of government.

        c. Against religious institutions.

    5. Crimes against the security of social resources.

        a. Against the security of communal property.

        b. Against the security of children.

        c. Against the security of animals.

It will be noted that Pound has included in his classification of interests a social interest in the general progress. Whether violations of such an interest are penalized with the criminal sanction is doubted. If there are such crimes, it may be necessary to include another group to cover this subject.[49]

This is the way the prudent scholar proceeds. Like the prudent merchant who has bought out his competitor, he begins with an inventory-taking, grouping all items in reasonable categories. He would not mix olive oil and shoe polish, he will list olive oil under fats or shortenings, and shoe polish under cleaning materials, or some such category. But to define the categories, to circumscribe them, that too is one of the principal tasks of the prudent scholar!

We are not particularly interested in whether or not Pound or MacDonald or Andrews were right in their classification schemes. What is of interest today is that there were scholars who were interested in classification schemes.[50]

But the classification and organization of the body of knowledge called criminal law is only the beginning. A deeper recognition and analysis of the component parts of any such classified and organized body of knowledge is the next important task; and here too we find a few scholars who have distinguished themselves.[51] Foremost among them are the late Professors Strahorn and Hitchler. Strahorn was a legal scholar of the best analytical tradition. He began by dividing each crime into three components: First, a stated socially damaging occurrence or criminal result (*corpus delicti*), which today we would designate as the criminal harm. He found this harm to correspond philosophically to the vengeance theory of punishment. Second, legally causative conduct, engaged in by the accused offender, i.e., conduct which is socially dangerous when committed by any person. He found this purposive conduct to correspond to the deterrence or social engineering theory of criminal law. Third, an indication that the offender possesses the requisite antisocial tendency or likelihood of recidivism, that is, a criminal intent or *mens rea*. He found this to correspond most nearly to the recidivism theory or the punishment-as-a-preventive theory of the criminal law. While the correlation of these three basic elements of the crime concept to the philosophical theories of criminal law is all but superficial, the recognition of the three basic elements is certainly a cogent discovery.

> This classification of the elements of criminality furnished an apt outline of the whole body of substantive criminal law. General principles of criminality underlying all specific crimes can thus be classified according to the particular element of criminality involved in their application and according to the correlative theory of criminology which seems to underly them. Specific crimes can be dissected and their particular elements discussed in their proper place in the outline of result, conduct, and intent.[52]

As tempting as it is at this point to inquire deeper into the theory advanced by Professor Strahorn, such cannot be our purpose. Suffice it to say that in the article here surveyed, and in several others, Professor Strahorn has provided us with classic articles that deserve to be preserved, read and re-read by all students of criminal law. Strahorn's writings are marked by a clear identification of basic issues and a desire to constantly relate these issues not only to what other scholars have said but also to criminological reality, as revealed by the writings and researches of criminologists. Strahorn was among the first of a new group of disciplined, informed, and realistic analytical scholars.[53]

The late Dean Walter H. Hitchler, of the Dickinson Law School, is closely akin intellectually to Professor Strahorn. His many articles are of a rare lucidity and clarity. He too concerned himself with an analysis of the crime concept, dissecting it with meticulous care. This must have been a disquieting undertaking at a law school which up to that time had been dominated by the 'practical' elements, and governed by judges.[54] Hitchler's analytical ambitions, and his recognition of the traditional common-law effort to frame the criminal law in terms of psychological realities—as best as the knowledge of the time would permit—caused him to advocate the addition of the irresistible impulse test to the M'Naghten Rules, so as to provide for a defense where the defendant lacked the requisite volitional power to form an intent to commit the offense in question.[55]

Preoccupation with the insanity test was commonplace among the scholars of the thirties. Indeed, nothing tests a scholar's power of analysis better than work on the insanity test. Among those who rendered an outstanding contribution in this area was Professor Edwin R. Keedy of the University of Pennsylvania. While he is perhaps best known through his work in criminal procedure, as Chairman of Committee B of the Institute of Criminal Law and Criminology at Northwestern University, he became quite involved in matters of substantive law, especially with insanity and criminal responsibility. He was one of the draftsmen of the famous insanity test proposal of the Institute previously quoted, which we must here repeat:

> No person shall hereafter be convicted of any charge when at the time of the act or omission alleged against him he was suffering from mental disease and by reason of such mental disease he did not have the particular state of mind that must accompany such act or omission in order to constitute the crime charged.[57]

This, indeed, constituted a superb proposal which fully catered for the demands of the law, while yet giving the medical expert the desired freedom to testify on the matter of the mental disease and its effect in terms of his own science. Professor Keedy ably defended this rule, for example, against Professor Ballantine who thought it far too general, and who, peculiarly enough, thought that the defense of insanity as expressed by Professor Keedy bowed too much to medical theory which might soon become obsolete.[58] If an analytically sound, *complete* reworking of the M'Naghten test were desirable, no test but that proposed by Keedy could fill such a place.[59] Keedy's interests were wide. He was a leading member of the criminal-law teaching fraternity, he showed as much interest in substantive law as in procedure, and was concerned with good working relations among scholars in America and all over the world.

A further scholar of renown for his work in criminal-law theory was Francis B. Sayre of the Harvard Law School. In 1927 Sayre became director of the so-called Harvard Institute of Criminal Law, to which we have found occasional reference in the literature, although no products of the Institute have revealed themselves.

Although well versed in Roman Law and the law of the civil-law countries, Sayre was firmly devoted to the common law of crimes, of which he proved himself a master by writing several articles which are cited to this day.[60] Despite an otherwise wide intellectual horizon, the fetters of traditionalism kept him chained to the common law, and his occasional analytical efforts were held back by these fetters. It was beyond Sayre's efforts to resolve the inconsistencies in the common law of crimes. Merely by way of example, he admitted that 'it is the very essence of our deep-rooted notions of criminal liability that guilt should be personal and individual. . . .'[61] Yet he willingly assented to the judicial importation of the tort concept of *respondeat superior* into the criminal law.[62] Elsewhere he recognized that *mens rea* for any one of a number of policy reasons, is of the essence of crime. Yet he willingly abandoned the concept in the so-called public welfare offenses, thus contradicting the very policy reasons he stated earlier.[63]

These few assessments will suffice to demonstrate that those criminal-law teachers who investigated the theory of criminal law did so with varying success, and from various vantage points. Some, like Strahorn, Hitchler and Keedy, achieved independence of thought and adequately penetrated the common law clichés. Others, like Sayre, were more tradition-bound and clung to the common-law-determined structure. Our list of those who have distinguished themselves through periodical contributions in the theory of criminal law in this pre-World War II era would not be complete without mention of Dean Albert J. Harno, equally well known as a legal educator and as a scholar of the criminal law. Among his memorable articles, showing erudition and learning, is his *Rationale of a Criminal Code*.[64] Combining the psychological awareness of the realist movement with the conservatism that had traditionally marked American criminal law scholarship, he wrote about codification:

> The study of aims must go deeply into the recesses of human behavior. and motivation. It must take into consideration social attitudes that prompt an insistent demand for severe punishment. The builders of a systematic code should weigh the dangers of fashioning one which is too far in advance of the mores of the time. It would be unsafe as well as unscientific for them to assume that the retributive theory of punishment is a dead issue. Let anyone who doubts this statement open his eyes to what is going on about him. Let him consider the motivation of the parent who chastises his child. . . . There can be no doubt that it would be preferable to give no consideration to the retributive theory in a schematic treatment of the subject of crime, for it is destructive of the ends which should be sought through a scientific modern code. Yet the desire for vengeance is so deeply rooted in the human psychology that it would be a serious mistake for the drafters of the code not to grapple with it.[65]

On the scholarly effort which must precede reorganization, reformation and codification of the criminal law, Harno said this:

> [T]he work of the draftsman should be preceded by searching investigations into the underlying causes for the social situations which appear to call for relief and then be followed by further studies to determine whether the definitions proposed are designed to meet the situation. In the substantive part of the code it is essential to define anti-social behavior; we must define crimes. But on what are these definitions to be based? Surely on social data, this involves determining what a social problem is and how to go about giving it relief.[66]

> The workers on a code will need to determine its scope. Obviously they cannot go into the minutiae of the criminal law. Indeed, it would be unfortunate if they did. They will need to determine what anti-social acts are to be included and to classify and define them, but other than that it would be well if they adopted a plan confining the code to statements of broad underlying principles and aims and to the establishment of an administrative scheme which would outline basic procedures. The definitions should be so conceived that they include sufficient elasticity to be adaptable to the ever-changing social and economic scene and to the advances in science. Of course it is impossible to foretell the future, but it is possible, in the drafting of a code, to contemplate future changes.[67]

This article signaled a new concern on the part of scholars for the ultimate task of codification of American criminal law. Much debate was yet to ensue on the topic, but the ultimate goal was within reach, and it was Harno who reopened the issue after Glueck had first raised it without results, as we shall note shortly.

Yet, this was not a firebrand type of criminal law scholarship. It was the conservative, cautious, prudent approach which, nevertheless, had progressive tendencies. Indeed, the criminal law scholar in the 1920s and 1930s, as symbolized by Dean Harno, retained his cool head in the midst of all the uproar created by the social sciences, especially psycho-analysis. To be sure, the scholars of the time between the wars did not reject psychology, psychiatry and sociology from their considerations. But they showed a certain reluctance to swallow everything which was set before them. All the revelations of the surveys, inquiries and commission reports of the 1920s and 1930s had not been convincing to Harno and his colleagues.[68] There were others, like Harno, who had the ability to go beyond the trial and appellate cases, and beyond the practitioner texts, but most contributed but a few articles, perhaps because they did not see the need for theoretical work in criminal law. But times were changing, a conceptionalism of sorts was winning the day, and youthful law professors who we shall mention next were in the forefront of the new development.

These are the young men who made the news in the academic world of the 1930s through intelligent and ingenious publications. These were the days when Professor Thurman Arnold, in his best flair of realism, published his 'Criminal Attempts—The Rise and Fall of an Abstraction',[69] when Professor Sheldon Glueck wrote 'The Principles of a Rational Penal Code',[70] when Professor Waite wrote his 'Irresistible Impulse and Criminal Liability', when Professor Miller—the author of such a dry student text—wrote a stimulating article on 'Criminal Law: An Agency for Social Control', when Professors Michael and Wechsler published their unsurpassed two-part article 'A Rationale of the Law of Homicide',[73] when Professor Edgerton published his superb analysis of corporate criminal liability,[74] and when many others contributed the article or two of their careers which are worth remembering. Whether these authors have been right or wrong with the views they espoused is insignificant. What is significant is their concern for 'first things', their analytical search for certainty and simplicity in a chaotic substantive law of crimes, and their rejection of superficial certainties. In my opinion, there are few final answers in the articles just listed, and even fewer in those not listed. But that each one brought us a bit closer to the goal, who can doubt? And that all, in the aggregate, exemplified a trend that must now be admitted.

6. *Scholarship in the History of Criminal Law*

We must not forget that this time of new intellectual excitement also produced an abundant crop of significant writings on the history of the criminal law. Professor Julius Goebel, in 1937, published his unforgettable *Felony and Misdemeanor*, followed in 1944 (with T. Raymond Naughten) by *Law Enforcement in Colonial New York*. Arthur P. Scott wrote *Criminal Trials in Colonial Virginia* in 1930, Raphael Semmes published *Crime in Early Maryland* in 1938. As early as 1923 George A. Washburne had written a significant historical study: *Imperial Control of the Administration of Justice in the Thirteen American Colonies*. Indeed, Roscoe Pound's *Criminal Justice in America* (1930) belongs in this category.

7. *Scholarship in Criminal Procedure*

Since this is primarily an account of scholarship in the law of crimes, only passing attention has been paid to scholarship in criminal procedure. But it would be remiss not to mention that the wholesome growth of scholarship spread to the procedure specialists as well. John Barker Waite's finest writings were produced in that era.[75] Lester Orfield, the unquestioned reigning monarch of criminal procedure scholars in America, began his long and distinguished career as a writer at that time. Besides many articles, he then produced two books on criminal procedure which are of lasting value.[76] It was this scholarship which found its finest expression in the American Law Institute's Code of Criminal Procedure in 1931, and in 1946 led to the streamlining of federal criminal procedure through the Federal Rules of Criminal Procedure,[77] in turn leading to procedural reforms in many states.

Part 3

THE PRESENT

CHAPTER VII

A Catalyzer, Common Law Scholarship and the Goal of Codification

1. *The Refugee Scholars—Catalyzers*

No sphere of human endeavor evolves unaffected by the cultural and political climate around it. Evolution itself jumps no phases. What happened before necessarily determines what will happen afterwards. Thus, the period of germination which we have described in the preceding chapter determined events. This was a good, a wholesome period, which made it possible for us today to work in an intellectual climate, and along lines of inquiry, which had never existed before in America. The present is an exciting time. Let us remember that we owe our good fortune to those who, through trial and error, set the stage for us today. We could deny to them the honorific title 'scholar of criminal law', for, by our present standards, what they did fell short of first-rate scholarship. But they conceived of themselves as scholars. We, too, conceive of ourselves as scholars, yet those after us may well deny us that title, for we may fall short of future standards. But we are closer to reaching the goal of a perfected instrument of social control than were those before us, and those after us will be closer yet.

It may not have been apparent to those of the previous generation what type and structure of scholarship would emerge from their efforts, and what 'schools' of thought and affiliation would develop. But by today, the scheme is quite apparent, and every one of today's 'schools' of criminal law scholarship is clearly traceable to some certain antecedent activities. More than that, we can virtually pinpoint the 'beginning' of the modern schools to specific events, specific books, specific persons.

But there is a need to explain why I felt so sure in drawing the dividing line between the past and the present. It is my contention that the appearance of dictatorial systems of law—or brute force—was an alarm which awakened Americans to the urgency of not only relying on a rule of law, but of putting it into a form which would withstand attack and assure its preservation. Once it is decided to

133

preserve something, why not put it into a form worth preserving? But there is another facet to the rise of oppression and the fall of the rule of law abroad, a facet which had a parallel in history. Historians have long maintained that the renaissance of central Europe in art as well as in law would never have been possible without the fall of the East Roman Empire. It was the refugee artists and scholars of Byzantium who fructified the thinking of continental Europeans in the fifteenth and sixteenth centuries. In a similar vein, the rise of totalitarian regimes in Europe had created a wave of refugees who were welcomed to our shores and whose skill and knowledge constituted a wholesome fructification of American thinking in the arts, the sciences and in law. To the legal scholars among them we shall now direct our attention.

The first of several waves of refugees from despotism reached us from Russia. It brought us, among others, Dr Vladimir Gsovski, Professor N. S. Timasheff, Professor Georges Gurvich and Dr Boris Brasol.

Dr Gsovski will be remembered as the Chief of the European Law Division of the Law Library of Congress (1957–1961), having theretofore served as Chief of the Foreign Law Section (1942–1957). From 1949 to 1960 he also held the post of Director of the Mid-European Project. Professor Kurt Schwerin, the Chairman of the Committee on Foreign Law of the Association of American Law Libraries, recently wrote in the memorial for Vladimir Gsovski:

> Dr Gsovski has played a leading part in the development of foreign law collections and of research in foreign law in this country. His numerous publications, particularly on Soviet Law and on the law of East European countries, have tremendously increased the knowledge and the facilities for study of these legal systems in the Western world.[1]

A prolific writer and profound scholar, Dr Gsovski wrote extensively on Roman, Civil and Comparative law, but his first love was the criminal law.[2] The *Highlights* were edited by him and served the criminal law profession well in constantly disseminating up-to-date information on the state of the criminal law in Eastern Europe. In 1947 he re-translated the German Criminal Code, with annotations.[3] In fine, Dr Gsovski was one of the pioneers of comparative studies in criminal law in America. His enthusiasm and competence sparked many others.

The second Russian refugee to be discussed is Nicholas Sergeivich Timasheff who, with a profound understanding of sociology, psychology and criminal law, put the comparative method to excellent use for the progress of American law and for American understanding of criminological problems. Among his principal works are *The Crisis in the Marxian Theory of Law* (1939), *An Introduction to the Sociology of Law* (1939) and various works on the topic of probation and punishment.[4]

Working sociologically, like Timasheff, Professor Georges Gurvich, who had emigrated to France, came to the United States during World War II and here completed his famous *Sociology of Law* in 1942.

The fourth outstanding member of the Russian group is Boris Brasol, about whom we have already written extensively.[5] Brasol's influence is important even though only a handful of people may have benefited by his outstanding work. More importantly, however, we should remember that Brasol is only one of the many refugee scholars who offered their insight to the thinkers of this country. He himself had benefited greatly from the European psychiatrists, especially the forensic psychiatrists, who found refuge on our shores. His work evidences the insight of a dozen or more psychiatric scholars of crime who came to America.

The second group of refugees, a small one, came from Italy. Nino Levi was perhaps its outstanding member. Levi co-operated with Professors Michael and Wechsler in the production of their remarkable coursebook on criminal law.[6]

Our third wave of immigrant scholars came from Germany, Austria, and other countries swallowed up by the Nazi machine. And indeed some of the greatest names in criminal jurisprudence were on the list of those whose wisdom and forthrightness Hitler could not tolerate. Mannheim and Grünhut went to England, where they have exercised a profound influence on the development of English thinking in criminal law. Honig went to Istanbul, Kantorowicz to Switzerland and thence to America. Goldschmidt found refuge in South America, and Heinitz in Italian anonymity. Thus, the best in criminal law scholarship of central Europe was soon transplanted all over the world.

In terms of sheer numbers, perhaps, American criminal law did not profit as much as other fields. The civilians fared much better in this respect, through the influence of Ernst Rabel, Max Rheinstein, Heinrich Kronstein, Stephen Riesenfeld, Albert Ehrenzweig, Walter Derenberg, Martin Domke, Arthur Lenhoff, Norbert West, Kurt Nadelmann, Edgar Bodenheimer, Ernst Levy, Eric Stein, Hans-Julius Wolff, Fritz Kessler, Rudolf Schlesinger, Wolfgang Friedmann, Walter Herzfeld, to mention only a few.

Though the criminal law and criminology contingent among the German refugees to America may have been small, its members were outstanding and influential scholars: Gustav Aschaffenburg,[7] the great master of forensic psychiatry; Hans von Hentig, who brought light into corners of criminology which had never before been illuminated; Helen Silving, expert in analytic criminal law and psychiatry; Otto Kirchheimer, who combined expertise in criminal law and political science;[8] Kurt Schwerin,[9] who master-minded the comparative law contributions in the *Journal of Criminal Law and Criminology*; Richard Honig,[10] who has participated in the Comparative Criminal Law Seminar at New York University, and now publishes extensively in Germany on American criminal law.

Most of these scholars will be discussed later but Hans von Hentig deserves immediate comment. None of the refugees to American shores fructified criminological thinking as much as von Hentig. *The Criminal and His Victim* (1948) started a whole new trend of thought in criminology, namely 'victimology', which maintains that crime can be properly understood only if one considers the victim as well as the perpetrator. In his *Crime—Its Causes and Conditions* (1947), von Hentig set a new high-water mark for criminological scholarship in this country. Von Hentig's students and followers may be found all over the world, and especially in America. His contributions to criminological periodical literature are among the most respected in the field.[11] Elsewhere, von Hentig's approach has been described as one of 'fact skepticism and historical realism'.[12] But American criminal law theory, too, benefited by von Hentig's work, not only through direct contributions,[13] but also through his criminological writings all of which rest on a thorough grounding in the theory of criminal law.

But there were many other German refugee scholars, not principally criminalists, who made significant contributions to our understanding of criminal law theory, our appreciation of foreign law and, through it, of our own law. We need think only of Hans-Julius Wolff's articles in the Michigan Law Review on German criminal law and procedure,[14] or those by Schwenck[15] and many others, most of which are distinguished from contemporaneous and comparable American articles by their greater conceptual clarity, logic, organization, and their facility of using helpful data from other disciplines. Even refugee scholars from dictatorial systems in our own hemisphere participated in the process of fructifying American thinking in criminal law. Among these, Sebastian Soler stands out.[16]

The last[17] wave came from Eastern Europe. From Poland, Leon Radzinowicz—today one of the world's most outstanding criminologists[18]—went to England, and Kazimierz Grzybowski to the United States.[19] The former exercises a paramount influence on the course of English criminology, the latter, with his encyclopedic knowledge of continental criminal law, keeps the profession in the USA abreast of developments abroad.[20]

In sum, American criminal law and criminology would not be the same without the influx of continental scholars. They have exercised a most wholesome influence on American thinking in criminal law and criminology. Through their writings and their teaching, the refugee scholars have demonstrated to us that progress can hardly be expected unless we put to good use the often superior methods and the experiences of foreign nations and of foreign scholarship. We shall return to this topic shortly, in connection with strictly American developments in comparative criminal law. Above all, however, as a group, the refugee scholars served as the necessary catalyzer for the transformation of incipient American criminal law scholarship into what it is today.

2. *About Contemporary Criminal Law Scholarship*

(a) *The Form of Scholarly Expression.* The mere form of scholarly expression will not serve us well as a criterion for classifying the activities of today's scholars in the criminal law. But a few words on that topic are appropriate. On the whole, the forms of expression have remained those of previous phases of development. That means, first of all, that the scholar employs the printed word. This is not to deny that, conceivably, some scholarship finds only oral expression. For the very sake of the academic profession, I hope that is so, for an appreciable portion of American teachers of criminal law has never published anything, or has published only so little that an evaluation cannot appropriately be made. The scholarship of the classroom, of bar committee-work, and of active participation in civil and social organizations—a burden on virtually every professor —is, therefore, not considered in this evaluation. Oral erudition, since it is not a submission to the scrutiny and criticism of the aggregate of scholars, is not considered 'scholarship' for the purposes of this study, and, perhaps, should not be considered scholarship at all.

Throughout the years discussed in this chapter, books remained the place where criminal law scholarship at its most mature level found its widest expression. Casebooks, of which sixteen or more in hard cover editions are competing on the national market today, take the lead over textbooks, of which there are currently four. Casebooks and textbooks together take the lead over other books, in terms of impact, and it remains to be seen how an annotated Model Penal Code will fit into the picture. The number of casebooks has increased significantly, and their standards have never been higher. The number of textbooks has decreased, with no loss to scholarship, but practitioners' texts are as mediocre as ever. Printed committee reports, code drafts, and similar publications, should be included in the category of books. Their number and quality has increased significantly over past eras. The number of other books on criminal law remains small—especially if compared with those published in England—but the few which have appeared are of extraordinarily high caliber.[21] There has been an increase in the number of book series, especially in England,[22] but also in the United States.[23] It appears that the 'little book', the monograph, is making its first significant appearance in American legal literature. Oceana Publications was the first to introduce this new medium in series form, and some of the volumes, judging by the reviews, are a welcome addition to the literature.[24]

A virtually new form of scholarly expression in our field is the hard-cover symposium, in the nature of the European *Festschrift*,[25] or as reprinted lectures delivered simultaneously,[26] or consisting of articles by the same[27] or different authors,[28] or consisting of papers written simultaneously on request.[29]

Many of the established book publishers have maintained their interest in the fields of criminal law and criminology; others have entered the field with a newly aroused interest in our subject.[30]

Some criminal law scholars and writers have produced popular books which, nevertheless, are worthwhile studies for the professional.[31]

The periodical literature has witnessed a boom without parallel in history. The number of legal and related periodicals has more than doubled in a generation. In line with the development in other fields, the number of specialized journals is rapidly increasing.[32] Likewise in line with general developments, the law review symposium has greatly added to the store of knowledge in criminal law and has become a favorite form of scholarly expression.[33]

In the last thirty years the number of articles of mature scholarship in law reviews has multiplied many times over all criminal law articles written during the entire previous history of American legal periodical publication. Several scholars have produced more than two dozen law-review articles on criminal law,[34] some many times that number. Some authors write exclusively or mainly for legal periodicals, others spread their output over the journals of the various criminological disciplines; some contribute to popular journals, while others regard this as beneath their dignity.

Student writing in legal periodicals remains what it always has been, only the bulk has increased. With few exceptions, student writing in legal periodicals, as competent as it may be, is necessarily directed to relatively narrow issues. Hence it lacks the benefit of an overall view of the problems of criminal law, crime as such, and crime in its relation to society. With few exceptions,[35] the student contributions of the past are not worth mentioning in an evaluation of mature American criminal law scholarship.

One novel form of periodical criminal law scholarship deserves special mention, the 'Survey'. Following the example of the *Annual Survey of English Law* (1928–1940), Dean Vanderbilt, at New York University, inaugurated the practice of publishing an *Annual Survey of American Law*, beginning in 1942. Each of these volumes contains a chapter, or two half-chapters, on criminal law and procedure.[36] By requiring a complete survey—and partial reporting—of the approximately 3500 reported appeals cases in criminal matters annually, and the statutes, codes, and scholarly works, the *Annual Survey* has performed a unique service to scholars and practitioners alike, and, not infrequently, has itself been a scholarly feat of no mean dimensions. The *Annual Survey* has sparked similar state-wide and court-wide endeavors in more than half of the states, and, while some of these surveys are but poorly written digests, some are of literary and scholarly value. In addition, several surveys covering longer periods of time belong to the better part of our literature in criminal law today.[37]

Lastly, in connection with 'periodical scholarship', it should be mentioned that many of the more prominent American law professors have seen fit to devote some of their energy to editorial functions on American and foreign legal and criminological journals. This service may not be as conspicuous as the writing of books and articles, but it is often more time-consuming and can be more influential. Editors set policies by accepting and rejecting manuscripts, by requiring revision and by setting editorial goals and standards. The names on the mastheads of American and foreign criminal law (and related) journals include many American scholars of the highest repute even before they obtained these editorial posts.

Since it is a popular belief that scholarship is identical with earned degrees—and, thus, theses produced—a few words on that subject seem to be in order. Relying on the very incomplete data listing theses placed on file compiled by the American Bar Research Center, of the about two dozen law schools granting advanced degrees in law, two-thirds did grant such degrees for theses in criminal law and closely related fields during the decade 1950–1960.[38] Twenty-three master's degrees were granted on the basis of criminal law theses by eleven law schools, variously designated as LL.M., M.C.J., LL.C.M., or—in the case of Fordham—M.A. Fordham granted four such degrees, Columbia, Southern California and Tulane three each, Indiana, N.Y.U. and Pennsylvania two each, Illinois, Kansas City, Michigan and Northwestern one each. Nine law schools granted doctorates, variously designated as J.S.D.,

S.J.D., L.C.D., LL.D. (Brooklyn), J.D. (S. Calif., Emory, Illinois) and Ph.D. (Fordham). Brooklyn heads the list with four, Georgetown, Illinois and Yale have two each, Emory, Fordham, Harvard, Northwestern and Pennsylvania granted one such degree. Brooklyn also granted two and Duke and Tulane one unspecified degree during that decade. Several of these theses were subsequently published, and have been considered where appropriate later on in this chapter. Unpublished theses, obviously, remained unconsidered.

To a much greater extent than ever before, the graduate degree seems to be regarded as an adjunct of scholarship in criminal law, though in itself it does not establish its holder as a scholar, nor is its absence inconsistent with scholarship. On the contrary, it has happened more than once that a J.S.D. holder regarded his degree as the terminal and termination of scholarship, rather than a starting point, while many without such a degree have produced many times the work required for it, and have, in fact, granted several such degrees to others. An evaluation of the personal data in the *Directory of Law Teachers in American Bar Association Approved Law Schools* for 1962 revealed the following interesting figures on scholarship and graduate degrees.

Of 63 criminal law and procedure professors with ten or more years of teaching experience in the field, 32 (one-half) have graduate degrees. In this group of 63, there are at least 26 teachers known for scholarly work outside their schools and states. Of these, only 8 have no graduate degrees, but these 8 are among the top echelon of law professors in the U.S.A.

Of 32 criminal law and procedure professors with six to ten years of teaching experience in the field, only 9 (less than one-third) have graduate degrees. In this group of 32 there are at least 11 teachers known for scholarly work outside their school and states. Of these, 8 (two-thirds) have no graduate degrees, and nearly all of these 8 have well-established reputations for scholarship.

Of 102 criminal law or procedure professors with less than six years of teaching experience in the field, only 30 (one-third) have graduate degrees. In this group of 102 there are at least 10 teachers known for scholarly work outside their schools and states. Of these only 3 have no graduate degrees, but these 3 have well-established reputations for scholarship.

It is to be assumed that the law schools where such degrees are obtained are likely to be centers of scholarly study and research. Which are these centers? The graduate degrees listed in the following statistics came from nineteen American universities and some foreign schools. It will be seen that of all the graduate degrees obtained by American criminal law professors, two schools (Harvard and Yale) granted more than one-half of the doctorates, and three schools (N.Y.U., Columbia and Harvard) granted almost one-half of all masters' degrees. The centers of graduate study consolidated and shifted after World War II. While Harvard and Yale still control the market for all doctorates, Harvard lost ground and N.Y.U. and Columbia gained and now control the market for masters' degrees, accounting together for almost one-half (N.Y.U. alone for one-third) of all masters' degrees.

Distribution of Graduate Degrees (98% in Law) by 71 (one-third) of the 209 Law Professors listed in the 1962 Directory of Law Teachers as Professors of Criminal Law or Procedure

	Institution Obtained	Master's Rank		Doctor's Rank	
1.	Brooklyn	—		3	
2.	Catholic U.	2		—	
3.	Chicago	—		1	
4.	Columbia	5	2 (tie)	3	
5.	Duke	1		—	
6.	Fordham	—		1	
7.	Georgetown	2		—	
8.	Harvard	5	2 (tie)	11	1
9.	Illinois	2		—	
10.	Michigan	3		2	
11.	Minnesota	1		—	
12.	National U.	1		—	
13.	N.Y.U.	11	1	—	
14.	Northwestern	2		—	
15.	Pennsylvania	3		—	
16.	St. John's	—		1	
17.	Virginia	1		—	
18.	Wisconsin	1		1	
19.	Yale	2		7	2
20.	Foreign	1		3	
		43		33	
		Top three schools have almost half		Top two schools more than half	

Distribution of Graduate Degrees obtained since
World War II, by American Professors of Criminal
Law or Procedure

Institution Obtained	Master's	Rank	Doctor's	Rank
1. Brooklyn	—		1	
2. Columbia	5	2	—	
3. Fordham	—		1	
4. Georgetown	2		—	
5. Harvard	2		4	1 (tie)
6. Illinois	2		—	
7. Michigan	3		—	
8. Minnesota	1		—	
9. N.Y.U.	11	1	—	
10. Northwestern	2		—	
11. Pennsylvania	3		—	
12. Virginia	1		—	
13. Wisconsin	—		1	
14. Yale	2		4	1 (tie)
15. Foreign	—		1	
	34		12	
	Two schools account for almost half, one for one-third		Two schools account for two-thirds	

(b) *The Emphasis of Scholarship.* In what follows, rather than to
use the mode or form of scholarly expression as a criterion for
classification of modern American scholarship in criminal law, we
shall look to the aims, hopes and aspirations, and the selected path
for reaching one's aims, as criteria. Some scholars work alone,
believing that thought concentration in the loneliness of one's
study, when the world at large is asleep, will yield the appropriate
result. Some want codification right now, others want it later, some
seek salvation through sociology, others through psychiatry. Some
regard the common law as wisdom eternalized, others feel a need
for shopping elsewhere. The one thing they all have in common,
virtually by definition, is the desire to improve our capacity to
control deviant man, and, thus, to prevent crime, especially repeated
crime, for the better securing of the values held in common by the

citizens of the nation. This is an important and desirable common goal, one which makes all those working for it members of the same fraternity, however great the differences of approach may be.[39]

Employing criteria of the nature just mentioned, a division of modern American criminal law scholars into several categories results. Membership of one category does not exclude membership of another as well. Indeed, one should think that the greater the participation of a given individual in the various approaches toward the goal, the greater is his scholarship, evidencing wisdom and broadmindedness. For if we have learned one thing from the previous generation, it is that monism in scholarship stands the best chance of leading to scientific blind alleys. Moreover, monism having been properly rejected in theories of criminal causation during the previous generation, it would seem to follow that the law's approach toward criminality cannot be monistic either.

These comments are not meant to imply that 'membership' in a given 'school' of thought without 'membership' elsewhere is indicative of monism. Not at all. For example, the group of 'codifiers' is anything but a monistic group. What causes me to regard them as a 'school' is their shared interest in the value of codification at this time. Obviously, they may differ widely in *what* is to be codified and how.

(c) *The Current Subject-Matter of Criminal Law Scholarship.* The subject-matter of criminal law scholarship has remained the same over the decades: crime and its prevention. This subject-matter is shared by all the non-lawyer criminologists, whose number, influence and specializations are on a constant increase. Among them, the sociologists have ordinarily been most readily accorded a pre-eminent position. But some investigators have found that in criminology a shift has taken place, in that criminological scholarship is slipping out of the hands of the sociologists.[40] I have not re-investigated this point. While probably accurate, still, 'all too often the term criminology is misused to designate the specific bailiwick of the sociologist'.[41] Sociologists wish it were so[42] and psychologists resent it. Social workers are pleased about the supposed development for the space deserted by sociologists will probably be taken by them. While all this might indicate that the scholar of criminal law remains confined to the positive law of crimes, he has increasingly absorbed enough extra-legal criminological knowledge to choose intelligently between competing criminological approaches, and to exercise discretion in the selection of whatever legal information he may need. More than that, increased criminological confidence on the part of the criminal law scholar has more and more gained him admission into the inner circles of the criminological professions, where occasionally he even assumes a leading role. While such boldness has been resented in some circles, it is being increasingly admired in others, particularly among those non-legal criminologists who have become aware of the fact that crime—the object of their interest—is a legal entity.

While the criminal law scholar has gained some ground, he has also lost some, at least temporarily. For some time the sphere of constitutional law had come to be more and more the specialty of the scholar of the political sciences, whether a Ph.D. from the outset or a political scientist turned lawyer. This has affected those aspects of criminal procedure which are primarily of constitutional significance. No political scientist would wish to acquire expertise in pleading criminal cases. But many have turned their attention to constitutional issues of criminal procedure. Some of the most significant books in this sphere have come from political scientists.[43] It is most regrettable that in the 1940s and 1950s the criminal procedure scholars did not concern themselves with the constitutional aspects of criminal procedure, but virtually abandoned the field to political scientists. When most needed, there was no (or not enough) scholarly guidance. The criminal justice profession, from the police officer to the supreme court justice, vainly looked for scholarly guidance when the flood of due-process demands broke the dam of tradition. Only during the flood, while the Supreme Court ground out dozens of decisions which completely changed state criminal procedure, did the scholarly branch of the profession respond with proposals for codification of minimum standards, of various sorts.[44] What an object lesson in the duties of scholarship!

There fortunately now exists a strong group of (mostly young) procedural constitutionalists, or constitutional proceduralists, who view the constitutional aspects of criminal justice as their prime concern.[45] But this group of experts is not necessarily identical with those who have been entrusted with the drafting of the minimum standards codes which should have been drafted a generation ago.

Even the late recognition of the need for codification of minimum standards of criminal justice, and of police duties, attests to the progress of the common law. Two generations ago, the profession would have accepted the courts' decisions on the matter as the final word. Today the profession wishes these final words to be placed into a coherent body of propositions.

While the political science scholar may have invaded the sphere of law, the criminal law scholar has invaded the sphere of politics. For over one hundred years, the term 'academic' had a derogatory connotation in America. There are indications in the political arena that this term is reverting to its original and positive meaning. Fifty years ago a 'professor' would have been laughed out of legislative halls. While President Wilson demonstrated that academic leanings and the power to handle political affairs need not be opposites, it took several more decades before the politicians realized that the legal theoretician's power of thought and analysis can be helpful in the political field. Professor Inbau—as an adviser—played a leading role in the Kefauver Crime Investigation, and Professor Ploscowe was instrumental in writing the Kefauver Report.[46] Today, there is hardly a significant piece of penal legislation enacted by Congress which has not first been submitted to the critical analysis of the academic criminal lawyer.[47] Conferences between academic and legislative lawyers have been initiated.[48] On judicial councils and similar agencies, the academic criminal lawyer can no longer be imagined absent.[49]

During the Roosevelt administration, and particularly during the war years, law professors by the dozens were placed in responsible positions within the agencies of the federal government, though only a negligible percentage of criminalists were in that group. Nor did any appreciable number of that group turn criminalists after their government experience. The Kennedy and Johnson administrations practiced a comparable use of legal academicians in responsible government posts, including that of the Attorney General and of the Director of the Office of Criminal Justice in the Department of Justice, a newly established office designed for quasi-academic work and liaison.[50] To the best of my knowledge, no specialist in criminal law has so far been placed in any responsible government post. But those academicians who now do hold responsible government posts in the criminal justice field will no doubt return to university life with a sense of urgency about matters of criminal law. Moreover, it is to be hoped that a successful experience with generalist academicians in government service will ultimately lead to the employment of criminal law specialists as well, so that the benefits of academic work in criminal law will accrue more immediately to the public benefit.

3. Scholarship and the Practical Lawyer

Where is the *situs* of scholarship? It may be assumed that the *situs* of immunological scholarship, as here understood, is in the university law schools. Our evaluation of criminal law publications bears this out. Apart from criminological scholarship of significance to criminal law, no major and sustained scholarship in criminal law has found a place outside the law schools, with the possible exception

—to be discussed shortly—of the American Law Institute, which, however, is so strongly influenced by law school scholars as to be virtually an adjunct of law school scholarship.

The vast majority of practitioners' texts on criminal law and procedure has not been produced by law professors. While a few of these have achieved a high standard of accuracy and completeness in their coverage of the law,[51] I have gained the impression that virtually no author of such a book aims at achieving scholarly standards. These works are exclusively guides and digests which, because they are geared to existing practices, perpetuate these practices. Given the rather minimal sophistication of contemporary practitioners these works may be viewed as inimical to everything which modern scholarship strives for. What has been said about these books in the preceding chapter can be incorporated here by reference as equally applicable to the practitioners' texts of the current generation.[52] The same comments are applicable to the occasional memoranda, Law Day speeches, after-dinner addresses, etc., by practicing attorneys, which have found their way into some law reviews. In our search we found not one law review article by a practicing attorney which would qualify as scholarly by the standard here adopted, or, perhaps, by any other definition of scholarship. However, in recent years a few judges have published books and articles of scholarly calibre,[53] as indeed the opinions of some of these judges display the scholar's analytical abilities.[54] Nor can judges be reasonably expected to be or act like scholars, as has already been argued. Judges, under the pressure of case loads, must dispose of specific issues before them. They cannot—as perhaps was possible three hundred years ago—concern themselves constantly with the growth of the law's compass and structure. Nor can the legislatures be expected to develop scholarship. The ordering function in law, thus, necessarily devolves upon the teachers.

However, if non-academic lawyers were to be kept away from all concern about the law's theoretical improvement, and were to be denied all understanding of the rudiments of its practical development, academic lawyers would isolate themselves and render themselves useless.

In combining scholarly erudition with the practical approach, the American Law Institute performs its most useful function. By bringing the top-ranking members of the bar together with the academicians, 'theory' rubs off on the practitioner, and 'practice' rubs off on the theoretician. The former is perhaps the more important aspect. The debates on the American Law Institute's Code of Criminal Procedure, a generation ago, and those on the Model Penal Code, for the past decade, may have been dominated by academicians—who ultimately drafted the Code—but the practitioners learned much that the law schools had not given them in their time and that practice could not teach them. This top echelon of the bar will perhaps serve as middlemen in conveying theoretical insight into the policy problems of the criminal law to their brethren on the local level.

Very recently the American Law Institute has undertaken to institutionalize and broaden this 'post-graduate' training in the policy problems of the criminal law. Under the able editorship of Professor Monrad Paulsen (*then* Coluambi), a series of well-conceived booklets has been published.[55] These booklets bring the relatively unsophisticated practitioner closer to the crucial policy issues of the criminal law, familiarize him with the intricacies of each proposition's involvement in every other, and introduce him to the 'cultured' discussions of the theoreticians. In short, the books are aimed at making better policy-makers out of criminal lawyers. While this will help them to become better practitioners, it will also increase their usefulness as potential workers for the betterment of criminal law. I see in this effort a very significant development, perhaps the first attempt to bring to the American bar that theoretical sophistication of which European bars have long been able to boast. For at least a century Italian, German, and French journals have been filled with highly sophisticated discussions of criminal theory, or, at least, of articles that are well grounded in theory. Here, then, is an indication that our craft bar may well be developing into a professional bar, of a competence comparable with that of the bars of Europe. In many respects, the efforts of the American Law Institute are paralleled by the educational efforts of several law schools, notably N.Y.U., which offer scholarly courses to members of the bar, hoping to create a 'scholarly' and 'cultural' outlook among those without whose help theoretical scholarship would be condemned to sterility.[56]

These scholarly efforts should be distinguished from similar activities which, while worth while, are *not* scholarly, though they do rely on the printed word. Thus, the Joint Committee on Continuing Legal Education of the American Law Institute and the American Bar Association publishes a periodical entitled *The Practical Lawyer—The Magazine for the General Practitioner*. Many interesting and well-written aritcles have appeared on its pages, nearly all of which are of the 'how-to' type.[57] The same committee has also published several booklets of interest to the practicing criminal lawyer,[58] but none of them make any pretense to scholarship and, instead, follow a 'how-to-do-it' approach.[59] These activities of the A.L.I. have their counterpart in those of the Practicing Law

Institute[60] and other organizations. Anything aiding the betterment of the practice of law should be welcomed. Indeed, one can note with considerable satisfaction that, increasingly, problems of concern to practicing attorneys are being approached by the law schools. Thus, Professor Murray Schwartz (U.C.L.A.), in behalf of the National Council on Legal Clinics, published an excellent case and materials collection designed to imbue law students with a feeling for ethical practices.[61] But all these efforts aimed at better practices do not amount to the practice of scholarship.

4. Current 'Common Law Scholarship'

Earlier in this book I have tried to demonstrate that the common law development in the English inns of court stands in striking contrast to the civil law developed at the continental universities. The one is a craftsman's law, the other a scholar's law. 'Common law scholarship', therefore, seems to be a contradiction in terms. Yet, the common-law nations, too, have produced studious lawyers who have investigated the *materia* of their interest and who, in various endeavors, have tried to make the best of it. Perhaps such studiousness—which may well be productive of written works—does not qualify as scholarship, if that concept implies the skillful employment of analytical and scientific methods for scientific purposes. But if law is 'a body of propositions having distinctive form [that] can be expounded in the manner of a rational science', then the common law of crimes, too, has had and has its scholars. Lawyers of the common-law world have frequently tried to expound their criminal law in a manner of a rational science. If, as has been argued, these efforts were less successful in England and America than they were on the European continent, the difference would be merely one expressible in terms of 'more successful' or 'less successful' scholarship.[62]

Jerome Hall, in a recent work, spoke of three levels of legal thought. At one extreme he found the 'heights of maximum generalization, where the "master science", jurisprudence, is enthroned'.[63] At the other extreme he saw 'the valley below, where positive law functions'.[64] And 'lying between positive law and jurisprudence is a distinctive body of generalizations which may be designated "legal theory" '.[65] 'For some purposes', Hall would stratify legal thinking in four levels, i.e., he would divide 'the valley below' into a lower valley where positive criminal law functions, and an upper valley, where 'the immediate elucidation of positive law' takes place. This would encompass 'the direct "low level" definition and clarification

of legal rules and doctrines with which case law is largely concerned'.[66] 'Low level' is, of course, a value judgment and not merely
a description of the activities of the elucidators of the common law
of crimes.

It is with these 'elucidators' that the current section is concerned.
Much, if not most, of the writing in the law reviews, student texts
and similar publications, is of this sort. A thousand and one articles
on the law of 'insanity' are demonstrative of this approach, and
learning, time and effort has been, and constantly is being, invested
in this type of 'low level' scholarship. This is a scholarship which
tacitly takes its given handicaps for granted. The common law
'scholars' are like the city fathers of a medieval walled city. They
will not take the walls down, and they will not alter the existing
zoning and road structure. They see their task in keeping the city
neat, in seeing to it that tramps get pushed out through the city
gate, that houses are properly repaired and painted, that the streets
and alleys of the city are appropriately named—and occasionally
renamed—that the city hall retains its impressive location on the
central square, in short, that all remains essentially as it is, and that
no revolutionary thoughts be introduced. Altogether, this is an
admirable undertaking, though a static rather than a dynamic one.
(The common law's dynamics emanate elsewhere, namely from the
courts and not the scholars.) Kant expressed his disdain for this
activity when he wrote:

> It is quite easy to state what may be right in particular cases (*quid sit
> juris*), as being what the laws of a certain place and of a certain time
> may say or may have said; but it is much more difficult to determine
> whether what they have enacted is right in itself, and to lay down
> a universal criterion by which Right and Wrong in general, and what
> is just and unjust may be recognized. All this may remain entirely
> hidden even from the practical jurist until he abandon his empirical
> principles for a time, and search in the Pure Reason for the sources of
> such judgments, in order to lay a real foundation for actual positive
> Legislation. In this search his empirical Laws may, indeed, furnish him
> with excellent guidance; but a merely empirical system that is void of
> rational principles is, like the wooden head in the fable of Phaedrus,
> fine enough in appearance, but unfortunately it wants brain.[67]

'Wooden head' or not, it remains the fact that the 'low level
writers' have performed a useful function of assembling, if not of
crudely sorting, the positive law. In fact, there is no distinct line
which separates the assembling and crude sorting function from
that to be performed by 'theory', as expressed by Hall. It is, then,
my own value judgment which caused me to treat of the bulk of

American criminal law writing in this section, and to treat of writings of greater sophistication a little later on.

The difference between Hall's two 'valley' levels of theoretical preoccupation can best be demonstrated by a comparison of the Kearney (5th) and Wingersky (6th) editions of Clark and Marshall's *Treatise on the Law of Crimes*.[68]

The fifth edition recorded, as faithfully as its author knew how, the positive law of crimes. There were not even attempted rationalizations. The book was as uninspired and uninspiring an account of the criminal law on the appellate level as can be imagined. But the author of the sixth edition found that 'a collision of ideas and concepts is gradually emerging and relentlessly demanding attention in the field of criminal law'.[69] Wingersky, unlike the mere legal warehouse custodian, found that 'spawned in self-complacent artificial isolation the snug certainty enbalmed in criminal law needs ventilation with fresh ideas and scientific techniques'.[70] Caught in the stream of these fresh ideas, the author then set out to contribute actively to the development. He rearranged the Blackstonian order of previous editions, selecting his own offense categorizations. The 'chief aim' of the book now became the presentation of 'broad outlines of basic substantive criminal law principles'.[71]

Yet such an undertaking is quite unorthodox, for, 'certainly, the American law student or graduate is still much more at home following Blackstone's lead in a search for some plausible reasons for any barely tenable proposition he may be called upon to support than he is when called upon to propose and support *à la* Bentham, a choice among all tenable propositions and their plausible supports'.[72]

The 'wooden head' approach, to borrow Kant's metaphor, describes the typical reaction to autocratic authority. The legal writer who accepts the limitations inherent in supreme court decisions is no different from the child that is satisfied with mommy's 'no, you may not have any ice cream—just because'. Why is the defendant not guilty of an attempt to receive stolen goods when the goods to be received were not stolen in fact? Because a supreme court said so? A book which gives no more of an answer than that is childish and worse than useless. Instead, today's lawyers should inquire into the reasoning which has gone into statutory and decisional law, examine it critically and determine whether the pat and stock-in-trade answers make any sense.

When a lawyer proposes to do more with his legal knowledge than to support and explain 'barely tenable propositions', and when a writer proposes to find and discuss 'broad outlines of basic . . . principles', he has left the bottom of the valley and ascended to a higher level. This is, then, no longer 'common-law scholarship'—it becomes plain scholarship, or, an expression 'in the manner of a rational science'.[73]

There is an enormous mass of low-level criminal law writing in our country. We need no further contributions to that mass, however studious they may be. We have had just about enough explanations of corporate criminal liability which tell us that a corporation cannot be imprisoned. And we have had about enough law-review space devoted to the question of whether or not M'Naghten, because of its old age, is outmoded in the post-Freudian era. There is no further need for discussions of whether a bingo card is a gambling device. And we have had the felony-murder doctrine explained forward and backward *ad nauseam*. Criminal-law scholars, as distinguished from other criminal-law teachers and law-review editors, have long recognized the utter futility of squandering time and talent on such activities.

But what alternatives are open to us? Some may conclude that not to write (and perhaps not to think) at all is the right step to take. Some may turn from charitable 'common-law' law-review writing to lucrative writing for popular magazines and tabloids. Some have concluded that it is not the article and the format of our standard type of legal literature that is useless, but the approach to the problems of criminal law by the *mass* of legal writers.

From this point, it will be my task to explain the activities of those who during this last decade have left the 'bottom of the valley' and have climbed higher in the canyon of criminal law scholarship.

5. *The Codifiers*

Would it not be logical to assume that any American criminal-law scholar who does not belong to the perpetuators and adorners of the *status quo* would be a 'codification' scholar? Perhaps it is true that all those who do not want to perpetuate the *status quo* are aiming at a 'proper' codification of our penal law. (The meaning of 'proper' is contentious, of course!) In fact, in the absence of indications to the contrary, we might well assume that there is certainly no strong 'school' of criminalists who propose a raising of the level of criminal law theory and practice without going the 'code way'. Indeed, few of today's prominent criminal-law scholars have not gone on record as advocating a code.

Beginning with the codification of the basic propositions of American criminal procedure in the American Law Institute's Code of Criminal Procedure,[74] a third wave of codifications began in America a generation ago. The true origins of this substantive codification wave are hard to identify. Perhaps it was the result of the urgings of Dean Pound or Wigmore.[75] Perhaps it was the result of all the criminological activities previously described; perhaps it was all that and the good fortune of having on the scene a group of young, eager and recently 'unemployed' law teachers—for, having completed the Code of Criminal Procedure, they were now longing for other deeds of valor.[76] In any event, at about this time the codification wave came rolling in. The first splashes of the wave came gently, almost prodingly. It was Sheldon Glueck who, a generation ago, published the first of a number of articles by distinguished scholars looking toward modern codification.[77] Louisianans, traditionally happy codifiers, responded with Marr's article on 'The Necessity of a Criminal Code for Louisiana'.[78] On the national scene Professor Gausewitz wrote his 'Considerations Basic to a New Penal Code' in 1936,[79] followed by J. Hall's 'Criminology and a Modern Penal Code',[80] Harno's famous 'Rationale of a Criminal Code'[81] and Wechsler's 'A Caveat on Crime Control'.[82] Never before had so many good people written so much good straight sense on the topic of codification.

Of course, there was no unanimity on the mode of proceeding. In fact, three schools of thought on the topic of codification emerged quite distinctly. The conservatives subscribed to Bishop's then half-a-century-old views, previously discussed. The conservatives wanted codification only after agreement might be achieved on our criminal law's 'elementary principles reduced to their smallest proportions',[83]—a task to be performed by the scholars.[84] The second and opposing view held that this waiting for agreement on the general principles, indeed any waiting (including that for criminological elucidation)[85] would delay codification efforts materially and to the detriment of the public. Hence, so it was concluded, codification—the best possible under the circumstances —should be tried right then and there. Some did exactly that.[86]

There emerged an ambitious third view, as thoroughly American as can be, of almost boundless confidence and spirit: This view takes it as true that our law is not yet systematized and reduced to its principles, and that criminology is far from being able to give us final answers. However, it concludes that it is just for those reasons that we should codify and, in doing so, achieve the penultimate perfection in theoretical schematization and systematization. The argument continues that we should use the best available criminological knowledge, but leave things flexible enough to permit ready improvement if and when new knowledge becomes available.

But we certainly cannot content ourselves with, in essence, casuistic-
ally repeating in code form all the cobwebbed nonsense which is
mixed in with the sound wisdom of the ages.

Of course, in the mid-thirties, when these contending views first
emerged, none of the then relatively young scholars was quite
audacious enough to start writing a code of national dimensions.
All agreed that some preparations had to be made. The remainder
of this section, however, shall be devoted to that man who, as it
appears in retrospect, took the straightest path toward codification
and who, thus, best represents the 'third view'. It seems that everything which Professor Herbert Wechsler—for he is that man—did
in his distinguished career—was aimed directly at preparing himself
for the task of a national codification.

Luckily, when Wechsler began his academic career as an assistant
at Columbia University, he found, in Jerome Michael, a mentor of
unusual qualifications. At that time Michael, together with Mortimer
Adler, was just putting the finishing touches to *Crime, Law and
Social Science*. Thus, the road-map prepared by Michael and Adler
was to lead Wechsler to the goal. What did this road-map indicate?
Just as they had blasted every past criminological undertaking,
they expressed dissatisfaction with everything ever done by the
practitioners and theoreticians of the criminal law. 'No attempt has
been made to clarify the subject matter of the criminal law by the
construction of a rational science', they said.[87]

> A rational science of the Anglo-American criminal law does not now
> exist. At most, there are fugitive articles in technical journals which
> aim at the clarification by rational analysis of some small portion of
> the total field. In method and purpose some of these articles are
> admirable; the traditional techniques of legal analysis are thoroughly
> rational. But these articles are isolated and fragmentary. They do not
> satisfy the need for systematic and comprehensive construction.
>
> Existing textbooks and commentaries are at best merely compilations
> of statutes and rules under conventional and uncriticised rubrics.
> The casebooks employed in legal instruction clearly exhibit the absence
> of any systematic analysis of the provisions of the criminal law. The
> textbooks and commentaries merely summarize a field of knowledge,
> more or less accurately.[88]

Overstating their case, Michael and Adler tagged the 'standard'
American treatises of Bishop, Wharton and McLain, as 'backward
American legal scholarship'.[89] This is a criticism which I cannot
support unless directed against the adulterated books which, in the
1930s, were masquerading under Bishop's and Wharton's names.

The codification ambitions of the American Law Institute came
under special attack. The Joint Committee on the improvement of

Criminal Justice had regarded the task of codification to be not dissimilar to the task of a restatement.[90] Michael and Adler had called this 'naive'.[91]

> The committee seem to be of the opinion that only empirical knowledge, in addition to the collection and comparative study of existing statutory material and interpretative descriptions, is needed to construct a code; and that empirical knowledge alone, 'facts', will answer the questions what *should* be the end of the criminal law, what behavior *should* be made criminal, and how criminals *should* be treated.[92]

What emerged from this criticism was the vision of a rational, wise statesman, equally at home in ethics and politics, law and especially criminal jurisprudence, the social sciences, history and foreign cultures. Michael and Adler's summary of 'the conditions of rational criminal legislation',[93] deserve to be read by all who aspire to codification scholarship. An ideal of Himalayan dimensions, it found its absolute contrast in the then realities of Washington, D.C., and the state legislatures. But no such ideal system was then possible, they said, because:

1. The specific interests deserving protection through criminal law in our society had not yet been defined; the aid of the rational sciences of politics and ethics had not yet been solicited.

2. The problems of empirical research had not yet been solved. Hence, it was then impossible to study the nature of the behavior to be prohibited and the actual effects of punitive and other treatment.

3. Knowledge of existing and past bodies of criminal law, especially through historical and comparative study, was totally inadequate, so that a vast reservoir of experience was not yet accessible.

4. Empirical knowledge of the administration of the criminal law, especially the treatment of offenders, was sketchy at best, no 'rational' studies having been made.[94]

> [T]he practical problems of the criminal law can be rationally solved only if we possess the kind of knowledge which criminology seeks, but has so far failed to give us. Conversely, the practical value of the knowledge which may some day be obtained in the fields of criminology and the other social sciences is primarily its utility in the direction of rational legislation and judicial administration.[95]

The first stop of Wechsler's trip along the route marked by this map was an article, in two installments, in which he and Professor Michael collaborated. 'A Rationale of the Law of Homicide',[96] became one of the best known law-review articles ever to be published. Hundreds of law students at Columbia University and elsewhere have both 'cussed' it for its length and praised it as a fabulous guide through all the major problem areas of the criminal law, from the theories of punishment and penal philosophy, to the intricate details of specific offenses and problems of administration. In short, in this article Michael and Wechsler attempted to remedy, at least partially, the four weaknesses highlighted in *Crime, Law and Social Science*.

The next step was a further joint undertaking by Michael and Wechsler: a casebook—nay, coursebook—which made all previous criminal law books look infantile: *Criminal Law and its Administration—Cases, Statutes and Commentaries*.[97] In scope and coverage, the book surpassed everything then in existence by a long shot. The book was widely acclaimed as the first expression of legal realism in a criminal-law casebook.[98] History and the comparative method received considerable attention. Seven years went into the making of this book, which was to be Wechsler's prolegomena to rational codification. 'University law schools cannot . . . content themselves with describing the law as it is or as it is declared to be in the immediate present. Their province also includes both the law as it will be and the law as it should be.'[99]

As significant as the book was to be as a way-station on the road to American codification, as a casebook it commanded only a relatively small market, and its methodology and approach have never been copied. One might say that the book was too good, because too voluminous and too sophisticated in approach for the average American law professor and the average American student body. The average criminal-law teacher wanted a volume to be taught from beginning to end. Michael and Wechsler's book, however, required the exercise of intelligent discretion in selecting from the vast amount of materials those which could be taught.[100]

There are two aspects of this book which deserve particular attention in our evaluation of the work as a way-station on the road to codification. First, the book deliberately chose a functional approach in its organization. This means, principally, that the authors chose 'to treat procedural matters collaterally, in the context of some substantive issue which they visibly affect'.[101] Beyond this refusal to preserve the substantive-procedural bi-partition of criminal law, the authors also ignored, for pedagogical reasons, the subdivision into a general and a special part. 'Principles' were not marked out as separate entities, while 'doctrines' were superbly presented—though usually in a dependent and often appended relationship.[102] Merely by way of example, 'the nature of an "Act" ' is explored under 'Differentiation of Non-Criminal From Criminal Homicides: Significant Factors', in the chapter on Homicide, the same chapter which also discusses the function of the executive, the court, and the jury in the administration of criminal justice.

While such an unusual organization may have its pedagogical value, it might have been predicted when this book appeared that a code prepared by the same author might tend toward the same type of functionalism, perhaps not by choice, but simply from habit. Moreover, unless antecedent labors clearly establish the basic principles of criminal law, it cannot be expected that such will appear in the subsequent code.

Secondly, the book evidenced a certain amount of impatience with criminology. Michael and Adler had demanded criminological accomplishments as a prerequisite for codification. But seven years later—seven years spent on *Criminal Law and Administration*, Michael and Wechsler had to note that criminology had made no significant progress. Did that mean that codification should be postponed? No! And here was the second major decision which was to effect the structure and shape of the code: 'We cannot wait for the last word in social science before taking a position.'[103]

Unquestionably, codification would have been begun earlier, had it not been for the holocaust of World War II. Following the war Professor Wechsler served on the prosecution staff of the war crimes trials in Nuremberg, whence he returned to Columbia with that maturity and sophistication in the practical aspects of the 'rational sciences' of ethics and politics which Michael and Adler had posited for their statesman-codifier of the criminal law.[104]

As soon as the turmoil of World War II had subsided, indications were received that the matter of codification had become acute, and that drafting was imminent. In 1952 it was announced that Professor Herbert Wechsler of Columbia University had been appointed by the American Law Institute as Chief Reporter of the Model Penal Code Project. Professors Louis B. Schwartz, of the University of Pennsylvania, and Paul W. Tappan and Morris Ploscowe of New York University, were appointed as Associate Reporters (Professor Schwartz later being promoted to a 'Reporter' of equal rank with Professor Wechsler).[105] The division of labor and responsibility was quite clear from the outset. Professor Wechsler retained ultimate responsibility for the whole project, and assumed direct responsibility for the provisions of the general part. Professor Schwartz assumed special responsibility for the provisions of the special part, and Professors Tappan and Ploscowe labored on the correctional or penological part. A staff of thirteen 'Special Consultants' was appointed, which, by 1962, included five prominent American criminal law professors, Allen, Collings, Knowlton, Paulsen and Remington,[106] the leading British scholar of criminal law, Professor Glanville Williams (Jesus College, Cambridge University), one of the leading American penologists, Sanford Bates, one of the leading

American forensic psychiatrists, Manfred Guttmacher, and one of the leading American sociological criminologists, Thorsten Sellin. During various phases of the work a number of research associates have been affiliated with the Model Penal Code Project, one of whom, Professor Yale Kamisar of Michigan, has become a leading scholar of criminal law administration.[107] A Criminal Law Advisory Committee, to which, at various times, forty prominent members belonged, discussed many issues presented by the preliminary drafts before these were presented on the floor of the Institute. Twelve of these are prominent criminal law professors, twelve are judges, nine are criminologists, three psychiatrists, two practicing attorneys, one a professor of English, and one a foundation representative.[108] Thus, a good portion of American criminal law professors served the Model Penal Code in one way or another.

With few exceptions, all judges known for scholarly opinions in criminal law were represented. The three prominent psychiatrists provided a cross-section of their profession. The criminologists represented all disciplines. These appointments not only put an enormous range of talent at the disposal of the Chief Reporter, but they also left any possible opposition force without essential leadership. Professor Jerome Hall of Indiana University was probably the logical choice for any conceivable opposition force when, having accepted the appointment to the Advisory Committee with reluctance, he resigned in 1955,[109] probably for no other reason than that in his opinion the preparation for codification had not proceeded far enough and that, to the extent that criminal law theory—Hall's own work—had resulted in the recognition of principles, it was not proposed to utilize these for the Model Penal Code.[110] The only other noticeable opposition was that by the National Council on Crime and Delinquency, heretofore known as the National Probation and Parole Association, whose able representative, Sol Rubin, intervened frequently, pressing for a more social-defense-minded approach in matters of sentencing. Unsuccessful in their efforts to influence the Model Penal Code, the N.C.C.D. then drafted its own Model Sentencing Act, with the co-operation of a large judicial advisory committee.[111]

Consequently, work on the code, financed by various foundation grants, proceeded smoothly and outwardly revealed no serious dissension. As each important code in history reveals the strong personality of its principal draftsman (for example, in England, Bentham's draft and Stephen's draft, Ferri's draft code of Italy, Radbruch's draft code of Germany), so does the Model Penal Code reflect the strong personality of Herbert Wechsler.

From time to time Mr Wechsler published his thoughts on codification in general, and on the progress of the Model Penal Code in particular. In 1952 he stated his approach for those not yet familiar with it: There must be a basic reconsideration of the main issues, of which there are three: (1) What behavior ought to be made criminal, and how should it be defined by the law? (2) What variations in the nature, circumstances or results of criminal behavior or in the character of the situation of the criminal should have the legal consequence of varying the nature of the offender's sentence? (3) What method of treatment ought to be prescribed or authorized in dealing with the offender?[112]

These questions are at once indicative of the 'functional', rather than analytical approach to the task. The 'systematic study of the penal law and its pervasive problems',[113] of which Wechsler spoke so frequently—and which, indeed, was accomplished—was systematic only in the sense of the direction indicated by the three questions. The road was to lead toward a systematic penal code, but not necessarily via a systematic penal science. '[S]ustained analysis, sorting the ethical, political, technical or practical aspects of problems from their scientific aspects, in the sense of the behavior sciences', all that was a code-end in itself, not an independent aid after which codification might be thought of.[114]

Perhaps Wechsler was always fully aware that the code might not find legislative recognition anywhere. In fact, there was a tendency—observable at all meetings—to prepare merely a restatement of criminal law, with choices among competing alternative solutions, but the more ambitious code-view appeared to triumph more frequently than not. 'The basic purpose', wrote Professor Wechsler '. . . is . . . to judge existing practice in the light of all the knowledge than can be obtained.'[115] Beyond that, the code's position is frequently the result of political compromise with a view toward political realities in the state legislature.

Major criminological research was neither planned nor undertaken. But, Wechsler commented,

> the project should, at least, permit the law to join with other disciplines in the production of a treatise on the major problems of the penal law and their appropriate solutions from which future legislation, adjudication and administration may be able to draw aid. The hope is to produce a commentary that will help to place the systematic literature of our penal law upon a par with that of well-developed legal fields.[116]

There was no change in approach as the project unfolded. The work proceeded steadily.[117] It is not easy for an outsider to gain familiarity with inside operations, but from what this author has been able to learn through presence at the meetings since 1955, and judging by the complete product, this code is exactly what might have been expected to result from Michael and Wechsler's casebook. The code's standards are just as high as the casebook's, and its limitations too are similar. The criticism here to be offered is in no way intended to detract from the magnitude and success of the code undertaking. The best code which could be hoped for under the circumstances did result. It will go down in history as one of the great codification efforts in criminal law, and it will rank on a par with some of the best draft codes of the past. In fact, in many places the codifier has transcended the limitations of the functional approach and solved the problems on the basis of principles. Thus, on the problem of strict liability, Wechsler had this to say:

> The kind of departure from sound principle involved in . . . strict liabilities is discovered in rethinking penal law. I know that the departure is defended as essential to effective regulation in a number of the areas involved. The defense fails with me and I am not unsympathetic to the regulators. If practical enforcement can not undertake to litigate the culpability of violators, I do not see how the enforcers rightly can demand the use of penal sanctions for the purpose. There are other weapons that can be employed such as injunctive orders or a civil penalty. Crime means condemnation and it is not right to pass that judgment if the bench can not declare that the defendant's act was wrong. This is a point that lawyers can not compromise.[118]

What a wonderful recognition of culpability as a principle! Yet a 'compromise' was in the offing, in derogation of the principle.[119] Strict liability was embraced by the Model Penal Code, though, by way of compromise, the type of offense in which absolute liability prevails is called a 'violation', and the punishment is limited to a fine.[120]

This one example demonstrates both the code's special strength and its greatest weakness. The strength lies in the recognition of the basic principles of criminal law—with an exception to be noted.

Thus, the principle of conduct, as a basic requisite of every crime, is recognized in Section 2.01: 'a bodily movement that otherwise is not a product of the effort or determination of the actor, either conscious or habitual,' is not voluntary conduct.[121]

With the exception of absolute liability, just noted, the principle of 'culpability' (*mens rea*) is fully recognized (Sec. 2.02).

The code's weakness, on the other hand, is the failure to apply these principles consequentially throughout. Occasionally the principles have simply been forgotten, or replaced by a compromising functionalism which is devoid of principles. This is demonstrated not only by the absolute liability provisions, but also by the rule of 'insanity'. Thus, when the draftsmen turned to the 'insanity' ('responsibility') formula, they disregarded the basic principles of conduct and *mens rea* and attempted to draft a *functional* formula (possibly by way of compromise among the advisory committee). Consideration of the two basic principles would have required a capacity doctrine to the effect that whenever 'mental disease or defect' rules out the capacity for the specified and requisite conduct, the defendant is not guilty of the crime charged.[122] Instead, the 'functional' formula of the code speaks of 'conduct' without capacity to appreciate the criminality thereof (or to act in accordance therewith), disregarding the fact that 'conduct' itself may be obliterated by mental disease or defect.[123]

In my opinion, 'functionalism' also played havoc with the culpability form of *recklessness* which, under the code, has been utilized to describe the frame of mind of the perpetrator of homicide all the way from manslaughter to murder. A more conservative code would take the analytical view and distinguish between intentional and non-intentional killings, as quite separate types of offenses.[124] So much for the code's shortcomings in the light of the recognized principles of criminal law, so necessary for a flawless statement of the doctrines.

The code also suffers from insufficient theoretical groundwork, resulting in a failure to discover and to state one principle altogether, that of 'unlawfulness', i.e., the *reus* in the phrase *actus reus*. By way of example, the draftsmen found it necessary, in a number of provisions, to reiterate such phrases as 'without legal privilege'[125] and 'except as authorized by law'.[126] The question then arises whether there might not be a principle inherent in all penal law by which legal privilege (or authority) serves as a general defense or exemption. Of course, there is, and such a general defense ought to be properly stated in the 'General Part' of the code, so as to make unduly repetitive phrases unnecessary. The same issue arose in a related matter, on the occasion of the American Law Institute debate of the Foreign Relations Law of the United States, when it was discovered that neither 'command of law' nor 'conflict of legal duties', had been included in the Model Penal Code.[127] In this connection it cannot be discussed whether 'authority of law' and 'conflict of legal duties' are independent principles or whether they are both merely aspects of the same or of kindred principles. The point simply is that, since no full clarity and agreement on principles existed to begin with, the resulting product could not be perfect by contemporary standards.

A similar criticism must be levelled at the statement of doctrines and other provisions on which social science research can be expected to yield fruitful information, but has not yet done so. The code embraced the concept of corporate criminal liability sweepingly, extended it to partnerships and unincorporated associations, and sanctioned the use of absolute liability in this connection.[128] There is no empirical evidence whatsoever which would suggest that this type of liability possesses any greater utility than personal liability for somebody acting through or in a corporation. Some aspects of the code's liability go even beyond the limits of existing law which, through trial and error, have at least proved not entirely useless. Almost forty years ago Professor Joseph A. Francis wrote: 'Until and unless it is demonstrated that the social good demands that corporations be held responsible for crimes, there is no sound reason for so holding them.'[129] There still is no such sound reason.[130] But the draftsmen were impatient. They felt they had to act right then, and while this may have been politically expedient there will be no method of evaluating the soundness of the decision until social science provides us with the data.

On the whole, however, the code is solid on the doctrines of criminal law, those practical statements of matters to be dealt with by courts which are directly derivable from principle, or, in turn, which are abstractions short of ultimate principles. Indeed, the doctrines were of special concern to Professor Wechsler, for, as he had explained in the *American Bar Association Journal*, 'basic doctrines governing the scope and measure of . . . liability have received small attention from the legislature and can not easily be renovated by the courts'.[131]

One of the strongest aspects of the code is, unquestionably, its forthright answer to Wechsler's first question: What behavior ought to be made criminal? The most widely publicized debates were those on this question. In 1956 the late Judges Hand and Parker debated whether the code should cover sexual activities among consenting adults committed in private. With Hand, the code ultimately answered with a resounding 'no'. Indeed, it is the sphere of the 'special part' in which the functionalist can work at his best. The voice of the community is detectable, it is caught and reflected in the code. The drafting of these provisions, however, is usually a bit cumbersome—or casuistic (reminiscent of the French Code). Too often the code reflects *the decided case, any* case likely to happen. It often lacks that abstractness which, while increasing the scope of coverage, is yet precise enough to serve as a general warning to the public. Penal code provisions must be broad enough to encompass even the unforseen case which, if he had thought of it, the legislator would have wished to cover. But the provision should circumscribe the situation type, and not list its incidents.

The Code is now before us in its entirety,[132] an unprecedented achievement of American scholarship in criminal law. The credit for it must go to its strong-willed originator, Herbert Wechsler, and his closest associates, Louis B. Schwartz, the late Paul W. Tappan, and Morris Ploscowe. While many people helped on the code, it has been my impression that the best in it is attributable to these four men. According to my personal observations, on the whole—and with few exceptions—the 'senior partners' (who perhaps attend the American Law Institute meetings principally for their superb cocktail parties, receptions and dinners), have not contributed significantly to the success of the code. More often than not the votes on the floor have not been either very intelligible or very intelligent. Most oral comments have come from the advisory committee members and a few other law professors and judges. In sum, the code is the scholars' work, and nobody else's.

For an entire decade the Code had been the principal object of American criminal-law scholars. Some, as just discussed, devoted much of their time to writing it, others to discussing it orally and in print.[133] The Model Penal Code has shaped careers of teachers, influenced the content and method of classroom work, and has become the guide for the criminal law knowledge and approach of many students. Colleagues abroad have listened in amazement when the word reached them that Americans—of all people—had undertaken to write a penal code.[134] They may not wish to copy the code or the American approach. Perhaps they are still ahead of us in many aspects. But in two respects they can surely learn from the code: (1) the determination of what ought to be subjected to the penal sanction in a modern industrial society and (2) the methods, ways and means which a modern society deems advisable for purposes of correction.[135]

The Code has already exerted an influence on adjudication and legislation. One of the outstanding examples of the impact on adjudication was the United States Supreme Court's adoption of the standard of obscenity as proposed by the American Law Institute,[136] and one of the outstanding examples of influence on legislation was Vermont's adoption of the code's insanity test.[137]

More importantly, in 1956 the Wisconsin legislature passed a new penal code for the State of Wisconsin. This code rests largely on the then available provisions of the Model Penal Code. Professor Frank Remington (of the University of Wisconsin),[138] a Special Consultant and Advisory Committee member of the Model Penal Code Project, 'served on the technical staff which prepared the [Wisconsin] code'.[139] The Wisconsin codifiers' objectives were not dissimilar to those of the Model Penal Code, going beyond the aims

of customary revision: simplification, de-formalization, harmoniza-
tion of substance and procedure, clarification of definitions and
defenses, systematization of substantive law and grouping into a
general and a special part, with logical and functional harm groups
in the special part.[140] Six years of research and drafting produced a
code which, by common-law standards, is admirable. Again, this
was a scholars' job, for the debates on the floor of the Wisconsin
legislature indicated that the good law-makers have little understanding of the objectives and contents of penal codes.[141] On the whole,
the code portrays the common-law thinking of its draftsmen. It
lacks the *elegantia juris* of continental codes, and is weak in engineering the general part, going not far beyond the experience-maxims
of case law. Nevertheless, the code is a legitimate step forward in
a common-law jurisdiction.[142]

Pursuing the legislative impact of the code, we note that Illinois
went several steps beyond Wisconsin in its codification. For Illinois
the Model Penal Code was not just an inspiration and suggestion
of method, it was a direct model. Illinois' is even more a scholars'
code than Wisconsin's. Professor Francis Allen,[143] of the Model
Penal Code Project, was the Chairman of the Drafting Sub-
Committee, and Professor Charles H. Bowman of Urbana, Illinois,
'has done yeoman service in putting this draft and the commentaries
in final form'.[144]

While deviating in many respects from specific provisions and in
some respects from the mechanical details of the Model Penal
Code (so as to accommodate state traditions and local demands),
the Illinois Code of 1961 resembles the Model Penal Code as only
a child can resemble its mother.[145] Hence, what has been said about
the Model Penal Code is equally applicable here. The contents of
the code are of less interest to us in this connection than the fact
that modern codification is possible in an American jurisdiction
ever since the Model Penal Code has pointed the way. This was
further demonstrated by new penal codes in Minnesota[146] and New
York,[147] which states did not profit as much from the Model Penal
Code as they should have.[148]

On Thursday, May 24, 1962, after ten years of hard labor, the
most significant decade in the history of American criminal law
scholarship came to a close, when the American Law Institute
passed a resolution adopting the Model Penal Code. Most of those
who voted in the affirmative still knew little about either codification
or criminal law scholarship. There was nothing in the resolution
which took cognizance of the giant effort of the draftsmen and of
the utter novelty of such an undertaking in a common-law nation.
Perhaps the two reporters felt it when they escaped a friendly but

largely meaningless standing ovation—as fast as they could, down the hotel lobby, and into an elevator—which took them up—up from the level on which the Model Penal Code had been approved.

Professor Wechsler has fulfilled the promise implicit in his past career. Criminal law scholarship, to him, meant the practical realization of research capacity, i.e., 'systematic inquiry designed to gain ideas, insights or information relevant to the solution of important problems of the field', with a shift of 'focus from the courts and their decisions to the legislatures and the task of legislation'.[149] Having produced this legislation—though it be moot— is this the end of Wechsler's scholarship in criminal law? It may be that Professor Wechsler will now turn his major attention to his second love, constitutional law and federalism, a field to which he has already made significant contributions.[150] Professor Schwartz, likewise, will be able to devote more time to his second love, a field with which his name and fame have long been associated, trade regulation. But it is not likely that their scholarly interest in the criminal law has come to an end with the completion of the Model Penal Code, though it would be idle to speculate on the direction which this interest may take.

There are, however, many criminal law scholars in America to whom codification has never been the current and principal interest. And while most of those prominently discussed in this section can be loosely grouped as belonging to the school of 'codifiers', nearly all of them have scholarly interests besides, follow paths of their own choosing, and, indeed, may have worked on the Model Penal Code only with reluctance and because it would have been unwise to refuse an invitation.

The next chapter will be devoted to all the efforts which were not aimed at immediate codification, though codification may ultimately be the goal of all of them.

CHAPTER VIII

The Lawyer and Interdisciplinary Scholarship

1. Criminal Justice Research

(a) *Massive Studies.* America has long been known as the land of contrasts. Even our attitudes in law seem to prove the point. Thus, one of the highest American creeds is that of the government of laws and not of men,[1] by which the founding fathers meant a government in which the passions and discretions of men in office are closely limited by laws defining their duties and prerogatives. Yet, probably in no country of the western world are there fewer, and less definitive, laws governing the duties and prerogatives of law enforcement and justice officials than in America. No country has broader standards governing law enforcement than America. 'Our genius seems to lie in the creation of great phrases like 'due process' or 'equal protection of laws', which can command general adherence precisely because they are equivocal', wrote Professor Schwartz recently.[2] Broad phrases like 'the public interest',[3] 'new deal', 'new frontier', or 'great society', have their origin in practical, vote-getting politics. The phrases stick when the vote-getting is no longer at stake; they become part of day-to-day politics and of our way of life. On the legislative level,[4] as much as at the other end of the polity, the law-enforcement level,[5] our governmental functionaries are accustomed to work with and under the vaguest possible standards and widest conceivable discretions—with the blessing of the public, as long as the standards and discretions carry the illusion of certainty through popularly understandable and intriguing catch-phrases. Yet—and here is another contrast—we operate with such ideological slogans while harboring an immense 'distrust of ideology'.[6] 'Our professors gleefully demonstrate that in any debatable case opposing parties will rely on one or more general principles, each of undoubted validity, although they lead in the particular case to opposite results.'[7] Only the Bible, I suggest—and perhaps the Delphic oracle—have permitted humanity similar material for forensic artistry.

It is no wonder, then, that some scholars of the criminal law would prefer to turn their research skills to the discovery of the puzzles inherent in such anti-ideological ideology, in so far as it affects criminal-law administration, while others continue their search for the discovery of those broad principles which will put an end to reaching opposite conclusions under the same or different principles. In this section we shall deal with the former group of scholars, those seeking certainty in the puzzle of slogans and manifestos, those seeking standards in the jungle of discretions, especially in law-enforcement.

That at present we have but few answers to the many puzzles inherent in criminal justice is attested to by the fact that the most basic of all law-enforcement manifestos has never been scientifically investigated. Worse yet, it is taken for granted by almost all scholars that the manifesto is a valid one and presents a legitimate collision of ideas. This manifesto, in other words, is so persuasive that it even fools the manifesto-hunters; it is that of the 'conflict among the objectives of efficient conviction of the guilty, successful rehabilitative treatment of deviant behavior, and fairness of procedure in dealing with suspected and convicted offenders'.[8] The first of these supposed conflicts—successful conviction versus rehabilitative treatment— would be a suitable topic for 'criminal justice' research, perhaps the most suitable and most important of all. We have but the vaguest notions on this conflict hypothesis of law enforcement; yet the historical method of legal research alone might yield valuable results.[9]

As for the conflict between successful rehabilitative treatment of deviant behavior and either or both of the other aims, it is not readily apparent how the conflict may come about. More frequently, the successful rehabilitation objective is deemed to conflict with the legitimate goals of retributive justice. But this, too, is only a surface conflict which in other nations has led to relatively successful theoretical solutions. The comparative research method might yield valuable clues for solutions in our own country.[10] A very recent investigation indicates that the supposed conflict, if it exists at all, has at least been deemed much greater than it probably is.[11] But much more research experience is needed before the matter can be regarded as resolved.

The research situation is a bit better as to another basic issue in the administration of criminal justice, that of discretion. A multitude of pre-war surveys, previously discussed, might well still hold useful data on the problem.

While, seemingly, we have left the era of massive studies, at least three such projects have been undertaken since World War II, and at least one of these, the American Bar Foundation Survey, to be discussed shortly, seems to lend itself to evaluations fruitful for a solution of the discretion issue. These three recent surveys, and a sampling of the many smaller ones which our American foundations have made possible, may be conveniently labeled 'Criminal Justice Research', to borrow the nomenclature chosen by Professor Remington in an article on that topic.[12] Professor Remington, for the sake of convenience, classified all research in criminal law into three categories, the third of which, I believe, is the one which, primarily, he regards as 'Criminal Justice Research', namely[13] 'the study of the process of administration by which the substantive criminal law is applied to cases which arise'.[14] As his discussion indicates, this would encompass the entire field of criminal law administration, from crime detection to sentence and correction. 'The major task for the future is to give increased attention to . . . [this] aspect of the criminal law.'[15]

This may sound a bit startling at the outset since, for generations, nearly all group and field research has been devoted to precisely that sphere, as discussed in previous chapters. The multitude of costly mass studies of the 1920s were of that nature—especially the Wickersham study—however ineptly they may have been carried out. Moreover, in our own time there is probably no self-respecting law school in the country which does not have its own criminal-justice project, of whatever scope and approach. Public and private agencies as well as the law schools are benefiting from a multitude of foundation grants available for criminal justice research. But perhaps all these studies are misdirected! Professor Remington singles out six directions which the new type of 'criminal justice research' should follow. The recurrent theme of all six directions is the study of responsibilities, discretions, and their limitations.[16] All six research directions rest on two implicit hypotheses: (1) That there is, in fact, a decisional conflict requiring the exercise of discretion in deciding upon alternative courses of action. As already indicated, the foundations of this hypothesis are not firm. But that, itself, ought to be the subject of the first and principal research efforts. (2) That conflicts—if there are such in fact—require for their solution the exercise of discretions broadly stipulated, as distinguished from guides and standards of relative certainty.[17] By way of demonstration, one might—as is customary in common-law jurisdictions—leave entirely undefined any duty or prerogative of a prosecutor to invoke the criminal process. This might be called the *laissez-faire* attitude of criminal prosecutions. This choice would rest on the assumption that since a law defines certain conduct as criminal, and since the election law provides for the election of a public prosecutor, the public prosecutor will invoke the criminal process whenever it appears that the law, defining conduct as criminal, has been breached and that somehow the public prosecutor, operating in the public limelight, will seek to satisfy the expectations of his electorate by applying the laws which seem to call for application.[18]

On the other hand, one could provide for extensive regulation of a duty to prosecute as soon as a given fact-probability appears— one which is easily verifiable by higher or co-ordinated authorities, leaving virtually no room for disagreement as to whether or not the condition for instituting proceedings has been met.[19] This would seem to be the chosen method of a regulated society.

It is suggested that the relative advantages and disadvantages of either system are themselves subject to investigation, i.e., either verification or disproof. Before we can suitably decide how discretions must be exercised, we should have the benefit of sociological examination of the hypotheses.

There had been practically no previous research on these two most fundamental issues of criminal justice until Professor Joseph Goldstein of the Yale Law School met the 'discretion' problem head on with his superb article on 'Police Discretion Not to Invoke the Criminal Process'.[20] This article is an outgrowth of a Ford Foundation Research Seminar on Criminal Law Administration, held at the University of Wisconsin Law School in 1958, with Professors Frank Remington, Francis Allen, William B. Harvey, Lloyd Ohlin, Richard Cloward, and Herman Goldstein. Professor J. Goldstein skillfully utilized and analyzed some of the data gathered by the American Bar Foundation Survey on Criminal Justice, to be discussed shortly. He came to the empirically well-founded conclusion 'that the police should not be delegated discretion not to invoke the criminal law. It is recognized, of course, that the exercise of discretion cannot be completely eliminated. . . . But . . . outside this margin of [unavoidable] ambiguity . . . responsibility for the enactment, amendment, and repeal . . . will . . . [be] retained where it belongs in a democracy—with elected representatives'.[21] I know that at least some of my colleagues regard Professor J. Goldstein's article as at least partially refuted by an article by another participant of the Wisconsin seminar, Professor Herman Goldstein, which, despite absence of documentation, contains a strong argument for a more discretion-oriented approach.[22] This, indeed, is the more traditional argument in Anglo-American countries.[23] We are here not interested in the merits of the argument, but in the fact that the argument has taken place, and that it could take place on the basis of facts gathered in a major empirical inquiry, thus proving the relative utility of factual investigations for purposes of solving basic problems in criminal justice.

In pursuit of factual information bearing on issues of the administration of criminal justice, three massive studies have been conducted since the close of the era of the giant surveys described earlier. The first was the enormous investigation conducted by Senator Estes Kefauver and his Senate Crime Investigating Committee, in 1950 and 1951.[24] The report confirmed nearly every suspicion about the tie-in between ward politics and organized crime, the extent and interest direction of organized crime, and its holds on the nation. Beyond that, it had little practical effect on the destiny of the nation —save in creating a presidential candidate. Nor did it exercise any significant influence on legal development in America, since it was not a scholarly effort, but a political enterprise in the nature of a fact-demonstration.[25]

The second massive investigation, this one in the nature of a spot-problem research enterprise, was conducted by the University of Chicago Law School into the functioning of the jury, in civil as well as criminal cases. This enormously costly, foundation-sponsored research used almost every conceivable research method. The project continued for ten years, and while it has been completed for some time, the conclusions have still been only sporadically published. As far as the criminal jury, in particular, is concerned, since only an occasional descriptive article on the study has been published, nothing can be concluded either about the research topic, or the methods employed.[26] But there can be little doubt that this study is likely to make or break the 'scientific method' in criminal justice research. No other study in either criminal or civil law has ever been so well conceived, prepared and executed as this. It is, therefore, worth quoting an observer of the University of Chicago project:

> The jury study project at the University of Chicago, under a Ford Foundation grant, embraced several years of intensive research. The material gathered is in the process of being summarized in a number of books covering such topics as: judge and jury in criminal cases, judge and jury in civil cases (comparing decisions of the judge and jury in these two situations); a report on the experimental jury work that was done, pin-pointing in great detail the behavior of the jury in several test cases, with emphasis on the social process; a report on post-trial juror interviews, influence of the juror's background on his decision of cases; the reputation and public image of the jury today; and a detailed report on a test criminal case involving the defense of insanity. These reports are eagerly awaited by all who are interested in judicial administration because they are expected to provide for the first time a reliable, empirical basis upon which to establish needed reforms in the use and procedures of juries.[27]

So far the only disappointing fact is that the evidence could not be made publicly available at an early time, with direct co-operation of those who carried out the research. For many phases of the research project years have passed, while the materials gathered dust. The original researchers have long since moved to other positions in far-away places. The jury material has become stale to most of them. Over a decade ago, this author prepared a voluminous research report for the jury project, embodying the results of comparative studies, historical, legal and sociological.[28] But by now that material has become quite alien to its author. It may be even more alien to un-initiated editors. This points to one of the most serious shortcomings of all massive research projects: the problem of staff turnover. More-over, the greater the amount of data gathered, the greater—in almost geometrical proportion—becomes the evaluation problem for new staff members. Nobody has as yet suggested a means of overcoming these difficulties, short of the obvious answer of appointing only research professors, and plenty of them, at high salaries with tenure.

The third massive fact-inquiry was that undertaken—with vast foundation support—by the American Bar Foundation, originally directed by Professor Arthur H. Sherry (California), with Professor Frank Remington (Wisconsin) as director of field research, and Professor Lloyd Ohlin, one of the nation's ablest sociological criminologists, as his aide. Among the consultants and advisors were two leading police experts, Bruce Smith and O. W. Wilson, and two law professors of extraordinary qualification in the field, Albert J. Harno and Fred E. Inbau. Its authors had a grandiose conception of their new and ultimate survey, as the 'Plan for Survey', published in 1955, shows.[29]

The new survey was intended to avoid the deficiencies of all previous surveys, all of which were listed in the 'Plan'.[30] Michael and Adler's admonitions had been closely studied, and the 'Plan' contained all but a pledge to follow such advice. Five methods were to be employed:

1. The method of direct observation.
2. The case history method.
3. The census method.
4. The administrative experiment.
5. The questionnaire.[31]

The study was not to concern itself with crime causation or substantive criminal law, nor was it meant to duplicate the efforts of other agencies, such as the American Law Institute. Instead, the survey was meant to gather data on and study

> The organization, administration, and operation of those agencies, bureaus and institutions engaged in the performance of police duties.

2. The organization, administration and operation of all those agencies, institutions and professional groups engaged in the prosecution and defense of criminal actions.

3. The organization, administration and operation of the courts and other judicial institutions which are charged with duties and responsibilities in the administration of criminal justice.

4. The organization, administration and operation of all the agencies and institutions concerned with the disposition of offenders through probation, sentence and parole and the processes by which their functions are exercised.[32]

The plan called for field research in selected jurisdictions, rendering a valid sampling.[33] Indeed, it was a very elaborate plan, on the broadest possible basis. The survey did not work on any specific hypothesis, nor was it intended to lead to any specific goals, other than the goal of revealing facts which may indicate the need for and type of improvements. Five years were contemplated for the survey. Thus the work was to be completed in 1959 or 1960. But half a decade later little information had become available on the results of the survey. It was generally understood to have yielded an enormous amount of useful data. Judging by the articles by Professors J. and H. Goldstein, this must have been so.[34] In the meantime, two substantial books on Arrest and Sentence have grown out of the Survey,[35] and others will no doubt follow. These first two volumes, written by Professors La Fave and Newman, went a long way toward appraising the interested public which had all but given up hope that anything would result from the Bar Survey. Both authors have skillfully exploited the gathered data and thus provided useful background material for legislative reform along liberal lines. They may also, and unwittingly, have set valuable precedents for similar research in criminal law proper. It is not known what other volumes and final reports are yet to follow. 'A pamphlet describing the status of the project and the availability of preliminary reports is available upon request by writing John C. Leary, Acting Administrator, American Bar Foundation, 1155 East 60th Street, Chicago 37, Illinois.'[36]

The criminal-justice research endeavors described so far, all of massive and long-term nature, were primarily studies of American conditions. To these three studies a fourth one has been recently added, namely, a 'Comparative Study of the Administration of Justice'. This research project has been created under the auspices of the Ford Foundation as a co-operative venture among a number of smaller law schools. The primary aim of the project was to prepare comparative law teaching materials which may be integrated into existing law-school courses in Civil Procedure

Criminal Procedure, and Evidence. The project was administered by Loyola University School of Law (Chicago) and had as participating law schools the following: Duke University School of Law, Louisiana State University Law School, University of Miami School of Law, University of Oregon School of Law, and Syracuse University College of Law.

The Study also aimed at substantially contributing:

> to the existing knowledge in the field of administration of justice, since for the first time a group of law teachers will be available with the knowledge and experience necessary to conduct research in depth in this area, and this project will make available the materials to make such research possible; . . . [and] most importantly, [it] will enable the members of the Bar to evaluate the operation of our own system in the light of what other nations are doing to solve common problems.

> The Study plans to survey over a four-year period the methods of the administration of justice currently in use in four geographical areas of the world.[37]

Areas of specific inquiry in criminal procedure have been broadly identified as: preliminary investigation, arrest, arraignment and pleas, search and seizure, confessions, nature and function of prosecutor, method of commencement, variation from method of civil trial, fact-finding agencies, sentencing and appeals.

The study has now been completed. The English-language literature of our profession has been enriched by a number of well-conceived law-review articles descriptive of foreign law and practice in the criminal justice field,[38] as well as an unusual casebook on American administration of criminal justice, which is nevertheless comparative in outlook since it incorporates foreign and comparative materials at every point at which American law and practice were deemed unsatisfactory.[39]

(b) *Spot-Problem Research*. The massive type of criminal justice research just described may be contrasted with the more modest spot-problem research projects which are designed to investigate, analyze or find improvements for one or but a few problem-spots in the administration of criminal justice. This type of research is relatively free from the inherent disadvantages of the massive research, namely the problems posed by personnel turn-over and 'material suffocation'. But its very nature, this type of research results in the collection of manageable amounts of data. Obviously, none of these studies is capable of being turned into a launching pad for a massive assault upon the very premises of criminal justice—at least none devised so far has been. But there is no reason why a master plan for such spot-problem research projects could not be devised so as to select a multitude of specified problems for research in diverse locations. For the time being, however, there is much duplication of effort, and many of the projects are directed to non-essential topics. Besides, as has already been stated, it is wasteful to spend time, money and energy on the proof of hypotheses whose veracity may be taken for granted, while the very fundamentals on which criminal justice rests have not been studied.

Perhaps never before in history has there been as much spot-problem research activity as in the last decade, and almost never before have the research designs been as practical in outlook as now.

As with growing affluence a society becomes more cognizant of those of its members who do not share in its wealth—throughout history revolutions have come about in this manner—the first criminal-justice problems to engage the attention of the researchers were those related to poverty, particularly bail. There is no other stage in the administration of criminal justice at which the difference between rich and poor had become as much a legislated imbalance as here. As early as 1927, Dean Arthur Beeley had demonstrated in Chicago that bail is an ideal subject for empirical inquiry in criminal justice.[40] Now, in the late 1950s and 1960s, the spot-problem researchers would begin with this topic.

Professor Foote has been associated with several such inquiries, the results of which have been published in recent years. He wrote:

Beginning in 1951, the University of Pennsylvania Law School undertook a policy of subsidizing summer research by selected students. Besides its value as an educational device, the result of this policy has been, in addition to the present bail report, the production of ten studies on varied aspects of the factual administration of the law.[41] Produced at a nominal cost,[42] this research policy has shown a remarkably high return on the dollar. These publications demonstrate both that a wide range of problems in the administration of our legal rules can be researched at a very low cost and that law schools can make a major research contribution through such utilization of their students.[43]

The New York bail study is the most ambitious of these summer research projects, and in addition to its research importance it has significant ramifications for legal education. . . .

Seven men with only a summer to spend on the job cannot exhaust a subject of such scope as the administration of bail in a city the size of New York. Despite such limitations of time and manpower, however, they have completed what is unquestionably the most authoritative study ever made of the effects upon the accused of the institution of bail. The work is based on a sample of more than 3,000 cases, comprising about half of the felony prosecutions instituted in three of New York City's counties in 1956. . . .

If conditional release pending trial is to be the norm under our system of criminal prosecution, this study makes it obvious that New York's administration of bail is falling far short of that goal. The authors of the study pinpoint some of the causes of this failure. . . .

[T]he most ironic finding in the whole study is the revelation that accused persons, whom our law presumed to be innocent and who are not to be punished, are confined pending trial under conditions which are more oppressive and restrictive than those applied to convicted and sentenced felons.

Another major contribution is the statistical data which gives us for the first time reliable information on the relationship between the levels of bail normally set for various crimes and the ability of defendants in different criminal categories to make bail at the differing levels. It has been implied that the amount of bail 'usually fixed' for a particular category of crime is prima facie reasonable bail. This data shows how far removed customary bail is in fact from bail that is reasonable in the context of the ability of most defendants to meet it.[44]

Foote conducted a similar study on the administration of bail in Philadelphia which, especially if it be considered that it cost the grand total of $1000, is a superb use of research skills.[45] The bail field-studies were followed up by a comparative bail symposium.[46]

The materials gathered on bail by Foote's studies constituted a more impressive body of facts than was available to most legislatures of the past when they embarked upon the passage of new laws. But even after Foote's studies, we lacked detailed information, on the basis of which an intelligent decision on the need for a money incentive to compel appearance in court could be reached in the first place and, if found to be necessary, on the basis of which predictions of bail risk could be made.

To remedy these defects,

the New York City bail project was inaugurated on October 16, 1961, in the Magistrate's Felony Court and the Court of Special Sessions. Six students from the evening division of New York University School of Law and staff members of the Vera Foundation began to interview defendants, to check out their stories, and, as amicus curiae, to recommend that certain of them be released on parole. They also began to gather information which perhaps will shed light on the administration of bail for the indigent accused in New York City.[47]

The students enjoyed the unexpectedly good co-operation of all officials concerned. All data were secured by means of a sophisticated questionnaire. Ultimately an overall evaluation of all these data was undertaken, and a prediction method for release without bail developed. The City of New York took over the operation of the bail project and is currently operating it successfully. There is no more convincing example of a criminal justice 'spot-problem' demonstration project than this one.[48]

It is no accident that most of the spot-problem research deals directly, or implicitly, with procedural problems that have civil liberties overtones. In the first place, there seems to be something dynamic in the personality of the civil libertarian which equally influences decisions to advocate reform and to engage in research. In the second place, small foundations frequently have special civil liberties interests. In the third place, civil liberties overtones happen to be quite popular. Indeed, at New York University School of Law there has been in operation a civil liberties institute, the Arthur Garfield Hays Civil Liberties Center. Besides services and instruction, the Center engages in research in civil liberties, selecting one or more topics for scrutiny and legal analysis, most of which are of direct interest to the criminal proceduralist.[49]

At the risk of being charged with local patriotism, I must refer to yet other research activities at New York University, not only because proximity has acquainted me with them, but also because, in the aggregate, more research of this type is carried on by the larger and national university law schools. On that level, however, the N.Y.U. research is not atypical of the research being conducted by comparable law schools.

Of particular interest in this connection are the research and clearing-house activities of the Institute of Judicial Administration. Among its published research are numerous reports dealing with various aspects of the administration of criminal justice, especially those bearing on judicial administration.[50] Typical is a recent pilot study of the 'Magistrates' Court and Special Sessions Court in Manhattan—Protection of Civil Liberties—Practices and Procedures'.[51] A number of observers surveyed—with permission—the principal functionaries in the courts under investigation and revealed their practices. Interviews likewise were had. The pilot study yielded an interesting report which succeeded in pinpointing areas in need of depth studies of the spot-problem type. More recently the Institute has assumed the direction of an American Bar Association study to formulate minimum standards of criminal justice.[52]

All these research projects, of the massive as well as the spot-problem type, are principally 'adjective' or administration studies. But their significance for the substantive law of crimes should not be underestimated. Although the impact may not be direct, it may still be pattern-setting in developing methods of inquiry into the problems of substantive criminal law, and particularly, in setting the mood for empiricism in substantive criminal law itself.

2. *The Sociological School of Criminal Law*

In comparison with the numerous criminal-justice research projects, those devoted primarily to the study of problems of the substantive law constitute a pitiful handful, and none is squarely directed to the fundamental premises of substantive criminal law.

Current research projects in substantive criminal law are primarily an outgrowth of the demands of the 'sociological school', or of 'legal realism'. More recently the phrase 'experimental jurisprudence' has been used to describe this type of research. Indeed, the few current studies are traceable to the influence of two pioneer works of this sort, Moore's parking studies and Hall's *Theft, Law and Society*. The relationship between substantive criminal-law studies and studies in other spheres of substantive law is a close one. Merely by way of example, the Weberian sociology of law, as advanced and further developed by Professor Max Rheinstein,[53] continues its influence on both criminal law and family law.[54]

This writer must take it for granted that his reader is familiar with 'the sociological study of law'.[55] In short, it is the study of the law in the books as it actually works or has worked on man in society. My use of both the present and the past tense indicates two different research goals and methods, the historical method (and goal), and the contemporary method, usually combining library and field research. In addition, there is a method which creates its own variables in order to test hypotheses. This may be called the method of experimental jurisprudence. This section, then, will be divided into three parts, each devoted to one of the three methods.

(a) *The Historical Method.* The historical method—although it had many forerunners—was pioneered for criminal law by Jerome Hall, but in a work which, at the same time, also pioneered the method for the study of the conditions of contemporary law: *Theft, Law and Society* (first edition 1935). Hall felt at that time that 'the need for scientific knowledge of interpersonal conduct in relation to law has become urgent in an age of tensions, conflicts and expanding controls'.[56] The book appeared in response to the demands of the sociological school and of the realists. At the same time, it seemed a natural reaction against the tendencies to create a philosophical social science. The result was a unique contribution to legal literature 'which did much to make us cognizant of the impact of social and economic conditions upon the historical development of those crimes involving property which are grouped under the popular term "Theft"'.[57]

Every teacher of criminal law is likely to have read Hall's *Theft, Law and Society*, so that the results of his substantive findings need not be reiterated. Some of them are of direct use to the legislator. Others, however, are meant for us as scholars. These can be conveniently summarized as follows: The most economical research method, the one likely to yield more fruitful results in relation to expenditure than any other, is the historico-sociological method of criminal-law research. One man, working alone with little more than a good library, paper, a pencil and a 75-Watt bulb, can shed more light on the inner workings, on the actual and supposed structure and content of the criminal law, and on the need for reform, than can a battery of research assistants working under the direction of a high-priced research director sitting in a mahogany panelled office—with indirect lighting. But the method which Hall pioneered requires stamina, perseverance and ingenuity, characteristics hard to obtain except in an era of depression and unemployment. *Plenus venter non studet libenter.* Since Hall completed his unprecedented and unequalled study, the United States has enjoyed a time of relative prosperity, with full employment and full stomachs for all lawyers worth their salt. It remains true, then, that Hall's continues to be the greatest historical contribution to practical sociological jurisprudence in American criminal law, and his study is deservedly characterized as 'a book of which American jurisprudence may be justly proud'.[58] But the reviewer who gave this characterization then continued:

[T]here is a pertinent lesson in the fact that the time and effort required to produce it have given the author some insight into the reasons for the lack of such studies. He confesses in the preface that without the opportunities and funds provided by Columbia and Indiana Universities, it could not have been written. Clearly, some effort is needed to make sure that wherever such opportunities and funds are available, they should not be wasted on mediocrity but be profitably invested in what is qualitatively significant and promising. In this case, they have been so invested.[59]

The proximity between criminal law and family law as agencies of social control—and as the resultants of social control—has caused a number of scholars of one branch to become interested in the other. A number of valuable studies, operating with methods similar to those developed by Hall, have resulted therefrom.[60] Indeed, one may be justified to speak of a revival of historical interest in law, as evidenced by the publication of such new journals as the *American Journal of Legal History* and the *Legal Historian*, and of such recent excellent historical studies—of great interest to the criminal lawyer—as George L. Haskins' *Law and Authority in*

Early Massachusetts, published in 1961, and Page's *Judicial Beginnings in New Hampshire 1640–1700*, published in 1959. Every year sees the publication of further solid articles shedding light on the hitherto obscure and vague aspects of the past in American criminal law and procedure.[61] This historical movement has its parallel in England, where it was sparked by Leon Radzinowicz' superb three-volume work *A History of English Criminal Law and Its Administration from 1750*, published in 1948 and 1957.

The sociological school was also partly responsible for the revival of studies in pure legal history, mentioned in Chapter VI above, and those in anthropological and archaic jurisprudence. K. N. Llewellyn and E. A. Hoebel's *The Cheyenne Way* (1941), and Hoebel's *The Law of Primitive Man* (1954) and *Man in the Primitive World* (1958), and a number of articles,[62] are the realist's response to a long line of purely historical[63] or purely ethnological[64] studies, and constitute a logical and necessary sophistication of early merely descriptive works.[65]

What can be expected of research with the ethnological or anthropological method? I think it is quite clear, as von Hentig keeps demonstrating in every piece of his writing, that we are still utterly in the dark on many of the most basic human instincts and urges of revelance to the criminal law. But if the theory of evolution holds true, and phylogenesis corresponds with ontogenesis, it follows that, by studying the actions and reactions of infant and adolescent societies, we can learn much about the behavior of contemporary infants and adolescents, or adults whose development has been arrested at, or who have retrogressed to, these states. Furthermore, we may be able to chart our course better for the future, for evolutionary theory suggests that man has increasingly become master over his own destiny. On the other hand, it is obvious that anthropological studies are farthest removed from anything promising quick and easy remedies.

(b) *The 'contemporary' method.* So-called only for want of a better title, this method is as sociological in approach as the historical method just described, but by contrast it collects and evaluates data of contemporary origin. In this sphere we may further distinguish between library research and field research. A listing of researches of the library type must again begin with Jerome Hall's *Theft, Law and Society*, in which he evaluates, legally and sociologically, all accessible data on the topics of receiving stolen property, automobile theft, embezzlement (in the second edition) and petty larceny (in the first edition). These studies demonstrate the essential unity of the social sciences. 'The basis of unification may be found in the common features of social problems and processes.'[66] The

Introduction to Hall's second edition is a splendid theorization of socio-legal research, and its propositions deserve to be adhered to by all who are about to embark upon a research career.

The number of lawyers who have undertaken socio-legal library research into contemporary problems is quite small. But an entire law review, *Law and Contemporary Problems*, is devoted to publications of essentially such research results, in symposium form. Several superb symposia on contemporary problems of criminal law have appeared therein,[67] though none of these has ever approached Hall's precedent, in terms of intensity and sophistication. To be particularly mentioned in this connection are various studies on the law and the social problem of abortion by Packer and Gampell[68] (who combined library research and field investigation), Calderone,[69] and Mills.[70] In addition, there have been a few such studies in the regulatory field,[71] and some in the sphere of sexual offenses.[72]

This just about exhausts a listing of socio-legal library research of the contemporary type, conducted and published by legal scholars. There are, of course, a number of studies undertaken on behalf of legislatures, looking toward reform, but most of these are lost in legislative proceedings and through the anonymity of the researchers.[73] Studies of this type should be awarded top priority because of their immediate usefulness for legislative improvement in the special part of the criminal law. Even though those studies may not—and most of those listed do not—measure up to the high standards of scientific research outlined by Michael and Adler, they are likely to yield preliminarily useful data to guide legislative choice between competing legislative alternatives.

As yet, there has not been developed in America an institution similar to the British Royal Commission Reports, which, since the time of Queen Victoria, have marked the birth or burial of most legislative reform in England. As has been noted earlier, a similar institution may well be in the making in our country. Indeed, we should have one. It is unthinkable that a nation as complex as the U.S.A. should go on making laws without prior fact ascertainments on the relationship between existing and projected law and the community it is meant to serve. This means that studies of this type should be encouraged. They are not costly and require merely a high standard of ingenuity and sophistication in criminal law and the subject to be investigated. Obviously, the higher the skill in the employment of the sociological methods of data gathering and evaluation, the better the result will be. But this observation is even more important for field research, especially in the sociology of criminal law, to which I shall now turn.

Among lawyers alone, and in the criminal law, as distinguished from its administration, such research was virtually unheard of until recently,[74] when Professor Beutel, then of the University of Nebraska, pioneered a new method. In his own words:

> In an effort to find the law which would be a fit subject for experimental research within the modest resources available, the writer and his students in a class in jurisprudence have conducted preliminary studies of the workings of various statutes picked almost at random. Many of those investigations have led into blind alleys. Others have indicated that the subjects chosen were too complicated for any but the most heavily endowed and continuous research. But in at least . . . four fields . . . , the preliminary studies seem to indicate that it is possible, without too much effort and expense, fruitfully to apply experimental methods of testing the operation and effectiveness of current statutes.[75]

The four studies were on the public health laws governing sterilization of barber-shop instruments, laws on use of tobacco by minors, statutes regulating the standard size for bricks, and codes governing plumbing. The results of the studies were startling. They revealed, *inter alia*, the ignorance of those regulated, the uselessness and obsolescence of the regulation, and the ineffectiveness of the regulatory method. Professor Beutel next turned to the hunt for bigger game: the bad-check statutes. And the results were again juridically significant and startling.[76]

Professor Beutel was as much glorified for his ingenuity as he was ridiculed for his naïveté.[77] His five 'jural laws', based on his four pilot studies and one major piece of research, have been the subject of much comment. These are the 'jural laws':

> Jural Law I: Laws will seldom be enforced literally either as they were written or intended.

> Jural Law II: In a changing society, inflexibility is likely to be the death of a law.

> Jural Law III: Obsolete and unenforced or unenforceable laws left on the books are likely to cause a spread of the breakdown of law enforcement into related areas.

> Jural Law IV: Severe punishment prescribed by law does not seem to deter crime any more than mild penalties.

> Jural Law V: Where there is competition between governmental units in law enforcement, that unit which most effectively meets the actual wants of the people governed tends to replace the less efficient, in spite of constitutional or legal limits to the contrary.[78]

Be the 'jural laws' valid or not, that is quite beside the point. What is important is the fact that Professor Beutel recognizes criminal law for what it really is: criminal law is social engineering, and it is not just social happening. There was never a period in the history of mankind when law was merely a social happening, however inept people may have been in their efforts to achieve their goals.[79] Cavers, in reviewing Beutel's work, wrote:

> Professor Beutel wants not merely to take research in law outside the law libraries; he would like to convert us into scientists and law into social engineering as literally as the refractory nature of the subjects and subject matter will permit. In his zeal for his vision of an experimentalist science of law, I think he may actually deter American law teachers from striving to widen their research activities and to diversify their research methods.[80]

Bravo for Professor Beutel! It is about time to deter those from the scholarly branch of the profession who have neither the skill, nor the stamina, nor the imagination to do anything but teach the same course forty times over from appointment to retirement. If a teacher becomes frightened by the enormousness of the job of social engineering through criminal law, let him quit. There can be no doubt whatsoever that Beutel *is* on the right track.

Beutel developed an order of proceeding in research and law improvement:[81]

1. The nature of the phenomena which law attempts to regulate should be studied. In particular, the social problem to which a specific law is directed should be carefully isolated and examined.
2. The rule of law or other method used to regulate the phenomena or intended to solve the social problem should be accurately stated.
3. The effect on society of adopting the rule should be observed and measured.
4. There should then be constructed a hypothesis that attempts to explain the reasons for this reaction.
5. This description, when broadened to apply to other analogous situations, might be considered a jural law that describes or predicts results which would occur on application of a similar regulatory law to similar problems.
6. If analysis shows that the law is inefficient, there could then be suggested new methods of accomplishing the originally desired result.
7. The proposed new law could be enacted and the process repeated.
8. A series of such adoptions of new laws and the study of their results might throw important light upon the usefulness of the underlying purposes behind the enactment, thus effecting a possible alteration in or abandonment of this objective, or in the long run, though this now appears doubtful, even induce a revision of our present scale of social and political ethics.

I should like to suggest that there is nothing wrong with the order of these eight steps, in so far as problems of the special part of criminal law are concerned. But it is to be noted that many of the problems are solvable by general principles—and these have become firm parts of our jurisprudence and have themselves been scientifically scrutinized, for example, problems like the affectability of man's character by education, the stimulability of man by threats of detriments (deterrence), the psycho-physiological nature of conduct, etc.[82]

Beutel's 'experimental jurisprudence' is as refreshing as it is exciting. Moreover, it is all-American in outlook. It is something on which our very history permits us to acquire superiority. Nothing like it has ever been tried abroad. It is alien to the traditions of continental lawyers, as alien to them as it is akin to the trial-and-error tradition of the common law.

Of course it is impossible to expect law schools to assume a major share of 'experimental jurisprudence' research burdens. In the first place, it is politically organized society which must decide on the *need* for this type of research. We can only urge it. In the second place, this type of research is a legislative responsibility. But if legislatures wish to utilize the summer-time services of 40,000 eager law students, and perhaps 3000 professors, let them make the bid. I think some of us should accept it.

No other research of this type has come to public attention as yet. This writer, with the aid of a research assistant, has completed a project financed by a foundation grant of $600, designed to study a form of petty larceny which had recently swept the country. The study was designed to test the means of transmitting a criminal idea and a criminal technique among juveniles found to be of pubescent age. The kind of theft in question was that of a given type of automobile hoodcrests of which, so the study showed, several hundred thousand had been removed. This research indicated that the hood fad originated among junior high school students in a few metropolitan areas, whence it spread to the suburbs, usually stopping at the commuting perimeter. The facts were ascertainable with relative ease, by spot counts of night-parked cars in various areas, and by the replacement sales of the automobile distributors, who had been gleefully co-operating. This study also throws new light on the causes of juvenile delinquency fad selections, and the termination of predatory crime.

The need for special skills in sociological methodology, statistics, and related subjects, makes it virtually mandatory for the investigator either to possess such skills himself, or to enter alliances with sociologists. Let us first discuss interdisciplinary research by teams of lawyers and sociologists. Following various earlier efforts, it has only been recently that such studies have been successfully undertaken on subjects relevant to the criminal law, though not necessarily involving major field research. Several books recently published by The Free Press of Glencoe, Inc., demonstrate that successful co-operation between lawyers and sociologists in criminal law is easily possible,[83] despite the severe shock which followed the first large-scale failure, and the untimely demise of the John Hopkins Institute of Law,[84] which had been designed to facilitate precisely that kind of co-operative effort.

The first major field research project to come to public attention was that of the Social Science Research Council Study, on violence in the metropolitan area of San Juan, P.R.,[85] which aimed, among other things, at finding the inter-relationship between criminal violence on the one hand, and the existence of a variety of social and situational factors on the other, among which the very factor of a criminal law and its enforcement was prominent.

The violence study was followed by several other research projects of the University of Puerto Rico's Social Science Research Center, under Drs Jaime de Jesus Torres and Franco Ferrocuti, into basic questions of the impact of penal laws on human behavior.[86] These studies deserve close watching, for, if successful, they may provide a blueprint for significant future work. This significance is due to the facts that, first, this type of research rests on a thorough ground-ing in the principles and aims of criminal law, as established so far, i.e., it takes certain propositions of positive criminal law as given data; and, second, it proposes to test not just a specific problem of the special part of criminal law, but the very bases on which ultimately all criminal law rests.

The next type of research is that by scholars equally at home in both sociology and law.[87] Unfortunately, there has been practically no invasion of the 'core area' of criminal law by such scholars,[88] but this has permitted just that much more attention to the 'pole' areas, namely delinquency at one end, and penology and corrections at the other.[89] The two names most prominently associated with this type of research are Tappan and Glueck. Paul W. Tappan's *Delinquent Girls in Court, Juvenile Delinquency, Contemporary Correction*[90] and other works give evidence of the highest competence in both disciplines. But Tappan's example also goes to show that the demands on the few scholars who possess this highest competence in two disciplines are so great as to constitute an unbearable surtax. Such talents can be utilized only in institutionalized settings, like that created by and for the Gluecks, or, indeed, a full-scale university-affiliated criminological institute,[91] or a separate school or academy,[92] or center of criminology.[93]

This leads us to a brief mention of the Herculean labors of the Gluecks, at Harvard University. In a long and distinguished series of widely known and acclaimed books,[94] the Gluecks studied groups of delinquents and offenders, comparing them with equal numbers of non-delinquents and non-offenders, and investigated every conceivable factor, biological as well as sociological, which might be thought to have a bearing on causes of delinquency or non-delinquency.

As early as 1943, they could proclaim:

We are thus led to the conclusion that it is not primarily or fundamentally either chance or the fear of punishment, but rather the presence or absence of certain traits and characteristics in the constitution and early environment of the different offender, which determines their respective responses to the different forms of treatment and determines, also, what such offenders will ultimately become and what will become of them. Those who behaved well, either during or after treatment, were, as a class, more favourably endowed by Nature and circumstanced by Nurture than were those who did not respond well.[95]

The Gluecks' work on prediction schemes for juvenile delinquency is both the most significant and the most controversial. A few excerpts will describe the nature of this work:

Varied Uses of Social Prediction Table
Because of the nature of the factors included in the Social Prediction Table, it can be applied at any age level ranging from 6 to 16 years. The question it is designed to answer is simply: 'Is the particular child about whom I am concerned probably a persistent juvenile delinquent or likely to become one?' Such checks of the Table as have been made to date would appear to substantiate the efficacy of the Table for this purpose. *Its efficacy when applied before the onset of overt evidence of maladapted behavior, however, is as yet to be determined,* but findings so far made are promising. [Emphasis added.][96]

Five factors were used to compose the prediction tables, and a 'delinquency score' was assigned for each factor, the score indicating the percentage of juvenile delinquency cases in which the factor was present:

Discipline of Boy by Father:	Score
Overstrict or erratic	72·5
Lax	59·8
Firm but kindly	9·3

Supervision of Boy by Mother:	
Unsuitable	83·2
Fair	57·5
Suitable	9·9

Affection of Father for Boy:
    Indifferent or hostile   75·9
    Warm (incl. overprotective)   33·8

Affection of Mother for Boy:
    Indifferent or hostile   86·2
    Warm (incl. overprotective)   43·1

Cohesiveness of Family:
    Unintegrated   96·9
    Some Elements of Cohesion   61·3
    Cohesive   20·6[97]

Based on these scores, it then became possible to determine the likelihood of persistent delinquency as follows:[98]

Score Class	Likelihood of Persistent Delinquency	
	Percentage of delinquencies occurring in this score class	Likelihood of delinquency
Under 200	8·2	Negligible
200–249	37·0	Low
250–299	63·5	More than an even chance
300 and over	89·2	High

Assuming successful validation of these tables (and the evidence to date permits of optimism in this regard), it should be evident that we are well on the road to completing a network of instrumentalities not only to predict recidivism of juvenile and young adult offenders, but their probable behavior *during* various forms of peno-correctional treatment—probation, probation with suspended sentence, correctional school, reformatory, prison, parole, as well as the age span in which satisfactory behavior is likely to occur among various types of offenders and in which recidivism ceases.[99]

The study of other factors, factor combinations and formulas, showed time and again that the selected five factor groups are vastly more important than any others.

But as the proof of the pudding lies in the eating, the proof of a prediction scheme, constructed on retrospective data evaluation, lies in successful prospective application. This has been done with the Glueck method in a number of instances. As Dr E. T. Glueck wrote in 1960, more and more studies here and abroad are validating the prediction tables. Uncertainties have been removed, especially in cases where ratings were difficult to assess. Today, after computer studies, prediction, with a high success score, is possible even where less than five factors are available for evaluation.

The largest validation effort is that currently being undertaken by the New York City Youth Board. A 1960 interim report, following a study of seven years duration (the children then being 12½ to 13 years old), showed that 94·6 per cent of the predicted non-delinquents were still non-delinquent, and 46 per cent of the predicted delinquents were already delinquent (and that prior to the age at which most confirmed delinquency is established!). Of 191 boys still non-delinquent, 176 or 89·7 per cent had been correctly predicted as non-delinquents; of 27 boys already delinquent, 17, or 63 per cent had been correctly predicted as delinquents.[100]

This is not the place to unravel the controversies that have raged about the Glueck studies. That many of the Gluecks' methods and findings are subject to legitimate criticism, no one can doubt.[101] At the same time, no other study has even approached the Gluecks' work in ingenuity, thoroughness, size, or scientific competency. Nor should we be frightened or even startled by the Gluecks' findings, for are they not merely validating statistically what humanity has suspected unscientifically for 3,000 years or longer, and what studies with other methods equally tend to confirm, namely, that mother-love and father-discipline are significant factors in building the character and constructing the emotional system of the child? It seems certain that the five-point prediction scale points to the very foundations of the moral and ethical qualities of criminal law and law abidance. While the Glueck studies await further scientific validation,[102] we may well be justified in pondering the next question: How do we secure for each child a healthy mother-love and a healthy father-discipline? Where can we break into the vicious circle of inferior mother-love and father-discipline, and crime and delinquency? How radically must the accustomed life cycle be tampered with? *The prospects of social engineering* are almost frightening when these questions are raised.

At this early stage in the evaluation of empirical scholarship in criminal law, the principal question is whether the thrust of the Glueck method is right and proper. There can be no doubt about the answer: Yes. Criminal law is meant to be the most awesome device for stimulating individual and community conduct into channels deemed desirable by the community. Well, then, what can be deemed superior to methods aimed at finding out how such conduct-responses can best be stimulated? Here is a vast opportunity for competent researchers, and all America is a vast laboratory.[103] Why not use it?

It would not be appropriate, however, to conclude this section on a hopeful note. All factors considered, what has been accomplished so far by the legal scholars of sociological bent is, in the aggregate, precious little. When only a few years ago I listened to a report by my eminent colleague and friend, the late Paul W. Tappan, on the status of criminological research in America, I considered him a confirmed pessimist. Now, however, having taken a closer look at all the research myself, I am close to agreeing with him. But I shall not yield that easily. If, among America's 250 criminal law professors, we could have only ten Beutels, ten Gluecks, and ten Tappans, we might be able to solve some of the core issues of criminal law, its principles, doctrines and specific rules.

The last type of research within this broad category is of 'experimental jurisprudence' in the narrower sense of the word, that is, under manipulation of variables. Only one such project of any significance has been carried out, that by Moore and Callahan.[104] Their study, ingeniously conceived, was aimed at finding out the social results of restrictive parking laws, whose time limitations were arbitrarily altered from time to time. Thus, in a shopping district parking-lot, it was found that 24 per cent of the parkers obeyed and 76 per cent violated a two-hour parking limit; 55 per cent obeyed and 45 per cent violated a fifteen-minute limit; 70 per cent obeyed and 30 per cent violated a thirty-minute limit; 52 per cent obeyed and 48 per cent violated an hour limit. Would it not appear that the easiest regulation might be that of the thirty-minute limit? This becomes even more convincing when we learn that at that limit 61 per cent of over-time parkers had left within ten minutes after lapse of the limit, while at the other limits, a considerably smaller portion of over-time parkers had left.

There are abundant opportunities for such socially and juridically significant research. What is the safest speed on a given highway? At what limits do the vast majority of drivers drive at unzoned—or zoned—highways?[105]

More important, however, what type of a stimulus does it take to get the citizenry to respond as they should? This question, of course, would test the theory of general prevention—completely untested by sociological research so far, though affirmed by many chance observations.

At whom is general prevention aimed? Broadly speaking at everybody. But the prohibition of deer-hunting out of season is obviously aimed only at deer-hunters, more particularly at those deer-hunters who are inclined to violate the law. Prohibition of short-weight selling is aimed at those who are engaged in weighing and selling, and particularly those who do not have enough conscience or natural restraint and who need an additional crutch of the law, an additional reminder that to do the wrong thing will lead to negative consequences. It is the task of the legislature in the first place to find that stimulus which will work on most of those who are tempted. But politicians obviously do not have the scientific skill to engage in that type of research.

There is no question but that a stimulus in the nature of an empty gesture cannot have much effect. In other words, certainly enforcement of a given law is a prerequisite of its effectiveness. But that severity has its importance as well can be easily demonstrated. If the city fathers decide to prohibit the parking of automobiles along the curb of various streets, they will have to consider what punishment to impose. Should they impose capital punishment for violators— if they had the power to do so—or will a $0.50 fine do? Certainly capital punishment would be much too outrageous for such an offense. No police officer would tag cars, no motorist would take the prohibition seriously, no court or jury would convict. On the other hand, if the punishment were a $1.00 fine, all motorists would conclude that the situation was ideal, for it costs $1.75 to park on the public parking lot next door. Hence, the right degree of punishment lies somewhere in the middle.[106]

However, and here is the rub, the proof of something as superficially obvious as the above example will come only from careful socio-legal research.

Moore and Callahan did their work at the Yale Law School, which was to maintain its interest in the inter-disciplinary approach to criminal law.[107] The Yale Law School has or had on its faculty a small staff of sociologists, charged with the task of developing the capacity of the law and of lawyers to apply behavioral science concepts.

> What is the purpose of developing the capacity to apply behavioral science concepts widely and fluently to legal problems? In addition to practical utility, the goal is to convey what might be called a sociolegal point of view. In this view, law is an instrument of social policy capable of permitting and encouraging certain activities, seeking to prevent others; it exists within a larger social context, including the historical circumstances giving rise to it and the social and personal consequences which it produces.[108]

As early as 1907, Roscoe Pound had counseled that 'the modern teacher of law should be a student of sociology, economics, and politics as well'.[109] Just now we are finally reaching that point, and only very gradually.[110]

It is to be expected that sociological research on problems of substantive criminal law will increase. But it is important that we give direction to such research. Not the marginal problems, but the core problems should be attacked first, and that means the very principles of criminal law which we take for granted, whether or not consciously or—for the most part—unconsciously.

Let us suppose, now, that a stage will have been reached at which every conceivable problem has been scientifically explored. Then what? Is it likely that we can, thereby, alter our criminal legislation for the more effective direction of human destiny? If not, why not? Many of us get frustrated about the conservatism and stubbornness of courts and legislatures to whom clear and irrefutable argument is addressed, and who do *not* respond accordingly. While there is something wholesome about the law's conservatism, even the most arch-conservative legislature will and must yield upon clear and over-whelmingly supported scientific proof of fact emanating from reputable sources. By way of example: the Kinsey reports strongly influenced the sexual offenses provisions of the Model Penal Code, and it, in turn, has already influenced the new criminal code of Illinois.[111]

There remains no reason why socio-legal studies in criminal law should not be undertaken, as long as we do not forget—as some sociologists are prone to do—that law, however rational it may tend to become, reflects the *values* as well as the wishes of the community, and such values themselves are observable and can be fathomed. This leads us to a discussion of the psychological or psychiatric school of criminology.

3. *The Psychological-Psychiatric School*

Having devoted some attention to interdisciplinary research as such in the foregoing section, I should like to come right to the point in the discussion of the psychological-psychiatric school of criminal law scholarship. On this topic it is difficult to withstand the temptation of treating forensic psychiatric theory at some length. But this is an assessment of criminal law scholarship, not of psychiatry. Hence, I shall proceed on the perhaps questionable assumption that the reader is generally familiar with the basic premises, methods and aims of psychiatry.

The era of spectacular claims, a phenomenon of the 1920s, previously described, is a matter of the past. Some of the wildest psychiatric eccentrics have either left this world or have been exposed and, thus, no longer constitute an acute danger to society and its criminal law. Psychiatrists, as well as legal scholars, have become considerably more responsible, often even conservative, in their claims and methods. In psychiatry this is largely due to better and more regularized training in mental and nervous diseases as well as in therapy, and also to the enormous advances in neuro-surgery and in neurology.[112]

While in the 1920s and 1930s the favorite sport of psychiatrists and lawyers consisted of heckling, nay, viciously attacking one another, with charges of utter stupidity, today's favorite sport is almost the reverse. With increased exposure to each other's theories, and with advanced knowledge in both fields as a result of such exposure, as well as through independent efforts, it is now quite customary for lawyers to take the psychiatrist's side and for psychiatrists to take the lawyer's side. This, of course, subjects them to attacks by those siding with the critics against whom the defender shielded the opposite profession. Merely by way of example, Dr Melitta Schmideberg, one of the world's foremost psychoanalysts in the correctional field, has drawn frequent criticism from lawyers, for defending the value structure and rules of the law. This writer has been severely criticized by a psychiatrist for defending psychiatrists against unfounded attacks by non-psychiatrists.[113]

Twenty years ago one of our foremost contemporary thinkers in criminal law, Professor Jerome Hall, could attack psychiatry for its premature claim to leadership while yet lacking some of the basic requisites of a science.[114] But even at that time it was possible for Hall to point hopefully to what looked like the tenets of an emerging scientific forensic psychiatry.[115] The development since Hall's criticism has been a most interesting one. While some sensationalist psychiatric writers have continued to deliver grist for the mills of non-psychiatric critics, there has been a strong current of responsible research and publication in psychiatry. This is bound to have its influence on lawyers' attitudes toward psychiatry. Perhaps it is too early to proclaim the triumph of reason over prejudice, but it seems to me that the reciprocal attitude of lawyers and psychiatrists is more and more becoming one of mutual understanding and even co-operation. Witness the recent symposium on 'Crime and Correction' in *Law and Contemporary Problems*. Professor John Barker Waite's article on 'The Legal Approach to Crime and Correction' evidences not only a desire to understand the psychiatric approach but also a readiness to accept psychiatric facts.[116] Dr Watson's contribution to this publication, 'A Critique of the Legal Approach to Crime and Correction', is a masterpiece of scholarly discipline and shows deep understanding of both the legal and psychiatric positions— perhaps even effecting a reconciliation between them.[117] Both lawyer and psychiatrist must indeed admit that among scholars and workers of that caliber a confident and intelligent co-operation is bound to be both possible and fruitful.

But while psychiatry is becoming more and more persuasive, the open-minded lawyer and law teacher must guard himself and his charges against swallowing uncritically all the revelations of behavioral science. It is obviously much easier for a competent psychiatrist than for a lawyer to distinguish between mature scholarship and pure sensationalism in the field. Besides, the sheer multitude of disagreements is confusing to the newcomer. When lawyers argue about legal-technical matter, there is usually a two-way split intelligible only to the insider. But when psychiatrists are in debate, the split of opinion is often as manifold as the number of psychiatrists present—and also is intelligible only to the insider. As yet, the legal profession viewed as a whole is relatively unconvinced that psychiatry's product is saleable merchandise. But lawyers willing to stop, look and listen, must at least admit that the product is taking shape and bound to be marketable sooner or later.[118]

Interdisciplinary scholarship in criminal law with the purpose of utilizing psychiatry in solving basic problems thus calls for greater expertise than any other interdisciplinary work, and this knowledge is possessed by few legal scholars. Only very few criminal-law academics have established a reputation for intimate familiarity with the intricacies of psychiatry.

But success in exploiting psychiatry for the good of criminal law may also be achieved by co-operative ventures between scholars of the two disciplines. The history of such co-operation begins at the Yale Law School. In the late 1920s, the then dean of the school, Robert Maynard Hutchins, had become enchanted with the methods of the behavioral sciences. He and Professor Slesinger re-examined various aspects of the law of evidence,[119] with the aid of

> data of basic behavioral processes, such as perception, emotion, and memory, in their relation to courtroom procedures and rules of evidence. The data was drawn mostly from largely unsystematized behaviorism. References were made largely to experimental investigations which, in the tradition of psychology, explored limited numbers of variables of the basic behavior processes in hypothetical contexts of unrealistically simple dimensions.[120]

The Yale tradition of behavioristic research was kept alive by Jerome Frank, Moore and Callahan, Lasswell, MacDougal, Harper, and many others, but in criminal law especially by Dession, Donnelly, and J. Goldstein. All of them kept psychiatrists and social scientists on the Yale law faculty, or on tap, from the 1930s.

The late Professor George H. Dession was among the first to fully recognize the contribution which psychiatry—and the behavioral sciences in general—can make to criminal law. Although displeased with the irresponsible attacks by some analysts on the fundamental conceptions of criminal law, Dession was nevertheless willing to conduct 'a thorough-going experiment . . . to demonstrate what may be expected from routine psychiatric diagnosis, treatment board sentences and institutional therapy within the framework of existing channels of disposition'.[121] Dession went at it, heart and soul. A succession of distinguished psychiatrists served on the Yale Law Faculty from then on, and Dession found more and more uses for psychiatry; thus his enthusiasm increased. After fifteen years of teaching at Yale, he published the final version of his teaching materials in the form of a casebook: *Criminal Law, Administration and Public Order* (1948), a book in which he drew heavily on the data of the social sciences, but warned that 'for their utilization by the lawyer a common frame of reference is required'.[122]

In this book, 'criminal sanctions . . . are conceived as a distinctively motivated sub-class of negative sanctions or collectively enforced deprivations of value; crime as a distinctively experienced sub-class of deviational or value-depriving behavior; and the role of sanctions as the economical use of value deprivation to achieve a net value gain'.[123] The book—and this itself is significant—was supported by grants from the Viking Fund, Inc., and the Social Science Research Council. Well organized, and quite clear in its organization and conceptualization of the criminal law, Dession's became the first major law book which not only demonstrated the utility of behavioral science data for the criminal law but which actually oriented its approach towards it. Yet actually few references to, and excerpts from, the literature of the behavioral sciences were included. Rather than subject his students to the raw data of behavioral sciences, Dession distilled them into the selection and organization of the legal materials in the book.

In the early 1950s Dession had become so convinced of psychiatry's contribution to the criminal law, that he proposed to abandon the idea of penal codes in favor of an ideologically enlightened correctional code. His testing-ground became the draft code for the Commonwealth of Puerto Rico which he was commissioned to produce, but, because of an untimely death, left uncompleted.[124]

Dession's invaluable work was continued by Professor Richard C. Donnelly, who assumed Dession's role as faithfully as one *pater familias* followed the other in Ancient Rome. Donnelly worked on the Puerto Rican draft code, carried on the criminal-law and behavioral sciences instruction program, and forced the evolution of the behavioristic criminal-law casebook. Since 1955,

lawyers and behavioral scientists at the Yale Law School are moving systematically through certain traditional areas of the law, such as criminal law, . . . with a view toward the preparation of teaching materials for the basic courses. These 'teams' are taking a new look at legal doctrines that make assumptions regarding human behavior. Once the assumptions are expressed, an effort is being made to ascertain what the state of behavioral science knowledge is—whether it confirms these assumptions, refutes them, or whether relevant material is non-existent.[125]

Donnelly's formulation of the objectives is one of the soundest statements yet made on the *real* contribution which psychiatry can make to criminal law: a re-examination of the doctrines! This means that we must tentatively take the doctrines—or, better yet, the principles, doctrines, and rules—of the criminal law for granted, state them with precision, and then scrutinize them under the magnifying glass of psychiatry.

Such a sober approach is in opposition to the wild-catting of psychiatrists who, before careful examination, denounce all law as irrational. It is likewise in opposition to the attitude of so many non-psychiatrists who, like George Bernard Shaw, regard psychiatry as 'all quackery and pornography'.[126]

Currently Dr Jay Katz,[127] a well-qualified psychoanalyst, serves on the faculty of the Yale Law School, in close co-operation with Professor Joseph Goldstein, who succeeded Professor Donnelly.[128]

Following a series a smaller publications,[129] the first major product of Yale's behavioristic approach to criminal law is now in print. It is a magnificent volume, containing more than twice the number of words contained in a standard casebook. The book is entitled *Criminal Law—Problems for Decision in the Promulgation, Invocation and Administration of a Law of Crimes*,[130] and is edited by R. C. Donnelly, Joseph Goldstein and a sociologist, R. D. Schwartz, now of Northwestern University. The book is naturally designed primarily to take the place of a casebook for the teaching of the basic law-school course in criminal law. Yet, by departing radically from anything to which law students have been exposed in the past, the book will probably find greater use in postgraduate than in undergraduate legal education. There are more than one million words in this NIMH (National Institute of Mental Health) -supported book, yet the standard crimes like burglary, arson and robbery are mentioned only in passing. Legal methodology, entities and categories have been largely discarded in favor of 'functional' questions. The legal textbook and periodical literature (except for *Yale Law Journal* citations) have been mostly ignored, while the literature of the behavioral sciences has received prominent attention. Perhaps we had expected too much from the pioneers at Yale. We had expected a perfect marriage of criminal law and psychiatry, and we received only one long legal-psychiatric interlude.

The entire first chapter (out of three) is devoted to 'The Case of Dr Martin', a Connecticut physician who achieved fame as an amateur therapist in treating disturbed children, and notoriety in using pederasty as his method of treatment. The Martin case then

C.L.S.—14

serves to launch a presentation of materials on the ethics of the medical profession in experimenting with human beings, and on the limits of permissible therapy.

In the other two chapters the authors re-examine many of the law's rules and maxims from the behaviorist's critical vantage point, with frequent attempts to relate the established concepts of psychiatry to those of the law.

The authors' criminological philosophy appears to be that of criminological positivism, with its quasi-deterministic attitude toward deviancy, and sympathy for permissiveness. This is demonstrated by the inordinate attention given to the District of Columbia's Durham Test of 'insanity', now discarded by legislation, and by the selection (and omission) of psychiatric and sociological authorities quoted in the book. Hans Illing recently wrote: 'Besides Glover, Bennet, et al., in England, and Rosow, Schmideberg, and a few others in this country, the analysts engaged in research in criminology are few'.[131] Yet of the four analysts mentioned, only one, Bennet, is represented in this book—with one quotation.

No doubt the book contains the material for fascinating work with students of law and the behavioral sciences; on a post-post graduate level, though, it solves few of today's burning issues of law and psychiatry. Nevertheless, this is a thought-provoking book, the largest shortcoming of which is that an unfavorable balance has been struck between law and the behavioral sciences, to the detriment of law and its students. In short, Dession's approach has been carried to an extreme by his followers. But whatever the merit of the book for instruction in criminal law, it is a valid attempt at subjecting criminal law to the scrutiny of the behavioral sciences.

Yale's idea of adding psychiatrists to law faculties was soon imitated by the University of Pennsylvania,[132] which appointed Dr Watson, an astute psychiatrist, to its law faculty. When Dr Watson left to join the law faculty in Ann Arbor, Pennsylvania added two able replacements to the faculty, Drs Lonsdorf and Leighton. It is too early to assess the value of such direct 'integration' of law and psychiatry with any degree of finality. No one will doubt, however, that some value inheres in the method, if only by increasing the awareness of each other's professional concerns and values.

Scholars at various other schools have made approaches to psychiatry, with mutual benefit. This holds true, particularly, for Boston University, New York University and Temple University, whose principal criminal-law teachers have closely co-operated with the Association for the Psychiatric Treatment of Offenders,[133] and other psychiatric groups and individual scholars. A number of psychiatrists and psychologists (for example, Drs Benjamin Karpman, Frederic Wertham, Melitta Schmideberg, Ralph Brancale, Robert Redmount, and others) have been invited to address criminal-law seminars and classes at New York University School of Law, and at many other law schools.[134] Professional and personal friendships have grown out of such pioneering efforts to learn from each other, and the scholarly literature of recent years reflects the better understanding thus gained.

Professor Henry Weihofen has emerged as the leading scholar in the field of forensic psychiatry, and serves as the most important link between the two professions.[135] While most of Professor Weihofen's writings are concerned with the practical matters of the defense of insanity, civil commitment procedures, and like topics, he has demonstrated that he is thoroughly familiar with psychoanalytic doctrine and its significance for the criminal law,[136] and that direct co-operation with level-headed psychiatrists can yield maximum benefits for the development of criminal law.[137]

The group of psychiatrically oriented criminal-law scholars is a small one as yet. Besides those already mentioned, and disregarding all those who have expressed only a fleeting interest in psychiatry, as well as those whose only contact consisted of work on the insanity test,[138] there are only two further scholars to be mentioned in this connection. Professor Helen Silving-Ryu, who has published outstanding contributions to criminal-law theory and who has also labored on a draft penal code for the Commonwealth of Puerto Rico, has gained a solid reputation for her expert perusal of psychoanalytic doctrine in her criminal-law publications.[139] Dr Robert Redmount has done similar work with the aid of clinical psychology.[140] Since we have been getting articles like those by the authors mentioned, we have moved quite a way from the era when all psychoanalytic contributions to criminal law could be compressed into a single footnote.[141] These new types of psycho-analytically-oriented article may begin with words shocking to the lawyer ('The most significant contribution of psychoanalysis to the understanding of mental processes is discovery of unconscious processes'), but they end with 'hope that the law may, within the limits of due process and the needs of protecting men's freedom, equality and dignity, utilize to the fullest extent the teachings of psychoanalytic psychology.'[142]

This assessment of the impact of psychoanalytical knowledge on criminal law, as reflected in its scholarship, would be incomplete without mention of Jerome Hall. Hall is not only a keen student of psychiatry, but also a watchdog against trespasses into the law's territory.[143] On more than one occasion he has proved his point.

That Hall has a point is demonstrated by the fact that even the leader of the Yale group, while advocating open-mindedness, warned against gullibility.[144]

But whom can the criminal-law scholar trust in the jungle of forensic psychiatry that grows thicker every day? Jeffery noted recently:

> One of the most damaging comments that can be made about the psychiatric position is that the psychiatrist in general ignores his critics. It is worth noting that, of the many Isaac Ray award books, most favor the psychiatric position.[145] The position taken by Hall,[146] Szasz,[147] East,[148] Wertham,[149] De Grazia[150] and others do not appear in these books.[151]

Well, then, this is quite a convenient guide. For if we look at the composition of the group which distributes these awards, and we find unreasoning partisanship among them—the kind of partisanship which convicts law without having examined it closely—it would follow that the criminal-law scholar intent upon objective legal-behavioral scholarship should shun their company. Needless to say, equally undesirable is the intellectual company of those who, in wild exaggeration of a few weaknesses and abuses, condemn all psychiatric participation in law reform. At the moment it appears as if those who are outside the main streams of American forensic psychiatry may at least have as much to offer as the Isaac Ray group. Why? On the whole, the 'out-group' members have studied the law as an instrument of social control and an embodiment of the social conscience of super-ego. They are not frightened by the law, for they know it, and it is startling unfamiliarity that breeds aggression.[152]

To the names of the three psychiatrists mentioned by Jeffery we could add many others,[153] like that of Dr Melitta Schmideberg, whose many writings have emphasized the value of law as a social restraint and as a keeper of social values. She speaks for many—but not the majority of her colleagues—when she calls for a 'rally round the law'. In a recent editorial in the *Journal of Offender Therapy* she emphasized again that psychiatry must support those values which carry our criminal law, and in turn, which our criminal law carries:

> Some premises must be assumed to be self-evident; namely that the aim of therapy is to cure and to socialize, and that, since the main cause of law-breaking lies in poor values, it is obviously the task of all therapy, education, and re-education to give and to develop normal social standards.[154]

It would be irresponsible to brand all psychiatrists as quacks, and as of no value—only harmful—to criminal law. We even must guard ourselves against dismissing the 'psychiatry' of those who come close to libelling the criminal law. The 'unconscious' with which Drs Menninger, Karpman and others are working is not 'invalid'' because these gentlemen happen to attack the criminal law. The 'unconscious' remains a valid conceptualization until disproved, and so far that has not occurred. Nor is all psychiatry useless because of the large disagreement which prevails in that profession, for if disagreement were the standard of usefulness, then all law and, twice over, all sociology would be useless. There is room for disagreement in any body of human knowledge, and, as to fact, agreement or disagreement may depend on the type and amount of evidence available. Moreover, when considering psychiatry, much that appears to the outsider as disagreement may be but minor variations, or, upon further investigation, may turn out to be matters of terminology. Thus, when one psychiatrist writes that 'no one would maintain that *all* criminals are mentally ill or abnormal',[155] and another maintains that all are ill or abnormal,[156] the seeming disagreement may be but a matter of semantics, totally insignificant for the law.[157] What does abnormal mean? Deviating from the norm! What if D deviates from the norm requiring driving below the speed limit? Does that make him committable to a mental institution? Does it excuse him from liability? If one psychiatrist wishes to call deviancy in traffic 'abnormal', just as he would call necrophilia 'abnormal', that is his privilege, and if another wishes to restrict 'abnormality' to serious ego-impairments, that is his privilege. I suggest, however, that Stafford-Clark and Karpman would agree that in the case of my motorist, institutionalization is not called for, whatever else they may disagree on.

The question of labelling is one of the most serious obstacles to a successful application of psychiatry to law. Suppose that all psychiatrists in the world were in agreement that X is a compulsive handwasher and Y is a psychopath, and both stand before the bar of the court charged with the sale of narcotics. Does it follow that X and Y should both be acquitted by reason of 'insanity'? 'Insanity' means nothing, and 'mental or emotional deviancy', or 'ego-impairment', are of interest to us in only two respects: Do such conditions have a substantial bearing on the subjects' *abnormality* as expressed in terms of act (*actus reus*) and intent (*mens rea*)? If not, the subjects are guilty of their offense when so proven. Then comes the more crucial question: How can we help these wards of the state, i.e., convicted offenders, who may have mental or emotional problems? That question may have little to do with the offense.[158]

Two conclusions will, I hope, be drawn from this argument:

(1) Actual or putative disagreement in the psychiatric profession and occasional vicious attacks by psychiatrists upon the law notwithstanding, psychiatry has produced a significant body of knowledge about the workings of the human psyche which entitles psychiatry to a voice in the shaping of the criminal law of the future. In this connection it is quite comforting to note that perhaps more of the law's age-old assumptions are affirmed than are disproved.[159]

(2) Some psychiatric claims to dominance over the criminal law are not well founded and speak of indescribable ignorance. It speaks of equal ignorance for lawyers to accept psychiatric pronouncements as definite statements of policy and law. Thus, it will remain for the law to decide whether a given defendant has committed an offense. 'Committed' means engaged in conduct which is described by a prohibited harm. Whether he has really engaged in such 'conduct' (or whether it was the uncontrolled behavior of St Vitus dance or of a paranoid patient), however, can be decided only with the help of those trained to diagnose mental illness.

With these recognitions, co-operation between law and psychiatry is possible and likely to be very beneficial, but only among those, of either discipline, who possess a gapless knowledge of their field, *and* who have conceptualized their branch of knowledge. Firmness in the concepts is necessary because experience in the courtrooms and conference rooms proves that no resolutions can be reached except after deep mutual study of the underlying assumptions and principles. Obviously, principles cannot be discussed in the heat of the firing line. Principles must be discussed at staff headquarters.

But currently there are no staff headquarters to speak of. There is in the entire United States not a single full-time project in operation which has as its aim the application of psychiatric insight to the criminal law, although the opportunities for this are abundant.

This concludes the account of that American criminal-law scholarship which has utilized the interdisciplinary approach. I wish it did not, for there are important sciences which have not yet been sufficiently incorporated in any comprehensive scheme of scholarly exploration of criminal law theory. Economics, for example, would appear to be a science which might hold relevant information, in terms of criminal causation as well as sanction application and the impact of crime on the nation's economy. But outside the anti-trust field,[160] no criminal-law scholar has explored these implications. Sociological criminology, on the other hand, is now in its second cycle of exploration of the relationships between crime and economics.[161] With the crime toll taking an ever-rising part of the nation's income,[162] and with the ever expanding penal regulation of economic endeavours, it is to be hoped that the interest in economics will increase among the scholars of the criminal law—for the betterment of the law as well as of the economy of the nation.[163]

It is my hope that this chapter has sufficiently indicated the relevant contribution which the interdisciplinary approach can make to the criminal law. A house of justice in which there is no room for the social and behavioral sciences is a house of prejudice, just as a building of correction without space for law is doomed to disintegrate—for want of a foundation and for want of a roof. This is a point which, as 'Taft's Skyscraper' indicates, seems to have escaped quite a few theoreticians.[164] (see plate facing p. 33)

The social sciences still do not meet the rigorous standards posited by Michael and Adler in 1933. But man is not only a social but also an experimentative animal. The shock of Michael and Adler's debunking has been overcome, and progress has been made. For England, incidentally, this shock did not come until 1959, when Lady Wootton of Abinger published her *Social Science and Social Pathology*, the impact of which on America thus far has been slight. But English criminal law and criminology scholars, too, will overcome this debunking—not, I hope, without learning from it. For have we not learned, above all else, that this social animal called man can survive in concert, even if every individual member alone could not? A blind man, a deaf man, and a dumb man stand a good chance of surviving—if they stand together. A blind criminal justice, a deaf forensic psychiatry and a dumb sociological criminology stand a good chance not only of survival—if they stand together—but also of bettering humanity's plight.

CHAPTER IX

Scholarship in Criminal Law Theory

Introduction

For a moment I was tempted to put the phrase 'pure law' into the title of this chapter, a not unnatural temptation, after having devoted the preceding chapter to interdisciplinary scholarship. But, on reflection, it appears that 'pure law'—with its Kelsenite implications—is non-existent in American criminal-law scholarship. Everybody in the small community of criminal-law scholars has one foot in one or several of the social sciences, and, moreover, nearly everyone views his strictly legal preoccupations in the wider context of jurisprudence, expressly or impliedly. Indeed, nothing is more inviting for the scholar of criminal law than to view the object of his preoccupation in the wider context of philosophy. On the European continent it has practically been a tradition for the professor of criminal law to hold a chair, or at least to lecture, in legal philosophy as well. The trend has been not nearly as pronounced in the U.S.A., though the most sensitive criminal-law scholars have also been inextricably involved in preoccupation with philosophical matters.[1] Indeed, the philosophical implications of criminal law are so vast that every one who does not feel them, and somehow tries to come to grips with them, is suspected of being a morally dull person. But this is not an account of philosophical scholarship, but of criminal-law scholarship. I shall proceed, therefore, under the assumption that the criminal-law scholar is not impervious to the challenges of philosophy, but shall leave these interests undiscussed except in so far as they bear directly on the discussion of the expressions of criminal-law scholarship itself.

The type of scholarship to be discussed in the two sections of this chapter in some respects is not unlike the 'common law "scholarship" ' discussed earlier. Its principal difference, however, is that it proceeds on a higher level of sophistication. It is criminal-law scholarship not of the common law, but upon the common law, with or without the aid of comparative studies. We shall turn, first, to a treatment of comparative scholarship in criminal law, because many of the incentives and drives for modern American criminal-law scholarship have indeed come from studies of foreign criminal law, with its considerably more developed theory.

1. Comparative Scholarship in Criminal Law

As the antecedents of contemporary comparative scholarship in criminal law have already been traced, and the impact of the refugee scholars assessed, it remains to describe the current phase, its expression and significance.

(a) *Comparative Criminal Procedure.* It was natural for the common-law scholar with comparative ambitions (beset by procedural problems of his own, and traditionally inclined to seek answers to vexing criminal-law problems in procedure) to turn principally to procedural studies. The trend was inaugurated by Morris Ploscowe's studies abroad, and the series of valuable articles he published afterwards, on French and West European Criminal Procedure.[2]

Professor Hazard, similarly, engaged in comparative criminal and civil law studies abroad, particularly in the Soviet Union. He likewise published a series of valuable articles and still keeps abreast of developments in the Soviet Union.[3]

These first modern comparative criminal-procedure publications coincided with those by the refugee scholars which we discussed earlier. World War II, the occupation of European countries, and the war crimes trials heightened the interest in studies of foreign and comparative criminal law, as, more recently, did the NATO Status of Forces Agreement and the increased interchange among nations. Several of these recent publications followed Ploscowe's and Hazard's models and some, indeed, are products of their students.[4]

In recent years it has also become customary to invite foreign scholars to contribute to English-language periodicals,[5] especially to symposia of international scope.[6]

Instruction in Comparative Criminal Procedure, in the nature of periodic or occasional lectures by visitors or local experts, has been instituted at many of the larger law schools, and a systematic seminar in Comparative Criminal Procedure has been offered by Professor Ploscowe at New York University for nearly two decades, and by Professor George at the University of Michigan for several years.

Such comparative studies of the institutions of criminal-law administration are essential, not only for purposes of improvement of the domestic system on the basis of foreign experience, but also in order to lay the foundations for that mutual respect which is necessary before nations can co-operate in the solution of the crime problem, through treaty or otherwise.[7] No case demonstrates this better than

> the Girard case where, through gross ignorance and stupidity in Washington, D.C., and elsewhere, especially on the part of the members of the legal profession, the relations between the United States and Japan became strained. The Japanese themselves finally destroyed the myth of inquisitorial Japanese criminal justice and calmed an unduly alarmed American public. If the American legal profession were properly enlightened on the principles of criminal justice abroad, no silly statements could have been made on the floor of Congress, no alarming stories could have appeared in the American press and American-Japanese relations never would have been strained.[8]

For these reasons, the recently increased emphasis on comparative criminal procedure must be wholeheartedly welcomed, and the recently launched Comparative Procedure Project deserves every possible support.[9]

(b) *Comparative Criminal Law*. 'Unlike the situation in the physical and biological sciences,' wrote Professor Hall, 'there have long been apparently insurmountable barriers to the construction of a science of law.'[10] But following the shrinkage of the world through improved communications and transportation facilities, today 'we are able for the first time in history to accumulate the data of jurisprudence on a world scale'.[11] But why should we do this? In order to learn that there is a law of murder and manslaughter in Burma and Germany as well as in the United States? In order to strive for a world law? What explains the increase in comparative criminal-law studies in America, in recent years?

> In science everybody realizes that it is simply foolish to attempt to discover again what somebody else has discovered already, unless, of course, the information on the first discovery is withheld. We lawyers of the common law have as little a monopoly on legal brains as our scientists have a monopoly on scientific brains. That we know now. Yet in both fields, science and law, including law teaching, we run around in circles like the horses in Jamaica or Wheeling Downs, fully equipped with blinders. All of us were probably shocked when we recently learned that some of our scientists had been working on problems of applied science, with the greatest urgency and secrecy, when in fact these problems had not only been solved behind the Iron Curtain, but had long been fully published there in scientific journals which nobody had read in this country.[12] The same holds true for law. I would not be so bold as to contend that foreign criminal law scholars and legislators have solved all problems about which we are completely

in the dark. But I certainly have found that on many questions, especially those of the general part of criminal law, our foreign colleagues are making much more sense than we do.[13]

But why should that be so? The answer has been suggested in the first chapter of this study: the European university tradition of law in continental countries, as opposed to our court traditions. While it may be improper to explain all the differences in result in terms of inductive (common-law) and deductive (continental) reasoning,[14] there is no question but that the European scholars have worked for centuries with the aim of reducing their law to a body of principles, while the common-law scholar, until recently, has given little thought to such principles and their inter-relationships. Certainly, then, the significance of comparative criminal law for today and the immediate future is that of an 'exhibit' on which criminal-law theory itself, and its method, can be investigated.

Whether with this purpose in mind or not, many American scholars have turned to the comparative method during the last generation. Hall's *General Principles of Criminal Law*[15] is one of the prime examples of the skillful use of foreign criminal-law experience. So is Hall and Mueller's casebook, which, although it quotes little foreign law, utilizes the continental method throughout in the systematic arrangement of the topics. As a matter of fact, all the leading casebooks have become comparative in outlook.

Examination of all current casebooks shows that, unquestionably, Michael and Wechsler's casebook has the largest number of foreign law references,[16] skillfully inserted, including large excerpts from English translations of the positivist-influenced Italian and Russian penal codes and that of Cyprus. The otherwise excellent 1956 supplement, unfortunately, is rather weak on foreign law.[17] Besides, a number of first rate articles on comparative criminal law has been published since.[18] Michael and Wechsler refer at various places, to the criminal law of France, Italy, Belgium, the Netherlands, the Soviet Union, Argentina, Germany, Switzerland, Austria, Sweden, Egypt, Palestine, Cyprus and Iraq.

Next there is Dession's casebook,[19] also quite strong on comparative law. Dession has a common feature with Michael and Wechsler: the footnote references are explanatory and not solely referral notes. Dession's use of foreign materials often tends to be more contrastive than comparative, which is evidenced by his frequent references to Soviet law. But the positivist approach seemed to have a special attraction for him, as indeed he was one of the best known advocates of a scientific or behavioristic approach to criminal law. The French references are principally to Garraud's 1934 edition of the *Précis de droit criminel*.[20] The most serious shortcoming of Dession's work is his omission of German law, though, fifteen years ago, this was perhaps politically understandable.

There is, next, a discreet but skillful use of foreign law references in Hall and Glueck's casebook,[21] as indeed, on a much smaller scale, there are a good number of casebooks which do refer to foreign materials occasionally.[22]

Until recently, however, it seemed improbable that in America a strong trend of comparative studies in substantive criminal law would materialize. The basis for such a development was largely wanting. Only a very small number of American criminal-law teachers had the benefit of instruction abroad. Of the refugee teachers only a very small number assumed teaching responsibilities in criminal law. Worse still, there is the enormous problem of the language barrier for Americans (nearly all the descendants of immigrants speaking foreign tongues) who have not distinguished themselves as linguists. According to a recent report of the Committee on Foreign Exchange of Law Teachers that among the roughly 2,500 teachers at American law schools, both full-time and part-time, there are, surprising as it may seem, only

92 who can lecture in French,
51 „ „ „ „ German,
47 „ „ „ „ Spanish,
15 „ „ „ „ Italian

and only very few who can lecture in Chinese, Danish, Dutch, Hebrew, Japanese, Lebanese, Norwegian, Portugese, Russian and Swedish.[23] But I should think that the number of those who can intelligently *read* a foreign language must be much larger. Nevertheless, a great number of our colleagues never had the opportunity to learn a foreign language properly, and relief is not in sight for some time to come.[24] Thus, many of our colleagues are barred from the most original approach to comparative law.

But time and again it has been demonstrated that even with an imperfect knowledge of foreign languages, comparative study in criminal law is possible and fruitful, through perusal of existing translations and other materials in the English language.[25] Nevertheless, for most criminal-law scholars, even the best among them, comparative studies were bound to remain the exception until materials in English became available in a systematic manner, and until the bases and working hypotheses of comparative law were more firmly established.

In the civil-law countries, in the meantime, the interest in American criminal law increased significantly. There the comparative method has long been employed, and language barriers are less significant.

The French, through Donnedieu de Vabres and Marc Ancel, as well as others,[26] the Latin Americans (Spanish) under Sebastian Soler, Jiménez de Asúa and Ricardo Levene,[27] and the Germans under Mezger, Schönke, Jescheck, and others,[28] have left no country or criminal-law problem unexplored. Their efforts, especially those of the Germans, are virtually unimaginable for Americans. They have translated nearly ninety criminal codes into German, including those of New York, California and Louisiana. Their monographic and periodical discussions, substantively and bibliographically, are inexhaustible. The Institute of Foreign and International Criminal Law, at the University of Freiburg, Germany, under the directorate of Professor Jescheck, has begun the second series of short texts (100–250 pages each) on the criminal law of all major countries of the world, primarily for the benefit of German criminal-law revision.[29] The French and Latin-American efforts have not been in progress for quite as long as the German endeavors which, in their present concentration, date back roughly sixty years, but they are equally thorough and useful.

It was natural, then, that American criminal-law scholars would be called upon to co-operate with colleagues abroad, through lecture series, visiting professorships and institute affiliations,[30] through editorial co-operation,[31] and particularly through contributions to foreign periodicals or book series.[32]

Necessarily, then, these scholars would reflect their foreign experience in their domestic work. Thus, just as the American literature on foreign criminal procedure increased, so did the literature on foreign substantive criminal law, by both native born and naturalized American scholars[33] and by foreign authors.[34] At a number of law schools, seminars on comparative criminal law have been held.[35] But, on the whole, up till now chance has governed the development of the comparative methods in American criminal law, so that, in 1957, this writer felt constrained to call for the establishment of an American institute of comparative criminal law.[36]

(c) *The Comparative Criminal Law Project at New York University.*
In 1958 New York University, with a traditional interest in comparative law, criminal law and, indeed—through Morris Ploscowe—comparative criminal procedure, announced the establishment of a Comparative Criminal Law Project, operating without foundation support.[37] The Comparative Criminal Law Project, acting with an advisory board on which many distinguished foreign and domestic scholars were serving,[38] endeavors (1) to acquaint American criminal lawyers with the system and method of criminal law outside the U.S.A., and (2) to acquaint foreign experts with the

American system. Both purposes rest on the proposition that an improvement of one's system—nay, even an appreciation of it—is academically impossible without comparison.

The Project employs three methods to achieve its aims: (1) seminar instruction (particularly with co-operation of foreign visiting scholars), (2) exchange of views, and (3) publications. The publication project is of particular interest in this context.

On the assumption that the availability of a good working collection of foreign criminal-law materials is essential before detailed work in comparative criminal law can be undertaken either at the Project, or anywhere else in America, two series were launched in which basic materials are published in English: *The American Series of Foreign Penal Codes*[39] and *Publications of the Comparative Criminal Law Project*.[40] Both the Project itself and the two publication series have been well received, judging by articles and reviews in the periodical literature. The only regrettable aspect of the Comparative Criminal Law Project, perhaps, is its late birth, for none of its publications could be utilized in the preparation of the Model Penal Code. However, the project serves a number of governmental agencies in an advisory capacity, among them the U.S. Senate Sub-Committee on Improvements in Judicial Machinery, as well as the U.S. Children's Bureau, and has published a series of comparative-law research papers which have had an impact on criminal justice reform.[41]

(d) *The American National Section of the International Association of Penal Law.*

The *Association Internationale de Droit Pénal* was founded in Paris in 1924, on French initiative, and soon absorbed the older *Internationale Kriminalistische Vereinigung*, which had been founded in 1866 by von Liszt (Germany), Prinz (Belgium), and von Hamel (Netherlands). Today it offers the sole permanent international forum for the scholarly discussion and resolution of the problems of criminal law, and serves as an advisory agency to the United Nations, as a *Category B* non-governmental organization (n.g.o.).

American efforts to join the international community of criminal-law scholars date back to the time prior to World War I, when the late Professor Keedy and his colleagues at Northwestern University formed the nucleus of an American group.[42] However, these efforts were frustrated by the intervention of World War I, and no serious renewed effort was undertaken thereafter, for lack of leadership, sponsorship and financial backing.

By 1957 nearly every important civilized nation of the civil-law world had joined the A.I.D.P. In that year the Soviet Union joined, appeared at the Congress in Athens with a large official delegation and made a determined effort to gain a respected place in the organization.[43]

It became plain, then, that the United States could no longer exclude itself from this important forum for the discussion of criminal policy. Hence, immediately upon its creation in 1958, the Comparative Criminal Law Project of New York University made a determined effort to facilitate the admission of the United States to the A.I.D.P. In preparation for the 1961 Congress the Project prepared a major policy paper on one of the topics selected by the A.I.D.P. for its next congress: *The Impact of Publicity Given to Crime and Criminal Proceedings.*[44] The author participated at a preparatory conference in Milan, Italy, in May 1959.[45] In May, 1960, at a planning session in Lisbon, Portugal, American interests were represented by Professor Canals (University of Puerto Rico).

After consultations with the American members of the International Advisory Committee of the Comparative Criminal Law Project, and with various other American teachers of criminal law, an American National Section of the *Association Internationale de Droit Pénal* was founded in December, 1960, was immediately accepted for temporary membership by the executive committee of the A.I.D.P., in Paris, and finally accredited at the Lisbon meeting in September, 1961. The membership of the American National Section now comprises well over one hundred American criminal-law scholars,[46] and is constantly being expanded by invitation to others who have distinguished themselves in the field.

At the 1961 Lisbon Congress of the Association,[47] a conspicuous delegation of eight American criminal-law scholars, capable between them of conversing in seven foreign languages, made a first impact on the world's criminal-law scholars 'in convention assembled'. Judging by the welcoming remarks and by subsequent publications, the American group made a rather favorable impression.[48] There is reason to believe that by being subjected to the systematic approach of continental scholarship, American criminal-law theory will benefit significantly through continued co-operation with the A.I.D.P. But beyond that, there are already numerous indications that continental scholars will be influenced by some of the functionalism and skepticism with which American scholars are imbued and which most European criminal-law scholars lack. For that reason, the national reports submitted by the American delegation were accorded more attention than those of most of the civil-law delegations.[49]

The American National Section submitted national reports on all of the four topics scheduled for international debate at the 1964 Congress of the Association, at the Hague, Netherlands.[50] The

American National Section, with the support of the Rockefeller Foundation, the American Council of Learned Societies, and the Comparative Criminal Law Project of New York University, also organized one of the four international preparatory conferences, on the topic of Offenses against the Family and Sexual Offenses, at Bellagio, Italy, in September 1963, an event which attracted world-wide attention.

The significance of the congresses of the A.I.D.P. should not be underestimated. The governments of the nations represented are keenly interested in the resolutions of the world's leading experts in criminal law and policy, and many of the resolutions are likely to sway parliaments in their legislative debates, as has happened repeatedly. But the principal significance of American participation in the activities of the International Association of Penal Law is the fact that such co-operation marks the entry of the common law into the mainstream of world development. The gulf between the common law and the civil law of crime has been bridged.

2. Synthetic Criminal Law Scholarship

This section is in direct sequence to Chapter VII, but indirectly it is a logical sequel to all the preceding chapters of this book because, by any standard, criminal-law theory is the most sophisticated form of criminal-law scholarship. It can come only—and in the United States it did come—after a period of factual and behavioristic research.

In chapter VII we described the efforts of individual scholars to grapple with the most fundamental propositions of criminal law. Most of those mentioned continued their work, and some younger scholars joined in, with a variety of articles in which the search for basic propositions is predominant.[51]

In 1938 Professor Weihofen joined his former teacher Kenneth Sears, to produce a quite reputable student text in the fourth edition of May's *Law of Crimes*,[52] but the attempt fell short of producing an organization of the principles. Burdick, in 1946, came much closer with his three-volume work *Law of Crime*. Although in the form of a practitioner's text, in substance it reached the high theoretical level of the early Wharton and Bishop editions, and, in some respects, surpassed them. Burdick knew exactly what he was doing: 'In bringing to the legal profession a new treatise on the substantive law of crime, it is pertinent to call attention to the fact that it is over half a century since Wharton and Bishop, the two most frequently cited American writers upon this subject, finished their labors.'[53] This is Professor Burdick's opening paragraph, and it is followed by a discussion of Wharton's and Bishop's pioneer work. Burdick's life history is almost as fascinating as that of Bishop's: law training in a practitioner's office in Connecticut in the 1880s, then the law school of Yale, and then teaching at the University of Kansas. 'There for forty-five years he has taught criminal law, a longer period, he believes, than any other law teacher has taught this subject.'[54] Burdick's horizon was world-wide. In *The Bench and Bar of Other Lands* (1939), he proved himself an able student of comparative law, and in *Principles of Roman Law and Their Relation to Modern Law* (1938) he evidenced an astounding acquaintance with ancient and modern civil law. But it was in his *Law of Crime* that he proved to be a true scholar of the theory of law. There he stated 'the fundamental principles governing the law of crime'.[55]

> From the time of Coke it has been emphasized that our law is based upon reason, and there can be no scientific jurisprudence in our law or in any other system of law unless logic and reason be the guides. The lawyer who has no other foundation for his cause than a case upon all fours hardly appreciates the science of his profession. A case may apparently be 'in point', but the reasoning upon which the decision was made may not satisfy a sound judicial mind.[56]
>
> This is a clear recognition of the superiority of a principled approach over a casuistic one.

Burdick walked down the right road, and he was by far more successful than most of his colleagues, but he did not quite reach the goal—for his vehicle was analysis, and analysis only. He did not use synthesis.

A generation before Burdick, John Henry Wigmore had outlined the steps of scholarly proceeding in criminal law.[57] The steps, according to Wigmore, are these:

1. The analytic process: 'tracing the logical implications of general principles as revealed in specific cases', i.e., the case-study process.[58]
2. The historic process.[59]
3. The legislative process.[60]
4. The synthetic process, i.e., 'the process of building up individual rules and principles into a consistent system—of being able to trace every rule backwards and upwards to its more and more general expressions and of harmonizing these. . . .'[61]

Common-law scholars, trained in case-analysis only, are, naturally, accustomed to the analytic method.[62] 'The synthetic process of thought is often dismissed . . . with the epithet of "speculative jurisprudence!" But its time must come, if our law is ever to be soundly reconstructed; and legal education must provide for this in its methods.'[63]

The writers and teachers who were active during these last thirty years may all have felt a desire to reach general conclusions and resolutions. While many worked at it, none succeeded until 1947, though Burdick came close to the goal. Only an insider could realize what was going on among criminal-law teachers at that time. For an outsider the situation appeared as dismal in 1944 as it had been in 1924 or in 1904. Thus, when a distinguished Argentinian criminal-law scholar visited the U.S.A. in 1944, he gave a blunt—and quite appropriate—lecture:

> A theory of penal law that does not succeed in building a system can neither aim at the dignity of a science, nor at the modest dignity of a university discipline.[64]

> I must express a certain measure of surprise, caused by the fact that in a country like the United States, of democratic feelings so deeply rooted, the University chair, with very few exceptions, should neither have exceeded the mere empiricism of the 'case system', nor have noticed the theoretical importance of a solid structure of the general part of criminal law on the basis of a consciously applied method. . . . [I]f the chair aspires to the truly constructive disinterested and scientific function that guides and does not serve empiricism, there is no other method except the compilation of a system.[65]

But Jerome Hall, as early as 1941, by recalling the tradition of Hale, Blackstone, Livingston and Bishop, had recognized that 'important progress in criminal law in its purely professional aspect, is inseparable from philosophic insight and scholarship'.[66] Hall meant to put 'philosophic insight and scholarship' to use in creating a 'science of criminal law' which would accord with the best recognitions of sociology and stand firmly grounded in ethics. In 1947, the first blueprint of the science was before us: *General Principles of Criminal Law*.[67] The best evidence of the significance of this work is, perhaps, the fact that this was the first and, generally, has remained the only American criminal law treatise which is deemed worthy of citation in continental textbooks. What made this such an unusual book?

Case analysis of a mass of data reveals certain problems which faithfully recur and which, on the whole, have been accorded equal treatment. Thus, if infants and mentally diseased persons are excused from liability, while 'normal' adults are not, the question naturally arises: what do infants and mentally diseased persons have in common that is not present in 'normal' persons? Positively stated: there is something necessary for each crime found in all normal people, but not found in infants and mentally diseased persons. Using this type of analysis for assembling the raw materials of a structure, Hall could then proceed to synthesize them, and the outline of a certain structure of criminal law appeared. The structure incorporated components of three distinct varieties. One of these components, consisting of 'the rules', or definitions of the various crimes, would correspond to the 'special part' of a continental penal code. But whereas the 'general parts' of continental codes contain only one further variety of propositions (an undifferentiated one, frequently intermingled with extraneous, e.g., procedural, propositions), Hall finds that 'general propositions' are of two varieties, which he calls principles and doctrines. But at this point we should let Hall speak for himself, by quoting from a convenient summary recently published:

By doctrines I mean such notions as those concerning mistake of fact and law, necessity, coercion, infancy, insanity, intoxication, solicitation, attempt and conspiracy. In order to have the substantive criminal law fully defined one needs to unite the special part with the doctrines. Having done so, and not until one has done that, one derives a complete definition of each crime. In sum, each crime has distinctive characteristics stated in the specific part, and general aspects stated in the doctrines.

Principles are broader generalizations than doctrines. There you ascend to a higher level of abstraction and, viewing the fusion of the specific part and the doctrines, you ask: what are the common ideas which run through this whole field of criminal law? The answer, I suggest, is that there are seven fundamental ideas, i.e., principles, which permeate and unify this branch of law. They are (1) legality, (2) harm, (3) act (effort), (4) *mens rea*, (5) the concurrence of the *mens rea* with the act to form the conduct, (6) causation, that is, a causal relationship between the conduct and the harm, and (7) the punitive nature of the sanction. These are the seven basic principles which comprise the foundation of the criminal law. . . .

The European scheme . . . fails to distinguish doctrines from principles. But doctrines differ from principles in very important ways. For example, the doctrine that an insane person does not commit a crime because he lacks the necessary capacity is surely a different kind of generalization from the requirement that there must be a *mens rea* in every crime, that there must be a harm, and so on. The specification of insanity as a qualification of the special part goes to the definition of a crime; it is essential to the correct legal definition of the specific crimes. But principles are much broader notions which may also be viewed as standing outside the positive law of crimes, serving as descriptive propositions of a criminal science. . . .

If some insight into the formal side, the architecture, of the criminal law has been given, it need only be added that this has practical importance for the lawyer because he cannot be familiar with every crime in the whole catalogue. He may never have had any occasion in law school or elsewhere to study the crime of counterfeiting or treason or many other crimes. But if one understands the principles of criminal law, one has the tools to work with and to analyze any crime. If he has this equipment he can ask, what is the relevant mental state in this crime, what is the harm, what conduct is required, what about the concurrence of the mental side with the conduct, and so on. The principles permit and require one to ask the correct questions about each crime. And, of course, so far as the relevance of this for constructing a science of criminal law is concerned, one has only to look at any book of physics to realize that most of the progress in the physical sciences is due to the formal side of those sciences. The laws of physics are organized into a system so that a mathematical physicist, for example, never goes into a laboratory. He works equations on paper and then the experimental physicist takes the theorist's conclusion and tests it in the laboratory. We shall never attain any such rigorous organization of criminal law, but that objective is nonetheless important.[68]

Hall's treatise was followed by a casebook[69] which soon gained acclaim as one of the most widely adopted teaching tools. But, for a while, Hall's colleagues remained aloof. To be sure, Hall's new theory—the first successful American synthesis of criminal law— was acclaimed, but there was no immediate rush to follow the lead. In 1953, six years after the *Principles*, the first casebook was published which followed Hall's suggestion of a synthesis of criminal law— Professor Snyder's *An Introduction to Criminal Justice* (1953). Professor Morrow wrote about the book:

> Professor Snyder has chosen, happily, in the opinion of this reviewer, to arrange his material so that general concepts affecting all criminal conduct will be studied thoroughly before any specific crimes are considered. This arrangement, consistent with that of European criminal codes and the more carefully planned codifications in this country, now seems well on its way to general acceptance.[70]

Thereafter, the idea became accepted that there is advantage in a theoretically sound approach, and that the theoretical approach should be given a try. Several scholars fell in line, though none with as radical and thorough a switch to synthetic jurisprudence as Hall had proved feasible and necessary. By way of example, while Professor Perkins' casebook of 1952[71] still followed the more established line, in 1957 he switched to a theoretically well-formed organization,[72] as did Hall and Glueck in their second edition (1958),[73] and, to some extent, Paulsen and Kadish in their entirely new book.[74] But Harno, in his fourth edition, retained the traditional approach,[75] and two other recent casebooks departed radically from either model.[76]

In the textbook market, too, the new theoretical orientation of American criminal-law scholarship became noticeable. For the first time in history, there are now two student texts which one can recommend to the students without whispering: Wingersky's *Clark and Marshall on Crimes* (6th rev. ed. 1958), and, particularly Perkins' *Criminal Law* (1957), the condensation of many years of sound and organized thinking.

Hall himself 'did not stop at positing his theory, but he constantly endeavored to explain the concepts in terms of which the theory is stated. Thus, at various places, he had dealt with each of the principles: legality,[77] harm,[78] conduct,[79] *mens rea*,[80] concurrence,[81] causation,[82] and punishment.[83] In 1958 he published a series of new and old studies in the volume *Studies in Jurisprudence and Criminal Theory*.[84] In 1960 there appeared the completely revised and much enlarged second edition of the *General Principles*.

While Hall's is, thus, the first American theory of criminal law—and has consequently become the most important individual stimulus for future development—it is not likely to be the final theory. Many questions remain unanswered, and friendly divisions of opinion on the scope of Hall's seven principles will continue to exist, for instance, whether *mens rea* is to be included within the concept of causation, to what extent *mens rea* absorbs other aspects of the mental process, by which principles such doctrines as accessoryship or attempt are to be explained, etc. I should think that Professor Hall himself would wish lively discussions to ensue and to continue on such problems, in the hope of reaching the ultimate perfection of American criminal-law theory. At this moment it is of relatively little significance on what specific issues there exists a split of opinion among the theoreticians, for all such differences pale in the face of the fact that American criminal-law thinkers are faced and concerned with a theory, and that this theory is being debated, criticised and improved. That is the big news for America, a common-law nation hitherto hostile to theory.[85] Even if Hall should turn out to be wrong in every particular—and that does not seem very likely—history has already proved him right in general: The evolutionary process of law in every civilized nation demonstrates that the road of law leads from case-law via theoretical scholarship to perfected codes, with various intermediate steps, frequently in the nature of casuistic codifications. Moreover, Hall stands corroborated by our own sages who, decades ago, felt the workings of this evolutionary process and framed their demands for an accelerated process of maturation by demanding a theory of law.

In view of the development toward a theory of crime and of criminal law it will become increasingly difficult for all but the country-schoolmaster counterpart of the American criminal-law teacher to persist in a purely casuistic and functional approach toward his subject.[86] At one time it was virtually the credo of criminal-law teachers—as of lawyers generally—that 'general principles do not decide concrete cases'. That time, I humbly suggest, is gone forever. A throng may still condemn criminal-law theory with the epithet 'conceptualism', which has become a rather derogatory term with the functionalists and so-called realists. For a long time all conceptualism has been regarded as an unnecessary or even false feat of intellectual acrobatics. But conceptualism may be true or false. A concept which accurately portrays life itself is no more false or useless than a photograph which accurately portrays the object on which the camera was focused. Just as a photograph may be helpful to mind and memory, a concept may be equally or more so. False are only those concepts which mock or ignore the nature which they ought to portray.

While we have long known that the number of principles and doctrines of our criminal law which are necessary for deciding concrete cases is considerably smaller than the number of appellate cases on record, it has only been in the middle of the twentieth century that we have begun to make an effort at culling them from the mass of the court reports. What we have found and learned is most encouraging, especially in light of the data which the natural scientists could make available to us. On the whole, our courts have reached just conclusions, though more on hunch than by actual insight. Here we can pinpoint the task which confronts us in the late twentieth century. We must stop working with hunches—we must turn to systematic search. Yes, ours is an old and established system of law. On the whole we have done pretty well over the centuries in operating on hunches. But now is the time, now we have the means, to turn to scientifically sound operations. What in the past we merely felt, should now be expressed—ready for use by all. Hunches have led to only superficially adequate solutions. Scientific work calls for analysis and search in depth, for systematic exploration to find and express all that is knowable. We criminalists have an exciting voyage of discovery before us. We know less of crime today than Columbus knew of the surface of the earth in 1492: Only the contours and crude intrinsic qualities are as yet apparent to us.

The novelty of the mid-twentieth century and of Hall's General Principles is simply that of insight and systematization. But not just in criminal law, not just in public law, not just in law, but everywhere, we can see the change which takes place on the American scene: the transmutation of our mode of life from the do-it-yourself, happy-go-lucky, hit-or-miss attitude in public life and technology to one of thorough scientific and planned advance to ever greater and more certain achievements. But in criminal law, as elsewhere, we can always plan only on and with the factor of life itself, never without or against it. That is what we know today.[87]

Research and Scholarship— A Look into the Future

That great master of history and teacher of historians, Ranke, taught that it is the historian's task to search and report events 'as they really happened'.[1] This book is not 'history' in Ranke's sense, because I have tried, in the description of each event and of each sequence of events, to find the lesson for the future. That makes this book a thesis, i.e., a verified hypothesis, based on impressions which I have gathered over the years. This book, thus, contains its own conclusions. These can be summarized in terms of (1) a tentative verification of the general law of the evolution of legal systems from case law to scholar's law to code law; (2) a tentative verification of the predictions and demands by American scholars of the nineteenth and twentieth centuries, in terms of a step-by-step forward move through various stages of research and scholarship, again beginning with case-law analysis, leading through various fact-type researches—historical, sociological, psychological, etc.— to analytical jurisprudence and, ultimately, to a synthetic jurisprudence of criminal law.[2]

Having reached the stage of scholarship in synthetic jurisprudence in America—a stage corresponding to a similar and still current European era which began there in the late nineteenth century— does it mean that we all should now concentrate on this type of scholarship? Not at all!

Some may wish to continue writing practitioners' texts, for they are needed, and it will take a long time before the new scientific approach in law—especially criminal law—will trickle down from the lofty heights of professorial studies to the practitioner in the court.

Some may wish to continue with primary emphasis on case analysis—and the analysis of practical reasoning which goes into the making of cases. That is good, for the case will remain one of the two principal objects of our attention for a long time to come. The case is 'popular' law, because it deals with the problems of the common man. And as long as we do not forget our obligation to the common man and his case, perhaps we can avoid the excesses of synthetic jurisprudence which have occurred in some European nations.

Some may wish to continue 'criminal justice research'. That is important because the finest system of penal laws is useless unless its application is ensured, and, as yet, we are far from having found the way to do so efficiently and with certainty. Moreover, the research methods currently being developed in criminal justice will ultimately inure to the benefit of criminal-law research.

Some may wish to continue fact-type research, sociological or psychological or, indeed, psychiatric. That is very important, because every part of the structure of a criminal-law theory must correspond to the realities established by the social and behavioral sciences, and much remains to be discovered.

Some may wish to continue work on codifications, and that is a matter of great practical utility. Any intelligent code—even if not yet conforming to a synthetic theory model—is better than the infantile collections of annotated statutes we find in most states.

But some should continue the work of synthesis in criminal theory, the latest and ultimate stage reached by legal scholarship in America, for it holds the key to efficient, i.e. potentially computerized regulation of human conduct, in terms which maximally correspond to the demands and experiences of mankind.

As far as the individual scholar is concerned, perhaps it will be good for every young man who wishes to walk the at times lonely and stormy path of criminal-law scholarship, to take his cue from the careers of a few of his elders: Is it not noteworthy that most of the accomplished scholars of criminal law passed the same way stations? Wechsler, Hall and Perkins, to name but three, began with 'realism', in the sense of fact-relatedness.[3] The young scholar might also take a hint from Professor Beutel as to how best to engage in the 'realistic phase' of a scholarly or research career, and Michael and Adler still provide one of the best standards for scientific research in criminal law.

Before, during or after the realistic phase, and usually after, there is a hard period of work with case analysis in the 'general part' of criminal law. This is the 'analytic phase', in which Wechsler, Hall and Perkins all engaged with great ardor, before proceeding to the next and final phase, that of ordering and synthesizing the insights they had gained during the analytic phase. In Wechsler's case this 'synthetic phase' resulted in the Model Penal Code, in Hall's case in the *General Principles of Criminal Law*, in Perkins' case it resulted in a work of great pedagogical value, his student text.

One may wonder about the step after synthesis. As I have

intimated, the American scholars' work in synthesis has only just begun, and it will take time before conclusions can be reached which can be agreed upon by most thinkers in the field. I have also indicated that Hall is that member of the senior group who has come closest to the goal. Once the synthetic work is generally regarded as complete, then, and only then, should we proceed to the stage of actively pressing for legislation by the body politic.

Finally, the question arises, *how* should we proceed from here? What forms should 'research' and 'scholarship' assume in order to accomplish its mission best? Should we practice team work? Should we work in large institutes? Should we engage in mass research? Should we farm out some of our work to social and behavioral scientists? Should we work in close conjunction with them? Should we prepare and equip ourselves as social and behavioral scientists? I would simply answer: That all depends. It depends on the phase in which the work is to be done, and work is to be done in every one of the three phases, the realistic, the analytical and the synthetic.

For the analytical and synthetic phase, it would not be wise to create large institutes and mass research projects. Here the scholar in the solitude of his study, may be able to do more than a whole army of field researchers. Perhaps every once in a while the analytical and synthetic scholars should also lock themselves up together in a 'think tank'.[5] Is it not tragic that the five or six leading scholars of American criminal law have never spent an hour together in common debate? Their juniors are happily ahead in this respect. In the summers of 1963 and 1966 more than two dozen young American criminal-law scholars met for four-week sessions at New York University and mercilessly debated the very issues with which this book has dealt. As yet there has been very little responsible issue-taking, in print, on each other's work. The tendency is to ignore the other's work, rather than to criticize it. Where there has been criticism, it has not always been appreciated. That must change. If the American credo 'divided we fall' has any contemporary meaning, it calls for a combination of brain-power, and for work in harmony, with mutual respect and for the mutual benefit of all scholars, and the singular benefit of all Americans.

For the realistic phase, however, the situation is a bit different. Here even the day-to-day work needs staffing and 'team work'. But it is doubtful whether massive studies of the type conducted in the 1920s and 1930s—and revived in the Bar Foundation Project—will yield benefits that stand in any suitable proportion to the investment. The late Karl Llewellyn put it nicely when he opined a few years ago that 'the large-scale enterprises have as their main hope of value the gathering, testing, development, discovery, or invention of those *basic* techniques which can enter into general use even when the large-scale enterprises themselves may have gone the way of Nineveh and Tyre'.[6] By now the 'basic techniques' have been pretty well developed. Why not employ them in the manner demonstrated by Beutel? 'Realistic' studies could be carried out by teachers and students at every one of the law schools of America, if not during the academic year, then during the long summer recesses. Such studies, in the aggregate, might cost but a fraction of the Bar Foundation Project, and, if well conceived—perhaps with some central guidance—might yield manageable amounts of useful data on small questions of great significance, with sharply defined concepts and hypotheses.[7] By way of example: Deterrence, as a prime aim of criminal law, has never been tested empirically. Suppose we stimulate a large number of conservatively budgeted studies on that topic. Each individual study would have to be selected with local opportunities in mind. In city A, a small community with law school A, there may have been a fad of 'drag races' among the high school crowd. City Hall now proposes to pass an ordinance and to take other measures in order to curb the dangerous fad. Why not let the law school co-operate in devising such measures? Then the results of these measures will have to be tested in practice. What happens if the ordinance is passed, *and* enforced by ten, twenty, or fifty police officers? What happens on the neighboring state highways and in the neighboring townships? In a large metropolitan area we are likely to find the seat of major industries. What happens to such an industry when Washington passes a new statute? How does the trucking industry react when the law is changed to prohibit full-capacity loading of liquid-fuel carriers? We may find out, for example, that safety hazards are increased by less than capacity loading. Now an imbalance arises: safety considerations and the economic worries of competitive standing in the carrier market versus financial loss through fines if the industry does not comply. How will the industry react? At what point of enforcement effort (again an economic consideration) will industry comply? What can we learn about the effect of deterrence, and about the execution of deterrent sanctions?

After many such small studies, let us go into the think tank to compare results. Perhaps we can find some proposition which seems to be generally applicable.

Lawyers cannot efficiently and effectively engage in direct experimental or validating studies on human beings, whether singly or collectively. This must be left to the behavioral and social scientists. But lawyers, with their age-old commitment to regulating human conduct for the best possible effectuation of smooth social living, have the duty of identifying the direction and scope of research to be conducted by those scientists, and of initiating such research. The criminal-law scholar must naturally participate in the research enterprise which he may have initiated. The chances of success for such a co-operation, especially with social scientists, are good indeed.[8]

If it were only a matter of identifying the scope and direction of criminal-law research, and of forming interdisciplinary teams to undertake the research task, the battle for the best possible American criminal law could be won handily. But life is not that simple. Just as the ancients could not do battle without having consulted the oracles, without having solicited the aid of the gods and without having made proper sacrifices, so today, the potential scholar of criminal law is dependent upon the good will of sages, the aid of the gods, and the sacrifices. The sages today sit in administrative posts of governments and universities, the gods sit on the boards of trustees of money-dispensing organizations, the sacrifices of the scholars tend to be of professional and familial nature, and often cut deeply into a scholar's pride and professional commitment. The sages are no wiser today than they were yesteryear, but they can be as powerful and as merciless. The gods of today are as little identifiable with the heavenly force above as were the heathen gods of then; in fact, rather than sitting above, today's gods sit at the foundations. As the workings of ancient oracles have remained mysterious, so are the criminal-justice grants of modern foundations. To give some guidance, to point to real needs, to appeal to reason, to overrule the spur-of-the-moment dictates of popular fancy in criminal-law research, I have written this book.

NOTES

(pp. xiii–9)

PREFACE

1. Quoted by Professor Sebastian Soler, in 'The Political Importance of Methodology in Criminal Law', 34 *J. Crim. L. and Crim.* 366, 367 (1944).
2. G. Mueller, 'Entwicklung und Stand der amerikanischen Strafrechts-wissenschaft' [1960], *Juristenzeitung* 465.
3. G. Mueller, 'Codification pénale aux Etats-Unis d'Amerique', *43 Rev. de Droit Pén. et de Crim.* 1 (1963).

INTRODUCTION

1. My comparison with medical history is based on Theodore H. Allen's *History of Medicine*, in *7 Science-History of the Universe* (1909).
2. Ibid. at 138.
3. Analogously, for the European continent see E. Schmidt, *Einführung in die Geschichte der deutschen Strafrechtspflege* 202–381 (1947).

CHAPTER I

1. In my discussion of the colonial period I have placed primary emphasis on the development in Massachusetts for, unquestionably, the Massachusetts experience has placed a more pronounced imprint on the American legal system than any other. But the Massachusetts experience is nevertheless quite typical. Thus, what has been said for Connecticut is virtually equally applicable to Massachusetts: 'Roughly speaking, New Haven's criminal laws were Mosaic or Biblical in origin; its civil and administrative acts were English in pattern, while in many cases the comparison of precept with precedent and the requirements of colonial life evoked indigenous legislation.' Charles H. Levermore, *Republic of New Haven: a History of Municipal Evolution* 153 (1886). On the whole, the development in the other colonies was not totally dissimilar, with the rather obvious exception of the colonies settled by the Dutch, the Germans, the Swedes, the French and the Spaniards, some of whom had no occasion to embrace English legal traditions for centuries. But even

among the English-settled colonies certain differences stand out rather clearly. See particularly R. B. Morris, *Studies in the History of American Law*, Introduction (2nd ed. 1958). In Massachusetts we should distinguish between Plymouth and Massachusetts Bay. The settlers of the former colony, as militant dissenters, had more occasion to distrust the common law than the settlers of the latter, who were mild dissenters. The Virginians never had any particular antipathy toward the ways and means of the common law, and when, in 1661, the Virginia General Assembly adopted the common law of England altogether, they simply ratified long-standing practice, initiated when in 1618 the Virginia Company had ordered the colonial governor to introduce the English common law. 1 Samuel E. Morison and Henry Steele Commager, *The Growth of the American Republic* 41 (4th ed. 1950). The corporate colonies, being tightly controlled from London, had little opportunity to disregard the common law. But in the Quaker colonies, the existing spirit of enlightenment was the cause for significant departures from the common law, especially in criminal law. See Morris, *op. cit.*; art. citing Fitzroy, 'The Punishment of Crime in Provincial Pennsylvania', *Pa. Mag. of Hist. and Biog.* (July, 1936), pp. 242–269; *The Burlington Court Book*, pp. xlviii, xlix. Rebellion against the common law, thus, was bound to be more widespread in the New England colonies than elsewhere. But all colonies had in common their devotion to the law of God, and their lack of experience in the truly professional solution of legal problems, as will be demonstrated. For Virginia see Sir J. Randolph and Edward Barraddall, *Reports on the Decisions of the General Court of Virginia, 1728–1741* (1909); for Maryland see J. H. Johnson, *Old Maryland Manors*, John Hopkins University Studies in Historical and Political Science vii (1883); for Delaware see *Court Records of Kent County Delaware: 1680 to 1705* (1959); for New Jersey see *Burlington Court Book of West New Jersey: 1680 to 1709* (1944), *Journal of the Courts of Common Right and Chancery of East New Jersey, 1683–1702* (1937); for New York see J. Goebel and T. R. Naughton, *Law Enforcement in Colonial New York 1664–1776* (1944); for Connecticut see Charles H. Levermore, *Republic of New Haven: A History of Municipal Evolution* 37 (1886); for Massachusetts see Emory Washburn, *Sketches of the Judicial History of Massachusetts* (1775). for New Hampshire see E. L. Page, *Judicial Beginnings in New Hampshire* (1959).

2. Goebel, 'King's Law and Local Custom in Seventeenth Century New England', 31 *Col. L. Rev.* 416, 422 (1931).

3. Ibid. at 425–426. On the Biblical orientation of colonial law see particularly Morris, op. cit. *supra* n. 1, at 21–41.

4. The book of Leviticus, however, served as a code of positive law in Virginia. See A. P. Scott, *Criminal Law in Colonial Virginia* 139 (1930).

5. For statutory references see Goebel, op. cit. *supra* n. 1, at 424–425,

n. 15, particularly reference to the 'Address' to the Plymouth Code of 1658 which, however, merely reflected long-standing policy. See also J. Goebel, *Cases and Materials on the Development of Legal Institutions* 265–269 (3rd ed. 1946); II *Plymouth Colony Records* 72–72 (Pulsifer ed. 1861). C. K. Burdick, I *The Law of Crime* 34 (1946).

6. George L. Haskins, *Law and Authority in Early Massachusetts* 56 (1960).

7. Ibid. at 124–125.

8. Ibid., loc. cit.

9. For example, W. L. Clark and W. L. Marshall, *The Law of Crimes* 23 (6th ed., Wingersky, 1958); Walter B. Miller, *Criminal Law* 30 (1934). It is more sensible to maintain that the first immigrants from England brought those principles of English common law along which seemed acceptable and useful to them in the situation of the new country. See, e.g., E. M. Dangel, *Criminal Law* 13 (1951). The correct position is presented by Haskins, op. cit. *supra* n. 6, at 185.

10. Haskins, op. cit. *supra* n. 6, at 37.

11. The five main events of the seventeenth century which led to the development of the 'rule of law' or 'legality' concept in English criminal law and procedure are the following:

    (1) The opposition of Lord Chief Justice Coke to King James I in 1616, as an expression of judicial independence toward the crown. This demonstration formed the basis for the development of judicial independence thereafter.

    (2) The Petition of Rights (1629), drafted with Coke's help and finally signed by King Charles. This law prohibits the application of martial law, restricts the crown's right to make arrests, and abolishes other interventions inconsistent with a rule-of-law concept.

    (3) The Habeas Corpus Act of 1679, which introduced an effective means of testing the legality of arrest and detention by the writ of habeas corpus.

    (4) The Bill of Rights, the constitutionally tremendously significant declaration of basic rights, 1687–1688, which, among others, provides that all royal prerogatives are subject to law; that petitions may be sent to the king without hindrance; that a standing army may not be maintained without authorization of parliament; that parliament shall enjoy full freedom of expression; that it may hold frequent sessions for the solution of grievances; and finally—of special significance for criminal law—that fines are to be sharply limited; that cruel and unusual punishments must not be imposed; and that bail shall become a matter of right.

    (5) The Act of Settlement, 1700, which finally guaranteed full judicial independence.

12. Haskins, op. cit. *supra* n. 6, at 56.

13. Ibid. at 203–204.

14. Ibid. at 199–200.

15. Ibid. at 204–205.

16. Ibid. at 208–209, 203.
17. Ibid. at 28–35.
18. Ibid. at 35.
19. Ibid. at 185.
20. Goebel, op. cit. *supra* n. 2, at 434.
21. Ibid. at 434–435.
22. Ibid., *passim.*
23. Haskins, op. cit. *supra* n. 6, at 4–7.
24. Ibid. at 75, 182.
25. Ibid. at 186.
26. Ibid. at 60.
27. Ibid. at 65, 189.
28. Ibid. at 182.
29. Ibid. at 137.
30. Ibid. at 178.
31. Ibid. at 137.
32. D. P. Corey, *The History of Malden, Massachusetts* 180–181 (1899), as cited by Haskins, op. cit. *supra* n. 6, at 134. See also Haskins, op. cit. at 178.
33. Haskins, op. cit. *supra* n. 6, at 178.
34. Roscoe Pound, *The Lawyer from Antiquity to Modern Times* 135–174 (1953). An admirable history of the legal profession in colonial America is Chroust, 'The Legal Profession in Colonial America' (pts. 1 and 2), 33 *Notre Dame Law.* 51, 350 (1958), pt. 3 in 34 ibid. at 44 (1959).
35. Raphael Semmes, *Crime and Punishment in Early Maryland* 36 (1938).
36. F. R. Aumann, *The Changing American Legal System* 46–47 (1940).
37. James, 'A List of Legal Treatises Printed in the British Colonies and the American States Before 1801', in *Harvard Legal Essays* (ed. Roscoe Pound) 160–161 (1934).
38. Aumann, op. cit. *supra* n. 36, at 43 et seq.
39. Haskins, op. cit. *supra* n. 6, at 174.
40. Ibid. at 35.
41. Ibid. at 177; and see particularly Goebel, op. cit. *supra* n. 2, at 434–443.
42. Roscoe Pound, *The Lawyer from Antiquity to Modern Times* (1953); ibid., *The Formative Era of American Law* (1938).
43. Ibid.
44. The first lawyers had received their legal training in England. During the eighteenth century it became possible to observe one's legal apprenticeship on America. But the standard of learning was extremely poor in America. See Morris, op. cit. *supra* n. 1, at 41–45. Able attorneys, and better popular regard for the legal profession, did not make their appearance until well into the eighteenth century. Roscoe Pound, *The Lawyer from Antiquity to Modern Times*, ch. 6 (1953); Albert J. Harno, *Legal Education in the United States* (1953); Chroust, op. cit. *supra* n. 34.
45. Randolph v. Blackmore, *Proceedings of the Maryland Court of*

Appeals 1695–1729 (ed. Bond and Morris, 1933), at 648; a prosecution for violation of the Navigation Acts, decided in 1696.

46. Goebel and Naughton, op. cit. *supra* n. 1, at 760.

47. Morris, op. cit. *supra* n. 1, at 15.

48. Thomas Lechford, *Plaine Dealing or News from New England* 86 (ed. 1867).

49. T. F. T. Plucknett, *A Concise History of the Common Law* 280 (5th ed., 1956).

50. Ibid. at 284.

51. Harold Potter, *An Historical Introduction to English Law and its Institutions* 36 (3rd ed., 1948).

52. Ibid. at 37.

53. *Supra* n. 11.

54. Potter, op. cit. *supra* n. 51, at 49.

55. Ibid. at 50.

56. Ibid. at 48.

57. Ibid. at 46.

58. Loc. cit.

59. Loc. cit.

60. Ibid. at 47.

61. Ibid. at 46.

62. Henry de Bracton, *De Legibus et Consuetudinibus Angliae* (about 1260). 'Bracton's Note Book' was not discovered until the nineteenth century, and published by Maitland at Cambridge.

63. Sir Edward Coke, *Institutes* (1628–1644), which in the third part treats of 'High Treason, and other Pleas of the Crown, and Criminal Causes' (1644).

64. Jerome Hall, *General Principles of Criminal Law*, 7, n. 10 (2nd ed., 1960).

65. Ibid. at 41–42.

66. Ibid. at 42.

67. Potter, op. cit. *supra* n. 51, at 45.

68. 2 Sir James Fitzjames Stephen, *A History of the Criminal Law of England* 206 (1883).

69. Plucknett, op. cit. *supra* n. 49, at 280.

70. Ibid. at 282.

71. Ibid. at 281.

72. Ibid. at 284.

73. 'An act does not make [the doer of it] guilty, unless the mind is guilty; that is, unless the intention be criminal. 3 Inst. 107.' *Black's Law Dictionary* 55 (4th ed., 1951).

74. The maxim will be discussed *infra, passim*. As far as Coke's contribution to the systematization of criminal law is concerned, it is nevertheless true that he is by far outdistanced by those who were to follow him one hundred years later. In general see Coke's *Third Institute* (1641).

75. Potter, op. cit. *supra* n. 51, at 52.

76. To the effect that Hawkins, the earlier author, may well have

plagiarized Hale, the later author, see Jerome Hall, *General Principles of Criminal Law* 7–8 (2nd ed., 1960).

77. C. K. Burdick, I *The Law of Crime* 24–25 (1946).

78. See section 5, *infra*.

79. Note that while Bentham's first English codification efforts coincided with Livingston's first American codification efforts, Stephen's second codification effort falls in the period of America's second codification wave. *Infra*, ch. 2, section 1. Stephen's Draft Code was appended to the Report of the Criminal Code Commission, published in 1879, and marked C.2345. See also Stephen's code-like *Digest of the Criminal Law* (1877, 5th ed. 1834).

80. C. S. Kenny, *Outlines of Criminal Law* (1902; 17th ed., Turner, 1958).

81. Glanville Williams, *Criminal Law—The General Part* (1953, 2nd ed. 1961).

82. Roscoe Pound, *The Spirit of the Common Law* 41 (1921), regards Coke's 'Summing Up' a convenient starting point for American legal history.

83. Haskins, op. cit. *supra* n. 6, at 135.

84. Waterman, 'Thomas Jefferson and Blackstone's Commentaries', 27 *Ill. L. Rev.* 629 (1933).

85. In general see also Radin, 'The Rivalry of Common Law and Civil Law Ideas in the American Colonies', in II *Law, A Century of Progress* (ed. Alison Reppy) 404 (1937).

86. 2 Sir James Fitzjames Stephen, *A History of the Criminal Law of England* 214–215 (1883).

87. 4 Sir William Blackstone, *Commentaries on the Laws of England* 1–2 (1769).

88. This thought would have to be verified by a close study of many American editions of English criminal law textbooks published during the nineteenth century.

89. 4 Blackstone, *Commentaries* 11 (1769).

90. Plucknett, op. cit. *supra* n. 49, at 287.

91. Hall, op. cit. *supra* n. 64, at 9.

92. The English reviewer of an American article on 'Law Reform in America', 4 *Legal Obs.* 67, 70 (1832), said 'we may here notice, that every English legal publication is reprinted in America; and it is not very creditable, either to the American editors or publishers, that this is generally done without any acknowledgement to the English author.' The author of the note disputed the American claim of having formed an independent American scholarship. The practise of publishing English works without authorization was not confined to law books and was simply part of the total piracy of English works in the nineteenth century in the absence of copyright protection.

93. See fifth American edition, from third London edition, by George Sharswood, 1845, two volumes.

94. See third American (Perkins) edition of *Chitty on Criminal Law*, reviewed at 16 *Am. Jur. and L. Mag.* 371 (1837).

95. 16 *Am. Jur. and L. Mag.* at 372.
96. This appointment may have been an anti-Blackstone move. See Waterman, 'Thomas Jefferson and Blackstone's Commentaries', 27 *Ill. L. Rev.* 629 (1933), and see text, *infra*.
97. Although law teaching in Transylvania University ceased, the law teaching in Lexington, Kentucky, was continued by the University of Kentucky, so that Lexington, Kentucky, may be said to be the city with the longest uninterrupted academic legal education in the United States.
98. In general see Albert J. Harno, 'The Law School—Centers of Legal Research and Scholarship', 12 *J. Legal Ed.* 193, 196, 197 (1959). In general, A. J. Harno, *Legal Education in the United States* (1953). On Jefferson and Chancellor George Wythe see J. W. Hurst, *The Growth of American Law—The Law Makers* 257, 258 (1950). Professor Hurst also discusses other early law teachers of the schools mentioned in the above listing. Butler's plan for New York University is given in Benjamin F. Butler, *Plan for the Organization of a Law Faculty, in the University of the City of New-York* (1835, ed. Niles and Marke, 1956). See also Currie, 'The Materials of Law Study', 3 *J. Legal Ed.* 331 (1951).
99. The lectures of James Wilson, professor of law at Philadelphia College, were published in 1804. See J. W. Hurst, *The Growth of American Law—The Law Makers* 258 (1950).
100. Harno, 'The Law Schools—Centers of Legal Research and Scholarship', 12 *J. Legal Ed.* 193, 196 (1959). In general see also C. Warren, *A History of the American Bar*, 332–365 (1913).
101. Letter from Chancellor Kent to Edward Livingston—Penal Code, 16 *Am. Jur. and L. Mag.* 361, 363 (1837). This letter was written on March 13, 1826.
102. Ibid. at 370.
103. See Letter, *supra* note 101, and 'Two Letters of Chancellor Kent', 12 *Am. L. Rev.* 479 (1873), directed to Livingston, and dealing with Livingston's penal code.
104. Albert J. Harno, *Legal Education in the United States* 24 (1953), dates Hoffmann's appointment 1816, and refers to Hoffmann's book as a 'worked out ... curriculum'. According to the *University of Maryland School of Law Bulletin 1963–1964*, p. 7, the first faculty of law, including David Hoffmann, was chosen in 1813, and the book is discussed as a 'recommended . . . course of study', p. 8. 'Regular instruction in law was begun in 1823.' Loc. cit.

   For Story's praise see Joseph Story, *Miscellaneous Writings* 91 (1852).
105. David Hoffmann, *Course of Legal Study* iii (1817). See also G. Mueller, 'Most Distinct and Lively Pictures', 49 *Law Lib. J.* 256 (1956).
106. F. R. Aumann, *The Changing American Legal System* 109 (1940).
107. H. Toulmin and J. Blair, *Review of the Criminal Law of the Commonwealth of Kentucky* (1804).

108. 4 *Encyclopedia Americana* 34–40 (1830).
109. Hogan, 'Blackstone and Joseph Story—Their Influence on the Development of Criminal Law in America', 40 *Minn. L. Rev.* 107 (1956).
110. See Harno, 'The Law Schools—Centers of Legal Research and Scholarship', 12 *J. Legal Ed.* 193–197 (1959).
111. See Moore, 'The Livingston Code', 19 (Part II) *J. Crim. L. and Crim.* 344, 346–347 (1928).
112. See Moore, op. cit. *supra* n. 111; see also Bibliography, ibid. at 363–366; for another Livingston Bibliography see Aumann, op. cit. *supra* note 110, at 123, n. 15.
113. Moore, op. cit. *supra* n. 111, at 360.
114. See Letter, *supra* n. 101, with a detailed criticism of Livingston's code, in which Kent demonstrates abundant knowledge of penal law and his adherence to the punitive school. See also Dillon, 'Chancellor Kent', 3 *Colum. L. Rev.* 257 (1903); 37 *Am. L. Rev.* 321 (1903); 26 *Nat. Corp. Rep.* 229 (1903).
115. B. M. Rothe, *The Daniel Webster Reader* 34 (1956).
116. 2 *Am. Rev. of History and Politics* 1–69 (1811).
117. Kempin, 'Precedent and *Stare Decisis*: The Critical Years 1800 to 1850', 3 *Am. J. Legal Hist.* 28 (1959). Unfortunately Mr Kempin did not have a word to say about precedent and *stare decisis* in criminal law. On the first American printed reports, books on pleading and foreign translations for practice in America, in general, see C. Warren, *History of the American Bar* 157–160 (1913).
118. F. R. Aumann, *The Changing American Legal System* 95 (1940), quoting from 36 *No. Am. Rev.* 396 (1833).
119. Nathan Dane, *A General Abridgement and Digest of American Law*, vols. 1–9 (1823, 1824, 1829).
120. The early nineteenth century saw a general cult of French law in America. The French codes were extolled. *Per contra*, statutes were passed against the citation of English precedent. Pound, op. cit. *supra* n. 35, at 180–181.
121. 9 Dane, op. cit. *supra* n. 119, at 630. State v. Hobbs, a New Hampshire case reported at 2 *Tyler* 380.
122. For an assessment of 'Criminal Procedure on the American Frontier', see an article with that title by Professor Blume, 57 *Mich. L. Rev.* 195 (1958), covering the Michigan Territory 1805–1825. This is an excellent and revealing discussion of the men who made the law at that time. Frontier law libraries are discussed at 245 and 247. See also Blume, 'Civil Procedure on the American Frontier, 1796–1805', 56 *Mich. L. Rev.* 161–167 (1957).
123. See Roscoe Pound, *The Spirit of the Common Law* 14 et seq. (1931). See also Pound, 'The Development of American Law and Its Deviation From English Law', 67 *L. Q. Rev.* 49 (1951).
124. Pound, 'The Development of American Law and Its Deviation From English Law', 67 *L. Q. Rev.* 49, 49–50 (1951).
125. Blume, op. cit. *supra* n. 122.

CHAPTER II

1. See, however, Martin Conboy, 'Federal Criminal Law', in I *Law, A Century of Progress* 295, 310 (1937), contending that until the revision of December 1, 1873, little federal statutory law had been added. Nevertheless, it is to be observed that by that time there were 227 sections in Title LXX, Crimes, and many federal penal statutes were, in fact, not included in Title LXX. Twenty years theretofore the situation was not materially different. See also Conboy, *supra*, for a general historical account of the growth of federal criminal law. For the growth of federal criminal law and enforcement agencies, see Arthur C. Millspaugh, *Crime Control by the National Government* (1937).
2. H. S. Sanford, *The Different Systems of Penal Codes in Europe* 8 (1854).
3. Ibid., loc. cit.
4. See 30 Stat. 58 (1897).
5. 31 Stat. 1181 (1901).
6. 35 Stat. 1088 (1909).
7. See Barron, 'Some Notes by the Revisers of the Federal Criminal Laws', 6 *Fed. B. J.* 141 (1945); Wright, 'Federal Legislation, Revision of Federal Criminal Laws', 33 *Geo. L. J.* 194 (1945); Zinn, 'Proposed Revision of Federal Criminal Law', 30 *A.B.A.J.* 49 (1944).
8. P.L. 772, 645 approved June 25, 1948, see H. R. Rep. No. 304, 80th Congress, 1st Sess., 1947.
9. Note, 'The Penal Code of New York', 1 *Alb. L. J.* 175 (1870). These shortcomings are explained by Mueller, 'Modernization of New York's Criminal Law and Procedure', *N.Y.L.J.*, February 17, 1961, p. 4.
10. Note, 'We Need a Criminal Code', 7 *Am. L. Rev.* 264, 266 (1872).
11. Ibid. at 267.
12. Ibid. at 264–265.
13. 20 *Cent. L. J.* 321–322 (1885).
14. Joel P. Bishop, 1 *Commentaries on the Criminal Law* iii (1868).
15. Graph and text taken from the fourth edition (1868) Volume I 630–631.
16. *Bishop on Criminal Law* (9th ed., Zane and Zollman, 1923), 2 vols.
17. Reproduced from 18 *Am. L. Rev.* 855 (1884).
18. Book Review, 'Bishop's New Criminal Law', 27 *Am. L. Rev.* 937 (1893).
19. We should keep in mind that American scholarship was at the time publisher-dictated. An enormous amount of piracy was in progress; and Bishop, who depended for his livelihood on his publications, suffered from it considerably. As near as we can ascertain, he himself never practiced it. See Bishop, 'The Common Law System of Reasoning—How and Why Essential to Good Government; What Its Perils, and How Averted', 22 *Am. L. Rev.* 1 (1888).

20. In the prefaces to the later editions the reader will find ample discussion of the insistence on ethics in legal research and publication.
21. Bishop, 'The Common Law System of Reasoning—How and Why Essential to Good Government; What Its Perils, and How Averted', 22 *Am. L. Rev.* 1 (1888).
22. Ibid. at 10.
23. Ibid., loc. cit.
24. Ibid. at 25–26.
25. Ibid. at 27–29.
26. Ibid. at 24.
27. See Book Review, 9 *Law Rep.* 385 (1847).
28. See also Jerome Hall, *General Principles of Criminal Law* 11 (2nd ed., 1960).
29. 22 *Am. L. Rev.* 421–422 (1888).
30. See 'Francis W. Wharton, LL.D., D.D., lawyer, publicist, editor, professor, author and clergyman', 18 *Case and Comment* 69 (1911).
31. Note, 'Honors to American Lawyers', 19 *Am. L. Rev.* 103 (1885). This criticism does not extend to Harvard's splendid support for criminological scholarship.
32. See Allen, Book Review, 27 *U. Chi. L. Rev.*
33. Wharton, 'Comparative Criminal Jurisprudence', 4 *Crim. L. Reg.* 1 (1883). For the review of a German criminal law book by Wharton see 26 *Atl. Monthly* 69 (1870), under the title: 'Criminal Law at Home and Abroad'. Wharton's criminal law comparisons received recognition as recently as 1960 in the New York case of People v. Reese, 25 Misc. 2d 959, 961, 212 N.Y.S. 2d 696, 698 (Dist. Ct. 1960).
34. The European influence is distinctly detectable in some of his articles, e.g., Wharton, 'Unsuitability of Means and Objects', 9 *Cent. L. J.* 42, 257 (1879).
35. Arthur E. Fink, *Causes of Crime, Biological Theories in the United States, 1800–1915* (1938); the reference is to Isaac Ray, *A Treatise on the Medical Jurisprudence of Insanity* (Boston, 1838).
36. See Wharton, 'Economy and Criminal Law', 3 *Crim. L. Mag.* 1 (1882).

CHAPTER III

1. In 1889, Dean Austin Abbott of New York University School of Law published his pattern-setting *A Brief for the Trial of Criminal Cases*, a book which, in subsequent editions, enjoyed considerable popularity among the practicing bar (see Austin Abbot, *Criminal Trial Practice*, 4th ed., Viesselman, 1939). Abbot's book led to many imitations on the state-wide level.
2. Emory Washburn, *Manual of Criminal Law* (Ewell, ed. 1877). Second edition 1878, third edition 1889.
3. Robert Desty, *A Compendium of American Criminal Law* V (1882).
4. George Luther Clark, *Handbook of Criminal Law* VI, St Paul, West Publ. Co. (1894).

5. Eulin McClain, *A Treatise on the Criminal Law* (Callaghan and Co., 1897), 2 vols. Professor McClain, A.M., LL.D., was Chancellor of the Law Department of the State University of Iowa.

6. Ibid. at 5.

7. Ibid. at VI.

8. Ibid. vol. 1, at 252.

9. J. B. Minor, *In Exposition of the Law of Crimes and Punishments* (1894). 'The most salient feature of Mr Minor's teaching was his analytical method.' Michie, 'John Barbee Minor', 7 *Green Bag* 401, 403 (1895).

10. Perhaps his prolific periodical writing is explained by his abhorrence of the numerous textbooks that were too often contradictory. See Brown, 'Too Many Law Books', 88 *Green Bag* 83 (1893).

11. Brown, 'Certainty of Punishment', 11 *Alb. L. J.* 282 (1875).

12. 9 *Crim. L. Mag.* 139 (1887).

13. Note, 'Nature and Definition of Crimes', 2 *Alb. L. J.* (1870).

14. Regina v. Tolson, 23 *Q. B. D.* 168 (1889).

15. Endlich, 'The Doctrine of *Mens Rea*', 13 *Crim. L. Mag.* 831 (1891).

16. Ibid. at 834.

17. Elliott, 'Proving Criminal Intent', 7 *Crim. L. Mag. and Rep.* 273, 274–275 (1886).

18. G.S.L.S., 'Malice and Morals in Law', 6 *Am. L. Reg.* 320 (1858).

19. See Note (Isaac Ray), 'The Law of Insanity', 4 *Am. L. Rev.* 236 (1869).

20. Loc. cit.. New York was one of these jurisdictions.

21. Note, 'Criminal Law and Insanity', 3 *N.J.L.J.* 232 (1880). This note constituted a criticism of Regina v. Higginson, 1 *C. and Kir.* 131 (1843), phrased substantially in terms of the M'Naghten Test.

22. This judgment, seemingly as summary as damning, rests on the study of hundreds of law review articles of that era. Several pages of demonstrative examples had to be cut to reduce the length of this book.

23. Benjamin F. Butler, *Plan for the Organization of a Law Faculty, in the University of the City of New York* (1835, ed. Niles and Marke, 1956), 25.

24. Ibid., loc. cit.

25. Ibid. at 26.

26. Ibid. at 27.

27. Ibid. at 27.

28. Ibid. at 28.

29. Ibid. at 29.

30. Ibid. at 27. Having prepared the 'Plan for the Organization of a Law Faculty, in the University of the City of New-York' in 1835, Butler assumed the post of Dean and Principal Professor at the Law School of New York University in 1838, and, presumably, used the instructional method he had created. There is some doubt as to whether many of his colleagues and successors used the same method. Hurst indicated that John Norton Pomeroy in 1865 turned to the

more modern case method, abandoning a type of lecture method in use before his time at New York University. J. W. Hurst, *The Growth of American Law—The Law Makers* 261 (1950).

31. Pound, 'Joseph Henry Beale', 56 *Harv. L. Rev.* 695, 696 (1943).

32. Bishop, 'The Common Law as a System of Reasoning; How and Why Essential to Good Government; What its Perils, and How Averted', 22 *Am. L. Rev.* 1 (1888).

33. One of Mr Bishop's blistering attacks against the practice of having junior research assistants write treatises which subsequently appeared under the name of some illustrious author.

34. Ibid. at 18.

35. Ibid. at 19–20.

36. Pound, 'Joseph Henry Beale', 56 *Harv. L. Rev.* 695, 696 (1943).

37. Beale, 'Development of Jurisprudence', 18 *Harv. L. Rev.* 271, 283 (1905).

38. Mallory, 'Philosophical Classification of Law', 1 *Am. L. S. Rev.* 137 (1904).

39. Mallory, 'The Theory of the American Digest Classification Scheme', 1 *Am. L. S. Rev.* 184 (1905).

40. Ibid. at 185.

41. Abbott's quotation could not be located.

42. As quoted by J. W. Hurst, *The Growth of American Law—The Law Makers* 262 (1950).

43. Yet the simplest remedy against the overflow of case-law, occasioned by useless publication of non-innovatory decisions, was not articulated for almost another century. In 1963, finally, the New York Bar leadership decided against continuation of indiscriminate publication of all decisions. See Flavin, 'Law Books Limited—Toward a Reduction in Opinions', 35 *N.Y. St. B. J.* 165 (1953).

CHAPTER IV

1. J. B. Ames, *Lectures on Legal History* 365 (1916), Lecture entitled 'The Vocation of the Law Professor', delivered in 1901.

2. Ibid. at 366–369.

3. Ibid. at 366–367.

4. Ibid. at 368–369.

5. Leon Radzinowicz, *In Search of Criminology* 63 (1961).

6. Eberhard Schmidt, *Einführung in die Geschichte der deutschen Strafrechtspflege* 352 (2nd ed. 1951).

7. Andenaes, *Introduction* to H. Schjoldager and F. Backer, *The Norwegian Penal Code* 1 (3 Am. Series of For. Penal Codes, 1961).

8. In lieu of many, see Beecher, 'Criminal Law Reform', 69 *Alb. L. J.* 26 (1907).

9. In general see Harry Elmer Barnes, *The Repression of Crime* 36 (1926).

10. Note, 'Crime in America', 118 *Law Times* 371 (1905).

11. Ibid.

12. See Sullivan, 'French Treatment of Juvenile Delinquents', 64 *Alb. L. J.* 386 (1902); ibid., 'The Salvation of Juvenile Delinquents', 64 *Alb. L. J.* 127 (1902); ibid., 'Ancient Modes of Determining Guilt or Innocence', 64 *Alb. L. J.* 396 (1902).

   L. D. Landrum was another writer who meets our general assessment. See, e.g., Landrum, 'Defective Administration of the Law', 64 *Alb. L. J.* 285 (1902); ibid., 'Temporary Emotional Insanity As A Defense Against a Charge of Crime', 56 *Cent. L. J.* 104 (1903).

13. Ferrari, 'The Public Defender, The Complement to the District Attorney', 2 *J. Crim. L. and Crim.* 704, 715 (1912).

14. Ferrari, 'Political Crime', 20 *Colum. L. Rev.* 308, 314–316 (1920).

15. Ferrari, 'Should Criminology Be Taught in the Law School?', 2 *J. Crim. L. and Crim.* 826, 830 (1912).

16. Ferrari, 'The Public Defender', *supra* n. 13 at 704.

17. See his publications, 'Society's Defense Against The Criminal', 63 *Alb. L. J.* 12 (1901); id., 'The Proposed Penal Code of the United States', 14 *Green Bag* 12 (1901); and others.

18. See Anderson, 'A Comparative Study of Feeble-Mindedness Among Offenders in Court', 8 *J. Crim. L. and Crim.* 428 (1917); id., 'The Laboratory in the Study and Treatment of Crime', 5 *J. Crim. L. and Crim.* 840 (1915); id., 'The Alcoholic As Seen in Court', 7 *J. Crim. L. and Crim.* 89 (1916); id., 'A Study of the Physical Condition of One Thousand Delinquents Seen in Court', 10 *J. Crim. L. and Crim.* 82 (1917), with C. M. Leonard; id., 'A Classification of Borderline Mental Cases Amongst Offenders', 6 *J. Crim. L. and Crim.* 689 (1916); id., 'Drug Users in Court', 7 *J. Crim. L. and Crim.* 903 (1917); and many other publications.

19. As quoted in Viner, 'The Intellectual History of Laissez Faire', 3 *J. Law and Econ.* 45, 68 (1960).

20. See Jerome Hall, *Crime and Social Progress* esp. 331–375 (1902); *contra:* G. Mueller, '*Mens Rea* and the Law Without It', 58 *W. Va. L. Rev.* 34, 35, 44–47 (1955).

21. Dillon, 'A Century of American Law', 22 *Am. L. Rev.* 30 (1888), esp. 43–44.

22. In general, Leon Radzinowicz, *A History of English Criminal Law*, vol. II, *The Movement for Reform*; vol. III, *The Reform of the Police* (1957); and G. Mueller, Book Review, 49 *J. Crim. L., C. and P. S.* 158, 159 (1958).

23. We have already mentioned Francis Wharton, the exception to the rule, i.e., a legal scholar who also acted as a criminologist.

24. See Arthur E. Fink, *Causes of Crime* 244–245 (1938).

25. Charles Caldwell, 'New Views on Penitentiary Discipline and Moral Education and Reformation of Criminals', 7 *Phren. J.* 384, 493 (Edinburgh, 1831–1832); id., *Elements of Phrenology* (1824). For bibliography see Fink, op. cit. *supra* n. 24, at 253, 267–268; biography, ibid., at 4, n. 6. Charles Caldwell, 1772–1853, founder of medical school at Transylvania University, Lexington, Ky. III *Dict. Am. Biog.* 406; Caldwell, *Autobiography of Charles Caldwell* (1855).

26. Benjamin Rush, *An Inquiry into the Effects of Public Punishment upon Criminals and upon Society* (1787); id., *Diseases of the Mind* (1811)—first psychiatric book published in America. For bibliography see Fink, op. cit. *supra* n. 24, at 259. Biography, ibid., at 49, n. 2. Benjamin Rush, 1745–1813, leading physician, signer of Declaration of Independence.

27. Isaac Ray, *A Treatise on the Medical Jurisprudence of Insanity* (1838). For bibliography see Fink, op. cit. *supra* n. 24, at 259, 293. Isaac Ray, 1807–1881, founder of American forensic psychiatry, whose book influenced the English judges in the famous M'Naghten case. Biography, Winfred Overholser, 'Isaac Ray', in *Pioneers in Criminology* ch. 6 (Mannheim ed. 1960), with exhaustive bibliography.

28. Doe, Charles, 1830–1896, Associate Justice (1859–1874), Chief Justice (1876–1896), Supreme Court of New Hampshire, opinions in 39 N.H.–68 N.H. Reik, *The Doe-Ray Correspondence: A Pioneer Collaboration in the Jurisprudence of Mental Disease*. Biography and bibliography, Kenison, 'Charles Doe', in *Pioneers in Criminology*, ch. 7 (ed. H. Mannheim, 1960); John Reid, *Chief Justice; The Judicial World of Charles Doe* (1967).

29. T. D. Crothers, physician, asylum superintendent and prolific periodical contributor who related criminality to inebriety, 1842–1918. Bibliography, Fink, op. cit. *supra* n. 24, at 254, 270–271. Biography, ibid., at 81, n. 21.

30. G. Frank Lydston, *The Diseases of Society* (1904); id., 'A Contribution to the Hereditary and Pathological Aspects of Vice', 46 *Chicago Med. J. and Exam.* 131 (1883). Bibliography, Fink, op. cit. *supra* n. 24, at 257, 285–286. G. Frank Lydston, 1858–1923, medical practitioner and surgeon, held chair in criminal anthropology, Kent College of Law, Chicago; latter-day phrenologist. Biography, Fink, op. cit. *supra* n. 24, at 16, n. 43. 11 *Dict. Am. Biog.* 513.

31. Harry Elmer Barnes, *The Repression of Crime* esp. 327 (1926).

32. For a brief assessment see the American Bar Association, *Administration of Justice Survey*; Arthur H. Sherry, *The Administration of Criminal Justice in the United States* 102–105 (1955).

33. John Howard, *The State of Prisons* (1777); id., *An Account of the Principal Lazarettos in Europe* (1789).

34. 4 Blackstone, *Commentaries* 11. Bentham, a student of Blackstone, followed his mentor's non-retributive approach but much more vigorously.

35. For general accounts on the competition between the Pennsylvania and the New York systems see G. O. Rusche and Otto Kirchheimer, *Punishment and Social Structure* 127–130 (1939); Harry Elmer Barnes, *The Repression of Crime* 162 (1936); Harry Elmer Barnes and N. K. Teeters, *New Horizons in Criminology* 505–545 (9th pr., 1950), to name but a few.

36. A. Lenz, *Die Anglo-Amerikanische Reformbewegung im Strafrecht* 16 (1908).

37. Ibid., loc. cit.

38. Lithner, 'Karl Roeder, ein vergessener Gefängnisreformer', 73 *Z. ges. Str. W.* 487 (1961).
39. Their report on the two competing American systems appeared in 1833: *Système Pénitentiaire aux Etats-Unis*, translated into English by Francis Lieber, as *On the Penitentiary System in the United States* (1833); translated into German by Nikolaus Heinrich Julius, as *Amerikas Besserungssystem* (1833).
40. See H. E. Barnes and N. K. Teeters, *New Horizons in Criminology*, op. cit. *supra* n. 35, at 537.
41. N. H. Julius, *Vorlesungen über Gefängniswissenschaft* (1837); id., *Die amerikanischen Besserungssysteme* (1837); id., *Nordamerikas sittliche Zustände* (1839).
42. G. M. Obermaier, *Anleitung zur vollkommenen Besserung der Verbrecher in den Strafanstalten* (1835).
43. Generally see Frank Freidel, *Francis Lieber, Nineteenth-Century Liberal* 216–218 (1947); T. S. Perry, *The Life and Letters of Francis Lieber* (1882); Francis Lieber, *A Popular Essay on Subjects of Penal Law and On Uninterrupted Solitary Confinement at Labor* (1838).
44. Carl J. A. von Mittermaier, *Gefängnisverbesserung* (1858).
45. Theodor Tellkampf, *Über die Besserungsgefängnisse in Nordamerika und England* (1844).
46. Lithner, op. cit. *supra* n. 38.
47. In general see Teeters, 'The First International Penitentiary Congresses 1846–47–57', 26 *Pris. J.* 191 (1946).
48. For a brief account of the history of probation, parole and good behavior systems, see Paul W. Tappan, *Crime, Justice and Correction* 539–549, 714–719 (1961).
49. Lenz, op. cit., *supra* n. 36, *passim.*
50. See Tappan, op. cit. *supra* n. 48, at 543–549, tracing the background of probation.
51. E.g., *Mass. Laws*, June 15, 1870, Chapter 359; *Michigan Law of 4/29/1873*, Chapter 171.
52. Tappan, op. cit. *supra* n. 48, at 387–389.
53. Editorial, 'Dr. Gault Retires as Editor-in-Chief of the Journal', 51 *J. Crim. L., C. and P. S.* 1–3 (1960). See also Editorial (Wigmore), 23 *J. Crim. L. and Crim.* 3 (1932).
54. The committee on translation of treatises on criminal law stimulated the Modern Criminal Science Series, published under the auspices of the American Institute of Criminal Law and Criminology.
    1. *Modern Theories of Criminality* by C. Bernaldo de Quiros, of Madrid. Translated from the Second Spanish edition by Dr Alfonso de Salvio, Assistant Professor of Romance Languages in Northwestern University. With an American Preface by the Author and an Introduction by W. W. Smithers, of the Philadelphia Bar.
    2. *Criminal Psychology* by Hans Gross, Professor of Criminal Law in the University of Graz, Austria, Editor of the Archives of Criminal Anthropology and Criminalistics, etc. Translated from the Fourth German edition by Dr Horace M. Kallen, Professor of Philosophy

in Wisconsin University. With an American Preface by the Author, and an Introduction by Joseph Jastrow, Professor of Psychology in the University of Wisconsin.

3. *Crime, Its Causes and Remedies* by Cesare Lombroso, late Professor of Psychiatry and Legal Medicine in the University of Turin, author of *The Criminal Man*, Founder and Editor of the 'Archives of Psychiatry and Penal Sciences'. Translated from the French and German editions by Rev. Henry P. Horton, M.A., of Ithaca, N.Y. With an Introduction by Maurice Parmelee, Associate Professor of Sociology in the University of Missouri.

4. *The Individualization of Punishment* by Raymond Saleilles, Professor of Comparative Law in the University of Paris. Translated from the Second French edition by Mrs Rachel Szold Jastrow, of Madison, Wis. With an Introduction by Roscoe Pound, Professor of Law in Harvard University.

5. *Penal Philosophy* by Gabriel Tarde, Late Magistrate in Picardy, Professor of Modern Philosophy in the College of France, and Lecturer in the Paris School of Political Science. Translated from the Fourth French edition by Rapelje Howell, of the New York Bar. With an Editorial Preface by Edward Lindsey, of the Warren, Pa., Bar, and an Introduction by Robert H. Gault, Assistant Professor of Psychology in Northwestern University.

6. *Crime and its Repression* by Gustav Aschaffenburg, Professor of Psychiatry in the Academy of Practical Medicine at Cologne, Editor of the *Monthly Journal of Criminal Psychology and Criminal Law Reform*. Translated from the Second German edition by Adalbert Albrecht. With an Editorial Preface by Maurice Parmelee, Associate Professor of Sociology in the University of Missouri, and an Introduction by Arthur C. Train, formerly Assistant District Attorney for New York County.

7. *Criminology* by Raffaelle Garofalo, late President of the Court of Appeals of Naples. Translated from the First Italian and the Fifth French edition by Robert W. Millar, of Chicago, Professor in Northwestern University Law School. With an Introduction by E. Ray Stevens, Judge of the Circuit Court, Madison, Wis.

8. *Criminality and Economic Conditions* by W. A. Bonger, Doctor in Law of the University of Amsterdam. Translated from the French by Henry P. Horton, M.A., of Ithaca, N.Y. With an American Preface by the Author, and an Editorial Preface by Edward Lindsey, of the Warren, Pa., Bar, and an Introduction by Frank H. Norcross, Justice of the Supreme Court of Nevada.

9. *Criminal Sociology* by Enrico Ferri, of the Roman Bar, and Professor of Criminal Law and Procedure in the University of Rome, Editor of the *Archives of Psychiatry and Penal Sciences, The Positivist School in Penal Theory and Practice*, etc. Translated from the Fourth Italian and Second French edition by Joseph I. Kelly, late Lecturer on Roman Law in Northwestern University, and Dean of the Faculty of Law in the University of Louisiana, and John Lisle, late

of the Philadelphia Bar. With an American Preface by the Author, an Editorial Preface by William W. Smithers, of the Philadelphia Bar, and Introductions by Charles A. Ellwood, Professor of Sociology in the University of Missouri, and Quincy A. Myers, formerly Chief Justice of the Supreme Court of Indiana.

55. See 'Crime and Immigration' (Report of Committee G, of the Institute), 4 *J. Crim. L. and Crim.* 523, 534–5 (1913).

56. See the 'Honoring John H. Wigmore' memorial number of the *J. Crim. L. and Crim.*, 32 *J. Crim. L. and Crim.* 261 (1941).

57. See van Hamel, 'The International Union of Criminal Law', 2 *J. Crim. L. and Crim.* 22 (1911).

CHAPTER V

1. Arthur E. Fink, *Causes of Crime* 211–239 (1938).

2. Henry M. Hurd, 'Imbecility with Insanity', 45 *Am. J. Insanity* 261 (1888).

3. Isaac N. Kerlin, 'The Moral Imbecile', *Proc. Nat. Conf. of Charities and Correction* 244 (1890).

4. Martha Louise Clark, 'The Relation of Imbecility to Pauperism and Crime', 10 *Arena* 788 (1894).

5. Walter E. Fernald, 'The Imbecile with Criminal Instincts', *Proc. Am. Medico-Psych. Ass'n* 363 (1908).

6. Charles W. Burr, 'Imbecility and Crime and the Legal Restraint of Imbeciles', 11 *Pa. Med. J.* 696 (1908).

7. Fink, op. cit. *supra* n. 1, at 218–219.

8. Ibid.; Hugo Münsterberg, *On the Witness Stand* 242–245 (1908).

9. Henry H. Goddard's long line of publications culminated in his book *Feeble-Mindedness, Its Causes and Consequences* (1914).

10. Ibid. at 9.

11. William Healy, *The Individual Delinquent* (1915).

12. Gault, 'Highlights of 40 Years in the Correctional Field—And Looking Ahead', 17 (1) *Fed. Prob.* 3, 3–4 (1953).

13. But the feeble-mindedness theory was recently revived: Frank E. Cooper, *A Comparative Study of Delinquents and Non-Delinquents* (1960). Dr McCord wrote of the book: 'The book suffers from several major handicaps. Perhaps the most critical fault is Dr Cooper's failure to include any of the studies of the last thirty-two years. . . . [I]t may serve only to shift public concern from major to minor—if not totally irrelevant—issues.' McCord, Book Review, 51 *J. Crim. L., C. and P. S.* 643, 644 (1961).

14. Fink, op. cit. *supra* n. 1, at 212.

15. Anon., 'Imbecility and Homicide: Case of Gregor MacGregor', 23 *Am. J. Insanity* 563 (1867).

16. Oliver Wendell Holmes, *The Common Law* 50 (1881).

17. Pieski, 6 (1) *J. Off. Therapy* 9 (May, 1962); 15 *Vand. L. Rev.* 671 (1962). For earlier attempts see Note, 'Mental Deficiency as Reducing the Degree of the Offense', 79 *U. Pa. L. Rev.* 209 (1930), and references therein.

18. Bogart, 'Asexualization of the Unfit', 29 *Medical Herald* 298 (1910); Committee Report (Hunter), 'Sterilization of Criminals', 5 *J. Crim. L. and Crim.* 514 (1914); Cook, 'The Innocent Criminal', 7 *So. Med. J.* 717 (1914); Foster, 'Hereditary Criminality and Its Certain Cure', 22 *Pearson's Magazine* 565 (1909); Parsons, 'The Prophylaxis of Criminality', 44 *Am. Practitioner and News* 348 (1910); Smith, 'Marriage, Sterilization and Commitment Laws Aimed at Decreasing Mental Deficiency', 5 *J. Crim. L. and Crim.* 364 (1914).

19. For the line of reasoning refuting the intelligence test theories, see Jerome Michael and Mortimer Adler, *Crime, Law and Social Science* 109–119, 160–169 (1933).

20. Cesare Lombroso, *Crime, Its Causes and Remedies* (1911); and see p. 108, *supra*.

21. August Drähms, *The Criminal: His Personnel and Environment* (1900), with an Introduction by Lombroso; Francis Alice Kellor, *Experimental Sociology* (1901); A. MacDonald, *Criminology* (1893), dedicated to Lombroso.

22. Fink, op. cit. *supra* n. 1, at 111.

23. Charles Goring, *The English Convict: A Statistical Study* (1913).

24. In general see Paul W. Tappan, *Crime, Justice and Correction* (1960), discussing the work of Kraepelin, Hooton, Sheldon, Kretzschmer, Maher and Gundlach, and others.

25. E. A. Hooton, *The American Criminal, An Anthropological Study* (1939); id., *Crime and the Man* (1939).

26. Sheldon Glueck and Eleanor T. Glueck, *Physique and Delinquency* (1956); id., *Unraveling Juvenile Delinquency* (1950).

27. Sheldon Glueck and Eleanor T. Glueck, *Physique and Delinquency* 217 (1956).

28. Louis Berman, *The Glands Regulating Personality* (1922); M. G. Schlapp and E. H. Smith, *The New Criminology* (1928); and see Podolsky, 'The Chemical Brew of Criminal Behavior', 45 *J. Crim. L., C. and P. S.* 675 (1955).

29. Dalnar Devening, as cited in 46 *Med.-Leg. J.* 64–65 (1929).

30. Paul W. Tappan, *Crime, Justice and Correction* 98, 99 (1960).

31. Maurice de Fleury, *The Criminal Mind* 115 (1901).

32. William A. White, *Insanity and the Criminal Law* (1923); id., *The Repression of Crime* (1925).

33. Robert H. Gault, *Criminology* 33 (1932).

34. William Healy, *The Individual Delinquent* (1915).

35. William Healy and Mary T. Healy, *Pathological Lying, Accusation, and Swindling* (1922); William Healy and Augusta F. Bronner, *Delinquents and Criminals: Their Making and Unmaking* (1926); William Healy, *Mental Conflicts and Misconduct* (1926); William Healy and Augusta F. Bronner, *Reconstructing Behavior in Youth* (1929); Franz Alexander and William Healy, *The Roots of Crime* (1935); William Healy and Augusta F. Bronner, *New Light on Delinquency and its Treatment* (1936).

36. Bernard Glueck, *Studies in Forensic Psychiatry* (1916); id., 'A Study

of 608 Admissions to Sing Sing Prison', [1918] *Mental Hygiene* (2) 85.

37. Sheldon Glueck's first work was *Mental Disorder and the Criminal Law* (1925).
38. Clarence Darrow, *The Pleas of Clarence Darrow* 27 (1924).
39. Ibid. at 71.
40. Ibid. at 73.
41. Ibid. at 74.
42. E.g., White, 'Need for Cooperation Between Lawyers and Psychiatrists in Dealing with Crime', 13 *A. B. A. J.* 551 (1927).
43. E.g., Menninger, 'Medico Legal Proposals of the American Psychiatric Association', 19 *J. Crim. L. and Crim.* 367 (1928).
44. Paul W. Tappan, *Crime, Justice and Correction* 113 (1960).
45. Gregory Zilboorg, 'Psychoanalysis and Criminology', in *Encyclopedia of Criminology* 398, 402 (ed. Branham and Kutash 1949).
46. Ibid., loc. cit. Note the use of the phrase 'if you will' by the free will-denying psychoanalyst.
47. Ibid. at 402. See also Gregory Zilboorg, *Mind, Medicine and Man* (1943); id., *Psychology of the Criminal Act and Punishment* (1954).
48. Benjamin Karpman, *The Sexual Offender and his Offenses* 218 (1954). For an earlier claim to that effect see Davis, 'The Psychology of Crime and the Stigmata of Degeneration', 19 *Case and Com.* 820, 826 (1913): 'Let us turn our jails and our penitentiaries into schools and hospitals.' And see also H. E. Barnes, *The Repression of Crime* (1926); id., *Battling the Crime Wave* (1931).
49. E.g., Benjamin Karpman, *Case Studies in the Psychopathology of Crime*, 4 vols. (1933–1957); id., *The Individual Criminal—Studies in the Psychogenetics of Crime* (1935); id., *The Sexual Offender and his Offenses; Etiology, Pathology, Psychodynamics, and Treatment* (1954); id. (editor), *Archives of Criminal Psychodynamics*.
50. Franz Alexander and Hugo Staub, *The Criminal, The Judge and the Public* (1931). See also the second edition published in 1956.
51. E.g., Zilboorg, op. cit. *supra* n. 43.
52. Karpman, Foreword to 'Symposium on Psychopathy', Special Issue, *Archives of Criminal Psychodynamics* ii (1961).
53. Preface to Benjamin Karpman, *The Individual Criminal: Studies in the Psychogenetics of Crime* at vii (1935). This book bears the following dedication (p. iii): 'Dedicated to Doctor William A. White, Teacher and Friend, whose broad sympathies and visions have inspired and encouraged me to do this work on behalf of our doubly unfortunate friends, The Criminal Insane.'
54. Preface to Benjamin Karpman, *The Individual Criminal: Studies in the Psychogenetics of Crime* at viii (1935).
55. Ibid.
56. According to a list on the title page of *Criminal Responsibility*, Charles Mercier's books included the following: *Nervous System and the Mind* (1902); *Psychology, Normal and Morbid* (1901); *Conduct and Its Disorders* (1900); *A New Logic* (1913); *Crime and*

Criminals (1919); *Causation and Belief* (1926). *Criminal Responsibility* (1926) was awarded the Swimey Prize, jointly given by the Society of Arts and the Royal College of Physicians, for the best book on medical jurisprudence (Introduction at 9).

57. Osman, Introduction to Charles Mercier, *Criminal Responsibility* at 7 (1926).
58. Preface to Charles Mercier, *Criminal Responsibility* at 3 (1926).
59. Osman, op. cit. *supra* n. 57, at 28–29.
60. Boris Brasol, *The Elements of Crime* (1927).
61. Ibid. at 186–223.
62. Ibid. at 31–185.
63. Ibid., see esp. the definition at 30.
64. Ibid. at 224–372.
65. John H. Wigmore, Introduction to Boris Brasol, *The Elements of Crime* at xiv (1927).
66. Preface to Boris Brasol, *The Elements of Crime* at ix (1927).
67. For one English response see Oliver C. M. Davis and F. A. Wilshire, *Mentality and the Criminal Law* (1935).
68. Weihofen portrayed a rebellious spirit in 'The Metaphysical Jargon of the Criminal Law', 22 *A. B. A. J.* 267 (1936). May's 4th edition was a work of a considerably more sober scholarship.
69. See Sheldon Glueck, *Mental Disorder and the Criminal Law* 110 (1925), also with citations to attacks upon the draft, and able defense by Professor Keedy. The topic of the insanity defense is more fully discussed in ch. V, sec. 1, *infra*.
70. But many legal-psychiatric court clinics had their origin in that era. E.g., Jacoby, 'Psychopathic Clinic in a Criminal Court—Its Uses and Possibilities', 7 *J. Am. Jud. Soc'y* 21 (1923); Olson, 'Psychopathic Laboratory', 4 *J. Am. Jud. Soc'y* 24 (1920); Shepard, 'Psychopathic Laboratory', 13 *J. Crim. L. and Crim.* 485 (1923); Note, 'Beginnings of a Psychopathic Laboratory in the Criminal Courts of Baltimore', 9 *J. Crim. L. and Crim.* 432 (1918).
71. L. Vernon Briggs, *The Manner of Man That Kills* (1921).
72. Mass. Laws of 1921, ch. 415.
73. Overholser, 'Psychiatry and the Law', in *Encyclopedia of Criminology* 394–398 (ed. Branham and Kutash, 1949).
74. The law, and a few similar statutes in other states, passed after the model of the Briggs Law, are discussed in Mueller, 'Procedure to Determine Responsibility and Fitness to Proceed in Criminal Cases', 3 *Crim. L. Rev.* 29 (1956).
75. Kreutzer, 'Re-Examination of the Briggs Law', 39 *B. U. L. Rev.* 188 (1959).
76. Ibid. at 204.
77. Sutherland, 'The Sexual Psychopath Laws', 40 *J. Crim. L. and Crim.* 543 (1950).
78. ' "[A]lthough the number of persons incarcerated under these statutes is relatively small very serious abuse of fundamental rights is prevalent", ' Jerome Hall, *General Principles of Criminal Law* 453

(2nd ed., 1960), citing Mihm, 'A Re-examination of the Validity of Our Sex Psychopath Statutes in Light of Recent Appeal Cases and Experience', 44 *J. Crim. L., C. and P. S.* 716 (1954).

79. Karpman, 'The Sexual Psychopath', 42 *J. Crim. L., C. and P. S.* 184 (1951), who prefers the term 'paraphiliac neuroses'.

80. Sutherland, *supra* n. 73, at 554.

81. Winfred Overholser, *Mental Hygiene* (1928).

82. Harry Elmer Barnes and N. K. Teeters, *New Horizons in Criminology* 323 (rev. ed. 1950).

83. 'An empirical science of psychology does not exist. . . . What is called theory in psychological literature is speculation and not analysis.' Jerome Michael and Mortimer Adler, *Crime, Law and Social Science* 80, 81 (1933).

84. Ibid.

85. Preface to Sheldon Glueck, *Mental Disorder and the Criminal Law* at xvii n. 1 (1925).

86. Jeffery attributes the trend of disparagement of criminal law to the positivists. See F. James Davis, Foster, Jeffery and Davis, *Society and the Law* 283–285 (1962).

87. Reproduced from Bettman, 'Report on Prosecution', *Nat'l Comm. on Law Obs. and Enf.*, No. 4, 47–49 (1931) [hereinafter cited as 'Bettman']. See also R. Moley, *Our Criminal Courts* (1930); Jerome Michael and Mortimer Adler, *Crime, Law and Social Science* 268 (1933); Harno, 'Some Significant Developments in Criminal Law and Procedure in the Last Century', 42 *J. Crim. L., C. and P. S.* 427, 442–443 (1951).

88. Felix Frankfurter, Preface to Cleveland Foundation, *Criminal Justice in Cleveland* at vii, ix (1922).

89. Ibid. at v.

90. Bettman, op. cit. *supra* n. 87, at 50.

91. Namely conclusions 1–7 and 9, recommending improvements in the police department, the prosecutor's office, the clerk of court's offices, the Municipal Court structure itself, in summary proceedings, in bar admission practice, in the juvenile court set-up, and replacement of the coroner by the medical examiner. Cleveland Foundation, *Criminal Justice in Cleveland* 649–652 (1922).

92. Ibid. at 651.

93. Paul W. Tappan, *Crime, Justice and Correction* 436 (1960).

94. Cleveland Foundation Survey, op. cit. *supra* n. 88, at 652.

95. Ibid. at 557–648.

96. Ibid. at 605. See Roscoe Pound, *Criminal Justice in America* (1930).

97. E.g., for the Illinois Survey, sponsored by the Illinois Association for Criminal Justice, the chapter on 'The Supreme Court in Felony Cases' was written by Albert J. Harno, dean of the College of Law of the University of Illinois and one of the leading authors in the field of criminal law. He also participated in writing the report on probation and parole for the same survey.

Professor, later Dean, Justin Miller (who subsequently wrote the

Hornbook on Criminal Law) was the executive secretary on the Minnesota Survey for part of the time. He was followed by Professor Wilbur H. Cherry, of the University of Minnesota School of Law. See Bettman, op. cit. *supra* n. 87, at 51–52.

98. R. Moley, *The Administration of Criminal Justice in Missouri* 3 (1926).
99. For a brief account see also Thompson, 'The Missouri Crime Survey', 12 *A. B. A. J.* 626 (1926).
100. Bettman, op. cit. *supra* n. 87, at 45.
101. Bettman, op. cit. *supra* n. 87, at 179 (conclusion no. 1).
102. Bettman, op. cit. *supra* n. 87, at 181.
103. Ibid. at 183 (no. 12).
104. Jerome Michael and Mortimer Adler, *Crime, Law and Social Science* 312 (1933).
105. Ibid. at 315.
106. Ibid. at 314, 315.
107. Ibid. at 314 n. 146.
108. Morris Ploscowe, 'A Critique of Federal Criminal Statistics', *Nat'l Comm. On Law Obs. and Enf.*, No. 3, Appendix A, at 199 (1931).
109. Report No. 13 (1931).
110. See 'Message from the President of the United States, January 13, 1930', *H. R. Doc.* No. 252, 71st Cong., 2nd Sess.
111. Ibid. at 2.
112. Ibid., loc. cit.
113. Report No. 13, *The Causes of Crime* at VII (1931).
114. Ibid. at XI–LXXI.
115. Ibid. at LXIX–LXXI. While Mr Anderson's theory may have tended toward the permissiveness of 'social defense', his proposed effort might well have revealed other conclusions than those he supposed to be forthcoming.
116. Ploscowe, op. cit. *supra* n. 108, at 142.
117. See American Bar Association Survey of Criminal Justice, and Kefauver Investigation *infra* at ch. VII, sec. 1, pp. 20, 24.
118. Harno, 'Some Significant Developments in Criminal Law and Procedure in the Last Century', 42 *J. Crim. L., C. and P. S.* 427, 441, 442 (1951).
119. Bruce, Burgess and Harno, 'A Study of the Indeterminate Sentence and Parole in the State of Illinois', 19 *J. Crim. and Crim.* (No. 1, Pt. II) at p. 305 (1928).
120. Ibid. at 6.
121. 3 *Dakota L. Rev.* 285 (1931).
122. 7 *Temple L. Q.* 63 (1932).
123. Currie, 'The Materials of Law Study', 3 *J. Legal Ed.* 331, 337 n. 9 (1951), citing *Handbook*, Ass'n of Am. L. Schools 33 (1928). And see Bordwell, 'Experimentation and Continuity in Legal Education', 23 *Iowa L. Rev.* 297, 305–308 (1938).
124. Compare Radzinowicz' account of criminology in the Netherlands. The law professors there have early taken the initiative in criminological pursuits. The sociologists have rarely entered the field.

C.L.S.—17

Leon Radzinowicz, *In Search of Criminology* 101 (1962). Whether such a total reversal of the American situation is healthy, however, is another matter.

125. *Report on the Causes of Crime*, No. 13, vol. II (1931). A subsequent, more refined work, is Clifford R. Shaw and Henry D. McKay, *Juvenile Delinquency and Urban Areas* (1942).

126. For a complete list of these prominent studies see Ploscowe, op. cit. *supra* n. 108, 'Reference List of Books and Articles Cited', 143–161.

127. Ibid. at 138, 139.

128. Ibid. at 138.

129. Michael and Adler, op. cit. *supra* n. 104, at 169. Ironically enough, in their preface the authors recorded their 'great indebtedness . . .to . . . Morris Ploscowe. . . .' Ibid. at xxviii.

130. Ibid. at 214.

131. Ibid. at 224.

132. Ruml, 'The Subject Matter of Criminology', in 'Crime, Law and Social Science: A Symposium', 34 *Colum. L. Rev.* 273, 276–277 (1934).

133. Llewellyn, 'On Crime, Social Science and Rationalism', op. cit. *supra* n. 132, at 277, 291.

134. Ibid. at 277.

135. Ibid. at 282.

136. McKeon, 'The Science of Criminology', in op. cit. at 291, 309.

137. Michael and Adler, op. cit. *supra* n. 104, at 87.

138. Ibid. at 83.

139. Ibid. at 65.

140. Ibid. at 64.

141. See also Thorsten Sellin, *Culture, Conflict and Crime, passim* (1938).

142. Ibid. at 24.

143. Ibid. at 23.

144. Paul W. Tappan, *Crime, Justice and Correction* (1960).

145. E.g., C. Ray Jeffery. See F. J. Davis, H. H. Foster, Jr., C. R. Jeffery and E. E. Davis, *Society and the Law* 283–285 (1962).

146. Ibid. at 305–306. And see ch. VII, *infra*, at note 40.

CHAPTER VI

1. See also H. W. Chaplin, *Cases on Criminal Law* (temp. ed. 1891; 2nd ed. 1896), with the editorial note: 'To accompany this volume: The Law of Crimes. By John Wilder May. Second Edition. Edited by Joseph Henry Beale, Jr.'

2. J. L. Knowlton, *Cases on Criminal Law* (1902). As far as ascertainable, there were no subsequent editions. In the same year there appeared a slim volume of *Cases in Criminal Procedure* as published by James H. Webb, of the Yale University 'Law Department'.

3. Also in 1935 there appeared W. E. Mikell's separate volume, *Cases on Criminal Procedure*. Mikell's *Illustrative Cases on Criminal Law*

(2nd ed. 1915), was designated as a 'Companion Book to Clark on Criminal Law (3rd ed.)'. It was one of the 'Hornbook Case Series' of the West Publishing Company.

4. When Goethe's Mephistopheles had knocked at law professor Faust's studio door for the second time, and for the second time the professor had shouted his 'enter', Mephisto's voice was heard to say: 'You'll have to call it thrice.'

5. (1) Roscoe Pound, 'What Can Law School Do For Criminal Justice?', paper read on December 29, 1926, before the round table meeting of the AALS in Chicago, reprinted in 6 *Am. L. S. Rev.* 127 (1927). (2) Pound, 'Toward a Better Criminal Law', speech before the conference of the American Bar Association, reprinted in 60 *ABA Rep.* 322 (1935). (3) Pound, Introduction to Rollin M. Perkins, *Cases on Criminal Law* at xiii (1950). Dean Pound addressed himself to the improvement of criminal justice on at least seventeen further occasions, but the other statements were not aimed directly at legal education. See Franklyn C. Setaro, *The Bibliography of the Writings of Roscoe Pound* (1942), items 102, 106, 110, 112, 141, 146, 172, 210, 212, 242, 265, 278, 281, 345, 363, 394, 428.

6. Pound, 'What Can Law Schools Do For Criminal Justice?', 6 *Am. L. S. Rev.* 127, 132 (1927).

7. Preface to Francis B. Sayre, *A Selection of Cases on Criminal Law* at vi (1927).

8. Roscoe Pound, Introduction to Sayre, op. cit. *supra* n. 7, at xxxviii.

9. Ibid. at xxxix.

10. Du Parq, 'The Place of Criminal Law in Legal Education', [1937] *J. Soc'y Pub. Teach. of Law* 31, 33.

11. The leading English casebook on criminal law includes a chapter on evidence in criminal cases. J. W. C. Turner and A. L. Armitage, *Cases on Criminal Law* (1953; 2nd ed. 1958). See Mueller, Book Review, 44 *J. Crim. L., C. and P. S.* 493 (1953); Foster, Book Review, 50 *J. Crim. L., C. and P. S.* 167 (1959).

12. Robert B. Patterson, *Jurisprudence—Men and Ideas of the Law* 537 (1953).

13. Ibid. at 556.

14. Ibid. at 554.

15. Loc. cit.

16. Ibid. at 554–555. See also F. James Davis, Foster, Jeffery and Davis, *Society and the Law* 374–377 (1962).

17. Pound, op. cit. *supra* n. 5. Roscoe Pound was not a 'realist'. Indeed, 'realism . . . that caldron of ideas was a witches' brew that revolted such moderate pragmatists as Pound and Cardozo': Patterson, op. cit. *supra* n. 12, at 538. But even a 'moderate pragmatist', or 'sociological jurisprudent', as Pound could well experience dissatisfaction with the existing state of affairs!

18. Edwin R. Keedy, *Cases on Administration of Criminal Law* (1928).

19. Hertzberg, Book Review, 42 *Harv. L. Rev.* 295 (1928). Other reviews at: 18 *Calif. L. Rev.* 336 (1928); 14 *Cornell L. Q.* 125 (1928); 24 *Ill. L.*

Rev. 498 (1928); 3 *Ind. L. J.* 576 (1928); 20 *J. Crim. L. and Crim.* 309 (1928); 27 *Mich. L. Rev.* 984 (1928); 14 *St. Louis L. Rev.* 446 (1928); 7 *Texas L. Rev.* 194 (1928); 76 *U. Pa. L. Rev.* 882 (1928). Having myself been instructed in criminal law administration with this book, I should say that it did not impress me as either overly liberal or overly practical.

20. Pound, Introduction to Perkins, *Cases on Criminal Law and Procedure, supra* n. 5, at XIII (1950). It is not quite apparent why Hughes' work—he was the first to have joined criminal law and procedure in one volume—was thought to be less successful. See Thomas W. Hughes, *Cases on Criminal Law and Procedure* (1922). After Sayre, it became customary to combine criminal law and procedure in one casebook, e.g., Warren B. Miller, *Illustrative Cases on Criminal Law* (Hornbook Case Series, 1934). This trend prevented the emergence of a separate criminal procedure casebook series. After Keedy's criminal procedure casebook, only four others were to appear on the market to date: C. A. Keigwin, *Cases in Criminal Procedure* (1939), see Stevens, Book Review, 27 *Geo. L. J.* 820 (1939); Edwin R. Keedy and Robert E. Knowlton, *Cases and Statutes on the Administration of Criminal Law* (rev. ed. 1955); B. J. George, Profitt and De Vine, *Statutes, Rules and Cases on Criminal Procedure* (2nd. ed. 1961); 2 vols., mimeographed. W. E. Mikell's book *Criminal Procedure* (3rd ed. 1935) was merely a separate edition of the procedural part of his casebook. On the local level, many mimeographed or even printed procedure casebooks have been published, e.g., F. E. Horack, *West Virginia Cases on Criminal Procedure* (1933); R. H. Kuh, *Materials for Course on Criminal Procedure* (N.Y.U., 1959); J. W. McKenna, *Cases and Materials on Criminal Law Procedures* (1960).

21. For a review of Mikell's Third edition (1935) see Harno, Book Review, 36 *Colum. L. Rev.* 1189 (1936). For other reviews, through several editions, see 12 *Chi.-Kent L. Rev.* 71 (1933); 18 *Marq. L. Rev.* 64 (1933); 22 *Calif. L. Rev.* 466 (1934); 1 *U. Chi. L. Rev.* 662 (1934); 47 *Harv. L. Rev.* 1085 (1934); 22 *Ky. L. J.* 655 (1934); 82 *U. Pa. L. Rev.* 880 (1934); 8 *St John's L. Rev.* 443 (1934); 7 *S. Calif. L. Rev.* 485 (1934); 20 *Va. L. Rev.* 603 (1934); 44 *Yale L. J.* 185 (1934); 14 *Chi.-Kent L. Rev.* 104 (1935); 24 *Geo. L. J.* 780 (1935); 20 *Iowa L. Rev.* 865 (1935); 21 *Iowa L. Rev.* 831 (1936); 24 *Ky. L. J.* 515 (1936); 1 *Mo. L. Rev.* 377 (1936); 11 *Notre Dame Law.* 242 (1936); 11 *St John's L. Rev.* 159 (1936).

22. Pound, op. cit. *supra* n. 5.

23. An entire criminal record was reprinted in the book, the purposes and aims of criminal law were stressed, notes and bibliographies were inserted, new and modern cases replaced ancient ones, and text was interspersed. See Morgan, Book Review, 4 *J. Legal Ed.* 473 (1952), who, as an evidence teacher, was not happy about the authors' trespasses into that field. Further reviews at 11 *Brook. L. Rev.* 116 (1941); 11 *Fordham L. Rev.* 123 (1942); 10 *Geo. Wash. L. Rev.* 258

(1941); 59 *Harv. L. Rev.* 1414 (1946); 31 *Ky. L. J.* 92 (1942); 3 *La. L. Rev.* 848 (1941); 15 *St John's L. Rev.* 350 (1941).

24. J. B. Waite, *Cases on Criminal Law and Procedure* (1931).
25. See Monroe, Book Review, 33 *J. Crim. L. and Crim.* 175 (1942).
26. Preface to C. E. Hughes, *A Treatise on Criminal Law and Procedure* III (1919).
27. Preface to Walter B. Miller, *Handbook of Criminal Law* at v (1934).
28. Ibid., loc. cit. Later on in the text the author refers to the revelations of the criminological research projects and the crime surveys. Ibid. at 10–15.
29. Morris Ploscowe, *Crime and Criminal Law*, in Vol. II of *The National Law Library* (1939). Other authors of the National Law Library were Professors Roscoe Pound, Howard L. Bevis, Francis S. Philbrick, Nathan Isaacs and Max Radin.
30. Preface to Morris Ploscowe, *Crime and Criminal Law*, op. cit. *supra* n. 29, at vii (1939).
31. Ibid. at ix.
32. See also A. E. Wood and J. B. Waite, *Crime and Its Treatment* (1941), a criminological textbook of the American Sociology Series. Professor Waite also gained wide recognition as a contributor to legal periodicals, especially in criminal procedure. For one of his finest articles on substantive law see his recently published 'The Legal Approach to Crime and Correction', 23 *Law and Contemp. Prob.* 594 (1958). For an assessment of Waite's casebook see *supra* n. 24.
33. J. B. Waite, *Criminal Law in Action* 9 (1934).
34. E.g., Harry Best, *Crime and the Criminal Law in the United States* (1930); Sheldon Glueck, *Crime and Justice* (1936).
35. Mueller, Bibliography of Local Practice Books on Criminal Law and Procedure, 59 *Law Lib. J.* 295 (1966).
36. R. A. Anderson, *Wharton's Criminal Law and Procedure* (5 vols., 1957).
37. Allen, Book Review, 27 *U. Chi. L. Rev.* 406 (1960).
38. E.g., Darrow, 'What to Do About Crime, A Stenographic Copy of an Address, Dec., 1926', 6 *Neb. L. B.* 117 (1928).
39. Hand, 'Have the Bench and Bar Anything to Contribute to the Teaching of Law?', 24 *Mich. L. Rev.* 466, 468 (1926).
40. Benjamin N. Cardozo, Introduction to *Selected Readings on the Law of Contracts* at ix (1931).
41. For a recent restatement of a similar view, long held by Judge Goodrich, see Goodrich, 'The Role of the Law School in a Democratic Society', [1956] *U. Ill. L. For.* 253, 259. See also Harno, 'The Law Schools—Center of Legal Research and Scholarship', 12 *J. Legal Ed.* 193, 200 (1959).
42. Rheinstein, 'Critique: Contracts to Make a Will', 30 *N. Y. U. L. Rev.* 1224 (1955). For further comments on law review scholarship see Mueller (editorial note), 'The West Virginia Law Review—Law Reviews and the Courts', 58 *W. Va. L. Rev.* 372 (1956); Mueller and Skolnick, 'Bar Reactions to Legal Periodicals: The West Virginia

Survey', 11 *J. Legal Ed.* 197 (1958); Friedman, 'A Comment on "Bar Reactions to Legal Periodicals: The West Virginia Survey" ', 11 *J. Legal Ed.* 384 (1959); Mueller and Skolnick, 'More on the West Virginia Survey', 12 *J. Legal Ed.* 249 (1959).

43. 14 *Ill. L. Rev.* 465 (1920).

44. Ibid. at 478.

45. Ibid. at 636.

46. Roscoe Pound, *Outlines of Lectures on Jurisprudence* 60 (4th ed. 1928). See also Cleveland Foundation, *Criminal Justice in Cleveland* 562 (ed. Pound and Frankfurter, 1922).

47. MacDonald, 'The Classification of Crimes', 18 *Corn. L. Q.* 524, 561 (1933).

48. Ibid. at 562.

49. Ibid. at 562–563.

50. Among the pioneer organizers and classifiers of the criminal law, Professor Alfred Le Roy Gausewitz, late dean of the University of New Mexico College of Law, deserves particular mention. See Gausewitz, 'Reclassification of Certain Offenses as Civil instead of Criminal', 12 *Wis. L. Rev.* 365 (1937).

51. While Professor Jerome Hall, who was to become the most outstanding exponent of the analytical approach in America, published several early analytical pieces at that time, ('Nulla Poena Sine Lege', 47 *Yale L. J.* 165 (1937); 'Criminal Attempt—A Study of Foundations of Criminal Liability', 49 *Yale L. J.* 789 (1940); 'Prolegomena to a Science of Criminal Law', 89 *U. Pa. L. Rev.* 549 (1941)), he really belongs to a later and more mature period and will be discussed *infra*, ch. IX.

52. Strahorn, 'Criminology and the Law of Guilt' (pts. 1, 2), 84 *U. of Pa. L. Rev.* 491, 600, 621 (1936); reprinted, 15 *Md. L. Rev.* 287, 327 (1955).

53. See also Strahorn, 'Probation, Parole and Legal Rules of Guilt', 26 *J. Crim. L. and Crim.* 168 (1935), which constitutes a step towards the integration of the legal normative and the behavioristic knowledge. See also Strahorn, 'The Effect of Impossibility on Criminal Attempts', 78 *U. Pa. L. Rev.* 962 (1930), an analytically sound and fact-conscious publication. See also Strahorn, 'Preparation for Crime as a Criminal Attempt', 1 *Wash. and Lee L. Rev.* 1 (1939) which indicates further sound, analytical and fact-conscious thinking.

54. For early writings by Walter H. Hitchler see 'Arson: As Affected by the Act of April 25, 1929', *P. L.* 767, 34 *Dick. L. Rev.* 131 (1930); 'Motive as an Essential Element of Crime', 35 *Dick. L. Rev.* 108 (1931); 'The Definition of Crime', 38 *Dick. L. Rev.* 207 (1934); 'The Physical Element of Crime', 39 *Dick. L. Rev.* 95 (1935). Hitchler is also reputed to have published a book dealing with the general principles of criminal law, but diligent research revealed no copy at the Dickinson Law School or the leading law libraries throughout the country.

55. Hitchler, 'Irresistible Impulse to Commit Crime', 35 *Dick. L. Rev.* 145 (1931).
56. But it did not even remotely approach the interest engendered by the Durham Rule of the mid-1950s. See Dorothy Campbell Tompkins, *Insanity and the Criminal Law: A Bibliography* (1960).
57. Keedy, 'Criminal Responsibility of the Insane—A Reply to Professor Ballantine', 12 *J. Am. Inst. Crim. L. and Crim.* 14 (1921), first stated in Keedy, 'Insanity and Criminal Responsibility', 2 *J. Am. Inst. Crim. L. and Crim.* 521 (1911). See also Keedy, 'Insanity and Criminal Responsibility' (pts. 1, 2), 30 *Harv. L. Rev.* 535, 724 (1916). For Keedy's later views see id., 'Irresistible Impulse as a Defense in the Criminal Law', 100 *U. Pa. L. Rev.* 956 (1952). The topic of the 'insanity' defense will be more fully discussed in ch. IX, sec. 1, *infra*.
58. Ballantine, 'Criminal Responsibility of the Insane and Feeble Minded', 9 *J. Am. Inst. Crim. L.* 485 (1919).
59. For Keedy's last article of significance to criminal theory see Keedy, 'Criminal Attempts at Common Law', 102 *U. Pa. L. Rev.* 464 (1954).
60. See Sayre, 'Present Significance of *Mens Rea* in the Criminal Law', in *Harvard Legal Essays* 399 (1934); '*Mens Rea*', 45 *Harv. L. Rev.* 974 (1932); 'Criminal Attempts', 41 *Harv. L. Rev.* 821 (1928); see also op. cit. *infra*., nn. 61–63.
61. Sayre, 'Criminal Responsibility for the Acts of Another', 43 *Harv. L. Rev.* 689, 717 (1930).
62. Ibid. at 717–719.
63. Sayre, 'Public Welfare Offenses', 33 *Colum. L. Rev.* 551 (1933). Sayre went as far as to advocate the abolition of the insanity and infancy defenses to statutory violations, so that infants and insane persons would be subject to criminal punishment. See Mueller, 'How to Increase Traffic Fatalities: A Useful Guide for Modern Legislators and Traffic Courts', 60 *Colum. L. Rev.* 944 (1960).
64. 85 *U. Pa. L. Rev.* 549 (1937).
65. Ibid. at 551, 552.
66. Ibid. at 561–562.
67. Ibid. at 559.
68. E.g., Harno, 'Some Significant Developments in Criminal Law and Procedure in the Last Century', 42 *J. Crim. L., C. and P. S.* 427, esp. 443 (1951). Occasionally Harno, especially in his younger years, was tempted to go along with as yet unproven scientific hypotheses, e.g., 'Medicine and the Law', 3 *U. Kan. City L. Rev.* 43 (1935), but with advancing age and wisdom he returned to sound propositions, e.g., 'Some Significant Developments in Criminal Law and Procedure in the Last Century', *supra* n. 68, regarding the irresistible impulse defense.
69. 40 *Yale L. J.* 53 (1930).
70. 41 *Harv. L. Rev.* 453 (1928).
71. 23 *Mich. L. Rev.* 443 (1925).
72. 43 *Yale L. J.* 691 (1934).
73. 37 *Colum. L. Rev*, 701. 1261 (1937).

74. Edgerton, 'Corporate Criminal Responsibility', 36 *Yale L. J.* 827 (1927).
75. This is a selected list of procedure articles by Professor Waite: 'Co-operation Between the Judiciary and the Police', 4 *Mich. State B. J.* 273 (1925); 'Incongruities in Michigan Statutes Regarding Punishments', 5 *Mich. State B. J.* 510 (1926); 'What is Being Done About Crime', 6 *Mich. State B. J.* 100 (1927); 'Code of Criminal Procedure: Problem of Bail', 15 *A. B. A. J.* 71 (1929); 'Some Inadequacies in the Law of Arrest', 29 *Mich. L. Rev.* 448 (1931).
76. Lester Orfield, *Criminal Appeals in America* (1939), followed by id., *Criminal Procedure from Arrest to Appeal* (1947).
77. See New York University, *Federal Rules of Criminal Procedure—Institute Proceedings*, Vol. VI (1946).

CHAPTER VII

1. Schwerin, 'In Memory of Vladimir Gsovski', 54 *Law Lib. J.* 165 (1961).
2. See Vladimir Gsovski and Kazimierz Grzybowski, *Government, Law and Courts in the Soviet Union and Eastern Europe* (2 vols., 1959).
3. Vladimir Gsovski, *The Statutory Criminal Law of Germany* (1947).
4. E.g., N. S. Timasheff, *One Hundred Years of Probation, 1841–1941* (1941); id., *Probation in Contemporary Law* (N.Y.U., 1941); id., 'The Dutch Prison System', 48 *J. Crim. L., C. and P. S.* 608 (1958); id., 'The Retributive Structure of Punishment', 28 *J. Crim. L. and Crim.* 396 (1937). See also his important article, 'What is the Sociology of Law?' [1937] *Am. J. Soc.* 43.
5. See ch. V, *supra.*
6. Preface to Jerome Michael and Herbert Wechsler, *Criminal Law and its Administration* at vi (1940).
7. Gustav Aschaffenburg, *Crime and Its Repression* (transl. Albrecht 1913); id., 'Psychiatry and Criminal Law', 32 *J. Crim. L. and Crim.* 3 (1941). See also Hans von Hentig, 'Pioneers in Criminology, II, Gustav Aschaffenburg (1866–1944)', 45 *J. Crim. L., C. and P. S.* 117 (1954); also in *Pioneers in Criminology* 327 (Mannheim, ed. 1960).
8. G. O. Rusche and Otto Kirchheimer, *Punishment and Social Structure* (1939); Otto Kirchheimer, *Political Justice* (1961); id., 'Criminal Omissions', 55 *Harv. L. Rev.* 615 (1942); id., 'The Act, The Offense and Double Jeopardy', 58 *Yale L. J.* 513 (1949).
9. Kurt Schwerin, *Classification for International Law* (1947); id., *Classification for International Law and Relations* (2nd ed. 1958); id., 'Biographical Services in Criminology', 41 *J. Crim. L. and Crim.* 254 (1950).
10. Richard Honig, *A Treatise on American Criminal Law* (in German), for the German series 'Mezger-Schönke-Jescheck, Das Ausländische Strafrecht der Gegenwart', vol. 4 (1963); see also Richard Honig, *Humanitas und Rhetorik in Spätrömischen Kaisergesetzen* (1960),

reviewed in Mueller, Book Review, 35 *Temple L. Q.* 116 (1961); Honig, 'Deutsche Strafrechtsreform im Lichte amerikanischer Rechtsgrundsätze', 70 *Z. ges. Str. W.* 616 (1958).

11. E.g., von Hentig, 'Redhead and Outlaw—A Study in Criminal Anthropology', 38 *J. Crim. L. and Crim.* 1 (1947); id., 'The Suspect: A Study in the Psychopathology of Social Standards', 39 *J. Crim. L. and Crim.* 19 (1948); id., 'The Criminality of the Negro', 30 *J. Crim. L. and Crim.* 662 (1940).

12. Note to von Hentig, 'The Problem of Returning to the Scene of the Crime', in *Essays in Criminal Science* 52 (ed. G. Mueller, 1961).

13. E.g., von Hentig, 'The Doctrine of Mistake, A Study in Comparative Criminal Law', 16 *U. Kan. City L. Rev.* 17 (1947); id., 'The Limits of Deterrence', 29 *J. Crim. L. and Crim.* 555 (1938).

14. Wolff and Shartel, 'Civil Justice in Germany', 42 *Mich. L. Rev.* 863 (1944); Wolff, 'Criminal Justice in Germany', 42 *Mich. L. Rev.* 1067 (1944).

15. Schwenck, 'The Administrative Crime, Its Creation and Punishment by Administrative Agencies', 42 *Mich. L. Rev.* 51 (1943); id., 'Criminal Codification and General Principles of Criminal Law in Germany and the United States—A Comparative Study', 15 *Tul. L. Rev.* 541 (1941).

16. Soler, 'The Political Importance of Methodology in Criminal Law', 37 *J. Crim. L. and Crim.* 366 (1943).

17. The Spanish refugee scholars of criminal law, for the most part, went to South America. Professor Jiménez de Asúa, probably the world's most prolific author on criminal law, lives in Argentina. Professor Lopez-Rey came to the United States through the United Nations, as Chief of the Section on Social Defense. Professor Emilio Gonzalez came to the United States after a stay in South America. All of them exercised some influence on both South American and North American criminal law. As to Jiménez de Asúa see Mueller, 'Causing Criminal Harm', in *Essays in Criminal Science* 167, 199 n. 15 (ed. G. Mueller, 1961); Mueller, 'On Common Law *Mens Rea*', 42 *Minn. L. Rev.* 1043, 1046 n. 14 (1958). As to Lopez-Rey, e.g., Lopez-Rey, 'Some Misconceptions in Contemporary Criminology', in *Essays in Criminal Science, supra*, at 300. As to Gonzalez, see Emilio Gonzalez, *The Argentine Penal Code* (Vol. 6, American Series of Foreign Penal Codes, 1963).

18. Leon Radzinowicz, *A History of the English Criminal Law and its Administration from 1750* (4 vols., 1948, 1956, 1957, 1968); and id., *In Search of Criminology* (1961); id., *Penal Reform in England* (1940; 2nd ed. 1946); ed., *Sexual Offences* (1957); ed., *The Journal of Criminal Science*; id., *Ideology and Crime* (1966).

19. Grzybowski, 'Main Trends in the Soviet Reform of Criminal Law', 9 *Am. U. L. Rev.* 93 (1960); id., 'Soviet Criminal Law Reform of 1958', 35 *Ind. L. J.* 125 (1960); id., 'Extraterritorial Effect of Soviet Criminal Law After the Reform of 1958', 8 *Am. J. Comp. L.* 515 (1959).

20. Grzybowski, 'New French Constitution', 8 *Am. J. Comp. L.* 214 (1959); id., 'Reform and Codification of Polish Laws', 7 *Am. J. Comp. L.* 393 (1958); id., 'Powers Trial and the 1958 Reform of Soviet Criminal Law', 9 *Am. J. Comp. L.* 393 (1958); and see note 19, *supra.*

21. E.g., Hall, Moreland, Tappan and others, to be commented upon below. See also Norval Morris and Colin Howard, *Studies in Criminal Law* (1964).

22. E.g., Leon Radzinowicz (ed.), Cambridge Studies in Criminology; Glover, Mannheim and Miller (eds.), The Library of Criminology. See Mueller, Book Review, 54 *Law Lib. J.* 188 (1961).

23. E.g., The Judicial Administration Series; Publications of the Comparative Criminal Law Project; American Series of Foreign Penal Codes. The increase has been greater in other fields of law and in the social sciences.

24. (1) Bi-lateral Studies in Private International Law; (2) The Legal Almanac Series; (3) Research in the Law Series. Oceana has also published separate monographs of interest, e.g., Joseph M. Snee and A. Kenneth Pye, *Status of Forces Agreements and Criminal Jurisdiction* (1957).

25. The first in criminal law: *Essays in Criminal Science* (ed. G. Mueller, 1961), dedicated to Dr R. H. Gault and the *Journal of Criminal Law, Criminology and Police Science*, on their fiftieth anniversary. The first in civil law: K. H. Nadelmann, A. T. von Mehren and J. H. Hazard, *XXth Century Comparative and Conflicts Law* (1961), dedicated to Prof. Yntema.

26. E.g., *Criminal Law Seminar* (ed. Julius Cohen, 1960), *Police Power and Individual Freedom* (ed. Claude R. Sowle, 1962).

27. Jerome Hall, *Studies in Jurisprudence and Criminal Theory* (1958); Francis A. Allen, *The Borderland of Criminal Justice* (1964); Helen Silving, *Essays in Criminal Procedure* (1964).

28. *Pioneers in Criminology* (ed. Mannheim, 1960); *Fundamental Law in Criminal Prosecutions* (ed. Harding, 1959); *Freedom and Responsibility* (ed. Morris, 1961); *The Sociology of Punishment and Correction* (ed. Johnston, Savitz and Wolfgang, 1962); *The Sociology of Crime and Delinquency* (ed. Johnston, Savitz and Wolfgang, 1962); *International Criminal Law* (ed. Mueller and Wise, 1965).

29. *Crime and Insanity* (ed. Nice, 1958); *Sociology of Crime* (ed. Roucek, 1961); *Crime in America* (ed. Bloch, 1961); *Sexual Behavior and the Law* (ed. Slovenko, 1965).

30. E.g., The New York Philosophical Library; The Free Press of Glencoe, Inc.

31. E.g., Morris Ploscowe, *Sex and the Law* (1961); paperback edition (1962).

32. The following have joined the theretofore sole American journal in the field of criminal law and criminology: *Crime and Delinquency* (formerly *NPPA Journal*); *International Journal of Offender Therapy* (formerly *APTO Journal*); *Archives of Criminal Psychodynamics*;

Federal Probation; Excerpta Criminologica; and—duplicating the name of a previously established Canadian journal—*The Criminal Law Quarterly* (of the American Bar Association). Many other journals in the English language are being published abroad, and many American journals are devoted to such related topics as police science, criminalistics and criminological research.

33. Simply by way of illustration, during the year 1960/61, the following law review symposia on criminal law were published (listing authors):

(1) 'Psychopathy, Part I', *Arch. Crim. Psychodynamics*, 389 (1961) (articles by Beardsley, Bender, Bergler, Bromberg, Dalman, Diamond, Edel, Fox, Gilbert, Guttmacher, Hodges, Jacob, Katzenelbogen, Kozel, Lipton, Maradie, Maughs, Mueller).

(2) 'The Cuyahoga County Juvenile Court', 10 *Clev.-Mar. L. Rev.* 507 (1961) (articles by Blackley, Columbro, Harpst).

(3) 'Psychiatry and the Law', 9 *Clev. Mar. L. Rev.* 399 (1960) (articles by Crawfis, Davidson, Eliasberg, Gokayt, Harder, Perr, Rood, Szasz).

(4) 'Selected Problems—California Business Regulation' [Criminal as well as civil], 12 *Hastings L. J.* 227 (1961) (articles by Ellis and McCloskey, Hederman and Dahlinger, Oppenheim).

(5) International Symposia Celebrating the 50th Anniversary of the Journal of Criminal Law, Criminology and Police Science:

(a) 'The Privilege against Self-Incrimination', 51 *J. Crim. L. C. and P. S.* 129 (1960) (articles by MacNaughton, Sowle, Wyman and foreign commentators).

(b) 'Police Detention and Arrest Privileges', 51 *J. Crim. L., C. and P. S.* 385 (1960) (articles by Foote, Remington, Wilson and foreign commentators).

(c) 'Police Interrogation Privileges and Limitations', 52 *J. Crim. L., C. and P. S.* 1 (1961) (articles by Inbau, Mueller, Weisberg and foreign commentators).

(d) 'The Exclusionary Rule Regarding Illegally Seized Evidence', 52 *J. Crim. L., C. and P. S.* 245 (1961) (articles by Allen, McGarr, Paulsen, and foreign commentators).

(6) 'The M'Naghten Test of Criminal Responsibility', 59 *Legal Aid Rev.* 2 (1961) (articles by Abrahamsen, Carr, Kuh).

(7) 'The Right to Counsel', 45 *Minn. L. Rev.* 693 (1961) (articles by Beaney, Boskey, Celler, Cuff, David, Douglas, Gordon, Kadish, McKesson, Pollit, Pollock, Rauh).

(8) 'Capital Punishment', 7 *N. Y. L. F.* 249 (1961) (recorded statements of a large panel).

(9) 'The Impartial Medical Expert' [Criminal as well as civil], 34 *Temp. L. Q.* 357 (1961) (articles by Griffen, Guttmacher, Levy, Polsky, Schroeder, van Dusen).

(10) 'Current Problems in Criminal Law I and II', 1960 *U. Ill. L. F.* 481; 1961 *U. Ill. L. F.* 1 (in honor of Dean Emeritus Albert Harno) (articles by Bennett, Kamisar, Mueller, Paulsen, Perkins, Remington, Rosenblum, Rubin, Weihofen).

During the year 1959/60, the following criminal law symposia were published in America:

(a) 'The Comparative Study of Conditional Release', 108 *U. Pa. L. Rev.* 290 (1960).

(b) 'Criminal Law', 38 *Texas L. Rev.* 819 (1960).

(c) 'Drunkenness and Alcoholism', 3 *Crim. L. Q.* 43 (1960).

(d) 'Juvenile Delinquency', 8 *J. Pub. L.* 499 (1959).

(e) 'The Mental Health Act', 1959, 23 *Mod. L. Rev.* 410 (1960).

(f) 'Psychiatry and Law', 9 *Clev.-Mar. L. Rev.* 399 (1960).

(g) 'Sex Offenses', 25 *Law and Contemp. Prob.* 215 (1960).

(h) 'The Wiretapping-Eavesdropping Problem: Reflections on The Eavesdroppers', 44 *Minn. L. Rev.* 811 (1960).

34. Professors Glueck, J. Hall, Mueller, Orfield, Perkins, Ploscowe, Silving, Wechsler, and Weihofen.

35. Some recent examples are: 'Developments in the Law: Criminal Conspiracy', 72 *Harv. L. Rev.* 920 (1959); 'Developments in the Law: Entrapment', 73 *Harv. L. Rev.* 1333 (1960); Dubin and Robinson, 'The Vagrancy Concept Reconsidered: Problems and Abuses of Status Criminality', 37 *N. Y. U. L. Rev.* 102 (1962); Symposium, 'Role of Common Law Concepts in Modern Criminal Jurisprudence', 49 *J. Crim. L., C. and P. S.* 250, 350, 415 (1958); Note, 'A Logical Analysis of Criminal Responsibility and Mandatory Commitment', 70 *Yale L. J.* 1354 (1961); Note, 'Amnesia: A Case Study in the Limits of Particular Justice', 71 *Yale L. J.* 109 (1961); Note, 'The Effect of Marriage on the Rules of the Criminal Law', 61 *Colum. L. Rev.* 73 (1961).

36. Contributors to the *Annual Survey of American Law, Criminal Law and Procedure* included Professors Darby, Ploscowe, McKenna, Teppen, Collings, and the author. State Surveys are now available for many states, including Colorado, Florida, Georgia, Kansas, Louisiana, Missouri, New Jersey, New York, North Carolina, Ohio, Pennsylvania, South Carolina, Tennessee, Virginia, and U.S. Supreme Court.

37. (1) Harno, 'Some Significant Developments in Criminal Law and Procedure in the Last Century', 42 *J. Crim. L., C. and P. S.* 427 (1951).

(2) L. Hall, 'The Substantive Law of Crimes—1887–1936', 50 *Harv. L. Rev.* 616 (1937).

(3) Warner and Cabot, 'Changes in the Administration of Criminal Justice During the Past Fifty Years', 50 *Harv. L. Rev.* 583 (1937).

(4) *Journal of Criminal Law and Criminology*, vol. 24, issue 1 (1933). Century-of-Progress essays.

38. American Bar Research Center, *Publication No. 1*, May, 1954, and supplements. Conceivably the list is incomplete, though all law schools were requested to report the theses filed. For purposes of this evaluation, the theses filed with the University of Idaho (undergraduate degree), with the U.S. Army Judge Advocate General's

School, and with the discontinued Northeastern law school, have been disregarded. These were little more than term papers.
39. This definition of scholarly purpose in criminal law, emphasizing crime control, is a bit dangerous in that it may lead to research emphasis on crime prevention at the expense of the broader aspects of criminal law, especially the understanding and conceptualization of crime as such. Several of the recently created institutes seem to have taken the narrower view of the definition, though it may be too early to document the point.
40. F. J. Davis, H. H. Foster, Jr., C. R. Jeffery and E. E. Davis, *Society and the Law*, 305–306 (1962):

> In the United States from 1920 to 1950 many sociology departments offered courses in criminology, based on sociological and psychological studies of criminals. Most of the textbooks published on criminology and penology have been written by sociologists. Today more and more of this work has been taken over by law schools and schools of social work. A good example of this shift is the one that occurred at the University of Chicago. During the 1920s and 1930s Chicago was the leader in criminological research because it had such men as Ernest Burgess, E. H. Sutherland, and Clifford Shaw. The last criminologist at Chicago was Lloyd Ohlin who is now a member of the New York School of Social Work at Columbia University. Very few sociologists today regard themselves as criminologists compared to thirty years ago. The 1960 program of the American Sociological Association does not include a section on criminology, and the subject appears under deviant behavior. This shift to law schools and schools of social work has given criminology a professional school orientation, which means practical problems in administration of criminal justice are emphasized. Schools of social work are especially interested in topics such as delinquency, probation and parole. Many such schools offer a graduate program in corrections for social workers interested in probation and parole. Here the emphasis is placed on penology rather than criminology.

41. G. Mueller, Introduction to *Essays in Criminal Science* at XVI (ed. Mueller, 1961).
42. Clinard, Book Review, 53 *J. Crim. L., C. and P. S.* 53, 54 (1962).
43. William Dienstein, *Are You Guilty* (1954); David Fellman, *The Defendant's Rights* (1958); Alan Barth, *The Price of Liberty* (1961).
44. The American Bar Association launched a project to study and formulate minimum standards of criminal justice. See Kaufman, 'Reform in Criminal Law: Have the Lawyers Lagged Behind?' 37 *N. Y. S. B. A. J.* 217, 219 (1965); Powell, 'An Urgent Need: More Effective Criminal Justice', 51 *A. B. A. J.* 437 (1965); Note, 'Minimum Standards for Criminal Justice Organization Completed', 3 *Am. Crim. L. Q.* 110 (1965); Goff, 'A.B.A. to Offer Guidelines for Criminal Justice', 40 (3) *Harv. L. Rec.* 16 (1965).

The American Law Institute is working on a model pre-arraignment procedure code. See A.L.I., 42nd *Annual Report*, at 15 (1965).
45. Since this is a survey of criminal law scholarship, these efforts in the

constitutional areas of criminal procedure cannot be separately evaluated, though the names of the principal workers in the field deserve mention: Professors Foote, Kamisar, George, Gowle, J. Goldstein, A. Goldstein, H. Goldstein, Donnelly, Knowlton, Paulsen, and others. Most of them tend to be identified with the civil rights wing, while another group of competent workers more often than not identifies itself with the prosecution's approach to constitutional law questions in criminal procedure. This group is headed by Professor Inbau, and it included Professors Collings, Kuh, Nodrud and others.

The limitation to substantive law also results in the exclusion from consideration of the prolific scholarship in criminal procedure represented by Professor Lester Orfield and others.

46. The Kefauver Report bears the following acknowledgement: 'The Committee wishes to express its appreciation to Judge Morris Ploscowe of New York City and the Commission on Organized Crime of the American Bar Association of which Hon. Robert P. Patterson is chairman, for their valuable assistance in the preparation of this report.' *Third Interim Report of the Special Committee to Investigate Organized Crime in Interstate Commerce*, 82nd Congress, 1st Sess. Rep. No. 307, ii (1951).

47. Merely by way of example: 'Wiretapping, Eavesdropping, and the Bill of Rights, Hearings Before the Subcommittee on Constitutional Rights of the House Committee on the Judiciary', 86th Cong. 1st Sess., pt. 3, July 9, 1959, with thirty-one professorial responses; *Report to the House Committee on the Judiciary*, 86th Cong., 2nd Sess., Committee Print, Feb. 1960, with eighty professorial responses.

48. Wofford, 'Notre Dame Conference on Civil Rights: A Contribution to the Development of Public Law', 35 *Notre Dame Law*. 328 (1960).

49. The United States Supreme Court Advisory Committee on Criminal Rules, appointed by the Chief Justice on April 4, 1960, has four professorial members, though by some incredible oversight this nation's leading academic expert on criminal procedure, Professor Lester Orfield, and the leading practical expert, Judge Holtzoff, were not among the appointees. 25 *F. R. D*. No. 3, i, ix (1960).

50. Lloyd, Justice Office: ' "A Dialogue" ', 40 (3) *Harv. L. Rec*. 1, 4 (1965); Vorenberg, 'The Office of Criminal Justice: Its Role and Its Relationship to State and Federal Law Reforms', 16 (4) *Harv. L. S. Bull*. 5 (1965).

51. E.g., L. I. Paperno and A. Goldstein, *Criminal Procedure in New York* (1960); E. Marks and L. I. Paperno, *Criminal Law in New York* (1961).

52. See Bibliography, op. cit. *supra*. Ch. VI, n. 35.

53. E.g., Mr Justice Douglas, Chief Justice Walter Schaefer, Chief Judge Kenison, Judges Holtzoff, Yankwich, Hofstadter, Bertel and several others.

54. Besides those mentioned in the preceding footnote, Judges Davidson

(Texas) and Hastie have consistently belonged to this group, as revealed by the case analyses undertaken in connection with the Annual Survey of American Law.

55. These are paper-bound handbooks, averaging approximately one hundred pages each, on the following subjects: Problems of a Criminal Defense; Police Interrogation; Electronic Eavesdropping; Assistance to the Indigent Accused; Discovery in Criminal Cases; Intoxication; Responsibility; Punishing Homicide; Obscenity; Sentencing (1962).

56. Among N.Y.U.'s courses and seminars within the general sphere of criminal law, open to members of the bar, are the following:

Criminal Law, Criminal Procedure, Problems in the Administration of Criminal Law, Law of Criminal Correction, Comparative Criminal Law, Comparative Criminal Procedure, International Criminal Law, Social Penal Legislation, Mental Disorder and Crime, The Bill of Rights, Model Penal Codes, Law and Psychology, Law and Sociology, Forensic Medicine, Juvenile Delinquency, The Indigent and the Criminal Law, and related subjects. See 'The Comparative Criminal Law Project', *N. Y. U. Law Center Bulletin*, Spring, 1961, p. 4, col. 1.

57. E.g., Polstein, 'How to "Settle" a Criminal Case', 8 (1) *Prac. Law.* 35 (1962).

58. E.g., M. Comisky, *Basic Criminal Procedure* (1958); Monrad G. Paulsen (ed.), (Joint Committee on Continuing Legal Education of the American Law Institute and the American Bar Association), The Problem of a Criminal Defense; The Problem of Police Interrogation, The Problem of Electronic Eavesdropping; The Problem of Assistance to the Indigent Accused; The Problem of Discovery in Criminal Cases; The Problem of Intoxication; The Problem of Responsibility; The Problem of Punishing Homicide; The Problem of Drafting an Obscenity Statute; The Problem of Sentencing (1961).

59. Mulder, Foreword to M. Comisky, *Basic Criminal Procedure* at iii (1958).

60. E.g., Wallace Mendelson, *Trial Practice-Criminal Cases* (rev. ed. 1955).

61. Murray Schwartz, *Cases and Materials on Professional Responsibility and the Administration of Criminal Justice* (1961).

62. Preface to Jerome Michael and Mortimer Adler, *Crime, Law and Social Science* at XI (1933).

63. Jerome Hall, *Studies in Jurisprudence and Criminal Theory* 8 (1958).

64. Ibid., loc. cit.

65. Ibid. at 9.

66. Ibid., loc. cit.

67. Immanuel Kant, *The Philosophy of Law—An Exposition of the Fundamental Principles of Jurisprudence as the Science of Right* 44 (1797, tr. W. Hastie, 1887). The matter is further discussed in Mueller, 'Criminal Theory: An Appraisal of Jerome Hall's *Studies in Jurisprudence and Criminal Theory*', 34 *Ind. L. J.* 206 (1959).

68. W. L. Clark and W. L. Marshall, *A Treatise on the Law of Crimes* (6th ed., Wingersky, 1958).

69. Preface to Clark and Marshall, op. cit. *supra* n. 68, at vii (1958).

70. Ibid., loc. cit.

71. Ibid. at 6.

72. Moran, 'Ethical Systems, The Human Sciences, and Legal Scholarship: An Excursive Evaluation of Glanville Williams' "The Sanctity of Life and the Criminal Law" ', 11 *J. Legal Ed.* 303, 315 (1959).

73. Preface to Michael and Adler, op. cit. *supra* n. 62, at xi.

74. Which inspired the promulgation of the Federal Rules of Criminal Procedure in 1946, and their recent adoption by many states.

75. Dating back to Wigmore, 'Nova Methodus Discendae Docendaeque Jurisprudentia', 30 *Harv. L. Rev.* 812 (1917), in which he describes six processes, the third of which, legislative process, he particularly advocated.

76. 'A joint committee representing the American Law Institute, The Association of American Law Schools and the American Bar Association have recommended that the Law Institute not only restate the "common law of crimes" but prepare a code of criminal law (Report of the Joint Committee on the Improvement of Criminal Justice, p. 15)." Michael and Adler, op. cit. *supra* n. 62, at 373 n. 61.

77. Glueck, 'Principles of a Rational Penal Code', 41 *Harv. L. Rev.* 453 (1928), reprinted in Sheldon Glueck, *Crime and Correction* 72 (1952).

78. 4 *Tul. L. Rev.* 18 (1929). At that time Louisiana law rested basically on James Workman's Crimes Act of 1805, revised as General Crimes Act, 1855, and as Revised Statutes, 1870, Livingston's draft of 1825 having not been successful.

79. (Pts. 1, 2) 11 *Wis. L. Rev.* 346, 480 (1936), one of the finest pieces of analytical and synthetic scholarship in criminal law. This paper was to play a significant role in the subsequent events leading to codification in Wisconsin. See V Wisconsin Legislative Counsel, *Judiciary Committee Report on the Criminal Code* ii (1953).

80. 27 *J. Crim. L. and Crim.* 1 (1936). See also J. Hall, 'Edward Livingston and His Louisiana Penal Code', 22 *A. B. A. J.* 191 (1936).

81. 85 *U. Pa. L. Rev.* 549 (1937) discussed at length in 'Mueller, The German Draft Criminal Code 1960—An Evaluation in Terms of American Criminal Law', [1961] *U. Ill. L. For.* 25, 25–39 (1961).

82. 27 *J. Crim. L. and Crim.* 629 (1937).

83. Bishop, 'The Common Law as a System of Reasoning—How and Why Essential to Good Government; What Its Perils and How Averted', 22 *Am. L. Rev.* 1 (1888).

84. As late as 1951, Jerome Hall, a member of this cautious school, wanted to emphasize scholarly and analytical work preceding codification attempts. 'The code should not be stressed in the early stages of the work.' Hall, 'The Proposal to Prepare a Model Penal Code', 4 *J. Legal Ed.* 91, 93 (1951). This view will be discussed in ch. IX, sec. 2, *infra*.

85. The various schools of thought seeking criminological refinement prior to codification will be discussed in ch. IX, sec. 2, *infra*.
86. Louisianians belonged to this school and were relatively successful. They did write and promulgate their code, under the very able direction of Louisiana law professors. See Louisiana State Law Institute, *Project of a Criminal Code for the State of Louisiana* (1942), prepared by Professors Dale E. Bennet (La. State University Law School), Clarence J. Morrow (Tulane University College of Law) and Leon Sarpy (Loyola University School of Law), with student and graduate assistance and the advice of Prof. Newman F. Baker of Northwestern University School of Law. See also Morrow, 'The Louisiana Criminal Code of 1942—Opportunities Lost and Challenges Yet Unanswered', 17 *Tul. L. Rev.* 1 (1942); id., 'Civilian Codification Under Judicial Review: The Generality of "Immorality" in Louisiana', 21 *Tul. L. Rev.* 545 (1947) and State v. Vallery, 212 La. 1095, 34 So. 2d 329 (1948); Bennett, 'The Louisiana Criminal Code, A Comparison with Prior Louisiana Criminal Law', 5 *La. L. Rev.* 6 (1942); id., 'Louisiana's Criminal Code of 1942', 20 *U. Kan. City L. Rev.* 208 (1952); Smith, 'How Louisiana Prepared and Adopted a New Criminal Code', 41 *J. Crim. L., C. and P. S.* 125 (1950). The Louisiana Code, luckily completed before the United States' entry into World War II, is a good piece of concise drafting, in the best tradition of Livingston and the spirit of the mid-twentieth century.

New York efforts at a new codification were not successful for a long time. See Rosenzweig, 'The Law Revision Commission and the Criminal Law—Unfulfilled Promise', 40 *Corn. L. Q.* 719 (1955). Notably, New York legislators have always avoided the scholars of criminal law. Very few have ever been invited to serve on criminal code commissions. The first annual report of the Law Revision Commission (1935) sounded very ambitious in terms of simplification of the criminal law, structural changes, consolidation and re-classification. What a Utopian undertaking for politicians and practicing lawyers! The most recent reform commission fortunately included Professor H. Wechsler. This commission submitted the draft of a new penal code: Proposed New York Penal Law, Senate Intro. 3918, Assembly Intro. 5376 (1964). The code was accepted by the 1965 legislature. See n. 147, *infra*.

Illinois' early efforts likewise remained unsuccessful. Proponents and opponents of codification fought their battles on extremely low intellectual levels. For a comment on the Draft Code, 59th General Assembly—House Bill No. 712, which failed to pass, see Note, 'The Draft Code of Criminal Law and Procedure', 30 *Ill. L. Rev.* 226 (1935); Stewart, '[Editorial] Notes on the Proposed New Illinois Criminal Code (House Bill No. 214, 60th G. A. 1937)', 2 *John Marsh. L. Rev.* 418 (1937). As will be described, Illinois' success came quite recently—and still early in comparison with other states—but as late as 1953, Illinoisians had been thinking more or less in terms of legislative patchwork. See Comment, 'Proposed Revisions in the Illinois Criminal Code', 48 *Nw. U. L. Rev.* 198 (1953).

87. Michael and Adler, op. cit. *supra* n. 62, at 373.
88. Ibid. at 371–372.
89. Ibid. at 372 n. 59.
90. *Supra* n. 76.
91. Michael and Adler, op. cit. *supra* n. 62, at 373, n. 61.
92. Ibid., loc. cit.
93. Ibid. at 376–382.
94. Ibid. at 376–378.
95. Ibid. at 384.
96. 37 *Colum. L. Rev.* 701, 1261 (1937).
97. 1940, Supplement 1956.
98. Riesman, 'Law and Social Science: A Report on Michael and Wechsler's Classbook on Criminal Law and Administration', 50 *Yale L. J.* 636 (1941).
99. Jerome Michael and Herbert Wechsler, *Criminal Law and its Administration* 1 (1940).
100. Preface to Michael and Wechsler, op. cit. *supra* n. 99, at V.
101. Ibid., loc. cit.
102. 'Principles' and 'doctrines' are explained *infra*, ch. IX, sec. 2.
103. Riesman, op. cit. *supra* n. 96, at 652.
104. See Wechsler, 'Issues of the Nuremberg Trial', 62 *Pol. Sci. Q.* 11 (1947).
105. See 1962 *A. L. I. Ann. Rep.* 1–2.
106. Francis A. Allen, University of Chicago; Rex A. Collings, Jr., University of California, formerly New York University; Robert E. Knowlton, Rutgers University; Monrad G. Paulsen, Columbia University, formerly University of Minnesota; and Frank J. Remington, University of Wisconsin.
107. Eleven 'Research Associates' are named as having served between 1953 and 1962: A. L. I., *Model Penal Code, Proposed Official Draft* at iv (May 4, 1962), from which all personnel data here discussed are taken.
108. The law professors are the following: Allen, Bennett, Dession (deceased 1955), Donnelly, Glueck, Harno, Hart, Michael (deceased 1953), Ploscowe, Remington, Sherry, and Waite. One of the judges, Joseph Sloane, and one of the practicing attorneys, Samuel Dash, are part-time law teachers. The judges are the following: Curtis Bok (deceased 1962), Charles D. Breitel, Edward J. Dimock, Gerald F. Flood, Stanley H. Fuld, Learned Hand (deceased 1961), Florence N. Kelley, Thomas D. McBride, John J. Parker (deceased 1958), Orie L. Phillips, Joseph Sarafite and Joseph Sloane. The criminologists are the following: Sanford Bates, James V. Bennett, Ernest W. Burgess, Kenneth D. Johnson, Lloyd Ohlin, Russell G. Oswald, Thorsten Sellin, Floyd E. Thompson (deceased 1960) and Will C. Turnbladh. The three psychiatrists are Lawrence Z. Freedman, Manfred S. Guttmacher and Winfred Overholser.

109. His name appears on the Advisory Committee roster through 1955 (Tent. Draft No. 4), but not thereafter.

110. See Hall, 'The Proposal to Prepare a Model Penal Code', 4 *J. Legal Ed.* 91 (1951).

111. The Model Sentencing Act may be found in a symposium, at 9 *Crime and Del.* 337 (1963). See also Murrah and Rubin, 'Penal Reform and the Model Sentencing Act', 65 *Col. L. Rev.* 1167 (1965).

112. Deviating from any precedent, it was also proposed, as a fourth objective, to deal with the 'organization of correction', i.e., the establishment and administration of correctional agencies, and their functions. Wechsler, 'The Model Penal Code Project of the American Law Institute', 20 *U. Kan. City L. Rev.* 205, 205–206 (1952); id., 'The Challenge of a Model Penal Code', 65 *Harv. L. Rev.* 1097 (1952), based on two memoranda prepared for the Advisory Committee on Criminal Law of the American Law Institute: *The Proposal to Prepare a Model Penal Code* and *The Possibilities of the Model Penal Code Proposal.*

113. Wechsler, 'The Challenge of a Model Penal Code', *supra* n. 112, at 1132–1133.

114. Ibid. at 1133.

115. Ibid., loc. cit.

116. Ibid. at 1130. Quaere: Which 'well-developed legal fields?'

117. For Wechsler's later reports see Wechsler, 'Legal Scholarship and the Criminal Law', 9 *J. Legal Ed.* 18 (1956); ibid., 'A Thoughtful Code of Substantive Law', 45 *J. Crim. L., C. and P. S.* 524 (1955); ibid., 'The American Law Institute: Some Observations on its Model Penal Code', 42 *A. B. A. J.* 321 (1956).

118. Wechsler, 'A Thoughtful Code of Substantive Law', 45 *J. Crim. L., C. and P. S.* 524, 528 (1955).

119. Mueller, '*Mens Rea* and the Law Without It', 58 *W. Va. L. Rev.* 34 (1955); id., 'On Common Law *Mens Rea*', 42 *Minn. L. Rev.* 1043 (1958).

120. Model Penal Code § 2.05 (Tent. Draft No. 4, 1955).

121. Model Penal Code § 2.01 (2) (d) (Tent. Draft No. 4, 1955).

122. In effect, the judges in M'Naghten had attempted to write precisely such a formula. See Mueller, 'M'Naghten Remains Irreplaceable: Recent Events in the Law of Incapacity', 50 *Geo. L. J.* 105 (1961).

123. Other problems of the code's responsibility test have been the subject of much oral and written debate. Among the principal points of attack is the code's refusal to take a *clear* stand on psychopathy. Sec. 4.01 (2) of Tent. Draft No. 4.

124. See Mueller, 'Where Murder Begins', 2 *N. H. B. J.* 214 (1960).

125. A.L.I., *Model Penal Code, Proposed Official Draft* (May 4, 1962), Sec. 250.11 (3) ('Cruelty to Animals').

126. Sec. 250.10. Abuse of Corpse. Sec. 250.2. Violation of Privacy.

127. A.L.I., *Foreign Relations Law of the United States, Proposed Final Draft* (1962), § 39, provides that whenever a state has legislative

jurisdiction, it may also exercise judicial jurisdiction, even though such exercise may require a person to engage in conduct which will subject him to (criminal) liability under the law of another state. In such cases, no matter what the defendant may do, he is likely to be punished by one of two interested states. During debate before the Institute, such a rule was regarded as harsh. But the debaters overlooked the fact that a common-law defense, recognized by the criminal law of all civilized nations, will take the sting out of this section. This is the defense of 'collision [or conflict] of [legal] duty', also sometimes called 'legal impossibility', or 'duress of law'. Contrary to what the discussants on the floor believed, nothing in § 39 prevents introduction of this defense by somebody who faces criminal punishment (e.g., for contempt), for failure to do an act abroad which he is ordered to do, in violation of foreign law.

The defense is not restricted to foreign law; there may be collision of legal duties even within domestic law. The *Model Penal Code* (§ 3.03) does not contain the defense. That should not make the draftsmen of the code feel unhappy, the German and other continental codes likewise do not contain the defense, but it is there recognized as a standard common-law defense, discussed by every textbook, affirmed in many decisions. Jürgen Baumann (*Strafrecht-Allgemeiner Teil* 277 (1961)) puts the defense in these terms: The defense exits: 'whenever the perpetrator chooses among two wrongs the smaller one, i.e., violates the smaller of the two legal interests, in order to preserve the higher one, or if he violates the smaller duty to fulfil the more important one. There always must be a real collision, i.e., there must not be a third way out.'

128. Sec. 2.07.
129. Francis, 'Criminal Responsibility of the Corporation', 18 *Ill. L. Rev.* 305, 323 (1924).
130. Mueller, '*Mens Rea* and the Corporation: A Study of the Model Penal Code Position on Corporate Criminal Liability', 19 *U. Pitt. L. Rev.* 21 (1957).
131. Wechsler, 'The American Law Institute: Some Observations on Its Model Penal Code', 42 *A. B. A. J.* 321 (1956).
132. A.L.I., *Model Penal Code, Proposed Official Draft* (May 4, 1962).
133. Very spotty biographic lists, omitting some articles critical of the code, have been published in the American Law Institute's Annual Reports, as follows: 1958: 15–16 (number of listed articles dealing with the M.P.C.); 1959: 21–26; 1960: 13; 1961: 8; 1962: 14.
134. The first report to the French was Schwartz, 'Le Projet du Code Pénal de l'American Law Institute', [1957] *Rev. de Sc. Crim. et de Droit Pén. Comp.* 37. A symposium publication dealing predominantly with the code, by some of the principal collaborators of the Model Penal Code and a few others (Schwartz, Sellin, Wechsler, Collings, Allen, Packer, Donnelly, Miller, Remington, Knowlton, Tappan, Nicolle), will appear as a parallel volume to the series: Marc Ancel, *Les Codes Pénaux Européens*. It has been prepublished in

English under the title 'Crime and the American Penal System' (ed. Schwartz), in the *Annals* (vol. 339, Jan. 1962).

135. See Symposium, 'Sentencing', 23 *Law and Contemp. Prob.* 399 (1958), especially articles by Tappan and Turnbladh. See also Rubin, 'Sentencing and Correctional Treatment Under the Law Institute's Model Penal Code', 46 *A. B. A. J.* 994 (1960). See also Wechsler, 'Correctional Practices and the Law', 17 (1) *Fed. Prob.* 16 (March, 1953).

136. Roth v. United States, 354 U.S. 476 (1957), accepting the standard of A.L.I., *Model Penal Code* § 207.10 (Tent. Draft No. 6, 1957), under which a publication is obscene if, to the average person, applying contemporary community standards, the dominant theme of the material taken as a whole appeals to prurient interests.

137. Vt. Stat. Ann. tit. 13, § 4801 (1) (1958); A.L.I., *Model Penal Code* § 4.01 (1) (Tent. Draft No. 4, 1955).

138. Mostly in preparation of the Wisconsin Code, Professor Remington published two articles, and co-authored many others: Remington, 'A Proposed Criminal Code for Wisconsin', 20 *U. Kan. City L. Rev.* 221 (1952); id., 'Criminal Law Revision—Codification vs. Piecemeal Amendment', 33 *Neb. L. Rev.* 396 (1954); Remington and Helstad, 'The Mental Element in Crime—A Legislative Problem' [1952] *Wis. L. Rev.* 644; Melli and Remington, 'Theft—A Comparative Analysis of the Present and the Proposed Criminal Code', [1954] *Wis. L. Rev.* 253; Remington and Ohlin, 'Sentencing Structure: Its Effect Upon Systems For the Administration of Criminal Justice', 23 *Law and Contemp. Probl.* 495 (1958); Remington, 'Liability Without Fault Criminal Statutes—Their Relation to Major Developments in Contemporary Economic and Social Policy: The Situation in Wisconsin (Introduction to a student research)', [1956] *Wis. L. Rev.* 625. See also Remington and Rosenblum, 'The Criminal Law and the Legislative Process', [1960] *U. Ill. L. For.* 481. The latter gives an excellent insight into the problems about which common-law scholars are particularly concerned when confronted with the task of codification.

139. Wisconsin Legislative Council, 1953 *Report* Vol. V, covering Judiciary Committee Report on the Criminal Code. Professor Young of the University of Wisconsin also served in that capacity.

140. Wisconsin Legislative Council, *supra* n. 139, at ii–iii; Platz, 'The Criminal Code', [1956] *Wis. L. Rev.* 350; Quayle, 'Criminal Law Revision in Wisconsin and Minnesota', 40 *J. Am. Jud. Soc'y* 88 (1956).

141. Platz, *supra* n. 140.

142. Wisconsin Criminal Code, Laws of 1955, ch. 696, effective July 1, 1956

143. Professor Allen has established a fine reputation for criminal law scholarship through participation in a variety of projects and through several solid law-review articles, among them 'Criminal Justice, Legal Values and the Rehabilitative Ideal', 50 *J. Crim. L.*,

C. and P. S. 226 (1959); 'Law and the Future: Criminal Law and Administration', 51 *Nw. U. L. Rev.* 207 (1956); 'The Supreme Court, Federalism, and State Systems of Criminal Justice', 8 *U. Chi. L. S. Record* 3 (Spec. Supp. 1958); 'The Supreme Court, Federalism, and State Systems of Criminal Justice', 8 *De Paul L. Rev.* 213 (1959); 'The Supreme Court and State Criminal Justice', 4 *Wayne L. Rev.* 191 (1958); most of which are reprinted in id., *The Borderland of Criminal Justice* (1964).

144. *Tentative Final Draft of the Proposed Illinois Criminal Code of 1961*, p. 7. Professor Fred E. Inbau, of Northwestern University, likewise served on the Drafting Sub-Committee. Ibid. at 6.

145. *Ill. Ann. Stat. Ch.* 38 (Smith-Hurd, 1961).

146. See *Minn. Stat. Ann.* §§ 609.01–618.21 (1964).

147. N.Y. Sess. Laws 1965, chs. 1030–1031.

148. See Note, 'Proposed Penal Laws of New York', 64 *Col. L. Rev.* 1469 (1964).

149. Wechsler, 'Legal Scholarship and Criminal Law', 9 *J. Legal Ed.* 18, 20 (1956).

150. Herbert Wechsler and Henry M. Hart, 'The Federal Courts and the Federal System' (1953); Herbert Wechsler, *Principles, Politics and Fundamental Law* (1961).

CHAPTER VIII

1. E.g., Preamble to Mass. Const.

2. Schwartz, 'The American Penal System: Spirit and Technique', 339 *Annals* 1, 6 (Jan. 1962).

3. Miller, 'The Public Interest Undefined', Foreword to Symposium: 'The Fundamental Concepts of Public Law', 10 *J. Pub. L.* 184 (1961). Glendon A. Schubert, *The Public Interest* (1960); Smith, 'Public Interest and the Interests of the Accused in the Criminal Process-Reflections of a Scottish Lawyer', 32 *Tul. L. Rev.* 349 (1958).

4. Remington and Rosenblum, 'The Criminal Law and the Legislative Process', [1960] *U. Ill. L. F.* 481 n. 2 (1960).

5. Miller and Remington, 'Procedures Before Trial', 339 *Annals* 111, 115 (Jan. 1962).

6. Schwartz, *supra* n. 2, at 6.

7. Ibid. at 6–7.

8. Remington, 'Criminal Justice Research', 51 *J. Crim. L., C. and P. S.* 7, 12 (1960), citing the opinion of Chief Justice Warren in Spano v. New York, 360 U.S. 315 (1959). That case, of course, dealt only with the supposed conflict between Remington's first and last objectives.

9. There is practically no American literature dealing specifically with the myth of the conflict between the public interest and the interests of the accused. A Scottish criminalist, however, denied the validity of the myth: 'it is submitted that the public interest, which is concerned with the suppression of crime and the maintenance of order, also comprehends an even more important end—the assurance of fair and impartial trial and pre-trial procedure.' Smith, 'Public Interest

and the Interests of the Accused in the Criminal Process-Reflections of a Scottish Lawyer', 32 *Tul. L. Rev.* 349 (1958). How little information on the supposed clash is available elsewhere as well was demonstrated at a symposium of the British Committee of Comparative Law, held at the University of Birmingham, U.K., in the fall of 1964, organized by Dr Smith, and devoted to the same topic as the above cited article, at which the principal European nations were represented. The author represented the United States. The papers delivered at this symposium have been published: J. A. Coutts (ed.), *The Accused* (1966).

The descriptive and purely argumentative literature on the supposed clash has grown with the increased attention which the Supreme Court has paid to the topic in recent years. But these decisions, arrived at under the pressure of the case and the case load, not having the benefit of legislative projection and scholarly depth analysis, likewise has not really contributed to the resolution of the puzzle, however much they have resolved the issues for positive law, for the time being.

10. 'The solution of the ensuing dilemma . . . in [many] . . . civil law countries, has been afforded by adherence to a dual approach, the so-called "dual-track" system, which consists in a systematic differentiation and separation of legal reactions to the delinquent individual.' Silving, ' "Rule of Law" in Criminal Justice', in *Essays in Criminal Science* 75, 103–104 (ed. Mueller, 1961), where the matter is fully discussed. See also Mueller, 'Crime, Punishment and Correction', 45 *Neb. L. Rev.* 58 (1966), for an attempted *single track* solution, under consideration of continental experience.

11. Daniel Glaser, *The Effectiveness of a Prison and Parole System* (1964).

12. Remington, op. cit. *supra* n. 8.

13. The other two categories of research in criminal law are these:

'(1) [T]he study of the function of the appellate court in the definition of what conduct is criminal; (2) the study of the function of the legislature in the definition of criminal conduct.' Remington, op. cit. *supra* n. 8.

Ad (1): Remington complains about (a) lack of scholarly attention to, in effect, the special part of the criminal law; (b) lack of judicial attention to the scholars' work. But Remington overlooks the constantly increasing significance of scholarly writing in both the general and special part of the criminal law. In the U.S. Supreme Court, and in the highest courts of principal states, hardly a thoughtful criminal law decision has been handed down during the past several years in which the views of scholars have not been relied upon. But this is a recent development. Remington demonstrates the lack of scholarly attention to problems of substantive law on the example of vagrancy. 'Because of the nature of the crime, vagrancy seldom reaches the appellate court and, for this reason, has been given little attention in legal research.' Ibid. at 9. But Mr Remington wrote this comment while perhaps no other crime was subject to greater judicial and scholarly scrutiny than that of vagrancy. See H. Warren Dunham, *Homeless Men and Their Habitats—A Research Planning Report* (1953); Lacey, 'Vagrancy and other Crimes of Personal Condition', 66 *Harv. L. Rev.* 1203 (1953); Foote, 'Vagrancy-Type Law and Its Administration', 104 *U. Pa. L. Rev.* 603 (1956); Perkins, The Vagrancy Concept', 9 *Hast. L. J.* 237 (1958); Sherry, 'Vagrants, Rogues and Vagabonds—Old Concepts in Need of Revision', 48 *Calif. L. Rev.* 557 (1960); Douglas, 'Vagrancy and Arrest on Suspicion', 70 *Yale L. J.* 1 (1960); Note, 'Use of Vagrancy-Type Laws for Arrest and Detention of Suspicious Persons', 59 *Yale L. J.* 1351 (1950); Comment, 'The Constitutionality of Loitering Ordinances', 6 *St. Louis U. L. J.* 247 (1960); the definitive scholarly analysis is Dubin and Robinson, 'The Vagrancy Concept Reconsidered: Problems and Abuses of Status Criminality', 37 *N. Y. U. L. Rev.* 102 (1962), discussing all recent cases. See also the decision of the U.S. Supreme Court in Thompson v. City of Louisville, 362 U.S. 199 (1960).

Ad (2): As to research on legislation defining criminal conduct, the thrust of Remington's argument is directed against poor legislative draftsmanship as well as frequent legislative refusal to deal with important problems, such as the requisite frame of mind of offenders. 'The immediate task is to do a more adequate job with the areas of the substantive law which have not been a matter of appellate judicial concern and those which have not heretofore received careful attention in legal research.' Ibid. at 11. It is not easy to differentiate this type of research from that included in Remington's first category. But be that as it may, the more customary complaint has been the opposite, namely that scholars deal precisely with those issues which are the rare concern of courts, i.e., the odd case, and not the bread and butter issue. Witness the enormous literature on insanity, an issue which arises in only a fraction of all criminal cases. But Professor Remington could note with satisfaction that the Model Penal Code, and his own and other state codifications, have already catered for the needs in this research area, though 'the long-run objective must of course be a continuing re-examination of the substantive criminal law in light of increasing knowledge about human behavior'. Ibid. at 11. That, with due respect, is one of the *really* needed types of research; to be discussed, *infra*, secs. 2 and 3. Comparative, analytic and synthetic research, not mentioned by Professor Remington, will be discussed in secs. 4 and 5, *infra*. For a very able recent discussion, arguing that, over the years, the position of the criminal defendant in court has become worse rather than better, see A. S. Goldstein, 'The State and The Accused: Balance of Advantage in Criminal Procedure', 69 *Yale L. J.* 1149 (1960).

14. Remington, op. cit. *supra* n. 8.
15. Ibid., loc. cit.
16. Ibid. at 16–17.
17. See Professor Remington's point (6): 'To what extent does protection

against arbitrary official action require a system of "checks and balances" as well as the promulgation of legal norms?' Remington, op. cit. n. 8, at 17. In another article, published almost simultaneously, Remington and Rosenblum are more specific on the issue of latitude, discretion and ambiguity by design or default. Remington and Rosenblum, 'The Criminal Law and the Legislative Process', [1960] *U. Ill. L. For.* 481 (1960). The current situation being what it is, the authors find that 'it becomes important to determine the basis upon which this kind of discretion is, and should be, exercised'. Ibid. at 497.

18. It is granted, of course, that most state laws are a bit more specific than that in requiring the application of the penal laws by the public prosecutor. The point simply is, that in most such laws there inheres a certain amount of discretion as to whether the criminal process ought to be invoked.

19. In world jurisprudence this is known as the legality principle, as distinguished from the opportunity principle.

20. J. Goldstein, 'Police Discretion Not to Invoke the Criminal Process: Low-Visibility Decisions in the Administration of Justice', 69 *Yale L. J.* 543 (1960), an article based on data gathered by the American Bar Association Survey 'The Administration of Criminal Justice in the United States'.

21. Ibid. at 587.

22. J. Goldstein, 'Police Discretion: The Ideal Versus the Real', 23 *Publ. Adm. Rev.* 140 (1963).

23. Pound, 'Discretion, Dispensation and Mitigation: The Problem of the Individual Special Case', 35 *N. Y. U. L. Rev.* 925 (1960); Breitel, 'Controls in Criminal Law Enforcement', 27 *U. Chi. L. Rev.* 427 (1960); Kadish, 'Legal Norm and Discretion in the Police and Sentencing Processes', 27 *Harv. L. Rev.* 902 (1962).

24. See Estes Kefauver, *Crime in America* (1952): 82nd Congress, 1st Session, Senate Report No. 307, Third Interim Report of the Special Committee to Investigate Organized Crime in Interstate Commerce, pursuant to S. Res. 202 (81st Congress).

25. The only scholar who participated to any material extent is Professor Morris Ploscowe (N.Y.U.), who wrote the final report.

26. Broeder, 'The Function of the Jury: Facts or Fiction', 21 *U. Chi. L. Rev.* 386 (1954); id., 'Report on the Jury Project', 26 *S. D. L. J.* 13 (1957); id., 'The University of Chicago Jury Project', 38 *Neb. L. Rev.* 744 (1959); James, 'Jury's Assessment of Criminal Responsibility', *J. Soc. Probl.* 57 (Summer 1959); James, 'Status and Competence of Jurors', 64 *Am. J. Sociol.* 563 (1959); Strodtbeck, James and Hawkins, 'Social Status in Jury Deliberations', 22 *Am. Sociol. Rev.* 713 (1957); Kalven, 'A Report on the Jury Project', *U. Mich. L. S.*, 1957; id., at 24 *Ins. Council J.* 368 (1957); id., 'The Jury, The Law and the Personal Injury Damage Award', 19 *Ohio St. L. J.* 158 (1958); Meltzer, 'A Projected Study of the Jury as a Working Institution', 287 *Annals* 97 (1953); Stone, 'The Jury as a Working Institution',

266   CRIME, LAW AND THE SCHOLARS (pp. 169–172)

44 *J. Crim. L., C. and P. S.* 776 (1959); Strodtbeck and James, 'An Attempted Replication of a Jury Experiment by Use of Radio and Newspaper', 21 *Pub. Op. Q.* 313 (1957); Strodtbeck and Mann, 'Sex Role Differentiation in Jury Deliberations', 19 *Sociometry* 3 (1956); Zeisel, 'The New York Expert Testimony Project: Some Reflections on Legal Experiments', 8 *Stanf. L. Rev.* 730 (1956).

See also H. Zeisel, H. Kalven and B. Buchholz, *Delay in the Court* (1959): 'The first book resulting from the Chicago Jury Study Project. A comprehensive, empirical analysis of causes of delay in a metropolitan court and probable success of various proposed remedies for some. This is the first thorough attempt at application of social science techniques to the study of a specific problem of law administration. The results are both interesting and useful.' F. James Davis, H. H. Foster, Jr., C. R. Jeffery and E. E. Davis, *Society and the Law* 225 (1962).

27. E. Davis, in F. James Davis, H. H. Foster, C. R. Jeffery and E. E. Davis, *Society and the Law* 219 (1962). A further volume on the Chicago Jury Study has appeared in the meantime.

28. G. Mueller, *Laymen as Judges in Germany and Austria* (Lithoprint for internal circulation, U. of Chicago, 1954). The study discussed the history of lay participation in the administration of criminal justice in Germany and Austria, and investigated its workings at various periods, under consideration of such factors as historical (political) events, (e.g., peace and war), the ethnic, religious and educational composition of various provinces, crop failures and price structures, etc., on the relation between jury and judge acquittals and jury and judge convictions.

29. Arthur H. Sherry, *The Administration of Justice in the United States—Plan for a Survey to be conducted under the auspices of American Bar Foundation* (1955); note, 'Administration of Criminal Justice', 19 *F. R. D.* 159 (1956).

30. Sherry, op. cit. *supra* n. 29, at 5–7.

31. Ibid. at 13, with descriptions of these methods at pp. 13–17.

32. Ibid. at 19.

33. 'During the survey, on-the-scene studies were made of the administration of criminal justice in three midwestern states—Kansas, Michigan and Wisconsin.' Miller and Remington, 'Proceedings Before Trial', 339 *Annals* 111, 112 (Jan. 1962).

34. *Supra*, nn. 20–22.

35. W. R. La Fave, *Arrest—The Decision To Take A Suspect Into Custody* (1965); D. J. Newman, *Conviction—The Determination of Guilt or Innocence Without Trial* (1966).

36. Remington, op. cit. *supra* n. 8, at 18, n. 35.

37. Clyde E. Sullivan, *The Comparative Study of the Administration of Justice* (mimeo., Chicago, 1962).

38. Administration of Criminal Justice Series:

(1) Pugh, 'Administration of Criminal Justice in France: An Introductory Analysis', 23 *La. L. Rev.* 1 (1962);

(2) Murray, 'The Proposed Code of Criminal Procedure of Guatemala', 24 *La. L. Rev.* 728 (1964);

(3) Murray, 'A Survey of Criminal Procedure in Spain and Some Comparisons with Criminal Procedure in the United States', 40 *N. D. L. Rev.* 7, 131 (1964);

(4) Hardin, 'Other Answers: Search and Seizure, Coerced Confessions, And Criminal Trial in Scotland', 113 *U. Pa. L. Rev.* 165 (1964);

(5) Huston, 'A Preliminary Survey of Criminal Procedure in Thailand', 16 *Syr. L. Rev.* 505 (1965);

(6) Murray, 'Criminal Procedure in the Federal District and Federal Territories of Mexico', 19 *U. Miami L. Rev.* 251 (1964).

39. F. C. Sullivan, P. Hardin, III, J. Huston, F. R. Lacy, D. E. Murray and G. W. Pugh, *The Administration of Criminal Justice—Cases and Materials* (1966).

40. Arthur Beeley, *The Bail System in Chicago* (1927).

41. Note, 'Philadelphia Police Practice and the Law of Arrest', 100 *U. Pa. L. Rev.* 1182 (1952); Note, 'The Administration of Divorce: A Philadelphia Study', 101 *U. Pa. L. Rev.* 1204 (1953); Note, 'Compelling Appearance in Court: Administration of Bail in Philadelphia', 102 *U. Pa. L. Rev.* 1031 (1954); Note, 'Criminal Registration Ordinances: Police Control Over Potential Recidivists', 103 *U. Pa. L. Rev.* 60 (1954); Note, 'Prosecutor's Discretion', 103 *U. Pa. L. Rev.* 1057 (1955); Foote, 'Vagrancy-Type Law and Its Administration', 104 *U. Pa. L. Rev.* 603 (1956); Note, 'The Philadelphia Constable', 104 *U. Pa. L. Rev.* 508 (1956); Note, 'Administration and Enforcement of the Philadelphia Housing Code', 106 *U. Pa. L. Ev.* 437 (1958); Note, 'Preliminary Hearings on Indictable Offenses in Philadelphia', 106 *U. Pa. L. Rev.* 589 (1958); Note, 'Curfew Ordinances and the Control of Nocturnal Juvenile Crime', 107 *U. Pa. L. Rev.* 66 (1958).

42. Previous studies have been financed by the Thomas Skelton Harrison Foundation, the Wiley C. Rutledge Memorial Fund for Studies in Law Enforcement and Individual Liberty (contributed by Jacob Kossman, Esq.) and the school's Alumni Annual Giving.

43. For an example of the application of the same policy in another law school, see Note, 'Metropolitan Criminal Courts of First Instance', 70 *Harv. L. Rev.* 320 (1956).

44. Foote, 'Foreword: Comment on the New York Bail Study', 106 *U. Pa. L. Rev.* 685, 688–689 (1958).

45. Note, 'Compelling Appearance in Court: Administration of Bail in Philadelphia', 102 *U. Pa. L. Rev.* 1031 (1954). See also Note, 'Bail Procedure and Weekend Arraignment Practice in the City Court of Buffalo', 7 *Buffalo L. Rev.* 427 (1958).

46. Articles by Schwartz, Foote, Smith, Dando and Tamiya, Bratholm, Vouin, 'The Comparative Study of Conditional Release', 108 *U. Pa. L. Rev.* 287–365 (1960).

47. Ares and Sturz, 'Bail and the Indigent Accused', 8 *Crime and Del.* 12,

15 (1962). Ares, Rankin and Sturz, 'The Manhattan Bail Project: An Interim Report on the Use of Pre-Trial Parole', 38 *N. Y. U. L. Rev.* 67 (1963).

48. Ibid. The Foote studies and the Vera-N.Y.U. projects have sparked enormous national interest in bail reform. For a listing of projects and publications see the following:

　(1) D. J. Freed and P. Wald, *Bail in the United States* (1964);

　(2) U.S. Dep't. of Justice and Vera Foundation, *National Conference on Bail and Criminal Justice* (1965);

　(3) Id., *Bail and Summons* (1966);

49. The Civil Liberties Center, New York University School of Law 7–8 (Pamphlet, 1961).

50. See the brochure, The Institute of Judicial Administration (1961).

51. Richard R. Korn and R. Simerman, *Magistrates' Court and Special Sessions Court in Manhattan—Protection of Civil Liberties—Practices and Procedures* (mimeo., 1961).

52. Note, 'Minimum Standards for Criminal Justice Organization completed', 3 *Am. Crim. L. Q.* 110 (1965).

53. Max Rheinstein, *Max Weber on Law in Economy and Society* (1954).

54. See Davis, Foster, Jeffery and Davis, op. cit. *supra* n. 27, at chs. 7 (and 8), discussing the work of Alexander, Bryce, Paulsen, Mueller, Gellhorn, Virtue, Glueck and others.

55. See the chapter with that title, by F. Davis, in Davis, Foster, Jeffery and Davis, op. cit. *supra* n. 27, at ch. 1.

56. Preface to Jerome Hall, *Theft, Law and Society* at v (2nd ed. 1952).

57. H. G. Reuschlein, *Jurisprudence—Its American Prophets* 447 (1951).

58. Horvath, Book Review (of the 2nd ed.), 2 *Am. J. Comp. L.* 109, 110 (1953).

59. Ibid.

60. Rheinstein, 'The Law of Divorce and the Problem of Marriage Stability', 9 *Vand. L. Rev.* 633 (1956) and other writings; Llewellyn, 'Behind the Law of Divorce', 32 *Colum. L. Rev.* 1291 (1932), 33 *Colum. L. Rev.* 249 (1933); Foster, 'Common Law Divorce', 46 *Minn. L. Rev.* 43 (1961); Mueller, 'Inquiry into the State of a Divorceless Society', 18 *U. Pitt. L. Rev.* 545 (1957); Morris Ploscowe, *Sex and the Law* (1951); id., *The Truth About Divorce* (1955).

61. Simply by way of example: Antieau, 'Natural Rights and the Founding Fathers—The Virginians', 17 *Wash. and Lee L. Rev.* 43 (1958); Blume, 'Criminal Procedure on the American Frontier: A Study of the Statutes and Court Records of Michigan Territory 1805–1825', 57 *Mich. L. Rev.* 195 (1958); Hubert, 'History of Jurisdiction and Venue in Criminal Cases in Louisiana', 34 *Tul. L. Rev.* 255 (1960); Hutt, 'Criminal Prosecution for Adulteration and Misbranding of Food at Common Law', 15 *Food, Drug and Cosm. L. J.* 382 (1960); Mueller, 'Compensation for Victims of Criminal Violence', 8 *J. Pub. L.* 218 (1959); Reid, 'A Speculative Novelty: Judge Doe's Search for Reason in the Law of Evidence', 39 *B. U. L. Rev.*

321 (1959); id., 'Of Men and Minks and a Mischievous Machinator', 1 *N. H. B. J.* 23 (1959).

62. Jeffery, 'The Development of Crime in Early English Society', 47 *J. Crim. L., C. and P. S.* 647 (1957); Mueller, 'Tort, Crime and the Primitive', 46 *J. Crim. L., C. and P. S.*, 303 (1955), and others.

63. Namely the works of Maine, Pike, Pollack, Maitland, Calhoun and others.

64. Namely the works of Malinowski, Diamond, Schultz-Ewerth, Mead and others.

65. Albert Kocoureck and John H. Wigmore, *Primitive and Ancient Legal Institutions* (1915); Wigmore, *A Kaleidoscope of Justice* (1941); John H. Wigmore, *A Panorama of the World's Legal Systems* (3 vols., 1928).

66. Jerome Hall, *Theft, Law and Society* xv (2nd ed. 1952).

67. Among recent symposia were 'Sentencing', 23 *Law and Contemp. Prob.* 399 (1958); 'Crime and Correction', 23 *Law and Contemp. Prob.* 583 (1958); 'Sex Offenses', 25 *Law and Contemp. Prob.* 215 (1960). A similar service is occasionally being performed by the *Journal of Public Law* (e.g., Symposium, 'Compensation for Victims of Criminal Violence', 8 *J. Pub. L.* 191 (1959)), and indeed many of the regular law reviews.

68. Packer and Gampell, 'Therapeutic Abortion: A Problem in Law and Medicine', 11 *Stan. L. Rev.* 417 (1959).

69. *Abortion in the United States* (ed. Mary S. Calderone, 1958), with amazing medical revelations. Cavan, Book Review, 50 *J. Crim. L., C. and P. S.* 171 (1959).

70. Mills, 'A Medicolegal Analysis of Abortion Statutes', 31 *So. Cal. L. Rev.* 181 (1958).

71. Remington, 'Liability Without Fault Criminal Statutes—Their Relation to Major Developments in Contemporary Economic and Social Policy: The Situation in Wisconsin', [1956] *Wis. L. Rev.* 625 (1956); 'Mueller, How to Increase Traffic Fatalities: A Useful Guide for Modern Legislators and Traffic Courts', 60 *Colum. L. Rev.* 944 (1960), a satirical article.

72. See Bibliography in G. Mueller, *Legal Regulation of Sexual Conduct* (Supp., 1961), particularly works by Tappan, Ploscowe, Radzinowicz and Caprio.

73. But see the California, Illinois and New Jersey Sex Offenders Reports, cited in Mueller, op. cit. *supra* n. 69.

74. Though the even more sophisticated type of research, employing artificial manipulation of variables, was pioneered by a legal scholar, Professor Moore, at the Yale Law School, to be discussed *infra*.

75. F. K. Beutel, *Some Potentialities of Experimental Jurisprudence as a New Branch of Social Science* 193 (1957). The title of the book is not fully descriptive of its contents. 'Experimental jurisprudence', as I understand the term, is restricted to the juridically significant manipulation of social and juridical variables to test hypotheses of

social control. But in his book Beutel discusses virtually all inter-disciplinary research efforts. However, inasmuch as Beutel advocates repetition of fact studies on the workings of laws after each enactment, following the recommendations of each previous evaluation, the whole process method may well be called 'experimental jurisprudence'.

76. Ibid. at ch. XIII.
77. One of the most sensible reviews is Cavers, 'Science, Research and the Law: Beutel's "Experimental Jurisprudence" ', 10 *J. Legal Ed.* 162 (1957).
78. Beutel, op. cit. *supra* n. 75, at 393–402, comments on each law omitted.
79. See Mueller, 'Tort, Crime and the Primitive', 46 *J. Crim. L., C. and P. S.* 303 (1955).
80. Cavers, *supra* n. 77, at 163.
81. Summary of the eight steps by Cavers, *supra* n. 77, at 165–166.
82. To be discussed in ch. IX, *infra*.
83. R. C. Donnelly, Joseph Goldstein and R. D. Schwartz, *Criminal Law* (1962), to be discussed in the next section; J. C. M. Paul and M. L Schwartz, *Federal Censorship: Obscenity in the Mail* (1962); F. James Davis, H. H. Foster, Jr., C. R. Jeffery and E. E. Davis, *Society and the Law* (1962).
84. Beutel, op. cit. *supra* n. 75, at 105–113.
85. Wallace and Canals, 'Socio-legal Aspects of a Study of Acts of Violence', 11 *Am. L. Rev.* 173 (1962).
86. Unpublished Annual Report of the Director of the Criminology Program, University of Puerto Rico, Nov. 1966; on file with the author.
87. I have omitted from discussion the juridically significant criminal-law field research by pure sociologists. There is a vast amount of activity in sociological criminology. But sociologists, not having any legal training, generally feel insecure in the 'core area' of criminal law. Hence, no significant sociological studies are available either in the general or special part of criminal law. But sociologists have shown much interest in the beginning and end—as distinguished from the center—of criminality. Hence, we find an abundance of studies devoted to juvenile delinquency at one end, and probation, parole, and corrections in general, at the other. Thus, on the question of probation success, fifteen major research projects could be recorded in 1955. (England, 'A Study of Post-probation Recidivism Among Five Hundred Federal Offenders', 19 (3) *Fed. Prob.* 10 (Sept. 1955), of which nos. 1–6 were concerned primarily with success or failure during probation, and nos. 7–15 with success or failure after probation. To England's study should be added:
   (1) John L. Sillin and Reuben L. Hill, 'Rural-Urban Aspects of Adult Probation in Wisconsin', 5 *Rural Soc.* 314 (1940).
   (2) Fred R. Johnson, *Probation for Juveniles and Adults* (N.Y., 1928).

(3) Elio Monachesi, 'A Comparison of Predicted with Actual Results of Probation', 10 *An. Soc. Rev.* 26 (1945).

(4) Elio Monachesi, *Prediction Factors in Probation* (Hanover, N.H., 1932).

(5) Frederick A. Moran, *Probation in New York State* (Albany, N.Y., 1923).

(6) U.S. Dep't of Justice, *The Attorney General's Survey of Release Procedures*, v. 2 (1939).

(7) Belle Boone Beard, *Juvenile Probation* (N.Y., 1934).

(8) Morris G. Caldwell, 'Preview of a New Type of Probation Study Made in Alabama' (*Fed. Prob.* June 1951).

(9) Irving W. Halpern, *A Decade of Probation, Court of Gen. Sessions* (N.Y., 1937).

(10) E. W. Hughes, 'An Analysis of the Records of Some 750 Probations', 12 *Brit. J. Ed. Soc.* 113 (1943).

(11) Alice D. Menkin, 'Rehabilitation of the Morally Handicapped', 15 *J. Crim. L. and Crim.* 147 (1924).

(12) Joseph P. Murphy, 'A Case Study to Test the Efficiency of Probation Treatment', 5 *Cath. Char. Rev.* 287 (1950).

(13) Jay Rumney and Joseph P. Murphy, *Probation and Social Adjustment* (New Brunswick, N.J., 1952).

(14) H. M. Stat. Off., *The Probation Service: Its Objects and Organization* (1938).

(15) *Report of the Commission of Probation on an Inquiry into the Permanent Results of Probation* (Doc. No. 421, Mass. Senate, Boston, 1924).

A discussion of all of the purely sociological studies is not within the ambit of this report, but the names of the most successful contemporary researchers deserve mention: Bates, Bloch, Cressey, McCord, Ohlin, Savitz, Sellin, Sutherland, Wolfgang, and others.

88. An exception is Paul W. Tappan, *The Habitual Sex Offender* (1950).

89. This, of course, is the subject which Mr. Justice Frankfurter urged the Supreme Court not to enter. (Frankfurter, in Gore v. United States, 357 U.S. 386, 393 (1958)). And Professor Remington considers it a fact 'that the whole field of sentence and correction is now largely outside the scope of appellate review'. Remington, 'Criminal Justice Research', 51 *J. Crim. L., C. and P. S.* 711 (1960). But the tide is turning, as has been demonstrated: Mueller, 'Penology on Appeal: Appellate Review of Legal But Excessive Sentences', 15 *Vand. L. Rev.* 671 (1962).

90. Paul W. Tappan, *Delinquent Girls in Court* (1947); id., *Juvenile Delinquency* (1949); id., *Contemporary Correction* (1951).

91. See the proposal by Leon Radzinowicz, *The Role of Criminology and a Proposal for an Institute of Criminology* (1964).

92. The School of Criminology, of the University of California (Berkeley), is the best example in point.

Sheldon Glueck has proposed the creation of a federal academy of criminal justice. See Davis, 'Model Act Envisions Criminal Law

Academies', *Harv. L. Rec.* 1, 4 (Feb. 25, 1965). Sen. Edward M. Kennedy (D., Mass.) introduced an appropriate bill in the Senate, and Rep. James C. Corman (D., Calif.) in the House, S. 1288, H. R. 6071, 89th Cong., 1st Sess. (1965).

93. The Center for the Study of Law and Society at the University of California (Berkeley) is now engaged in various field studies of aspects of the administration of justice and of delinquency. Careful selection of skilled researchers from various disciplines and insistence on the employment of sober methods is likely to yield fruitful results. See Annual Reports of the Center for the Study of Law and Society.

94. Sheldon Glueck and Eleanor T. Glueck, *500 Criminal Careers* (1930); *Later Criminal Careers* (1937); *Criminal Careers in Retrospect* (1943); *One Thousand Juvenile Delinquents* (1934); *Five Hundred Delinquent Women* (1934); *Juvenile Delinquents Grown Up* (1940); *After Conduct of Discharged Offenders* (1945); *Unraveling Juvenile Delinquency* (1950); *Delinquents in the Making* (1952); *Physique and Delinquency* (1956); *Predicting Delinquency and Crime* (1959).

95. Sheldon Glueck and Eleanor T. Glueck, *Criminal Careers in Retrospect* (1943).

96. E. T. Glueck, 'Spotting Potential Delinquents: Can it be Done?' 20 (3) *Fed. Prob.* 7, 12 (Sept. 1956).

97. Ibid. at 9.

98. Ibid., taken mostly from *Unraveling Juvenile Delinquency* (1950). See also E. T. Glueck, 'Status of Glueck Prediction Studies', 47 *J. Crim. L., C. and P. S.* 18 (1956), with a discussion of prediction of recidivism as well as detection of potential delinquents.

99. Glueck, 'Status of Glueck Prediction Studies', *supra* n. 95, at 22.

100. E. T. Glueck, 'Efforts to Identify Delinquents', 24 (2) *Fed. Prob.* 49, 54 (June, 1960).

101. E.g., Lopez-Rey, 'Some Misconceptions in Contemporary Criminology', in *Essays in Criminal Science* 3 (ed. G. Mueller, 1961).

102. Validation studies are currently taking place in New York City, Japan, Israel and elsewhere.

103. Cf. Leon Radzinowicz, *In Search of Criminology* ch. VII (1962).

104. Moore and Callahan, 'Law and Learning Theory: A Study in Legal Control', 53 *Yale L. J.* 1 (1943).

105. Mueller, 'How to Increase Traffic Fatalities: A Useful Guide for Modern Legislators and Traffic Courts', 60 *Colum. L. Rev.* 944, 948–949 (1960).

106. The matter is discussed at length in Mueller, 'The Public Law of Wrongs—Its Concepts in the World of Reality', 10 *J. Pub. L.* 203, 205–214 (1961).

107. A matter to be discussed further in the next section.

108. R. D. Schwartz, 'The Law and Behavioral Science Program at Yale: A Sociologist's Account of Some Experiences', 12 *J. Legal Ed.* 91, 98 (1959).

109. Pound, 'The Need of a Sociological Jurisprudence', 19 *Green Bag* 607, 611 (1907).

110. See also Ellingston, 'A Sociologist's Participation in Criminal Law Instruction', 8 *J. Legal Ed.* 207 (1955); Rose, 'Problems in the Sociology of Law and Law Enforcement', 6 *J. Legal Ed.* 191 (1953); Morris and Turner, 'The Lawyer and Criminological Research', 44 *Va. L. Rev.* 163 (1958), a superb assessment of the situation, with the advice: 'What is needed in American skills is sociological research directed towards questions of immediate relevance to the criminal lawyer's roles; questions which are answered in Europe from theoretical premises untested by research data.' Ibid. at 183.

111. *Ill. Ann. Stat.* ch. 38, § 11 (Smith-Hurd, 1961).

112. Simply by way of example, the 'interpretative cortex', which holds, and, on stimulation, compares past recorded impressions (memory) with present reality, was not discovered until 1957, by Dr Wilder Penfield. *N. Y. Times*, Nov. 24, 1957, § 1, p. 11, cols. 6–7.

113. Cleckley, Book Review, 26 (1) *Fed. Prob.* 69 (1962), reviewing *Archives of Criminal Psychodynamics*: Symposium on Psychopathy (ed. Karpman), with article by Mueller, 'The Failure of Concepts of Criminal Theory in Judging the Psychopathic Offender?', at 558 (1961).

114. Jerome Hall, *General Principles of Criminal Law* 526 et seq. (1947).

115. Ibid. at 534 et. seq.

116. 23 *Law and Contemp. Prob.* 594–610 (1958).

117. Ibid. at 611–632.

118. This and the two preceding paragraphs have been excerpted from my article, op. cit. *supra* n. 113.

119. Hutchins and Slesinger, 'Some Observations on the Law of Evidence' —'Spontaneous Exclamations', 28 *Colum. L. Rev.* 432 (1928); 'Memory', 41 *Harv. L. Rev.* 860 (1928); 'Competency of Witnesses', 37 *Yale L. J.* 1017 (1928); 'Consciousness of Guilt', 77 *U. Pa. L. Rev.* 725 (1929); 'State of Mind to Prove an Act', 38 *Yale L. J.* 283 (1929); 'State of Mind in Issue', 29 *Colum. L. Rev.* 145 (1929); 'Family Relations', 13 *Minn. L. Rev.* 625 (1929).

120. Redmount, 'A Pantoscopic View of Law and Psychology', 10 *J. Legal Ed.* 436, 444 (1958).

121. George H. Dession, 'Psychiatry and the Conditioning of Criminal Justice', 47 *Yale L. J.* 319, 329 (1938).

122. George H. Dession, *Criminal Law, Administration and Public Order* IV (1948).

123. Ibid. at V. The terminology is that of the functionalists, especially Professor Harold D. Lasswell, who, in the preparation of the book, had 'been more than generous with criticism and suggestion'. Ibid., loc. cit. Generally see Lasswell and McDougal, 'Legal Education and Public Policy: Professional Training in the Public Interest', 52 *Yale L. J.* 203 (1943); McDougal and Lasswell, 'The Identification and Appraisal of Diverse Systems of Public Order', 53 *Am. J. Int'l L.* 1 (1959).

124. Besides his incomplete code, see *Comment*, Professor Dession's 'Final Draft of the Code of Correction for Puerto Rico', 71 *Yale L. J*

1050 (1962). Dession's scholarly legacy includes a host of sound and valuable—albeit tentative—articles. See Dession, 'Psychiatry and Public Policy', 5 *Buffalo L. Rev.* 48 (1955); id., 'The Technique of Public Order: Evolving Concepts of Criminal Law', 5 *Buffalo L. Rev.* 22 (1955); id., 'Sanctions, Law and Public Order', 1 *Vand. L. Rev.* 8 (1947); id., 'Psychiatry and Public Policy', 18 *Psychiatry* 1 (1955); id., *Psychiatry and the Law* (1955); id., 'Justice After Correction', 25 *Conn. B. J.* 215 (1951); id., 'Deviation and Community Sanctions', in Paul H. Hoch and J. Zubin (eds.), *Psychiatry and the Law* 1 (1955); Dession and Lasswell, 'Public Order Under Law; The Role of the Advisor-Draftsman in the Formation of Code or Constitution', 65 *Yale L. J.* 174 (1955). And see the Dession Memorial Issue, 5 *Buffalo L. Rev.* 1–115 (1955).

125. Donnelly, 'Some Comments Upon the Law and Behavioral Science Program at Yale', 12 *J. Legal Ed.* 83, 89 (1959).

126. Clifford R. Shaw, *The Crime of Imprisonment* 47 (1946).

127. Who succeeded Dr Lawrence Freedman, a prolific writer and scholar. See Freedman, 'Conformity and Non-Conformity', in *Psychiatry and the Law* 45 (ed. Paul H. Hoch and J. Zubin, 1955).

128. See Katz, 'The Law and Behavioral Science Program at Yale: A Psychiatrist's First Impressions', 12 *J. Legal Ed.* 99 (1959), an account of the difficulties of imparting to law students what to them is an unorthodox body of knowledge.

129. E.g., Lasswell and Donnelly, 'The Continuing Debate Over Responsibility: An Introduction to Isolating the Condemnation Sanction', 68 *Yale L. J.* 869 (1959), containing some excellent thoughts.

130. R. C. Donnelly, Joseph Goldstein and R. D. Schwartz, *Criminal Law—Problems for Decision in the Promulgation, Invocation, and Administration of a Law of Crimes*, New York (The Free Press of Glencoe, Inc., 1962). Pp. XXVII, 1169.

131. Illing, Book Review, 53 *J. Crim. L.*, *C. and P. S.* 80, 81 (1962).

132. See 'Law School Developments' (Watson, Foote, Levin, Kalven), 'The Law and Behavioral Science Project at the University of Pennsylvania' (papers presented at the Law and Medicine Round Table, at the Annual Meeting of the Association of American Law Schools, San Francisco, Cal., on Dec. 29, 1957), 11 *J. Legal Ed.* 73 (1958). See also Watson, 'Reflections on the Teaching of Criminal Law', 37 *U. Det. L. J.* 701 (1960); Watson, 'A Critique of the Legal Approach to Crime and Correction', 23 *Law and Contemp. Prob.* 611 (1958).

133. Professor William Curran (Boston University), Director of the Law-Medicine Institute, served as Legal Consultant to the Massachusetts Chapter (Donald Hayes Russell, M.D., Chairman); Professor Samuel Polsky (Temple University) has closely cooperated with the New York Chapter (Irving Barnett, Ph.D., Chairman), and this writer serves as the Secretary and one of the editors of the *Journal of Offender Therapy*.

134. E.g., The University of Pittsburgh (through Professor Henry H.

Foster, Jr.); The University of Texas, Western Reserve University, Harvard University, The University of Maryland, and others.

135. See his books *Insanity as a Defense in Criminal Law* (1933) and *Mental Disorder as A Criminal Defense* (1954), which 'is in substance a second edition'. Perkins, Book Review, 5 *U. C. L. A. L. Rev.* 174 (1958).

136. Henry Weihofen, *The Urge to Punish* (1956).

137. E.g., Manfred S. Guttmacher and Henry Weihofen, *Psychiatry and the Law* (1952); id., 'Mental Incompetency', 36 *Minn. L. Rev.* 179 (1952). On various occasions Professor Weihofen has also co-operated with Dr Winfred Overholser, e.g., 'Commitment of the Mentally Ill', 24 *Tex. L. Rev.* 307 (1946); 'Mental Disorder Affecting the Degree of Crime', 56 *Yale L. J.* 959 (1947).

138. Nowadays one must have published on this topic, else one is no one. See Dorothy Campbell Tompkins, *Insanity and the Criminal Law: A Bibliography* (1960).

139. Silving, 'Psychoanalysis and the Criminal Law', 51 *J. Crim. L., C. and P. S.* 19 (1960); id., 'Mental Incapacity in Criminal Law', [1961] *Current Law and Social Problems*, 1. See also 5 *J. Off. Ther.* 1 (1962); id., 'Rule of Law in Criminal Justice', in *Essays in Criminal Science* 77 (ed. G. Mueller, 1961); id., 'Testing of the Unconscious in Criminal Cases', 69 *Harv. L. Rev.* 683 (1956); and other writings on topics of the criminal law in which Dr Silving brought her psychoanalytic insight to practical application, e.g., 'The Oath' (pts. 1, 2, 68 *Yale L. J.* 1329, 1527 (1959); 'Euthanasia: A Study in Comparative Law', 103 *U. Pa. L. Rev.* 350 (1954); 'Victims of Criminal Violence', 8 *J. Pub. L.* 236 (1959); and her writings with Ryu, e.g., 'Error Juris: A Comparative Study', 24 *U. Chi. L. Rev.* 421 (1957).

140. Redmount, 'Some Basic Policies Regarding Penal Policy', 49 *J. Crim. L., C. and P. S.* 426 (1959); id., 'A Pantoscopic View of Law and Psychology', 10 *J. Legal Ed.* 436 (1958); id., 'Values, Concepts, and the Assessment of Personal Deviancy', [1961] *Duke L. J.* 355 (1961); id., 'Psychological Discontinuities in the Litigation Process', [1959] *Duke L. J.* 571 (1959).

141. Jerome Michael and Mortimer Adler, *Crime, Law and Social Science* 81 (1933).

142. Silving, 'Psychoanalysis and the Criminal Law', 51 *J. Crim. L., C. and P. S.* 19 and 33 (1960). But it is not just the opening and the closing paragraphs that are of significance, it is the thoroughness and good will with which legal principles are 'psychoanalyzed' by Dr Silving that makes her contributions so remarkable.

143. Jerome Hall's central ideas on law and psychiatry are now conveniently available, in ch. 13 of *General Principles of Criminal Law* (2nd ed. 1960).

144. Donnelly, 'Some Comments Upon the Law and Behavioral Science Program at Yale', 12 *J. Legal Ed.* 83 (1959).

145. 1952 Dr Winfred Overholser, *The Psychiatrist and the Law* (1953);

1953   Dr Gregory Zilboorg, *The Psychology of the Criminal Act and Punishment* (1954);
1954   Hon. John Biggs, Jr., *The Guilty Mind* (1955);
1955   Prof. Henry Weihofen, *The Urge to Punish* (1958);
1956   Phillip Roche, M.D., *The Criminal Mind* (1959);
1957   Prof. Manfred Guttmacher, *The Mind of the Murderer* (1960);
1958   Alistair W. Mac Lloyd (not yet published);
1959   Dr Maxwell Jones (not yet published);
1960   Hon. David L. Bazelon (not yet published);
1961   Prof. Sheldon Glueck, *Law and Psychiatry: Cold War or Entente Cordiale* (1962);
1962   Karl Menninger (not yet published).

Dr Jeffery must have had the foregoing Isaac Ray Award lectures in mind. The next following lectures are added for the sake of completeness. In my opinion, Dr Jeffery's criticism does not apply to them.

1963   Hon. Morris Ploscowe (lectures delivered at Vanderbilt University during the academic year 1962/3);
1964   Hon. Justin Wise Polier, Family Court, City of New York (not yet published);
1965   Dr Georg Stürup (lecture delivered at the University of Pennsylvania, 1966).

146. Jerome Hall, *General Principles of Criminal Law* ch. 13 (2nd ed. 1960); 'Psychiatry and Criminal Responsibility', 65 *Yale L. J.* 761 (1956); 'Responsibility and the Law: In Defense of the McNaghten Rules', 42 *A. B. A. J.* 917 (1956); 'Mental Disease and Criminal Responsibility—M'Naghten Versus Durham and the American Law Institute's Tentative Draft', 33 *Ind. L. J.* 212 (1957); 'Mental Disease and Criminal Responsibility', 45 *Colum. L. Rev.* 677 (1945); Hall and Menninger, 'Psychiatry and the Law—A Dual Review', 38 *Iowa L. Rev.* 687 (1953). See also the following:

H. A. Davidson, *Forensic Psychiatry* (1952).

Dession, 'Psychiatry and the Conditioning of Criminal Justice', 47 *Yale L. J.* 319 (1938).

Edwards, 'Diminished Responsibility—A Withering Away of the Concept of Criminal Responsibility?', in *Essays in Criminal Science* 309 (ed. G. Mueller, 1961).

Morris, 'The Defences of Insanity in Australia', in *Essays in Criminal Science* 273 (ed. G. Mueller, 1961).

Mueller, 'M'Naghten Remains Irreplaceable: Recent Events in the Law of Incapacity', 50 *Geo. L. J.* 105 (1961); 'The Failure of Concepts of Criminal Theory in Judging the Psychopathic Offender', 4 *Archives of Criminal Psychodynamics* 558 (1961); 'The German Draft Criminal Code 1960—An Evaluation in Terms of American Criminal Law', [1961] *U. Ill. L. F.* 25 (1961); 'Irreconcilibility of Guilt Concepts', 5 (2) *J. Off. Therapy* 1 (1961); 'The Public Law of Wrongs—Its Concepts in the World of Reality', 10 *J. Pub. L.* 203, 244–250 (1961).

Silving, 'Mental Incapacity in Criminal Law', in *Current Law and Social Problems* 3–88 (1961).

Dorothy Campbell Tompkins, *Insanity and the Criminal Law: A Bibliography* (1960).

United Nations, 'Inquiry on the Treatment of Abnormal Offenders in Europe', No. 12, *Int. Rev. Crim. Policy* 3 (1957).

Henry Weihofen, *Mental Disease as a Criminal Defense* (1954).

147. E.g., Thomas S. Szasz, 'Psychiatric Expert Testimony—Its Covert Meaning and Social Function', 20 *Psych.* 313 (1957); id., 'Psychiatry, Ethics and the Criminal Law', 58 *Colum. L. Rev.* 183 (1958); id., 'Contribution to the Philosophy of Medicine', 97 *A. M. A. Arch. Int. Med.* 5 (1956); id., 'Some Observations on the Relationship Between Psychiatry and Law', 75 *Arch. Neur. and Psychiat.* 297 (1956); id., 'The Problem of Psychiatric Nosology', 114 *Am. J. Psychiat.* 405 (1957); id., *The Myth of Mental Illness* (1961); id., *Pain and Pleasure* (1957).

148. Sir Norwood East, *Society and the Criminal* (1951); id., 'Legal and Medical Advances in Criminology', in *The Roots of Crime* (ed. East, 1954); id., *An Introduction to Psychiatry in the Criminal Courts* (1927).

149. F. Wertham, 'Psychoauthoritarianism and the Law', 22 *U. Chi. L. Rev.* 336 (1955); id., Book Review, 22 *U. Chi. L. Rev.* 569 (1955); id., *Dark Legend* (1941); id., *The Show of Violence* (1949); id., *Seduction of the Innocent* (1954); id., *The Circle of Guilt* (1956); and others.

150. De Grazia, 'The Distinction of Being Mad', 22 *U. Chi. L. Rev.* 339 (1955); id., 'Crime Without Punishment: A Psychiatric Conundrum', 58 *Colum. L. Rev.* 746 (1952); Book Review, 62 *Yale L. J.* 679 (1953).

151. F. James Davis, H. H. Foster, Jr., C. R. Jeffery and E. E. Davis, *Society and the Law* 295 (1962).

152. Besides those already mentioned, see also Franz Alexander and Hugo Staub, *The Criminal, The Judge and the Public* (rev. ed. 1956); J. Biggs, *The Guilty Mind* (1955); Julius Cohen, *Murder, Madness and the Law* (1952); Karl Menninger, *The Human Mind* (3rd ed. 1943); P. Reiwald, *Society and its Criminals* (tr. James, 1950); P. Q. Roche, *The Criminal Mind* (1958); Gregory Zilboorg, *The Psychology of the Criminal Act and Punishment* (1954); Hacker and Frym, 'The Legal Concept of Insanity and the Treatment of Criminal Impulses', 37 *Calif. L. Rev.* 575 (1949).

153. Brancale, 'Diagnostic Techniques in Aid of Sentencing', 23 *Law and Contemp. Prob.* 442 (1958); W. Bromberg, *The Mold of Murder: A Psychiatric Study of Homicide* (1961); Bromberg and Cleckley, 'The Medico-Legal Dilemma, A Suggested Solution', 42 *J. Crim. L., C. and P. S.* 729 (1952); Hervey Cleckley, *The Mask of Sanity* (1941); H. A. Davidson, *Forensic Psychiatry* (1952); id., 'Irresistible Impulse and Criminal Responsibility', 1 (2) *J. For. Sci.* 1 (1956); Davidson, 'Criminal Responsibility: The Quest for a Formula', in *Psychiatry and the Law* (ed. Hoch and Zubin, 1955); Havelock Ellis and A. F.

Brancale, *The Psychology of Sex Offenders* (1956); Erickson, 'Psychiatry and the Law: An Attempt at Synthesis', [1961] *Duke L. J.* 30 (1961), with valuable bibliography; Glover, 'Medico-Psychological Aspects of Normality', 23 *Brit. J. Psychol.* 165 (1932); Guttmacher, 'The Psychiatric Approach to Crime and Correction', 23 *Law and Contemp. Prob.* 633 (1958); Knight, 'Determinism, Freedom and Psychotherapy', 9 *Psychiatry* 251 (1946); L. S. Kubie, 'Social Forces and the Neurotic Process', in *Explorations in Social Psychiatry* 769 (ed. Alexander H. Leighton, John A. Clausen and D. W. Wilson, 1957), and other writings by Kubie; John M. Macdonald, *Psychiatry and the Criminal Law* (1958); W. L. Neustatter, *Psychological Disorder and Crime* (1953); Winfred Overholser, *The Psychiatrist and the Law* (1953); Overholser and Weihofen, 'Mental Disorder Affecting the Degree of a Crime', 56 *Yale L. J.* 959 (1947); id., 'Psychiatry's Contribution to Criminal Law and Procedure', 12 *Okla. L. Rev.* 13 (1959); Rubin, 'A New Approach to M'Naghten vs. Durham', 45 *J. Am. Jud. Soc'y* 133 (1961); Waelder, 'Psychiatry and the Problem of Criminal Responsibility', 101 *U. Pa. L. Rev.* 378 (1952).

This list is both too short and too long, in support of my statement. It is meant to indicate the range of the psychiatric spectrum within which sensible collaboration for legal scholars may be found.

154. Schmideberg, Editorial, 6 (1) *J. Off. Therapy* 1, 12 (1962). Among Schmideberg's countless recent articles, the following are particularly noteworthy: 'Criminal Psychiatry Based on Offender Therapy and Cooperation with the Courts', 1 *Exc. Crim.* 371 (1961); id., *The Borderline Patient, American Handbook of Psychiatry*, ch. 21 (1959); id., 'Making the Patient Aware', 6 *Crime and Del.* 255 (1960); id., 'Psychotherapy of Juvenile Delinquents' 1 (2) *Int'l Res. Newsl. Ment. H.* 3 (1959); id., 'Danger of Indiscriminate Permissiveness', 1 *Psychosom.* 208 (1960); id., 'Principles of Psychotherapy', 1 *Compr. Psychiat.* 186 (1960); id., 'Psychiatric Study and Psychotherapy of Criminals', 5 *Progress in Psychother.* 156 (1960); id., 'Multiple Origin and Functions of Guilt', 30 *Psychiat. Q.* 471 (1956).

155. David Stafford-Clark, *Psychiatry To-Day* 221 (1952).

156. Benjamin Karpman, *The Sexual Offender and his Offenses* 562 (1954).

157. The example is one of many chosen by Hakeem, 'A Critique of the Psychiatric Approach to Crime and Correction', 23 *Law and Contemp. Prob.* 650, 658 (1958).

158. These ideas are further developed in Mueller, 'The Public Law of Wrongs—Its Concepts in the World of Reality', 10 *J. Pub. L.* 203 (1961); id., 'The Failure of Concepts of Criminal Theory in Judging the Psychopathic Offender?', *supra* n. 143; id., 'M'Naghten Remains Irreplaceable: Recent Events in the Law of Incapacity', 50 *Geo. L. J.* 105 (1961); id., 'Irreconcilibility of Guilt Concepts', 5 *J. Off. Ther.* 1 (1961); and other writings.

159. E.g., Diamond, 'With Malice Aforethought', 2 *Arch. Crim. Psychodyn.* 1 (1957), comparing Bentham's and Freud's pain and pleasure concepts.

160. Only one of the leading American criminal law scholars has established an equal reputation for outstanding work in the field of legal regulation of business: Professor Louis B. Schwartz, of the University of Pennsylvania. See Schwartz, 'Institutional Size and Individual Liberty: Authoritarian Aspects of Bigness', 55 *Nw. U. L. Rev.* 4 (1960); id., 'New Approaches to the Control of Oligopoly', 109 *U. Pa. L. Rev.* 31 (1960); id., 'Highlights of the Final Report of the Attorney General's National Committee to Study the Antitrust Laws—The Schwartz Dissent', 1 *Antitrust Bull.* 6 (1955); id., 'Committees, Politics, Scholarship and Law Reform: Antitrust Studies in Perspective', in 'Report of the Attorney General's Committee on Antitrust Law—a Symposium', 104 *U. Pa. L. Rev.* 145, 153 (1955); id., 'Legal Restriction of Competition in the Regulated Industries: An Abdication of Judicial Responsibility', 67 *Harv. L. Rev.* 436 (1954).

161. The first cycle included such significant contributions as Arthur C. Hall, *Crime and Its Relation to Social Progress* (1901); see also Sullivan, 'The Salvation of Juvenile Delinquents', 64 *Alb. L. J.* 127 (1902); and William Adrian Bonger, *Criminality and Economic Conditions* (tr. Horton, 1916).

The second cycle began with E. H. Sutherland, *White Collar Crime* (1949). See also Lane, 'Why Businessmen Violate the Law', 44 *J. Crim. L., C. and P. S.* 151 (1953); Mueller, 'Equal Injustice Under Law', 10 (1) *Challenge—The Magazine of Economic Affairs* 6 (1961), also at *Wall Street Journal*, Oct. 23, 1961, p. 10, col. 3–5, also at *Maryland Motor Transport News*, Feb. 1962, pp. 5, 28–31; id., 'A Criminologist's Thoughts about the Economic Planner's Weapon', in Helmut Schoeck and James W. Wiggins (eds.), *Central Planning and Neomercantilism* (1964).

162. Collings, 'Criminal Law and Administration', in *1957 Annual Survey of American Law* 93 (1958).

163. So far, the new *Journal of Law and Economics*, edited by Professor Aaron Director, at the University of Chicago, has not featured a single article devoted exclusively to economic aspects of penal law.

164. Donald R. Taft, *Criminology* (1950), reproduced with permission of the Macmillan Company, New York.

CHAPTER IX

1. (1) Allen, 'Criminal Justice, Legal Values and the Rehabilitative Ideal', 50 *J. Crim. L., C. and P. S.* 226 (1959); and see the articles by Dession and with Lasswell, nn. 118–121, ch. VII, *supra*.

(2) Jerome Hall, *Readings in Jurisprudence* (1938); id., *Living Law of Democratic Society* (1949); id., 'Reason and Reality in Jurisprudence', 7 *Buffalo L. Rev.* 351 (1958); id., 'Plato's Legal Philosophy', 31 *Ind. L. J.* 171 (1956), now ch. 3 in *Studies in Jurisprudence and Criminal Theory* (1958); id., *Integrative Jurisprudence in Interpretations of Modern Legal Philosophies* 313 (ed. Sayre, 1947).

(3) Mueller, 'Criminal Theory: An Appraisal of Jerome Hall's Studies in Jurisprudence and Criminal Theory', 34 *Ind. L. J.* 29, 207 (1959); id., 'To the Memory of Ernst Seelig', 47 *J. Crim. L., C. and P. S.* 539 (1957); id., 'The Problem of Value Judgments as Norms of Law: Answer of a Positivist', 7 *J. Legal Ed.* 185 (1955).

(4) Helen Silving, 'Law and Fact in the Light of the Pure Theory of Law,' in *Interpretations of Modern Legal Philosophies* 642 (ed. Sayre, 1947); 'Positive Natural Law', 3 *Natural L. F.* 24 (1958); 'Testing of the Unconscious in Criminal Cases', 69 *Harv. L. Rev.* 683 (1956); 'From the Sublime to the Ridiculous: A Study of Legal Symbolism', 30 *Tul. L. Rev.* 269 (1956); 'Twilight Zone of Positive and Natural Law', 49 *Calif. L. Rev.* 477 (1955); 'Jurisprudence of the Old Testament', 28 *N. Y. U. L. Rev.* 1129 (1953); 'Plea for a Law of Interpretation', 98 *U. Pa. L. Rev.* 499 (1950); 'The Unknown and the Unknowable in Law', 28 *Calif. L. Rev.* 352 (1947).

(5) Orville C. Snyder, *Preface to Jurisprudence* (1954).

(6) Herbert Wechsler, *Principles, Politics and Fundamental Law* (1961).

The philosophical implications of criminal law are demonstrated with particular persuasiveness in Edmond Cahn, *The Predicament of Democratic Man* (1961); id., *The Moral Decision* (1956); id., *The Sense of Injustice* (1949).

2. Ploscowe, 'Development of Inquisitorial and Accusatorial Elements in French Procedure', 23 *J. Crim. L. and Crim.* 372 (1932); id., 'The Administration of Criminal Justice in France', 24 *J. Crim. L. and Crim.* 712 (1933); id., 'Jury Trial in France', 29 *Minn. L. Rev.* 376 (1945); id., 'The Investigating Magistrate (Juge d'Instruction) in European Criminal Procedure', 33 *Mich. L. Rev.* 1010 (1935); id., 'Measures of Constraint in European and Anglo-American Criminal Procedure', 23 *Geo. L. J.* 762 (1935); id., 'Expert Witness in Criminal Cases in France, Germany and Italy', 2 *Law and Contemp. Prob.* 504 (1934); id., 'The Development of Present-Day Criminal Procedures in Europe and America', 48 *Harv. L. Rev.* 433 (1935); cf., id., 'An Examination of Some Dispositions Relating to Motives and Character in Modern European Penal Codes', 21 *J. Crim. L. and Crim.* 26 (1930). See also the articles by Woods, 'The French Correctional Courts', 23 *J. Crim. L. and Crim.* 20 (1932); id., 'The French Court of Assizes', 22 *J. Crim. L. and Crim.* 325 (1931); id., 'The Efficiency of French Justice', 15 *A. B. A. J.* 162 (1929).

3. Hazard, 'Reforming Soviet Criminal Law', 29 *J. Crim. L. and Crim.* 157 (1938); Hazard and Stein, ' "Exterior Treason"—A Study in Comparative Criminal Law', 6 *U. Chi. L. Rev.* 77 (1938); Hazard, 'Soviet Socialism and Embezzlement', 26 *Wash. L. Rev.* 301 (1951); id., 'Soviet Criminal Procedure', 15 *Tul. L. Rev.* 220 (1941).

4. Simply by way of example, here are some of the better recent studies in comparative criminal procedure:

Appleton, 'Reforms in Japanese Criminal Procedure Under Allied Occupation', 24 *Wash. L. Rev.* 401 (1949);

Sybille Bedford, *The Faces of Justice* (1960);

Hauser, 'Comparative Law: The Criminal Law in France', 45 *A. B. A. J.* 807 (1959);

Kock, 'Criminal Proceedings in France', 9 *Am. J. Comp. L.* 253 (1960); id., 'The Machinery of Law Administration in France', 108 *U. Pa. L. Rev.* 366 (1960);

Meyer, 'German Criminal Procedure: The Position of the Defendant in Court', 41 *A.B.A.J.* 592 (1955);

Meyer, 'The Japanese Inquest of Prosecution', 64 *Harv. L. Rev.* 279 (1950);

Mueller, 'Resocialization of the Young Adult Offender in Switzerland', 43 *J. Crim. L. and Crim.* 578 (1953);

Shoham, 'Sentencing Policy of Criminal Courts in Israel', 50 *J. Crim. L., C. and P. S.* 327 (1959);

Joseph M. Snee and A. Kenneth Pye, *Status of Forces Agreements and Criminal Jurisdiction* (1957);

Schwenck, 'Comparative Study of Laws of Criminal Procedure in NATO Countries under the NATO Status of Forces Agreement', 35 *N. C. L. Rev.* 358 (1957).

For a study in comparative penology see Bates, 'One World in Penology', 38 *J. Crim. L. and Crim.* 565 (1948); Berman, 'The Comparison of Soviet and American Law', 34 *Ind. L. J.* 559 (1959); Hazard, 'Soviet Socialism as a Public Order System', 53 *Am. Soc. Int'l L. Proc.* 21 (1959).

5. E.g., Vouin, 'The Protection of the Accused in French Criminal Procedure' (pts. 1, 2) 5 *Int'l and Comp. L. Q.* 1, 157 (1956); id., 'Illegally Obtained Evidence', 91 *Int'l Crim. Pol. Rev.* 241 (1955); Delaume, 'Jurisdiction over Crime Committed Abroad: French and American Law', 21 *Geo. Wash. L. Rev.* 173 (1952); Gagnieur, 'The Judicial Use of Psycho-Narcosis in France', 39 *J. Crim. L. and Crim.* 663, and 40 *J. Crim. L. and Crim.* 370 (1949); Abe, 'Criminal Procedure in Japan', 48 *J. Crim. L., C. and P. S.* 359 (1957).

6. In the following two recent symposia, the names of foreign participants have been italicized:

'Conditional Release Pending Trial', 108 *U. Pa. L. Rev.* 287 (1960) (articles by *Bratholm, Dando* and *Tamiya*, Foote, *Smith, Vouin*).

'The Impartial Medical Expert' [criminal as well as civil], 34 *Temp. L. Q.* (1961) (articles by Griffen, Guttmacher, Levy, Polsky, *Schroeder*, van Dusen).

In the following symposia, seven foreign experts contributed one short paper on each of the subjects: (Messrs. G. Arthur Martin, Canada; Glanville L. Williams, U.K.; Robert Vouin, France; Walter R. Clemens, Germany; Haim H. Cohn, Israel; Haruo Abe, Japan; Anders Bratholm, Norway.)

International Symposia Celebrating the 50th Anniversary of the *Journal of Criminal Law, Criminology and Police Science*.

(a) 'The Privilege against Self-Incrimination', 51 *J. Crim. L., C. and P. S.* 129 (1960) (articles by McNaughton, Sowle, Wyman).

282   CRIME, LAW AND THE SCHOLARS (pp. 200–204)

(b) 'Police Detention and Arrest Privileges', 51 *J. Crim. L., C. and P. S.* 385 (1960) (articles by Foote, Remington, Wilson).

(c) 'Police Interrogation Privileges and Limitations', 52 *J. Crim. L., C. and P. S.* 1 (1961) (articles by Inbau, Mueller, Weisberg).

(d) 'The Exclusionary Rule Regarding Illegally Seized Evidence', 52 *J. Crim. L., C. and P. S.* 245 (1961) (articles by Allen, McGarr, Paulsen).

These four symposia are now available in book form, *Police Power and Individual Freedom* (ed. Claude R. Sowle, 1962).

7. See Mueller, 'International Judicial Assistance in Criminal Matters', 7 *Vill. L. Rev.* 193 (1962).

8. Mueller, 'The Teaching of Comparative Law in the Course on Criminal Law', 49 *J. Crim. L., C. and P. S.* 101, 11 *J. Legal Ed.* 59 (1958).

9. See publications cited n. 38, ch. VIII, *supra*.

10. Jerome Hall, *Studies in Jurisprudence and Criminal Theory* 103 (1958).

11. Ibid., loc. cit.

12. *N. Y. Times*, Nov. 24, 1957, § 1, p. 1, p. 12, col. 3.

13. Mueller, 'The Teaching of Comparative Law in the Course on Criminal Law', 49 *J. Crim. L., C. and P. S.* 101, 102, 11 *J. Legal Ed.* 59, 61 (1958).

14. Hall, op. cit. *supra* n. 10, at 111.

15. 1st ed. 1947; 2nd ed. 1960.

16. Jerome Michael and Hubert Wechsler, *Criminal Law and Its Administration* (1940).

17. Herbert Wechsler, 1956 Supplement to Michael and Wechsler, *Criminal Law and Its Administration* (1956).

18. Apart from those mentioned, attention is called to Ryu, 'The New Korean Criminal Code of October 3, 1953', 48 *J. Crim. L., C. and P. S.* 275 (1957); Ryu and Silving, 'Error Juris: A Comparative Study', 24 *U. Chi. L. Rev.* 421 (1957); Ryu, 'Causation in the Criminal Law', 106 *U. Pa. L. Rev.* 773 (1958); id., 'Problems of Criminal Attempts', 32 *N. Y. U. L. Rev.* 470 (1957).

19. George H. Dession, *Criminal Law, Administration and Public Order* (1948).

20. René Garraud, *Précis de Droit Criminel* (15th ed. 1934).

21. L. Hall and S. Glueck, *Cases on Criminal Law and Enforcement* (2nd ed. 1958), e.g. p. 60.

22. Mueller, *supra* n. 8.

23. AALS, *Program and Reports of Committees* 85 (1957).

24. Recently published figures on language training in the Soviet Union show that 40 per cent of all students in secondary schools study English, 40 per cent German and 20 per cent other languages. 65 per cent of all students in institutions of higher learning study English. While these quantitatively impressive figures do not tell us anything about the quality of foreign-language teaching in Russia, they will nevertheless serve as a stimulus for increasing language

training in the United States, especially in view of the recent Soviet advances in science which are, directly or indirectly, attributable to this educational achievement. See U.S. Office of Education, Division of International Education; Dep't of Health, Education and Welfare, 'Education in the U.S.S.R.' 74 (*International Education Relations Branch Bull. No. 14*, 1957).

25. See Charles Szladits, *A Bibliography on Foreign and Comparative Law—Books and Articles in English* 324, 346 (Parker School of Foreign and Comparative Law, 1955); 2nd vol. (1962). On the importance of Dr Szladits' work see Dainow, 'The Civil Code and the Common Law', 51 *Nw. U. L. Rev.* 719, 732, n. 32 (1957); Mueller, Book Review, 58 *W. Va. L. Rev.* 213 (1956).

26. Donnedieu De Vabres, *Traité de Droit Criminel et de Législation Pénal Comparée* (3rd ed. 1947), and other works. The extensive French literature on comparative and foreign criminal law is at present being further enriched by publication of all foreign criminal codes in French translation. See 1 Marc Ancel and Yvonne Marx, *Les Codes Pénaux Européens 1956*, covering Germany, Austria, Belgium, Bulgaria, Denmark and the Danish Code of Crimes for Greenland, Volume 2 (1957) covers Spain, Finland, France, Greece, Hungary, Iceland and Italy. Volume 3 (1958) covers Liechtenstein, Luxembourg, Monaco, Norway, Netherlands, Poland and Portugal. Separate volumes have been published on Great Britain, Ethiopia and the Soviet Union. Publisher is the Centre français de droit comparé, 28 rue St-Guillaume, Paris, France.

27. J. Jiménez de Asúa and F. Carsi Zacarés, Codigos Penales Ibero Americanos (2 vols. 1946) and other works. E.g., Levene, 'Situacion Actual Del Derecho Penal Norteamericano', 23 *Jurispr. Arg.* 1 (1961); see also Introduction to Gonzalez-Lopez, 'The Argentine Penal Code' (6 *Am. Ser. For. Pen. Codes*, 1963); Introduction to G. Mueller, *Derecho Penal–Sus Concepciones en la Vida Real* (Buenos Aires, 1963).

28. The majority of the excellent German works on foreign and comparative criminal law have come from the Institut für ausländisches und internationales Strafrecht, at the University of Freiburg i.B., Germany, formerly under Professor Schönke, and now under Professor Jescheck. Among the most important of the Institute's publications are the series of translations of foreign penal codes in the German language (*Sammlung ausländischer Strafgesetzbücher*), presently numbering eighty volumes, the collection of texts on foreign criminal law (*Das ausländische Strafrecht der Gegenwart*), covering in the first three volumes Argentina, Austria, Chile, Denmark, England, Greece, Japan, Yugoslavia and Finland, as well as monographs, periodical contributions (*Auslandsrundschau, in Zeitschrift für die gesamte Strafrechtswissenschaft*) and bibliographic materials. The East Germans have likewise begun comparative efforts in criminal law, though in a rather one-sided manner.

29. See n. 28, *supra*. Of special interest are the comparative studies contained in the *Materialien zur Strafrechts-Reform*, which the

government has published over the past several years, preparatory to a new German penal code.

30. Prof. L. B. Schwartz (principally France); Prof. Jerome Hall (Far East, Germany, France and other countries); Prof. G. O. W. Mueller (Germany, Spain, and Italy); Prof. B. J. George, Jr. (Far East); Prof. R. Knowlton (Burma); Prof. J. M. Canals (France, Italy); Prof. L. B. Orfield (Scandinavia); Prof. P. W. Tappan (Scandinavia and Low Lands), etc.

31. Prof. H. Wechsler, *Revue Internationale de Droit Pénal*; Profs. Paul W. Tappan and Gerhard O. W. Mueller, *Quaderni di Criminologia Clinica*, etc.

32. Besides those to be mentioned in the next following section, see Hall, 'Ignorantia Legis', 26 *Rev. Int. de Droit Pénal* 293 (1955); id., 'International Criminal Law', 1 *Aktuelle Fragen des Internationalen Rechts der Schriftenreihe der Deutschen Gruppe der AAA* 82 (1957); id., 'Strafrechtstheorie', 73 *Z. ges. Str. W.* 385 (1961); id., 'The Three Fundamental Aspects of Criminal Law', 8 *J. Crim. L.* (Tokyo) 1 (1957); and others. Schwartz, 'Le projet de Code pénal de l'American Law Institute', [1957] *Rev. de Sc. Crim. et de Droit Pénal Comp.* 37. Mueller, 'Das amerikanische Bundesstrafrecht', 69 *Z. ges. Str. W.* 37 (1957); id., 'Entwicklung und Stand der amerikanischen Strafrechtswissenschaft', [1960] *Jur. Z.* 465; id., 'Zensur und Selbstkontrolle der Massenmedien in den Vereinigten Staaten', in Löffler, Cron, von Hartlieb, Stammler and Mueller, *Selbstkontrolle von Presse, Funk und Film*, 30 (1960); id., *Eine amerikanische Stellungnahme zum Entwurf eines Strafgesetzbuches E* 1960 (1961), also published at 72 *Z. ges. Str. W.* 297 (1961); id., 'Il Fallimento Delle Concezioni Della Teoria Criminale Nel Giudicare il Delinquente Psicopatico', 3 *Q. di Crim. Clin.* 195 (1961); id., 'Psycho-Pathologie et "Pachydermologie"' 16 (n.s.) *Rev. Sc. Crim. et de Droit Pén. Comp.* 535 (1961); id., 'Codification pénale aux Etats-Unis d'Amerique', 43 *Rev. de Droit Pén. et de Crim.* 1 (1963); id., *Derecho Penal – Sus Concepciones en la Vida Real* (Buenos Aires, 1963). A symposium to which many of the leading participants of the Model Penal Code Project have contributed has been translated into French, Marc Ancel and Louis B. Schwartz, 'Le systeme pénal des Etats-Unis d'Amerique' (Paris, 1964). In English: Schwartz (ed.) 'Crime and the American Penal System', 339 *Annals* (1962), with contributions by Schwartz, Sellin, Wechsler, Collings, Allen, Packer, Donnelly, Remington, Knowlton, Bennet, Tappan and Nicolle.

33. Omitting those mentioned elsewhere, e.g., Canals, 'Classicism, Positivism and Social Defense', 50 *J. Crim. L., C. and P. S.* 541 (1960); Grzybowski, 'Soviet Criminal Law Reform of 1958', 35 *Ind. L. J.* 125 (1960); Schwartz, Foreword, 'The Collection of European Penal Codes and the Study of Comparative Law', 106 *U. Pa. L. Rev.* 329 (1958); George, 'An Unresolved Problem: Comparative Sentencing Techniques', 45 *A. B. A. J.* 250, 23 *Fed. Prob.* 27 (1959); id., 'Sentencing Methods and Techniques in the United States',

26 (2) *Fed. Prob.* 33 (1962); Mueller, '*Mens Rea* and the Corporation', 19 *U. Pitt. L. Rev.* 21 (1957); id., 'The German Draft Criminal Code 1960—An Evaluation in Terms of American Law' [1961] *U. Ill. L. For.* 25; Silving, 'Testing of the Unconscious in Criminal Cases', 69 *Harv. L. Rev.* 683 (1956); id., 'Euthanasia: A Study in Comparative Criminal Law', 103 *U. Pa. L. Rev.* 350 (1954); id., 'The Oath' (pts. 1, 2), 68 *Yale L. J.* 1329, 1527 (1959); id., 'Victims of Criminal Violence', 8 *J. Pub. L.* 236 (1959); id. (with Ryu), 'Error Juris: A Comparative Study', 24 *U. Chi. L. Rev.* 421 (1957); Miller, 'A Comparison of the Basic Philosophies Underlying Anglo-American Criminal Law and Russian Criminal Law', 23 *U. Kan. City L. Rev.* 62 (1955); id., 'Responsibility—In Criminal Law and In Treating Juvenile Offenders', 23 *U. Kan. City L. Rev.* 267 (1955); Hazard, 'Codifying Peaceful Co-existence', 55 *Am. J. Int'l L.* 109 (1961); id., 'UNESCO and the Law', 4 *Record* 291 (1949); id., 'World Organization for Comparative Law', 2 *J. Legal Ed.* 80 (1949); Berman, 'The Comparison of Soviet and American Law', 34 *Ind. L. J.* 559 (1959); id., 'Law as an Instrument of Mental Health in the United States and Soviet Russia', 109 *U. Pa. L. Rev.* 361 (1961).

34. Karev, 'The Forthcoming Reform of USSR Criminal Law', *Harv. L. Rec.*, May 1, 1958, p. 1; Ancel, 'The Collection of European Penal Codes and the Study of Comparative Law', 106 *U. Pa. L. Rev.* 334 (1958); Dando, 'Basic Problems in Criminal Theory and Japanese Criminal Law', 35 *Ind. L. J.* 423 (1960); Ryu, 'Contemporary Problems of Criminal Attempts', 32 *N. Y. U. L. Rev.* 1170 (1957); id., 'Causation in Criminal Law', 106 *U. Pa. L. Rev.* 773 (1958); id., 'The New Korean Criminal Code of October 3, 1953', 48 *J. Crim. L., C. and P. S.* 275 (1957); id. (with Silving), 'Error Juris: A Comparative Study', 24 *U. Chi. L. Rev.* 421 (1957); Andenaes, 'General Prevention—Illusion or Reality', 43 *J. Crim. L., C. and P. S.* 176 (1952); id., 'Determinism and Criminal Law', 47 *J. Crim. L., C. and P. S.* 406 (1956); id., 'Recent Trends in the Criminal Law and Penal System in Norway', 5 *Brit. J. Del.* 21 (1954); Battaglini, 'The Exclusion of the Concourse of Causes in Italian Criminal Law', 43 *J. Crim. L., C. and P. S.* 441 (1953); Hazard, 'Soviet Commentators Re-Evaluate the Policies of Criminal Law', 55 *Colum. L. Rev.* 771 (1955).

One of the most significant contributions to the American literature of comparative criminal law was the bilingual Criminal Law symposium of the Revista Juridica de la Universidad de Puerto Rico (27 *Rev. Jurid. de la Univ. de P. R.*, 1957/8), to which many illustrious criminalists from common-law as well as civil-law countries contributed (Herzog, Del Vecchio, Jimenez de Asua, Morrow, Williams, Nuvolone, Silving, Ferracuti, and others).

35. E.g., U. of Penn. Law School: Professors Foote and Damaska (Yugoslavia), 1961/62; Yale Law School: Professor Silving, 1958/59; University of Michigan Law School: Professor George and guests; N.Y.U.: see n. 37 *infra*.

36. Mueller, 'The Teaching of Comparative Law in the Course on

Criminal Law', 49 *J. Crim. L., C. and P. S.* 101, 109, 11 *J. Legal Ed.* 59, 70–71 (1958).

37. See 'Comparative Criminal Law Project', *N. Y. U. Law Center Bulletin*, Spring, 1961, 4–5, 7, for a report.

38. *International Advisory Committee*: *Argentina*: Ricardo Levene h., Sebastian Soler; *Brazil*: Heleno Claudio Fragoso; *Canada*: John Ll. J. Edwards; *Denmark*: Stephen Hurwitz; *France:* Marc Ancel, Henri Feraud; *Germany*: Hans von Hentig, H. H. Jescheck; *Great Britain:* Leon Radzinowicz, Glanville Williams; *Italy:* Benigno di Tullio; *Japan:* Shigemitsu Dando; *Korea:* Paul K. Ryu; *Netherlands:* J. M. Van Bemmelen; *Norway:* Johs. Andenaes; *Spain:* Federico Castejon; *Switzerland:* Jean Graven, H. F. Pfenninger; *United States of America:* Francis A. Allen, José M. Canals, B. J. George, Jr., Jerome Hall, Albert Hess, Manuel Lopez-Rey, Roy Moreland, Norval Morris, Lester B. Orfield, Rollin M. Perkins, Morris Ploscowe, Frank J. Remington, Louis B. Schwartz, Arthur H. Sherry, Helen Silving, Herbert Wechsler. The author is Director of the Project.

39. American Series of Foreign Penal Codes:

    1. *The French Penal Code*, translated by Jean F. Moreau and Gerhard O. W. Mueller, with an introduction by Marc Ancel, 1960.

    2. *The Korean Criminal Code*, translated and with an introduction by Paul K. Ryu, 1960.

    3. *The Norwegian Penal Code*, translated by Harald Schjoldager and Finn Backer, with an introduction by Johs. Andenaes, 1961.

    4. *The German Penal Code*, translated by Gerhard O. W. Mueller and Thomas Buergenthal, with an introduction by Horst Schröder, 1961.

    5. *The Turkish Code of Criminal Procedure*, translated by the Legal Research Institute, the New York University Faculty Team, the Judge Advocate's Office of the Joint United States Military Mission for Aid to Turkey, William Belser, Yilmaz Altug and Tugrul Ansay, edited by Charles Tenney and Mustafa T. Yücel, with an introduction by Feyyaz Gölzüklü, 1962.

    6. *The Argentine Penal Code*, translated by Emilio Gonzalez-Lopez, edited by Frederick W. Danforth, Jr., with an introduction by Ricardo Levene, 1963.

    7. *The French Code of Criminal Procedure*, translated and with an introduction by Gerald L. Kock, 1964.

    8. *The Japanese Draft Penal Code*, 1961, with an introduction by Juhei Takeuchi, 1964.

    9. *The Turkish Criminal Code*, translated by the Judge Advocate's Office of the Joint United States Military Mission for Aid to Turkey, *et al.*, with an introduction by Nevzat Gürelli, 1965.

    10. *The German Code of Criminal Procedure*, translated by Horst Niebler, with an introduction by Eberhard Schmidt, 1965.

    11. *The German Draft Penal Code*, 1960, translated by Neville Ross, with an introduction by Eduard Dreher, 1965.

    12. *The Austrian Penal Act*, translated by Norbert D. West and

Samuel I. Shuman, with an introduction by Roland Grassberger and Helga Nowotny, 1966.

13. *The Israeli Criminal Procedure Law*, with an introduction by Professor U. Yadin, 1967.

40. Publications of the Comparative Criminal Law Project of New York University: Volume 1. *Essays in Criminal Science* (ed. G. O. W. Mueller, 1961); Volume 2. *International Criminal Law* (ed. G. O. W. Mueller and E. M. Wise, 1965); Volume 3. *The General Part of the Criminal Law of Norway* by Johs. Andenaes, Dr. Jur. (translated by Thomas P. Ogle, 1965); Volume 4. *Japanese Criminal Procedure* by Shigemitsu Dando (translated by B. J. George, Jr., 1966). All published by Fred B. Rothman and Co., S. Hackenseck, N.J., and Sweet and Maxwell, Ltd, London, U.K.

Another type of publication is produced by the Comparative Criminal Law Project, i.e., monographs, articles and other papers, prepared by staff and students, frequently arising out of consulting activities. Among them are the following:

Comparative Criminal Law Project, Newsletters 1–11 (1959–1966); chapters 'Etats-Unis: Droit Pénal', in *Annuaire de Législation Français et Etrangère* (n.s.), vols. 1957–1966 (translations of summaries of the *Annual Survey of American Law—Criminal Law and Procedure*); G. Mueller, *Eine Amerikanische Stellungnahme zum Entwurf eines Strafgesetzbuches* (Bonn, Germany, 1961), also at 73 *Z. ges. Str. W.* 297 (1962); in English translation: 'The German Draft Criminal Code 1960—An Evaluation in Terms of American Criminal Law' [prepared by the Project, with the advice of Profs. Honig, Schröder, Edwards, Moreland, Perkins and Sherry], [1961] *U. Ill. L. F.* 25; Kröger and Mueller, 'The Meeting of Two Police Ideas: Anglo-American Experiments in West Germany', 51 *J. Crim. L., C. and P. S.* 257 (1960); 'The Comparative Criminal Law Project', 8 (3) *N. Y. U. L. C. Bull.* 4 (1961); anon., 'Le "Comparative Criminal Law Project" ', 16 *Rev. de Sc. Crim. et de Droit Pénal Comp.* 414 (1961); Mueller, 'American Experiences in the Penal Regulation of Road Traffic—The Real Lesson for European Legislators' (*6th Int'l Cong. of Comp. Law*, Hamburg, 1962); id., ' "The Devil May Care"— or Should We?: A Re-examination of Criminal Negligence' (paper prepared for the Seventh International Congress of Comp. Law, Uppsala, Sweden, 1966), 55 *Ky. L. J.* 29 (1966); id., 'Beweisverbote im amerikanischen Strafprozess', in *Verh. d. 46. deut. Juristentages*, Bd. 1, Teil 3A, 33 (1966).

41. Mueller and Le Poole, 'The United States Commissioner Compared with the European Investigating Magistrate', *Memorandum No. 1 to the U.S. Senate*, p. 33 (mimeo. 1966); also published in *Hearings Before the Subcommittee on Improvements in Judicial Machinery of the Committee on the Judiciary, United States Senate, 89th Congress, 2nd Session, on the United States Commissioner System, February 8 and 9, 1966*, Part 3, pp. 285–295; Mueller and Le Poole, 'Judicial Fitness: A Comparative Study', *Memorandum No. 2 to the U.S.*

Senate, p. 36 (mimeo. 1966); Mueller and Le Poole, 'Appellate Review of Legal but Excessive Sentences: A Comparative Study,' *Memorandum No. 3 to the U.S. Senate*, p. 35 (mimeo. 1966); also published in *Hearings Before the Subcommittee on Improvements in Judicial Machinery of the Committee on the Judiciary, United States Senate, 89th Congress, 2nd Session, S. 2722. of March 1 and 2, 1966*, Washington, D.C., U.S. Government Printing Office, 1966, pp. 86–100; Mueller, Le Poole and Wang, 'Non-Punitive Detention: A Comparative Study', *Memorandum No. 4 to the U.S. Senate*, p. 36 (mimeo. 1966); Mueller and Le Poole, 'Jurisdiction over Crimes Committed Aboard or With Aircraft', *Memorandum No. 5 to the U.S. Senate*, p. 37 (mimeo. 1966); Mueller, Le Poole and Edwards, 'The Protection of the Criminal Defendant and of the Integrity of the Administration of Criminal Justice Against Prejudicial Mass Publicity', *Memorandum No. 6 to the U.S. Senate*, p. 36 (mimeo. 1966); Edwards, 'Preliminary Investigation by Magistrates in Great Britain and Canada', *Memorandum No. 7 to the U.S. Senate*, p. 35 (mimeo. 1966); Poole, 'Correctional Consolidation', *Memorandum No. 8 to the U.S. Senate*, p. 15 (mimeo. 1966).

42. *Supra*, p. 121.

43. One American report was filed for that Congress: Allen, 'La Responsabilité Pénale des Sociétés Privées en Droit Américain', 28 *Rev. Int'l de Droit Pénal* 9 (1957).

44. Mueller, 'Problemes Soulevés Par La Publicité Donnée aux Infractions et Aux Poursuites Criminelles', 32 *Rev. Int'l de Droit Pénal* 373 (1961). Force, 'Mémoire Sur le Droit en Vigueur aux Etats Unis', 32 *Rev. Int'l de Droit Pénal* 395. For a shorter, combined version in English, see Mueller, 'Problems Posed by Publicity to Crime and Criminal Proceedings', 110 *U. Pa. L. Rev.* 1 (1961).

45. See Mueller, 'Etats Unis', in Centro Nazionale di Prevenzione e Difesa Sociale, *Les Problèmes Posés Par La Publicité Donnée Aux Actes Criminels et Aux Procedures Pénales* 71 (1960, rev. ed. 1961).

46. The founding members were the following:

Prof. Francis A. Allen	University of Michigan
Prof. José Canaes	University of Puerto Rico
Prof. Caleb Foote	University of Pennsylvania
Prof. B. J. George, Jr.	University of Michigan
Prof. Jerome Hall	Indiana University
Dr Albert G. Hess	National Council on Crime and Delinquency
Prof. Roy Moreland	University of Kentucky
Prof. G. O. W. Mueller	New York University
Prof. Lester B. Orfield	Indiana University
Prof. Rollin M. Perkins	University of California
Prof. Morris Ploscowe	New York University
Prof. A. Kenneth Pye	Georgetown University
Prof. Frank J. Remington	University of Wisconsin
Dr M. Schmideberg	Ass'n Psych. Treatment of Offenders

Prof. Louis B. Schwartz	University of Pennsylvania
Prof. Thorsten Sellin	University of Pennsylvania
Prof. Arthur H. Sherry	University of California
Prof. Helen Silving	University of Puerto Rico
Prof. Paul Tappan	University of California
Prof. Herbert Wechsler	Columbia University

47. See Conference Reports at 10 *Am. J. Comp. L.* 319 (1961); 53 *J. Crim. L., C. and P. S.* 72 (1962).

48. E.g., Jescheck, 'Der VIII. Internationale Strafrechts-Kongress vom 21–27 September 1961' in *Lissabon*, 74 *Z. ges. Str. W.* 183 (1962).

49. George, 'Sentencing Methods and Techniques in the United States', 25 (2) *Fed. Prob.* 33 (1962); Mueller, op. cit. *supra* nn. 44, 45; Remington, 'Les Méthodes et les procédés techniques employés dans l'élaboration de la sentence pénale', 31 *Rev. Int'l de Droit Pénal* 45 (1960).

50. Symposium, 'American Papers for the International Congress of the International Association of Penal Law', 32 *U. K. C. L. Rev.* 1–173 (1963).

51. Hitchler, 'Homicide-Degrees of Murder: Wilful, Deliberate and Premeditated Killings', 51 *Dick. L. Rev.* 183 (1947), 22 *Pa. B. Ass'n Q.* 34 (1950); id., 'The Killer and His Victim, and Felony Murder', 53 *Dick. L. Rev.* 3 (1943); id., 'Murder in the First Degree', 54 *Dick. L. Rev.* 353 (1950); id., 'Uncomfortable Murders', 55 *Dick. L. Rev.* 139 (1951); Klein and Hitchler, 'Common Law Misdemeanor Doctrine', 59 *Dick. L. Rev.* 343 (1955); Strahorn, 'Criminology and the Law of Guilt', 15 *Md. L. Rev.* 287 (1955); Snyder, 'Liability for Negative Conduct', 35 *Va. L. Rev.* 445 (1949); id., 'Who is Wrong about the M'Naghten Rule and Who Cares?', 23 *Brookl. L. Rev.* 1 (1956); id., 'False Pretenses—Harm to Person From Whom Thing Obtained', 24 *Brookl. L. Rev.* 1 (1957); Roy Moreland, *A Rationale of Criminal Negligence* (1944); id., *The Law of Homicide* (1952); Harno, 'Intent in Criminal Conspiracy', 89 *U. Pa. L. Rev.* 624 (1941); Perkins, 'The Doctrine of Coercion', 19 *Iowa L. Rev.* 507 (1934); id., 'Partial Insanity', 25 *J. Crim. L. and Crim.* 175 (1934); id., 'Negative Acts in Criminal Law', 22 *Iowa L. Rev.* 659 (1937); id., 'Ignorance and Mistake in Criminal Law', 35 *U. Pa. L. Rev.* 35 (1939); id., 'A Rationale of *Mens Rea*', 52 *Harv. L. Rev.* 905 (1939); id., 'Parties to Crime', 89 *U. Pa. L. Rev.* 581 (1941); id., 'The Law of Homicide', 36 *J. Crim. L. and Crim.* 391 (1946); id., 'Non-homicide Offenses Against the Person', 26 *B. U. L. Rev.* 119 (1946); id., 'The Civil Offense', 100 *U. Pa. L. Rev.* 832 (1952); id., 'Self-Defense Re-Examined', 1 *U. C. L. A. L. Rev.* 33 (1954); id., 'Criminal Attempt and Related Problems', 2 *U. C.L.A.L. Rev.* 319 (1955); and others; Taylor, 'Partial Insanity as Affecting the Degree of Crime—A Commentary on Fisher v. United States', 34 *Calif. L. Rev.* 625 (1946); von Hentig, 'The Doctrine of Mistake', 17 *U. Kan. City L. Rev.* 17 (1947).

52. Kenneth C. Sears and Henry Weihofen, *May's Law of Crimes* (4th ed. 1938).

C.L.S.—20

53. Foreword to C. K. Burdick, The *Law of Crime* at v (1946).
54. Ibid. at vii.
55. Ibid., loc. cit.
56. Ibid. at vii–viii.
57. Wigmore, 'Nova Methodus Discendae Docendaeque Jurisprudentiae, 30 *Harv. L. Rev.* 812 (1917).
58. Ibid. at 822.
59. Ibid. at 823.
60. Ibid., loc. cit.: a very disputable inclusion at this point.
61. Ibid. at 824.
62. For that matter, all the casebooks published after 1939 and before 1949 were analytically sound, some more so than others, but none was successful in synthesis: Harno's second edition (Albert J. Harno, *Cases and Materials on Criminal Law and Procedure*, 1939); Michael and Wechsler's (J. Michael and H. Wechsler, *Criminal Law and its Administration*, 1940); Hall and Glueck's second edition (L. Hall and Sheldon Glueck, *Cases and Materials on Criminal Law*, 1940); Robinson's (J. J. Robinson, *Cases on Criminal Law and Procedure*, 1941)—an unusually good analytical book, but unsuccessful in the market; Waite's second edition (J. B. Waite, *Cases on Criminal Law and Procedure*, 1947); and Dession's (George H. Dession, *Criminal Law, Administration and Public Order*, 1948).
63. Wigmore, *supra* n. 57, at 824.
64. Soler, 'The Political Importance of Methodology in Criminal Law', 34 *J. Crim. L. and Crim.* 366, 367 (1944).
65. Ibid. at 369.
66. Jerome Hall, 'Prolegomena to a Science of Criminal Law', 89 *U. Pa. L. Rev.* 549 (1941), subsequently ch. 1 in *General Principles of Criminal Law* (1947, 2nd ed. 1960).
67. The vast majority of reviews recognized the complete novelty of Hall's approach and acclaimed the book. The general opinion of the profession can best be gleaned by consulting several reviews of the second edition, particularly those of Gooderson, [1962] *Cambr. L. J.* 118, Lord Chorley, 25 *Mod. L. Rev.* 604 (1960), and Sir John Barry, 4 *Sid. L. Rev.* 28, 31 (1962), who called it 'the most valuable synthesis, the most consistently erudite, constructive and civilized dissertation upon the philosophy and theory of criminal law it has been this reviewer's good fortune to read'.
68. Hall, 'The Three Fundamental Aspects of Criminal Law', in *Essays in Criminal Science* 159, 160, 162–163 (ed. G. Mueller, 1961). This chapter is based on an article previously published at 8 *J. Crim. L.* 1 (Tokyo, 1957). As Hall's jurisprudential, historical and sociological interests have been mentioned earlier, these aspects of his theory will not be discussed at this point.
69. Jerome Hall, *Cases and Readings on Criminal Law and Procedure* (1949), Supplement (1963); now Hall and Mueller, *Cases and Readings on Criminal Law and Procedure* (2nd ed. 1965).
70. Morrow, Book Review, 6 *J. Legal Ed.* 132, 133 (1953).

71. But, as may be recalled, it was this edition to which Roscoe Pound wrote the introduction in which he demanded that students should be given a 'sound fundamental grasp of law principles'. Pound, Introduction to Rollin M. Perkins, *Cases and Materials on Criminal Law and Procedure* XIV (1952).

72. Rollin M. Perkins, *Cases and Materials on Criminal Law and Procedure* (2nd ed. 1958).

73. Jerome Hall and Sheldon Glueck, *Cases on Criminal Law and Its Enforcement* (2nd ed. 1958).

74. Monrad C. Paulsen and S. H. Kadish, *The Criminal Law and Its Processes* (1962), combining the functional and the theoretical approach.

75. Albert J. Harno, *Cases and Materials on Criminal Law and Procedure* (4th ed. 1957).

76. Fred E. Inbau and Claude R. Sowle, *Cases and Comments on Criminal Justice* (1960), a good book, especially for those wishing to stress procedure more than substance, which has been inordinately slighted; Donnelly, Goldstein and Schwartz (1952), discussed *supra*, ch. VIII sec. 3.

77. Jerome Hall, *General Principles of Criminal Law* ch. 2 (1947, 2nd ed. 1960).

78. Ibid. at chs. 3 and 4, especially in terms of completed and inchoate harm, though the concept as such was briefly explained in Hall, *Cases and Readings on Criminal Law and Procedure* 45–46 (1949).

79. Hall, op. cit. *supra* n. 77, *passim*, especially chs. 7–9.

80. Ibid. at chs. 5–6, 10–14; Hall, 'Ignorance and Mistake in Criminal Law', 33 *Ind. L. J.* 1 (1957); Hall, 'Ignorantia Legis', 28 *Rev. Int'l De Droit Pénal* 293 (1955).

81. Jerome Hall, *Cases and Readings on Criminal Law and Procedure* 70–73 (1949).

82. *Studies in Jurisprudence and Criminal Theory* ch. 10 (1958).

83. Hall, op. cit. *supra* n. 77, at ch. 15.

84. See Mueller, 'Criminal Theory: An Appraisal of Jerome Hall's *Studies in Jurisprudence and Criminal Theory*', 34 *Ind. L. J.* 206 (1959).

85. That a similar development may well be taking place in England is attested to by the fact that Professor Glanville Williams, the most astute British criminal-law scholar since Bentham and Stephen, has now published the second edition of his *Criminal Law—The General Part* (2nd ed. 1961).

86. The English, so it seems, have come to the same conclusion. Six years after Hall published his *General Principles*, Glanville Williams came out with his superb analytical treatise *Criminal Law—The General Part* (2nd ed. 1961), which, as Lord Chorley suggested, 'provides in a number of ways an even clearer elucidation and is certainly a worthy rival to the American volume'. Book Review, 25 *Mod. L. Rev.* 604 (1962).

87. This and the preceding two paragraphs are the concluding para-

graphs of a major study constituting the writer's attempt to present a synthetic theory of criminal law, along the lines suggested by Hall. Mueller, 'The Public Law of Wrongs—Its Concepts in the World of Reality', 10 *J. Pub. L.* 203 (1961).

CONCLUSION

1. Ferdinand Schevill, *Six Historians* 126 (1956).
2. With minor deviations in the prognosticated path, it is amazing that all of the past sages are in basic agreement on the order of development. E.g., compare Hohfeld, 'A Vital School of Jurisprudence and Law: Have American Universities Awakened to the Enlarged Opportunities and Responsibilities of the Present Day', in Wesley N. Hohfeld, *Fundamental Legal Conceptions* 332 (ed. Cook, 1923) and Wigmore, 'Nova Methodus Discendae Docendaeque Jurisprudentiae', 30 *Harv. L. Rev.* 812 (1917). As has been discussed, others have established a similar order.
3. Herbert Wechsler, ch. VII, sec. 5, *supra*; Jerome Hall, text at nn. 121, 122, in ch. V, *supra*, and ch. IX, *passim*; Rollin M. Perkins: see his work in procedure, especially with and for law enforcement, e.g., his articles especially between 1924 and 1933; his *Iowa Criminal Justice* (1932), with a fine use of criminal statistics, and his *The Elements of Police Science* (1942).
4. E.g., see Braden, 'Legal Research: A Variation on an Old Lament', 5 *J. Legal Ed.* 39 (1952); Allen, 'History, Empirical Research, and Law Reform: A Short Comment on a Large Subject', 9 *J. Legal Ed.* 335 (1956); Kalven and Tyler, 'The Palo Alto Conference on Law and Behavioral Science', 9 *J. Legal Ed.* 366 (1959); Hurst, 'Research Responsibilities of University Law Schools', 10 *J. Legal Ed.* 147 (1957); Godfrey, 'Some Notions for a Regime of Woodshed Legal Research', 13 *J. Legal Ed.* 1 (1960); and others.
5. The closest thing to a 'think-tank' experiment has been N.Y.U.'s Ford Foundation sponsored four-week summer workshop on Criminal Law and Administration, in August, 1963, with nearly thirty young criminal-law professors, several visiting foreign criminal-law professors included, and Professors Ricardo Levene, Gerhard O. W. Mueller, Henry H. Foster, Jr., Norval Morris, Monrad Paulsen, Morris Ploscow, Herbert Wechsler, and Glanville Williams, Journal of Criminal Law, Criminology and Police Science. as faculty. This experiment was repeated in the summer of 1966, with an equally distinguished international faculty.
6. Llewellyn, 'On What Makes Legal Research Worth While', 8 *J. Legal Ed.* 399, 421 (1956).
7. Currie, 'The Materials of Law Study', 8 *J. Legal Ed.* 1, 74–75 (1955):

> The greatest of the manifold difficulties associated with the assimilation of nonlegal materials seems to me to have been the lack of any sharp conception of the purpose to be served by such materials and, more particularly, the frustrations and defections which resulted when the

more ambitious conceptions of the goal were disapproved . . . The tendency to ask the wrong questions of other disciplines and to expect too much of the replies is persistent.

8. Professor Jeffery recently said this about the major difficulties confronting the criminological scholar in our time:

> First, there is the problem of integrating the sociological approach to criminal behavior as symbolized by Sutherland's theory of differential association, with the psychological approach, as symbolized by Freud's theory of neurosis. The second problem is that of integrating a legal theory of crime with a theory of criminal behavior. Crime is a three-dimensional problem: legal, psychological, and sociological.

Jeffery, 'An Integrated Theory of Crime and Criminal Behavior', 49 *J. Crim. L., C. and P. S.* 533 (1959). See also Jeffery, 'The Structure of American Criminological Thinking', 46 *J. Crim. L., C. and P. S.* 658 (1956).

Index